SPURNPOINT was built in 1908 for Robert Rix of Hull by A. Hall & Co., Ltd., of Aberdeen
Her registered dimensions were 125.3′ x 21.1′ x 8.8′ and the tonnages were 235 gross and
88 nett.

WILD ROSE aground in the River Dee near Queensferry. The fast flowing tides
sometimes lead to groundings but the vessels usually refloated on the next tide
Registered dimensions were 100.9′ x 18.0′ x 8.8.′ Tonnage 104 gross. Built 1883.

Also in this Series

OLD TIME STEAM COASTING

Spargo & Thomason

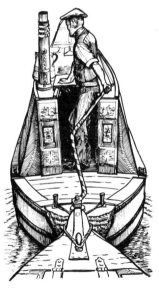

TALACRE leaving Point of Ayr Colliery, North Wales.

Plate 2

STEAM COASTERS
and
Short Sea Traders

Second Edition

Charles V. Waine, Ph.D.

ASTERIA was built in 1891 for Wm. Robertson

Illustrated by the Author

WAINE Research

Publications

To:
The British Steam Coaster
and all who worked with them.

4 MOUNT BATTOCK was built in 1939 by J. Lewis & Sons Ltd., of Aberdeen and is seen here at the coal wharf adjacent to the shipyard. Registered dimensions were 140.9′x 25.6′x 9.6′ and the tonnages were 396 gross, 154 nett and 448 deadweight.

© C.V. Waine.

Published by:

Waine Research,
Mount Pleasant,
Beamish Lane,
Albrighton,
Nr. Wolverhampton

First Published 1976.
Reprinted 1977.
Second Edition 1980.

ISBN 0 905184 04 1.

Printed & Bound in England.

Also in this series:

The Complete Book of
    CANAL & RIVER NAVIGATIONS
  by E.W. Paget-Tomlinson.

A Survey of
  MERCANTILE HOUSEFLAGS & FUNNELS
  by J.L. Loughran.

Preface

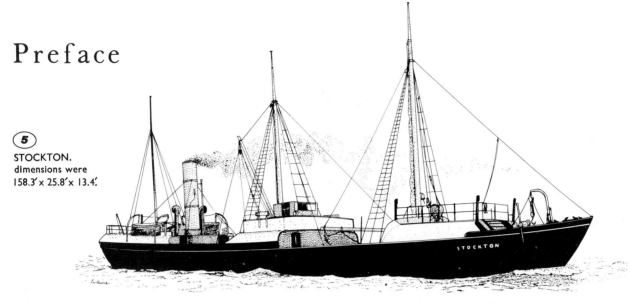

⑤

STOCKTON.
dimensions were
158.3′ x 25.8′ x 13.4′.

Coasters never attracted the public gaze as Liners did and yet they often led much more adventurous lives, so this book is about the coasting tramp which carried cargo from anywhere to anywhere else, around the British Isles and nearby Continent. Following in the wake of schooners and brigs, they carried coal for our fires, corn for the bread, bricks for the walls, slates for the roofs and stone for the roads. Many were little more than one hundred feet in length, often the largest vessels able to navigate the winding channels and reach tiny quays with inches to spare. But all that is left of the many steam coasters are their graceful names like PEARL, SNOW QUEEN and THE LADY BELLE; just memories on old men's lips. As one seaman recalls, they had been struggling against a westerly gale in the Channel for many hours, trying to cover the last few miles to Penzance, each wave sweeping the whole of the foredeck and preventing the crew reaching their bunks and food lockers. All were tired and hungry. Then astern, they saw a large ship rapidly gaining on them. It was one of the Atlantic Greyhounds proceeding as if on a mill pond.

Despite the rigours of the coasting life, they had certain compensations, for the ships were often in port and most voyages were short. This particularly applied to the men of the East Coast colliers who got home to Newcastle most weeks. Many of these vessels carried more than a million tons of coal to London during their often long lives of thirty or forty years service. In both World Wars coasters suffered heavy losses of men and ships, carrying essential supplies. In the Second World War, they went to the rescue of the army at Dunkirk and over three hundred and fifty of them returned four years later, to take part in the Normandy Landings. Though they endured considerable risks, the coasting men took it all in their stride, as usual, and the operation was a great success. Afterwards coasters quietly returned to their normal round of voyages.

A great variety of designs was used and these are described and illustrated here with actual General Arrangement drawings from the various shipyards. Their steam machinery is also fully illustrated and the complexities of a complete engine room are unravelled. Steam coasters were usually smartly kept and the colours of some of the leading owners are illustrated. This book would not have been possible without the help and encouragement of past and present shipowners who gave up their valuable time to answer questions and search out old plans, photographs and documents featured in the text. Extra material came from the collection of the National Maritime Museum (50, 51, 52, 100b, 101, 105, 106b), Merseyside County Museums (26, 27, 42, 66, 78, 86, 92) and Kingston upon Hull Museums (91, 131a, 141, 149a). I am indebted to the Trustees of the museums for allowing these reproductions, and Messrs David Lion, Michael Stammers and Edward Paget-Tomlinson respectively, for their help in selecting material from the collections. My friends P. N. Thomas (69, 70, 94, 98, 113a), Don Smith (13a, 13b, 85, 118) also kindly loaned material for reproduction in this revised third printing. Shipyards also kindly provided plans as follows; Goole Shipbuilding & Repairing Co. Ltd. (97), Cochrane & Sons Ltd. (71) and Austin & Pickersgill (133b).

Many shipping agents and crew members of steam coasters also helped with details about the ships with which they worked, especially Captain Roberts of Llanfaethlu and Captain Fellows of Connah's Quay and Captain O. G. Spargo of Birkenhead. Mr. Ross and Dan McDonald provided much of the material for the chapter on Clyde 'puffers' while Peter Norton kindly researched some of the Liverpool shipping. Messrs John Clarkson, Alex. Duncan, Jimmy Hartery, Dick Scott and F.R. Sherlock kindly delved into their collections and came up with one or more photographs which enabled me to prepare the perspective sketches and check the details for the colour plates. Lastly but not least, thanks are due to Mr. Tom Coppack for reading the text from the shipowners point of view and my various friends in the field of Naval Architecture for doing their best to eliminate any technical errors. Finally I am always interested to hear from anyone who has worked in or with steam coasters.

C.V. Waine, Ph.D.,
Albrighton, July 1980.

Collier built 1852 [4].

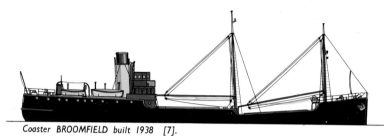

Coaster BROOMFIELD built 1938 [7].

Coaster BELFORD built 1920 [6]

Coaster THE DUCHESS built 1924 [8].

Coaster CALATUM built 1908 [6].

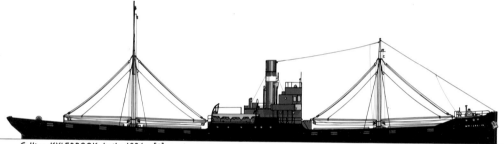

Collier KYLEBROOK built 1924 [9].

Clyde 'Puffer' AILSA built 1904 [5].

Up-River Collier BRIMSDOWN built 1951 [10].

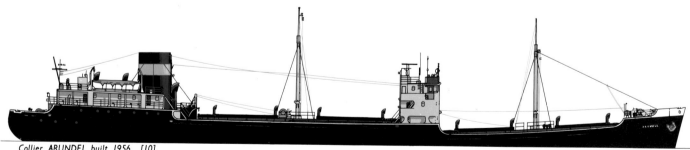

Collier ARUNDEL built 1956 [10].

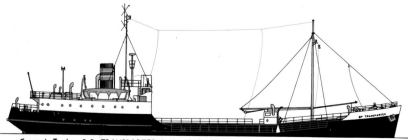

Coastal Tanker B.P. TRANSPORTER built 1945 [11].

Plate 6.

Scale 0 _____ 50ft

The numbers in brackets indicate the chapter (opposite) in which the type is described.

Contents

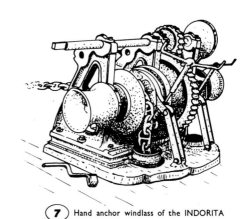

7 Hand anchor windlass of the INDORITA

NOTES: ◄━━━━━━━━━━━━━━━━━━━━━━━━━━━━━━━━━━━

Figure numbers in the text are indicated thus: (24) and correspond with the page number on which it occurs. Pipes on Plate 42 are indicated by starred numbers thus: 34* in the text.

Original scales are indicated on many drawings in words. As all of the drawings have been reduced from the original size, the scale bars must be used for determining all dimensions.

In Chapter 12 the name of many ships is followed by the gross tonnage and the last two figures from the year of build, so the number 124/99 would indicate a ship of 124 gross tons built in 1899.

S.S. CLINT
PROFILE & DECK PLANS

This plan was submitted for Lloyd's approval in 1896 by J Fullerton & Co. of Glasgow. Suggested modifications to the steelwork are shown in red. The boiler was probably raised to improve access to the underside. The iron deck was more durable. Registered dimensions were 125.0' x 20.0' x 9.0' and tonnage 197 gross.

0 ____ 20 feet

⑧

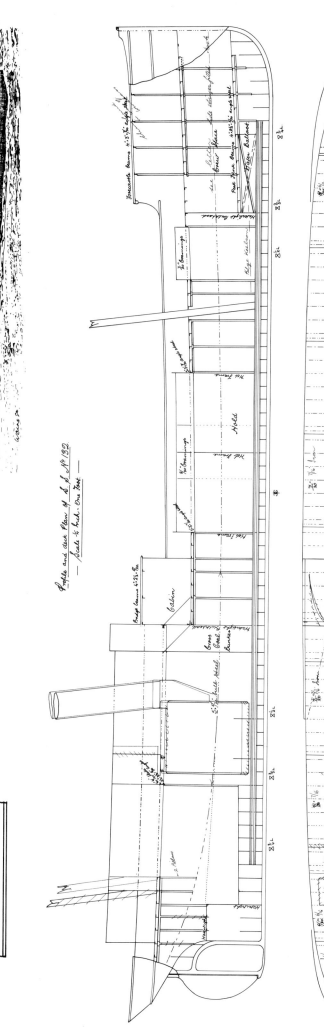

Profile and deck Plans of S.S. N° 132
— Scale ½ Inch. One Foot —

1.

Outline

9 DERWENT, built in 1883.

The steam coaster, once a familiar sight around the coasts of the British Isles is now but a memory. However, these vessels made an important contribution to the rise of Britain as an industrial power. When the first steam colliers appeared, the paddle steamer had long been established in the passenger and cargo liner trades, but it was not until the advent of the screw propellor in the 1830's, coupled with compact machinery, that an efficient small cargo ship could be built. As this propelling machinery was in the stern, the prime central part of the hull was now available for cargo carrying. In addition, screw machinery was lighter, less costly and less prone to damage (paddle floats were often damaged when they struck drift wood). Among the first users of steam coasters was the North East coal trade to London. The coal was traditionally carried in brigs. These two-masted vessels needed large crews as they were square rigged, and could not, because of this rig, proceed effectively against the wind. Thus in a period of adverse winds, coal stocks of London merchants might become very low, and then when the wind changed dozens of brigs would arrive and choke the Thames, vying with each other for the insufficient discharging berths available. It was soon realised that the trade could be efficiently regulated by the use of steam coasters, despite the extra cost of building. They could also make many more voyages per year than a sailing vessel. Even so, many sailing ship owners were quick to point out that the wind was free and coal was not.

Several steam colliers were built in the 1840's, but the vessels did not attract much public attention until the very successful JOHN BOWES was built in 1852. The first vessels were closely similar to schooners in design, but were mostly built of iron for increased strength (19b). It also reduced the fire risk. Although these vessels proved good carriers, like the schooners and brigs before them, they usually needed ballast if they were to make passages empty, especially in rough winter seas and there were few return cargoes for the north-east. This meant laboriously loading sand, chalk or shingle ballast and then discharging this on arrival. The use of water ballast was suggested and various arrangements tried. The forerunner of the modern cellular double bottom was suggested by Mr. McIntyre who was manager of Palmer's yard on the Tyne. He fitted various colliers with tanks along the bottom of the holds, which became known as McIntyre tanks. The steamers carried a full outfit of sails and often sailed to conserve fuel, as coal consumption was high in these early vessels.

No sooner had the steam collier been shown to be viable, than competition from another quarter became significant, that of the railways who rapidly established themselves as the main carriers of coal to London. This competition checked the collier fleets for a number of years. Sailing brigs and snows were much cheaper than steam vessels and so continued to be used where delivery time was less important. As late as 1892, Stephenson Clarke purchased several sailing vessels for their coal trade to Shoreham. They were not finally displaced by steam until 1898. A similar pattern prevailed elsewhere with steam coasters and schooners existing side by side in several fleets for many years. This was possible because steam was used where rapid delivery was required and this could be combined with fast loading and discharge. The schooner with its small crew and lower capital outlay could load and discharge cargo at a more leisurely pace and still be profitable. Steam vessels had great advantages in areas of strong tides, narrow passages and canals, so they soon became established in the Western Isles of Scotland, but were limited to a length of sixty-six feet if they were to use the Forth and Clyde Canal. Because of this, small coasters were a particular feature of that area. In the North East Coast coal trade the size of vessel rapidly increased as there were no such exacting restrictions.

Throughout the 1860s and 1870s vessels similar to JOHN BOWES were built, still retaining a big spread of canvas. However, changes begun in the 1870s were to become clearly defined in the 1880s. The most important change was the introduction of the raised quarter deck which had two advantages for the designer. Firstly it gave increased engine room height for the higher-pressure cylindrical boilers and vertical compound and triple expansion engines associated with them, then coming into use. The low pressure, box-like boilers and v-type oscillating engines of the earlier steamers were lower. Secondly, it was found convenient to extend this deck forward into the cargo space and increase the cargo capacity. The design as used in the 1920s may be considered the typical British coaster (19c). The screw steamer with engines amidships was also becoming common, mainly because designers felt the machinery weight in the stern would be excessive, in these larger ships. Also

10 KNOTTINGLEY was built in 1907 for the Wetherall S. S. of Goole. Registered dimensions were 195.0′ x 32.6′ x 11.4′

it avoided the change in trim of the vessel as the bunker coal was consumed. The raised quarter deck was often used in these vessels to make up the cargo space lost due to the long shaft tunnel (19d). This type had become popular in the North East Coast coal trade by the 1890s. Both these designs continued to be used for the remainder of the steam era with only slight modifications. Sail area was reduced and square sails discarded by the 1880s, but gaffs were used on fore-and-aft sails until the 1890s. The officers at first had their accommodation in the stern, but during the 1880s it began to appear under the navigating bridge which by now had become a much more substantial structure. The bridge was either placed amidships or aft, depending on the type and size of the vessel. Most vessels over 140 feet in length, with the engines aft, had the bridge amidships, usually at the forward end of the raised quarter deck. The engineers were always adjacent to the engine room with the firemen and seamen forward. Such then was the design for the bulk cargo trades such as coal, timber, stone and grain.

The screw steamer was also adopted for the cargo liner trades, such as those operated by the General Steam Navigation Company, Coast Lines and its predecessors and the Clyde Shipping Company. For this general cargo trade, a greater hold volume is required as parcels of cargo are generally more bulky for a given weight, are often fragile and may not be stacked to any great extent. To give more volume, two or more decks are usually built into these vessels (19e, f). The general cargo often included perishables to be picked up and dropped at several ports. Thus rapid loading and unloading was essential. This was achieved by fitting a full outfit of derricks and sometimes steam deck cranes in addition. The larger vessels usually had engines amidships. The railways and road transport slowly took the coastal trade, but rates remained favourable and coastal liner services operated until the 1960s and are the subject of a companion volume to this book.

Steam coasters were slower in appearing on the Irish Sea and the first significant building did not begin until the 1880s to handle the expanding trade associated with iron and coal. Prior to this, small cargo steamers had mainly been confined to the Bristol Channel. The West Cumberland iron and steel trade from Maryport and Whitehaven encouraged owners such as Hine Bros., and W.S. Kennaugh to purchase steam coasters, while the trade from Glasgow supported such leading owners as William Robertson. Irish coal merchants also began to look to steam for the Irish coal trade. In Liverpool one of the early coasting firms was J.J. Mack, soon to be followed by a host of others in the 1890s. The small steam coaster also became a feature of some East Coast fleets for the coal trade to the East Coast of Scotland. The large colliers with engines amidships looked to the Baltic timber trade or the Spanish iron-ore trade for summer employment when the demand for coal fell off.

Cargoes increased in variety and destination as the 20th Century was reached, prices of steamers fell and encouraged more owners to build, but continental voyages with uncertificated masters were restricted to Elbe-Brest limits by the various Merchant Shipping Acts, though summer voyages further afield were usually allowed. Road improvement, spurred on by the appearance of the motor car, increased the demand for roadstone. Coastal quarries built jetties for steam coasters to carry away their stone to the main coastal towns. Thus steam coasters helped build the roads which eventually took their trade. Building of steam coasters continued, while schooner building had virtually stopped by 1910.

During the First World War, freight rates rose rapidly and all coasters were fully employed while building prices rose to three to four times the pre-war figures, but owners continued to order ships because of the high freight rates offering. As the war neared the closing stages most owners were predicting a buoyant market as reconstruction got into its stride and ordered larger coasters to meet the expected demand from merchants for larger cargoes to be moved. The rapidly expanding electrical undertakings on the Thames also needed more tonnage. In the slump which actually ensued, owners who had contracted for ships at high prices and taken delivery, were faced with mortgage repayments which they were unable to meet on the income from lower freight rates. Many companies failed or had to drastically reduce their fleets. However those owners who had hung back, found virtually

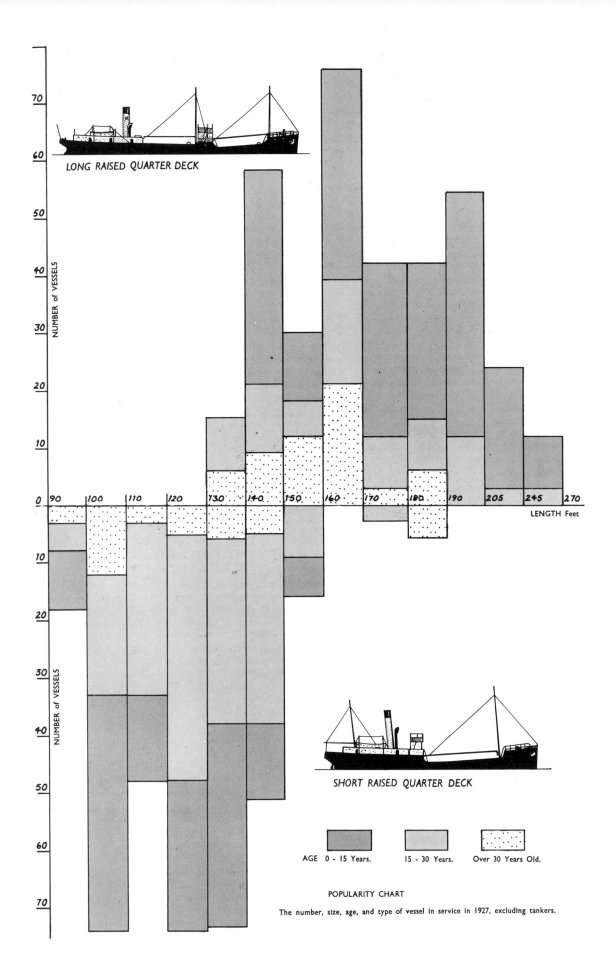

LONG RAISED QUARTER DECK

NUMBER of VESSELS

NUMBER of VESSELS

90 100 110 120 130 140 150 160 170 180 190 205 245 270

LENGTH Feet

SHORT RAISED QUARTER DECK

AGE 0 - 15 Years.   15 - 30 Years.   Over 30 Years Old.

POPULARITY CHART

The number, size, age, and type of vessel in service in 1927, excluding tankers.

Plate 11

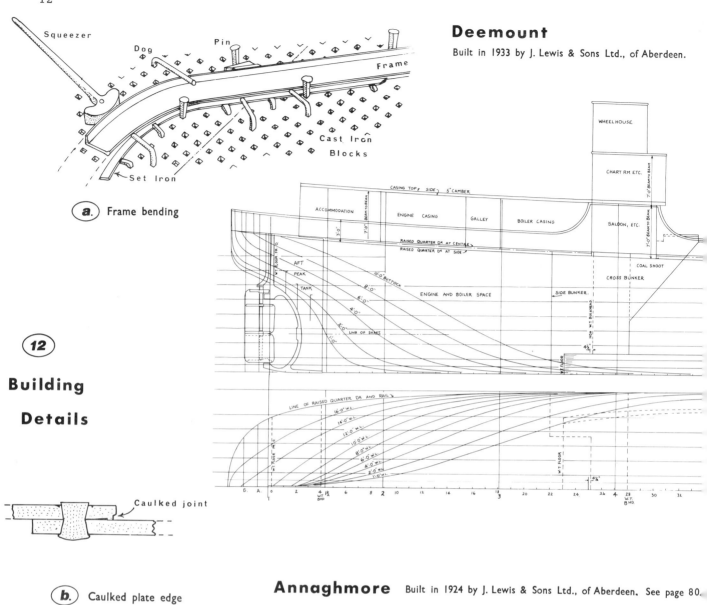

Squeezer

Dog

Pin

Frame

Cast Iron
Blocks

Set Iron

a. Frame bending

Deemount

Built in 1933 by J. Lewis & Sons Ltd., of Aberdeen.

WHEELHOUSE

CHART RM. ETC.

7'-0" BEAM TO BEAM

CASING TOP 2 SIDE 5" CAMBER

ACCOMMODATION

ENGINE CASING

GALLEY

BOILER CASING

SALOON, ETC.

7'-0" BEAM TO BEAM

BEAM TO BEAM

3'-0"

7'-0" BEAM TO BEAM

RAISED QUARTER DK AT CENTRE

RAISED QUARTER DK AT SIDE

COAL SHOOT

W.T. FLOOR FR. 40

AFT

PEAK

TANK

10'-0" BUTTOCK

8'-0"

6'-0"

4'-0"

2'-0"

1'-0"

LINE OF SHEET

ENGINE AND BOILER SPACE

CROSS BUNKER

SIDE BUNKER.

NON W.T. BULKHEAD

W.T. BULKHEAD

4½"

W.T. FLOOR

LINE OF RAISED QUARTER DK AND RAIL

16'-0" W.L.

14'-0" W.L.

12'-0" W.L.

10'-0" W.L.

8'-0" W.L.

6'-0" W.L.

4'-0" W.L.

2'-0" W.L.

1'-0" W.L.

W.T. FLOOR

W.T. FLOOR

4½"

B. A. 0   2   4   ½   6   8   2   10   12   14   16 18 3   20   22   24   4   26 28 W.T. 30   32
                  ½   18   22   26 B.HD.
              W.T.   3
              BHD.

12

Building

Details

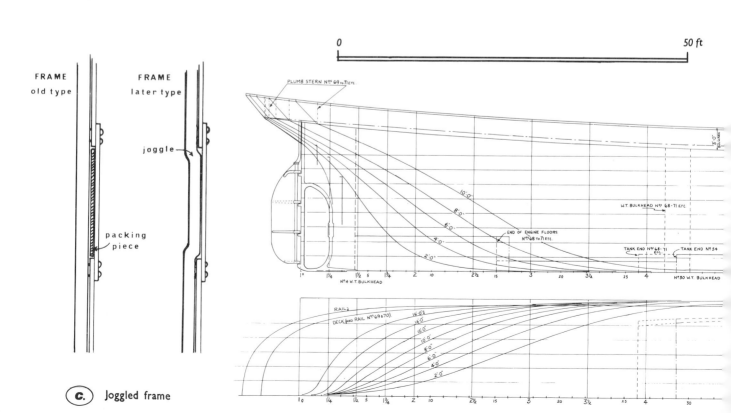

Caulked joint

b. Caulked plate edge

Annaghmore Built in 1924 by J. Lewis & Sons Ltd., of Aberdeen. See page 80.

0   50 ft

FRAME
old type

FRAME
later type

joggle

packing
piece

PLUMB STERN Nos 69 to 71 ETC.

3'-0"
BULKHEAD

10'-0"

8'-0"

6'-0"

4'-0"

2'-0"

W.T. BULKHEAD Nos 68-71 ETC.

END OF ENGINE FLOORS
Nos 68 to 71 ETC.

TANK END Nos 68-71
ETC.

TANK END No 54

1'-0"   1¼   1½   1¾   2   10   2½   15   3   20   3½   25   4
No 4 W.T. BULKHEAD   No 30 W.T. BULKHEAD

RAIL

DECK AND RAIL Nos 69 & 70

16'-0"

14'-0"

12'-0"

10'-0"

8'-0"

6'-0"

4'-0"

2'-0"

1'-0"   1¼   1½   5   1¾   2   10   2½   15   3   20   3½   25   4   30

c. Joggled frame

S S Nº 129
LINES   PLAN

DIMENSIONS

LENGTH B.P. _____ 165'-0"
BREADTH MLD. _____ 27'-0"
DEPTH MLD. _____ 12'-1½"

— Scale :- ¼" = 1 Foot :—

13a

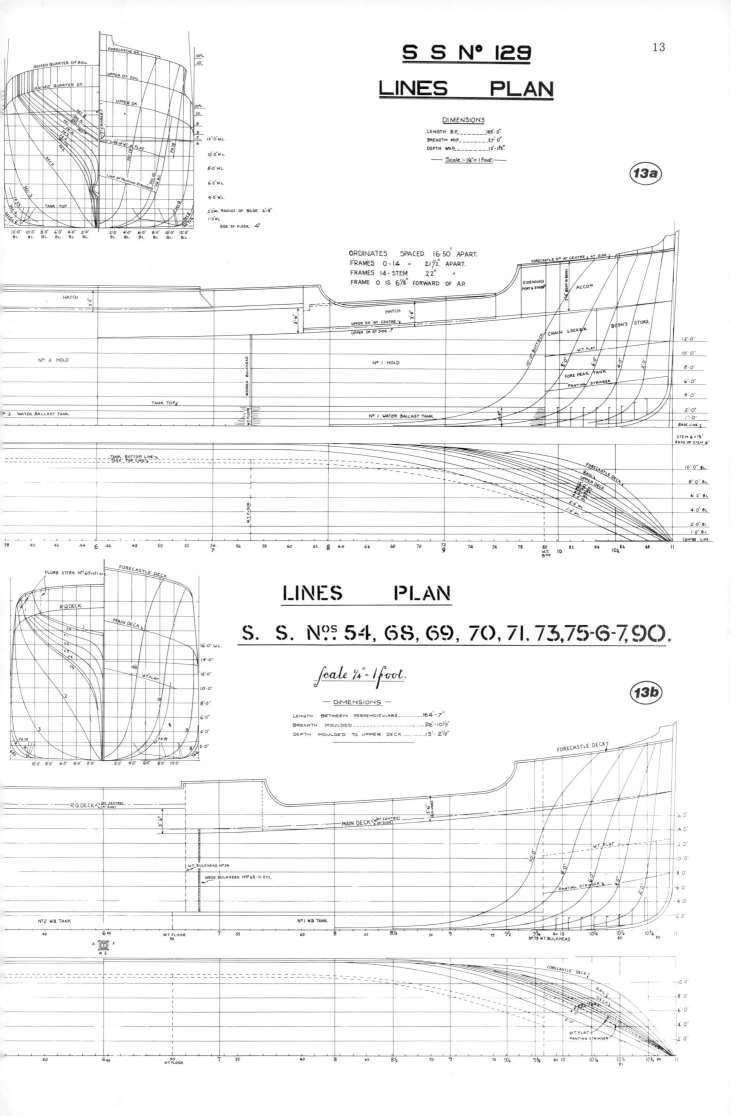

ORDINATES   SPACED 16·50' APART.
FRAMES 0-14   "   21½" APART.
FRAMES 14-STEM   22"   "
FRAME 0 IS 6⅞" FORWARD OF A.P.

LINES   PLAN

S. S. Nᵒˢ 54, 68, 69, 70, 71, 73, 75-6-7, 90.

Scale ¼" = 1 foot.

— DIMENSIONS —

LENGTH BETWEEN PERPENDICULARS _____ 164'-7"
BREADTH MOULDED _____ 26'-10½"
DEPTH MOULDED TO UPPER DECK _____ 13'-2½"

13b

new ships on the market at around a quarter of the price for which they had been built a few months earlier. Low freight rates continued for the next ten years. However, better placed owners found shipyards desperate for work, quoting very favourable prices of about one third of those quoted at the peak in 1919, and so new coasters were built during the 1920s. The final reckoning came for shipyards and owners alike at the end of the decade. The slump in rates became even more severe and many of the shipyards, which had built good coasters for many years closed down, never to be reopened. It is hard to pick out any particular yard, but perhaps the closing of John Fullerton's yard at Paisley, which had built many fine coasters for the British fleets, marked the turning point for the steamer.

The steam coasters were well built for the most part and had long lives. The 1927 Lloyd's Register lists over seven hundred vessels belonging to and trading around the British Isles. They ranged in length from sixty-six feet to about two hundred and seventy feet, but the majority were less than one hundred and ninety feet in length as can be seen from the popularity chart (page 11). Many companies which had managed to struggle through the 1920s found themselves in difficulties and such well known fleets as that of Richard Hughes of Liverpool passed into the hands of the Banks who continued to operate the fleet in the hope of recovering their money as mortgages. Many older coasters were laid-up never to trade again. During the 1930s strong competition from Dutch motor coasters caused forward look-ing British owners to take note; the oil engine was by now reliable and showed good savings on manpower and fuel/engine weight and so they could carry more cargo on a smaller draft.

The first motor ships had appeared by 1910, initially as auxiliaries and then by degrees, to fully powered motor coasters. These early engines were not very reliable and a set of sails was usually kept handy. At this time they were mainly used where the shallow draft and increased cargo capacity outweighed the mechanical problems. These oil engines also gave a new lease of life to the old schooner as they could be easily fitted to them. When the wind was favourable fuel could be saved and when it was not, time could be saved. They soon proved a match for the small steam coaster in many trades on the Irish Sea and were not finally eliminated until the 1950s. They offered no competition to the larger coaster, but by the 1930s reliable engines were available for larger vessels and the Dutch were first to take advantage of them. The same path was followed by progressive British owners in the 1930s as freight rates improved slightly, but building prices still remained favourable. The large engines-aft collier also appeared on the East Coast at this time and proved considerably more efficient than the vessels with engines amidships that it replaced.

With the arrival of World War II all the remaining laid up coasters were pressed into service, but this time freight rates were fixed by the Government at a little above pre-war levels. This time losses of coasters were much more serious, but some losses were made up by the building of a series of standard vessels of various types. By the end of the war, those steamers which had survived were in need of considerable maintenance which was hampered by the fact that everyone wanted the limited drydocking space available. The steam coaster's decline, begun in the 1930s continued, but the North East Coast coal trade remain-ed faithful to the steam collier. However, the coal mines were nationalised and coal exports virtually stopped, while the nationalised gas and electricity undertakings built up a sizeable fleet, although management was largely left in the hands of Stephenson Clarke. Even in this stronghold of steam, motor vessels became increasingly numerous.

The design of these motor ships closely followed steamship practice at first but by the end of the 1950s, the bridge had been moved aft. This saved the expense of separate central heating systems introduced during the 1940s and reduced cable runs and pipework for indi-vidual wash basins with running water which were becoming general in the officers' accom-modation. In addition it cleared the deck for easier cargo working. The only loss was visi-bility forward and the officers isolation from the engine room noise. Coal burning steamers were often converted to burn oil which was now significantly cheaper than coal by the mid-1950s and in any case good firemen were almost unobtainable, but Asian crews were able to manage oil burners with little training. In addition those coasters still engaged in carry-ing coal to power stations and gas works began to decline, as the stations themselves were converted to burn oil.

However, the slump did not immediately occur as had been expected from previous ex-perience and coasters were fully employed. The costs of loading and discharging general cargo rose and the regular coastwise services of Coast Lines and others declined rapidly. Coast Lines expanded their interests in road transport while the Dundee, Perth & London Shipping Company looked to the tramp trades to employ their ships. Traditional collier owners began to build motor tankers at this time while Rowbothams of London expanded their fleet of clean products tankers to meet the rising demand from oil companies. The price of steam coasters fell further towards the end of the 1950s as freight rates dropped and running costs rose. Many were sold to foreign owners or sold for scrap. Some new companies sprang up as in the 1930s, tempted into shipping by the low prices and, like the 1930s, most did not last long. Many steam coasters found a new lease of life as sand and gravel dredgers for the construction industry as quarries on land were unable to meet the demand. They could often dredge their cargoes within river limits and so did not have to meet the Board of Trade requirements for sea-going vessels, but could carry their cargoes directly to the centres of cities such as London, Liverpool and Dundee. The trade had originally been deve-loped in the Bristol Channel where specialised steamers were built in a number of cases. The trade was prosperous and the steamers were soon replaced by new motor ships in many cases. Thus, by the 1960s the steam coaster had all but vanished from the Irish Sea and only lingered on in the East Coast coal trade.

2.

⑮ GERTIE under construction in 1902.

Building & Repairing Steam Coasters

Steam coasters were built throughout Britain by shipyards large and small. The yards were most numerous around the Clyde, Tyne and Wear as the map (17) shows. Many of the smaller yards built a few vessels when trade was good and then closed down or continued as repairers when there was a slump. The effects of the cyclical nature of trade are particularly noticeable here and few builders survived for any great length of time. Shipowners could refrain from ordering ships for considerable periods as the steam coaster was built to last and a service life of thirty to forty years was normal; a wonderful tribute to their often long defunct builders.

A shipyard needs firm gently sloping ground adjacent to sheltered water, which is at least ten to twelve feet deep at high tide. Such conditions commonly occur among the many rivers and harbours throughout the British Isles. Since most coasters were built of steel, a site near a steel mill was advantageous, but many yards survived in more remote areas where the cost of transporting raw materials has been offset by lower labour and other costs. The Dublin Dockyard Company, which operated from 1901 to 1923, was typical of a shipyard in use during the main coaster building period. The yard was set up by Mr. Scott, who had been managing director of S. McKnight & Co., of Ayr and Mr. Smellie who left the design department of Denny's to join Mr. Scott in the venture. They leased the site of the yard (the North West corner of the Alexandra Basin) from the Dublin Dock Board who were keen to see a shipbuilding and repairing industry set up in Dublin to enhance the facilities of their port. There was a disused repair yard there, but the site was cleared and construction of new buildings began in December 1901. The first owner to entrust the yard with an order was Captain Rowland of Liverpool and the steam coaster GERTIE (15) was launched for him on the 4th of October 1902 and delivered on the 10th of November.

The first step in the successful building of a steam coaster was the work of the designing and estimating department in the drawing office. As shipowners often decided to proceed with a new ship very suddenly, shipbuilders had only a few days in which to prepare plans, specifications and costs if they were to be in the running for the contract. Consequently this work required much experience backed up by carefully compiled data from previous ships. The careful shipowner of this period specified his vessel in some detail thus: deadweight carrying capacity, draft, cargo space, speed, fuel consumption and any special strengthening required. The designer needed to check carefully the way in which the dimensions were specified as there are a number of different ways of defining them. He also had to consider the various regulations laid down in the Merchant Shipping Acts.

Firstly there is DEADWEIGHT TONNAGE, that is the actual weight of cargo and fuel which will sink the ship in the water to the load line on the side of the ship. The load a ship is allowed to carry is, for example, greater in summer than in winter. This is because a greater reserve buoyancy is needed to allow the ship to lift easily to the heavy seas liable to be encountered in winter. Thus the deadweight will depend on the freeboard assigned. Of course the actual weight of cargo carried will also depend to some extent on the weight of fuel needed for the voyage. DISPLACEMENT is the actual weight of water displaced by the presence of the ship. Two figures are commonly used, light displacement which is the weight of the empty ship and loaded displacement which is the total weight of ship plus cargo and all stores etc. The figures are rarely on record for steam coasters.

The commonly quoted tonnage figures are based on volume and here one ton is equivalent to 100 cubic feet of enclosed space. This volume measure is very old and appears to have come from the word 'tun' meaning a large wine cask. One of the main commodities moved by sea was wine and so a standard wine cask was a conventional measure for ships. The foundations for the modern tonnage measurements were laid down in the Merchant Shipping Act of 1854 which resulted from the work of a Royal Commission under George Moorsom and so is sometimes referred to as the Moorsom System. In the Act, the value of the ton for volume measurements was fixed at 100 cubic feet and two official measures were laid down, gross tonnage and nett tonnage. GROSS TONNAGE is the total permanently enclosed volume of the ship less certain deductions such as water ballast tanks, the wheelhouse, galley and

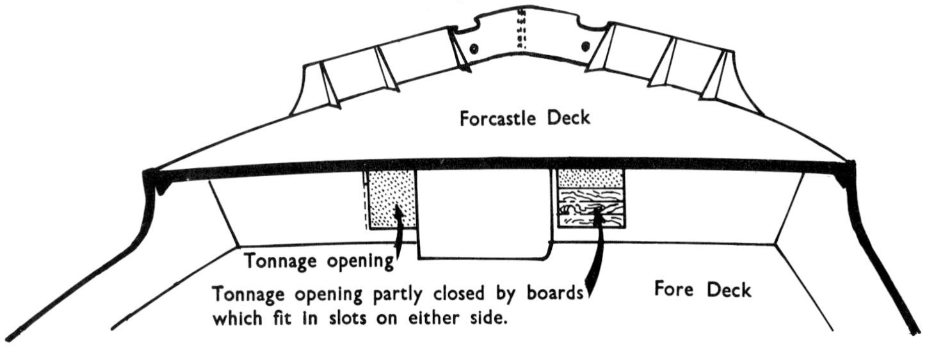

Forcastle Deck

16

Tonnage opening
Tonnage opening partly closed by boards
which fit in slots on either side.

Fore Deck

lavatories. Deductions were introduced to encourage owners to provide proper galley space and discourage open bridges. Also a second deck incompletely enclosed against the sea could obtain exemption. The opening, known as a TONNAGE OPENING had to conform with certain requirements. Tonnage openings into forecastles are often fitted in ships with crew accommodation aft. They may be temporarily closed with loose boards which drop into slots on either side of the opening and still remain exempt (16). Exemptions are only allowed above the tonnage deck which is defined as the main deck in single decked ships and the second permanently enclosed deck from below in multi-decked ships. The volume of a ship below this deck is the UNDER DECK TONNAGE. The NETT TONNAGE, the second official tonnage, is defined as the gross tonnage less non-earning spaces such as accommodation, an allowance is also given for engine and machinery space. This tonnage was used to calculate port and dock dues as well as light dues. Owners expected builders to keep this tonnage as low as possible for the ship. Over the years various adjustments to the regulations have been made to prevent bad design features arising in ships. Two other common volume measurements are the GRAIN capacity in cubic feet of the hold and the BALE capacity which excludes the space obstructed by the ship's framing.

There are several dimensions usually recorded for ships and perhaps the length causes the most confusion as this is measured in a number of ways. REGISTERED LENGTH was measured from the fore side of the tip of the stem bar to the after side of the stern post or rudder stock if there was no rudder post. LENGTH BETWEEN PERPENDICULARS (or LENGTH B.P.) is usually used by owners when contracting with a builder for a new vessel. It is the length from the after side of the stern post to the fore side of the stem bar/upper deck intersection (projected if necessary). Latterly it has become synonymous with LLOYD'S LENGTH which is measured from the after side of the rudder post to the fore side of the stem bar or plating on the summer loadline. LENGTH OVERALL is measured from the foremost tip of the stem to the aftermost tip of the overhang of the stern. REGISTERED BREADTH is also the EXTREME BREADTH measured over the plating. However, in coasters, it is often not the extreme breadth as they generally have several inches of belting on each side. MOULDED BREADTH is measured across the frames, excluding the thickness of the plating. REGISTERED DEPTH (DEPTH OF HOLD) is measured from the top of the ceiling in vessels with ordinary floors and double bottomed ships or from the tank top, if no ceiling is laid, to the top of the deck beams amidships. MOULDED DEPTH is measured from the underside of the deck at the side of the ship to the underside of the shell plating (top of keel).

DRAFT is the absolute minimum depth of water for the vessel to float. The usual draft quoted is the SUMMER DRAFT which is the draft of the ship when loaded to the summer load line. The loadline mark came into use in 1870, but it did not have the force of law and most owners continued to load their ships as they thought fit. However this was overcome by the first Merchant Shipping Act of 1876 which was the work of Samuel Plimsoll. This laid down regulations regarding the freeboard of all ships and the mark L⬡R replaced the mark L◇R which had been introduced in 1870. The regulations have been amended from time to time to suit new types of vessel and to take into account improvements like steel hatch covers, winter and summer, and cargoes such as timber.

Each designer had his own methods for preparing the basic hull design, but the final result was three views of the hull, each at right angles to the other (13a, b). The sheer plan shows the rise fore and aft of the decks and shape of the stem and stern. Lines showing the shape of the ship at different breadths (the bow and buttock lines) are also drawn in and the positions of the sections of the body plan and the water planes of the half-breadth plan are also indicated. The half-breadth plan shows the shape of the water line at different drafts. The body plan shows the shape of sections indicated on the sheer plan and half-breadth plan. The forward sections are always shown on the right and the after sections on the left. The designer always kept margins to a minimum in order to be competitive with other yards.

Having fixed the dimensions; weight, cost of steelwork and its assembly, could be established, followed by the joiners' and shipwrights' timber requirements. Plumbing and floorings were then taken into account. Meanwhile machinery estimates were prepared or tenders obtained from leading machinery builders. Finally labour costs of all departments were allowed for. The quotation, together with a proposed general arrangement drawing, and sometimes a model and rigging plan, were sent to the shipowners.

If the yard's provisional plans were accepted, detailed work could begin. The lines plan was then used to determine the displacement accurately at the proposed loadline. The empty weight was then calculated accurately by adding up the weight of all the steelwork and equipment required. The difference gave the weight of cargo that could be carried. Similarly a

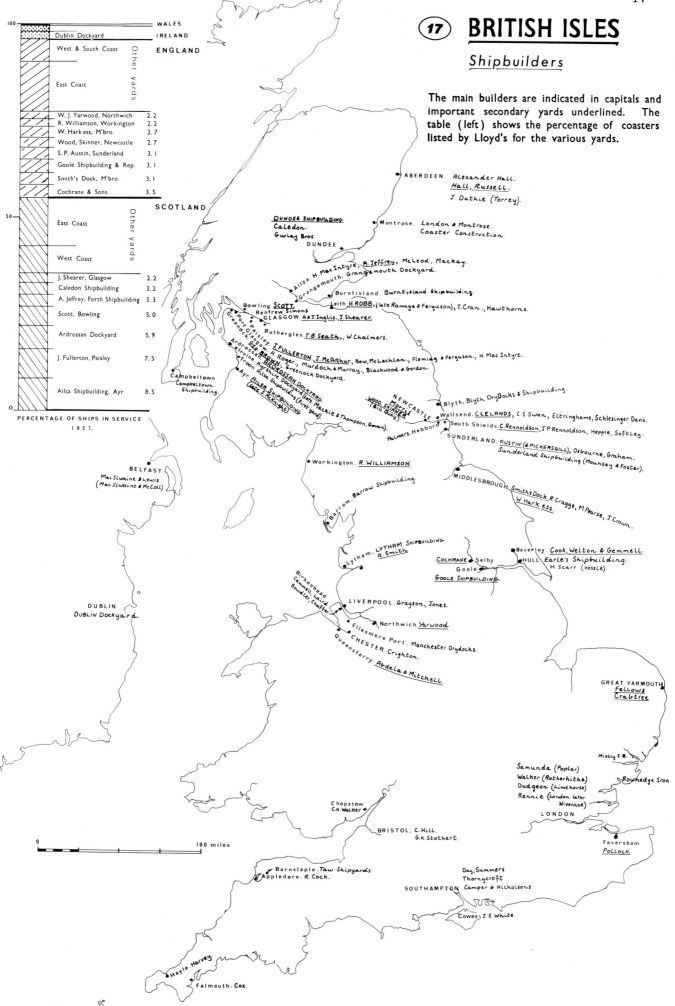

The main builders are indicated in capitals and important secondary yards underlined. The table (left) shows the percentage of coasters listed by Lloyd's for the various yards.

WALES
IRELAND
Dublin Dockyard
West & South Coast
ENGLAND
East Coast
Other yards

W. J. Yarwood, Northwich	2.2
R. Williamson, Workington	2.2
W. Harkess, M'bro.	2.7
Wood, Skinner, Newcastle	2.7
S. P. Austin, Sunderland	3.1
Goole Shipbuilding & Rep.	3.1
Smith's Dock, M'bro.	3.1
Cochrane & Sons	3.5

SCOTLAND
East Coast
Other yards
West Coast

J. Shearer, Glasgow	2.2
Caledon Shipbuilding	3.2
A. Jeffrey, Forth Shipbuilding	3.3
Scott, Bowling	5.0
Ardrossan Dockyard	5.9
J. Fullerton, Paisley	7.5
Ailsa Shipbuilding, Ayr	8.5

PERCENTAGE OF SHIPS IN SERVICE
1927.

ABERDEEN. *Alexander Hall.*
Hall, Russell.
J. Duthie (Torrey).

DUNDEE SHIPBUILDING
Caledon.
Gurlay Bros.
DUNDEE

Montrose. *London & Montrose.*
Coaster Construction.

Alloa. H. MacIntyre. A. Jeffrey, McLeod, Mackay.
Grangemouth. Grangemouth Dockyard.
Burntisland. Burntisland Shipbuilding.
Bowling SCOTT. Leith H.ROBB, (late Ramage & Ferguson), J.Cran., Hawthorns.
Renfrew Simons
Port Glasgow GLASGOW. A & J. Inglis, J. Shearer.
Greenock Rutherglen. T.B.Seath., W. Chalmers.
Paisley. J. FULLERTON, J. McArthur, Bow, McLachlan., Fleming & Ferguson., H. MacIntyre.
Ardrossan ARDROSSAN DOCKYARD.
Irvine. Ayrshire Dockyard. A. Roger., Murdoch & Murray., Blackwood & Gordon.
Troon Ailsa Shipbuilding (first yard). Greenock Dockyard.
Ayr. AILSA SHIPBUILDING (late Mackie & Thompson, Govan).
(late J. McKnight)

NEWCASTLE
WOOD SKINNER MORRISON
(Bill Quay)
Palmers. Hebburn.

Blyth. Blyth Dry Docks & Shipbuilding.
Wallsend. CLELANDS, C.S. Swan, Eltringhams, Schlesinger Davis.
South Shields. C. Rennoldson, J.P. Rennoldson, Hepple, Softley.
SUNDERLAND. AUSTIN (& PICKERSGILL), Osbourne, Graham.
Sunderland Shipbuilding (Mounsey & Foster).

Workington. R. WILLIAMSON.

Barrow. Barrow Shipbuilding.

MIDDLESBROUGH. Smith's Dock, R. Craggs, M. Pearse, J. Crown.
W. Harkess.

Lytham. LYTHAM SHIPBUILDING
R. Smith.

COCHRANE Selby
Goole
GOOLE SHIPBUILDING.

Beverley. Cook, Welton & Gemmell.
HULL. Earle's Shipbuilding.
H. Scarr (Hessle).

Birkenhead
Cammell Laird
Bowdler, Chaffer
LIVERPOOL. Grayson, Jones.
Northwich. Yarwood
Ellesmere Port. Manchester Drydocks.
Queensferry CHESTER. Crighton.
Abdela & Mitchell.

BELFAST
MacIlwaine & Lewis
(MacIlwaine & McColl)

DUBLIN
DUBLIN DOCKYARD.

Chepstow
C.H.Walker.

BRISTOL. C. Hill.
G.K.Stothert.

Barnstaple. Taw Shipyards
Appledore. R. Cock.

Hayle. Harvey
Falmouth. Cox.

GREAT YARMOUTH
Fellows
Crabtree

Mistly S.B.

Rowhedge Iron

Samunda (Poplar)
Walker (Rotherhithe)
Dudgeon (Limehouse)
Rennie (London later Wivenhoe)
LONDON

Faversham
Pollock

Day, Summers
Thornycroft
SOUTHAMPTON Camper & Nicholsons

Cowes. J. S. White.

0   100 miles

detailed check was made to see that the hold volume met the owner's requirements. As most coasters were expected to carry a full cargo of coal about forty-four cubic feet of hold space were allotted per ton of cargo. The strength and stability were taken care of by following Lloyd's rules. Vessels built in the 1880's tended to have small hatches, high bulwarks and small freeing ports, so a large weight of water could accumulate on deck and seems to have been one of the causes of vessels foundering at that time. Regulations requiring larger freeing ports were introduced and the tendency to fit larger hatches with higher coamings also helped by reducing the area of deck on which seawater could accumulate.

By 1900 much of the steelwork was being drawn out on paper or on a model rather than being left to the men on the building berth to mark out and cut as they went along. The model was usually made at a scale of one quarter of an inch per foot and was known as the half-block model. It was used to determine accurately the length of the curved plates and the position of the butts in the plating, so that they were clear of obstructions. In earlier times smaller yards often made a model rather than a lines plan. Careful planning of the construction by the drawing office was normal practice by 1900 and allowed maximum utilisation of the yard's plant, and a better eye could be kept on the work so that it met owner's requirements and generally speeded construction. The general arrangements department of the drawing office elaborated the provisionally approved plans to produce a rigging plan (20) and the general arrangement plan which showed profile and decks (21). The amount of detail shown varied considerably from yard to yard. Often it is these provisionally approved plans, showing the ship as designed, rather than as finally completed, that have survived and this is why there are often small differences between the plans and photographs of the actual ship. However it was normal for ships to be progressively modified to meet changing service requirements and standards during their often long, service lives.

The engine room was next planned in detail together with the bunkering arrangements. Then all the accommodation was fitted in and in later vessels, provisions made for the extensive plumbing and wiring. Plans were also made for the efficient steering, anchoring, mooring, navigating and ventilating of the ship together with lifeboats and other safety equipments. These finalised details were usually resubmitted to the owners and to the Classification Society (usually Lloyd's) as well as the Board of Trade. In earlier times the vessels were often built without reference to the societies.

The steel and ironwork department of the drawing office will have prepared the midship section (22) and strength plans showing all the scantlings (dimensions) of all transverse and longitudinal members of the hull structure for approval by Lloyd's who made alterations if required as was the case for CLINT (8). Details of the stern frame and rudder were also submitted. The midship section gives details of the riveting; welding never became very important in steam coasters as it took some time for all the technical difficulties to be solved and bring welding up to the same reliability as riveting. The weight savings in welding are significant, since the plates do not need to be overlapped and angle lugs are not needed either, and it was left to the motor coaster to exploit welding to the full.

Once the plans were approved, then offsets and other details could be passed to the mould loft where the loftsman drew out the vessel's lines full size in chalk on the black painted floor. He also faired out any irregularities which appeared in the lines when drawn out full size. All was now ready for transferring the lines to the scrieve board. This was a specially laid floor on which the loftsman marked out the frames of the ship, decks and other details, using a scrieving knife to cut the lines into the wood. When this had been done the floor was taken up and relaid near the frame bending blocks to guide the frame bending gangs. On approval of the steelwork plans, the materials were ordered from the steelworks, as far as possible in the sequence in which they were to be used. These orders covered plates, sections, angles, tubes and rods, making the minimum allowance for machining. If the vessel was being built for classification with Lloyds, then all the steel would have been tested and approved by a representative of Lloyds at the steelworks. While delivery was awaited, detailed frabrication plans were made giving full instructions for the making of frames, floors, beams, inner bottom, ballast tanks, engine and boiler seatings, deck stringers and so on. The shell expansion plan was also prepared on which the plates for the ship were shown flattened out (Plate 124). All the plate dimensions were indicated on this plan together with openings for washports and other details.

The Dublin Dockyard had its own electric, hydraulic and pneumatic power plants. The hydraulic power (water under high pressure) was used to operate machines such as the manhole punch, heavy section cutter and beam bender. Pneumatic power (compressed air) was by this time used for the power hand tools for work on the ship of drilling, riveting, caulking and plate edge trimming. The mould loft usually occupied the upper floor of the joiners shop which was particularly convenient, since numerous wooden templates (or moulds) were prepared from the mould loft drawing. These templates were skeleton frameworks of thin wood, which showed the shape of the plate and the position of the rivet holes. The templates were then used by the ironworkers to cut out the steel plates and sections to the required shape. The ironworkers department, the heart of the shipyard, was by far the largest of the workshops. The sheds were fitted out with plate and angle furnaces with their accompanying frame bending blocks and a variety of machines. In the latter part of the 19th century, the keel and frames were carefully erected and faired, then templates were taken from them for stringers, deck plates, tank tops and shell plating. However by 1900, lofting and drawing office methods had become accurate enough for the templates to be made in the mould loft and so work on preparing the plates could proceed even before the frames were made.

Plate 19

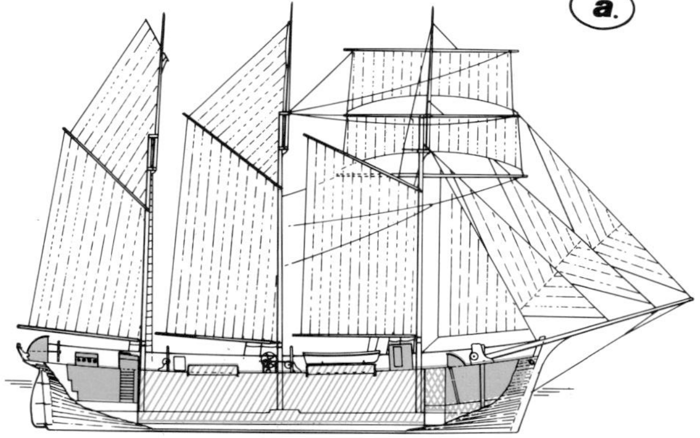

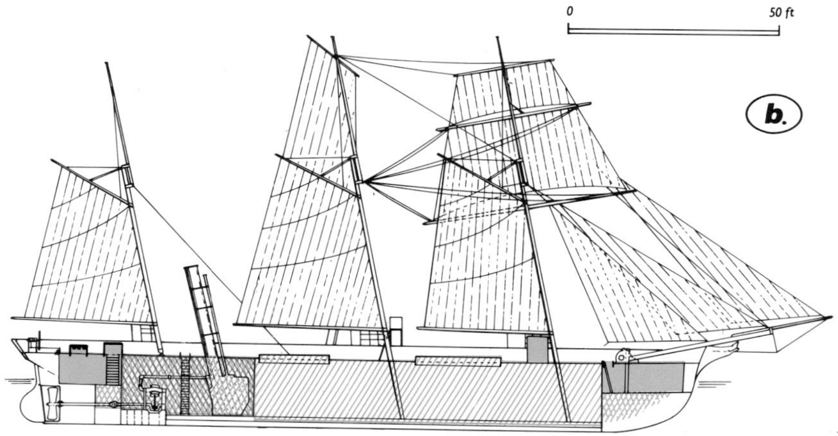

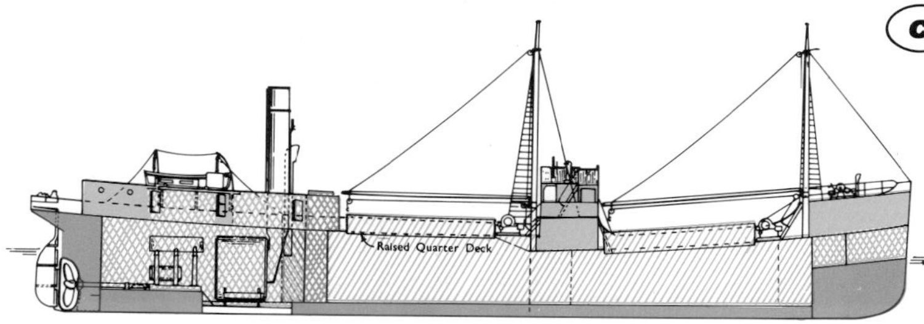

50 ft

0

Top KATHLEEN & MAY   Middle SCREW COLLIER (1852)   Bottom KEMPTON

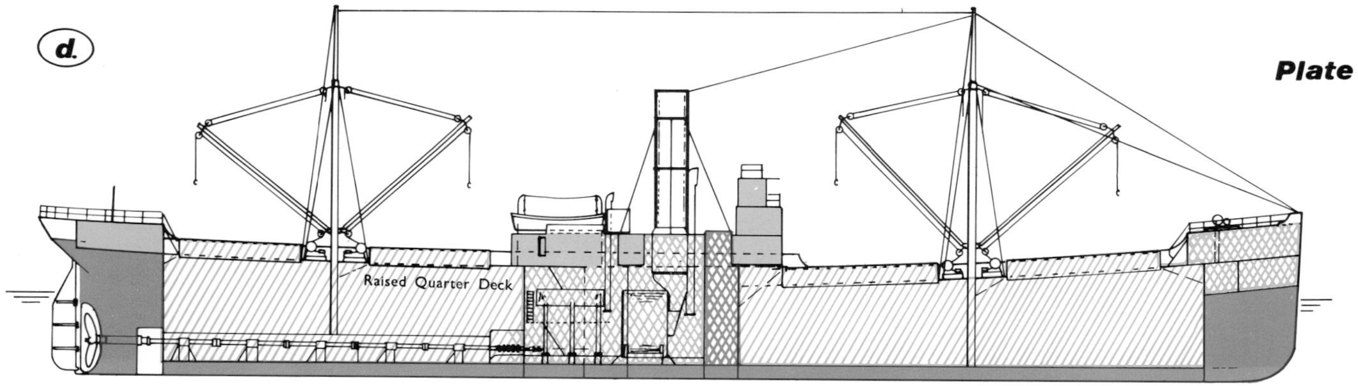

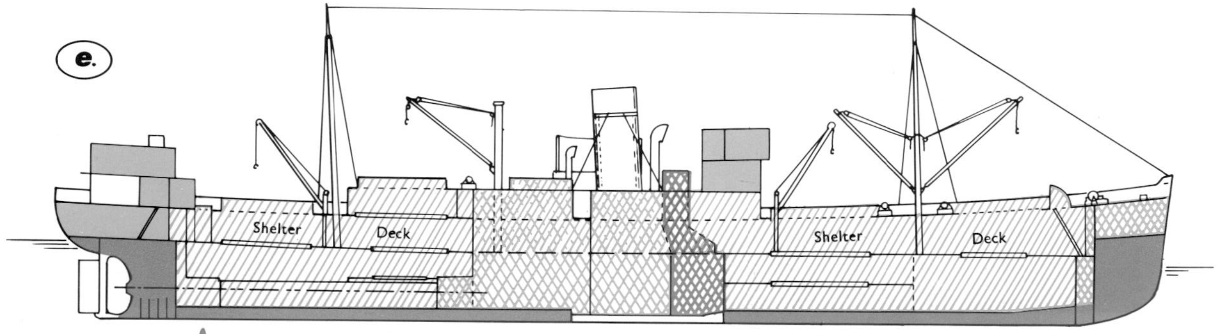

Raised Quarter Deck

Raised Quarter Deck

Shelter Deck

Shelter Deck

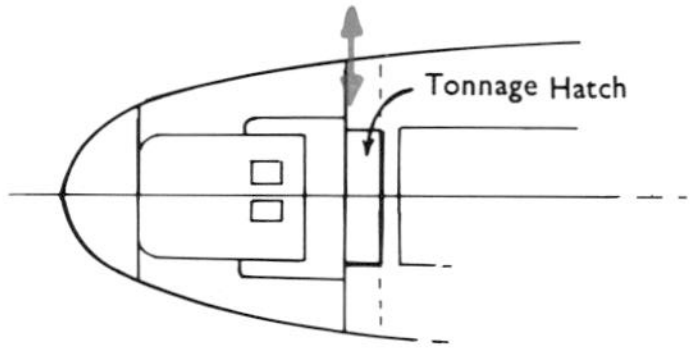

Shelter Deck

Tonnage Hatch

CARGO SPACE		
MACHINERY, STORES		
CREW		

CROSS BUNKER		
SIDE BUNKER		
WATER BALLAST		

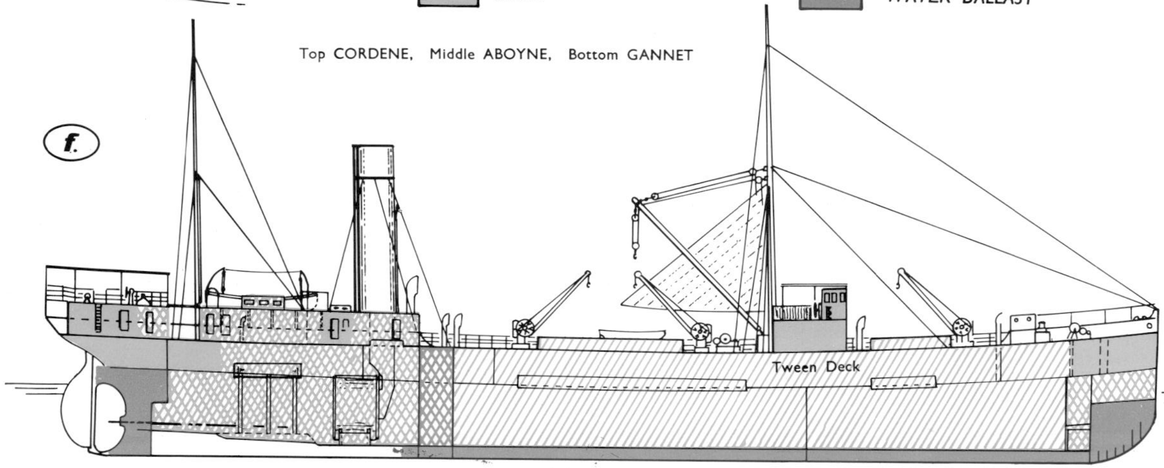

Top CORDENE,   Middle ABOYNE,   Bottom GANNET

Tween Deck

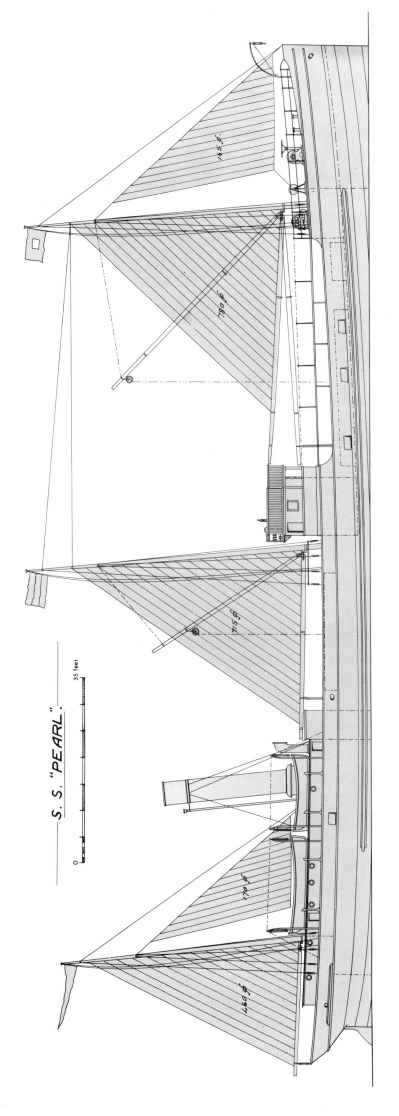

— S.S. "PEARL" —

35 feet

S.S. PEARL
RIGGING PLAN

20 Original plan drawn at John Shearer & Sons yard for PEARL built in 1896 for William Robertson also of Glasgow. Sails were generally set but are rarely seen in photographs as they were lowered on the approach to port. Registered dimensions were 185.0 x 29.1' x 10.8' and tonnages 678 gross, 700 dwt.

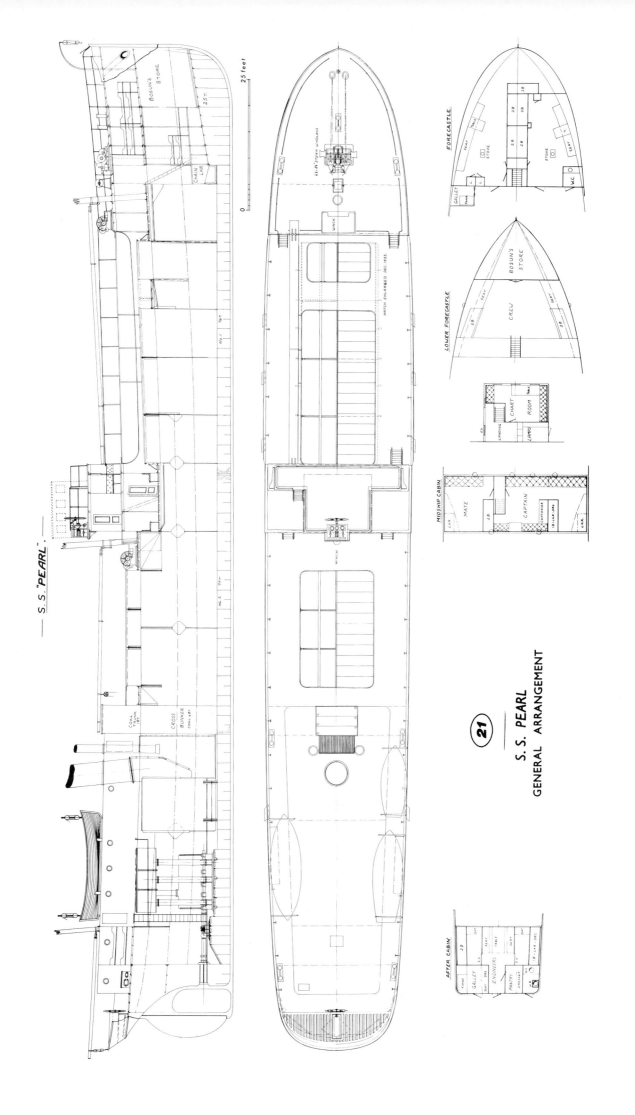

— S.S. "PEARL" —

25 feet

0

FORECASTLE.

LOWER FORECASTLE.

MIDSHIP CABIN.

AFTER CABIN.

21

S. S. PEARL
GENERAL ARRANGEMENT

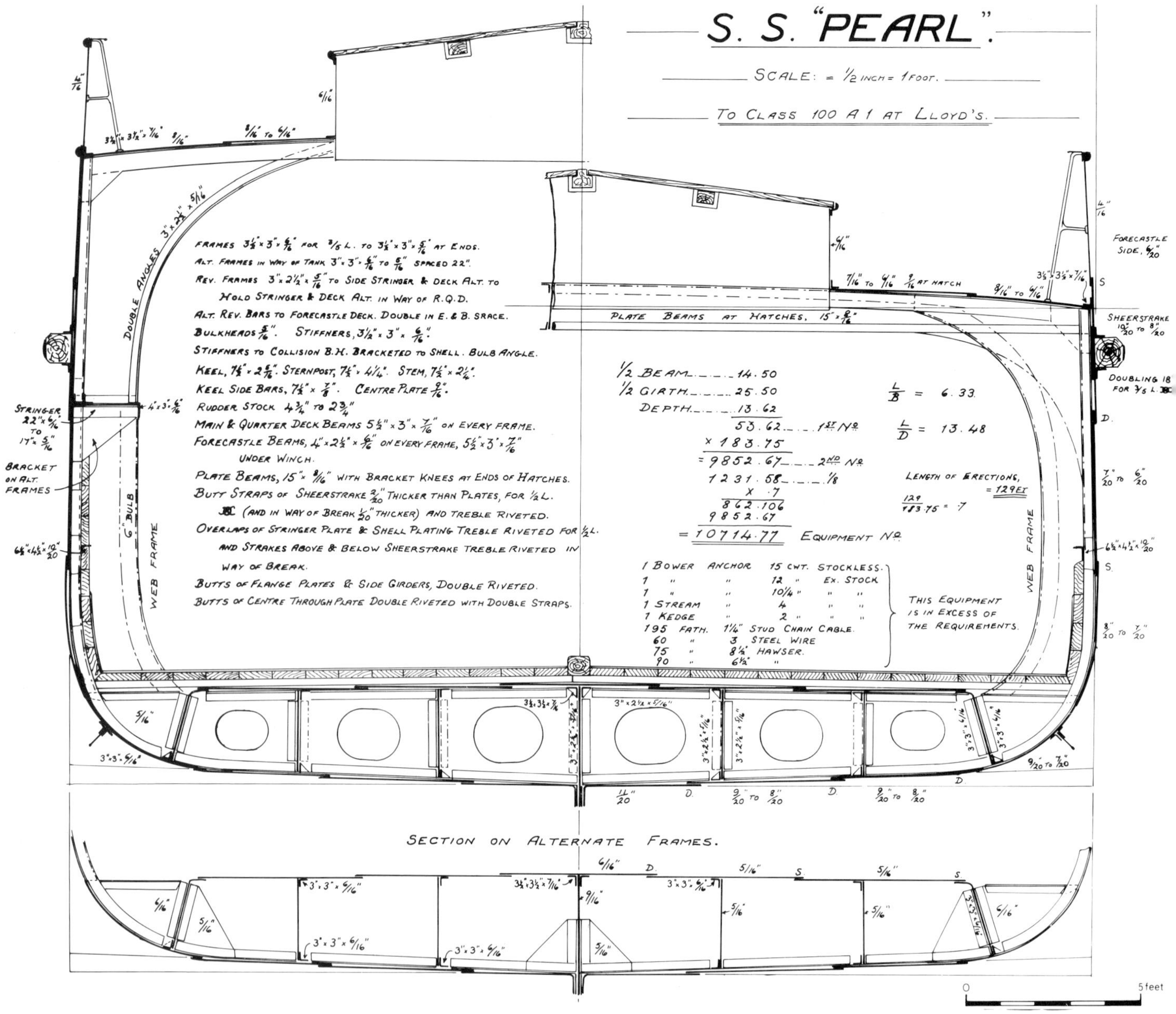
S. S. "PEARL".
SCALE: = 1/2 INCH = 1 FOOT.
TO CLASS 100 A 1 AT LLOYD'S.
FRAMES 3½"x 3" x 6/16" FOR 3/5 L. TO 3½" x 3" x 5/16" AT ENDS.
ALT. FRAMES IN WAY OF TANK 3" x 3" x 6/16" TO 5/16" SPACED 22".
REV. FRAMES 3" x 2½" x 5/16" TO SIDE STRINGER & DECK ALT. TO HOLD STRINGER & DECK ALT. IN WAY OF R.Q.D.
ALT. REV. BARS TO FORECASTLE DECK. DOUBLE IN E. & B. SPACE.
BULKHEADS 5/16". STIFFENERS, 3½" x 3" x 6/16".
STIFFNERS TO COLLISION B.H. BRACKETED TO SHELL. BULB ANGLE.
KEEL, 7½" x 2⅝". STERNPOST, 7½" x 4¼". STEM, 7½" x 2¼".
KEEL SIDE BARS, 7½" x 7/8". CENTRE PLATE 9/16".
RUDDER STOCK 4¾" TO 2¾"
MAIN & QUARTER DECK BEAMS 5½" x 3" x 7/16" ON EVERY FRAME.
FORECASTLE BEAMS, 4" x 2½" x 6/16" ON EVERY FRAME, 5½" x 3" x 7/16" UNDER WINCH.
PLATE BEAMS, 15" x 8/16" WITH BRACKET KNEES AT ENDS OF HATCHES.
BUTT STRAPS OF SHEERSTRAKE 2/20" THICKER THAN PLATES, FOR ½ L.
(AND IN WAY OF BREAK 1/20" THICKER) AND TREBLE RIVETED.
OVERLAPS OF STRINGER PLATE & SHELL PLATING TREBLE RIVETED FOR ½ L. AND STRAKES ABOVE & BELOW SHEERSTRAKE TREBLE RIVETED IN WAY OF BREAK.
BUTTS OF FLANGE PLATES & SIDE GIRDERS, DOUBLE RIVETED.
BUTTS OF CENTRE THROUGH PLATE DOUBLE RIVETED WITH DOUBLE STRAPS.
PLATE BEAMS AT HATCHES. 15" x 8/16"
½ BEAM 14.50
½ GIRTH 25.50
DEPTH 13.62
53.62 1ST No
x 183.75
= 9852.67 2ND No
1231.58 1/8
x 7
862.106
9852.67
= 10714.77 EQUIPMENT No
L/B = 6.33
L/D = 13.48
LENGTH OF ERECTIONS, = 129 FT
129 / 183.75 = .7
1 BOWER ANCHOR 15 CWT. STOCKLESS.
1 " " 12 " EX. STOCK
1 " " 10¼ "
1 STREAM " 4 "
1 KEDGE 2 "
195 FATH. 1¼" STUD CHAIN CABLE.
60 " 3 STEEL WIRE
75 " 8½" HAWSER.
90 " 6½" "
THIS EQUIPMENT IS IN EXCESS OF THE REQUIREMENTS.
DOUBLE ANGLES
STRINGER 22" x 6/16" TO 17" x 5/16"
BRACKET ON ALT. FRAMES
6" BULB
WEB FRAME
FORECASTLE SIDE, 6/20
SHEERSTRAKE 10/20 TO 8/20
DOUBLING 18 FOR 3/5 L.
SECTION ON ALTERNATE FRAMES.
0
5feet

22 Midship Section of PEARL built 1896. The calculation on the right was used to determine the size of anchor required by Lloyd's. Later vessels dispensed with side stringers.

Perhaps the most exacting work was that of heating and bending the long bars of angle iron, for the frames. The frame bending gang first took a long strip of iron, about one inch by a quarter of an inch thick called the set-iron, to the scrieve board and bent it to the shape required for the frame as shown by the line cut into the board. The set-iron was then taken to the bending blocks; large iron grids with holes about six inches apart. The shape was marked out on the grid, making due allowance for the shrinkage of the frame bar, with a liberal supply of pins, dogs and collars placed in suitable holes in the grid (12a). In addition, details of bevelling to suit the curving in of the plating towards the ends of the ship were noted. While this was being done, the frame bar was heated until red-hot in the furnace. As soon as all the pins were in place, it was pulled out and immediately set upon by the frame bending gang in order to bend it round the pins and dogs before it had time to cool and stiffen, using hand levers and tongs. The men had to use all their speed, skill and concentration to shape it immediately, since it could not be returned to the furnace once bending had begun. Where the bevel was particularly complex, at the bow and stern, the bar was taken from the furnace and bevelled first, reheated and bent to shape. Joggling of the frames was general by this time to avoid using packing pieces (12c). This was done cold, as by this period the quality of the steel was satisfactory for cold working. The rivet holes were also punched prior to bending.

Plates were prepared by rolling them with flattening rolls if required, then the appropriate template from the mould loft was used to mark out the edges of the plate and the rivet holes. The plates were then lifted by a small crane on to the shearing and hole punching machine. The shears were then used to cut the plate to size. The shears and punch could make up to thirty-five strokes per minute on some machines, and so operators had to be very agile moving the plate as they had less than two seconds to arrange the next cut, or move it on to the next hole to be punched. About 80,000 rivet holes were required for a coaster of 500 gross tons. The plate edges were later smoothed off using an edge planing

Plate 23 The steam tanker PASS OF MELFORT of 708 gross tons. (above).

BRONZITE loading coal from compartment boats at Goole. (below).

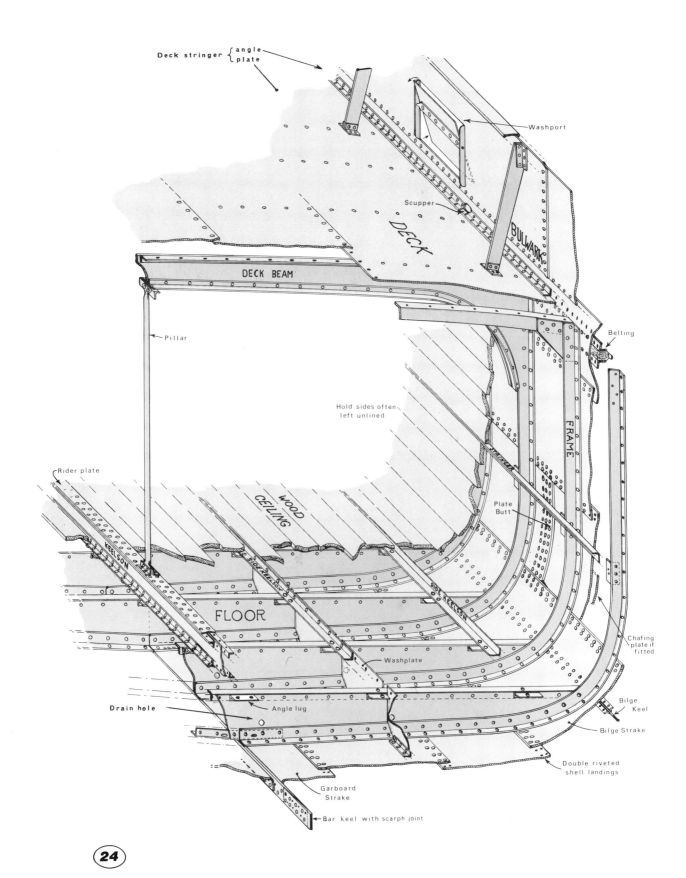

Deck stringer { angle
              { plate

Washport

Scupper

DECK

BULWARK

DECK BEAM

Pillar

Belting

Hold sides often
left unlined

FRAME

Rider plate

WOOD
CEILING

Plate
Butt

KEELSON

SIDE KEELSON

FLOOR

Chafing
plate if
fitted

Washplate

Angle lug

Bilge
Keel

Drain hole

Bilge Strake

Double riveted
shell landings

Garboard
Strake

Bar keel with scarph joint

(24)

**CUT - AWAY SECTION THROUGH
A COASTER WITH OPEN FLOORS.**

Built to Lloyd's Classification. Registered dimensions were 142.3′ x 26.1′ x 11.3′. Washplates are fitted to
prevent debris in the bilges from sliding back and forth with the motion of the vessel and damaging
the bottom plates. Note drain holes to allow water to reach the pump suction wells.

SIDE INTERCOSTAL KEELSON

FLOOR PLATE   CENTER THROUGH PLATE

TANK MARGIN PLATE

KEEL PLATE

FRAME LEGS

25 Ship with a double bottom under construction in Dublin Dockyard. Note the lugs on the centre through plate for attaching the floors. Similarly lugs have been riveted to the tank margin plate to attach the frame legs, one of which is being riveted to the bilge bracket plate by the riveter in the foreground while, to the left, rivets are heated ready for use. A pile of completed frame legs lies on the right. Workers beyond the frame legs are shoring up the centre through plate and behind them a shipwright erects a launching platform for the vessel in the background.

machine. If the plate was to have more than a slight curvature, it was put through the plate bending rolls. The various components were assembled on skids at the head of the building berth and riveted together to form sub-assemblies which were then erected. Hydraulic riveters exerting a pressure of up to forty tons were used to give the best results. Meanwhile the keel bars were drilled ready for riveting, and since the maximum length of bars available was about fifty feet, the ends were scarphed together after positioning on the building blocks. The shipwrights would have erected the blocks according to instructions from the drawing office. The usual slope of building blocks was five-eighths of an inch per foot. The height of the blocks was usually about four feet six inches spaced four feet apart, so that riveters could easily work under the ship. Heavy piles about fifteen inches square were driven into the ground under the line of the blocks and baulks of timber called ground ties laid on top to support the keel blocks. Considerable care was taken to see that the blocks were correctly positioned since they supported the ships considerable weight while it was being constructed.

Once the keel bar was completed, the garboard strakes were riveted into place, followed by the frames and floors, in a vessel without a double bottom (24). Where a flat plate keel was being used, the plates for this were laid first, followed by the centre-through-plate and then by the floors which were usually already riveted to the frames. The frames were erected from the stern towards the bows and deck beams temporarily attached with additional support from timber shores and light timbers forty to fifty feet long called ribbands, clamped along the frame tops to add extra support. After the frames were in position, they were adjusted until perpendicular to the keel, often called "horning". The method of erecting complete transverse frames cannot be used for vessels with double bottoms, which became general for larger coasters during the 1880s, and so the sequence was, keel plates, centre-through-plate, floors, tank margin plate and frame legs (25). Though most of the plates could be made from the mould loft templates, the complex shapes at bow and stern were usually made from templates taken from the ship, after the frames were in place. The deck and shell plating were then begun, the shell plating was usually begun with an in-strake near the bilge and then, when several in-strakes were in place, the out-strakes were put on. The riveting was started at the mid-point working outwards, so that if the holes were not quite true, the error would be spread equally over both sides. The plates were then made watertight by expanding the edge with a caulking tool (12b). Decks were usually begun with the deck stringer plate and stringer angle (▒). Deck beams were laid off from the screive board and also given the correct camber (or round-up), commonly quarter of an inch for every foot of midship beam. In earlier times they were bent hot but by 1900 most yards had machines capable of bending them cold. Brackets (beam knees) were then fitted to each end. Prior to fitting, holes were punched in the beam for riveting on the deck plates or bolting down the

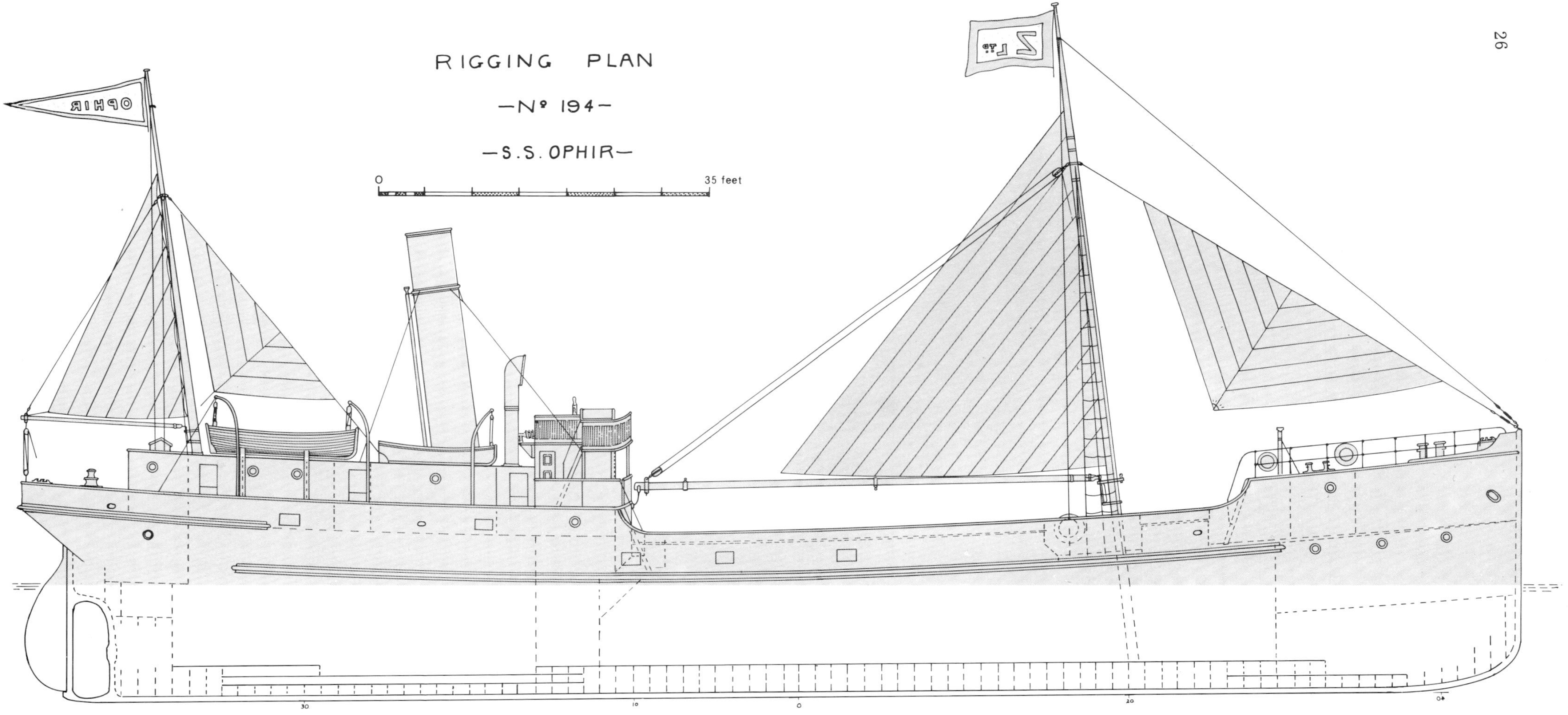
RIGGING PLAN
—Nº 194—
—S.S. OPHIR—
0
35 feet
OPHIR
Z Lᵀᴰ
30
10
0
20
40

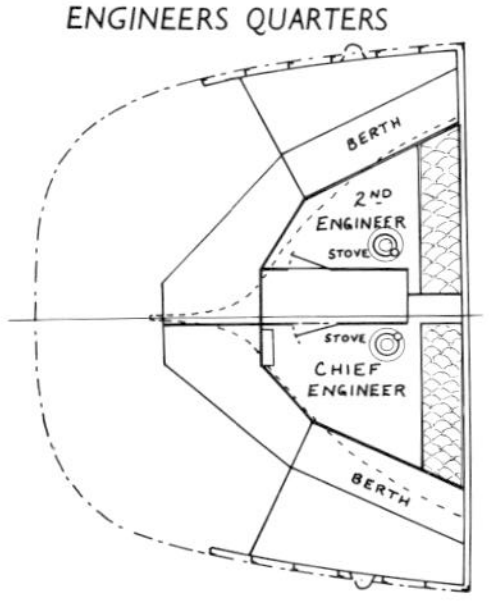
ENGINEERS QUARTERS
BERTH
2ND ENGINEER
STOVE
STOVE
CHIEF ENGINEER
BERTH

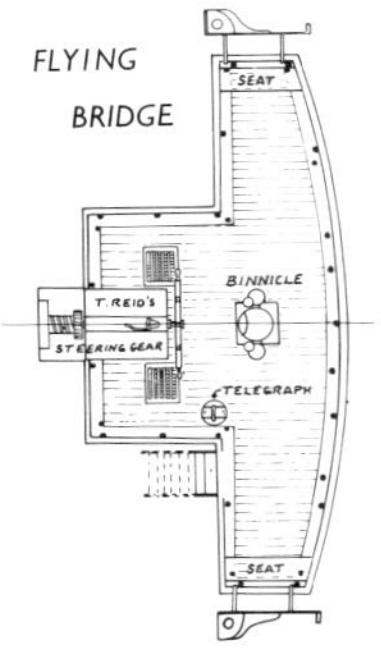
FLYING
BRIDGE
SEAT
BINNICLE
T REID'S
STEERING GEAR
TELEGRAPH
SEAT

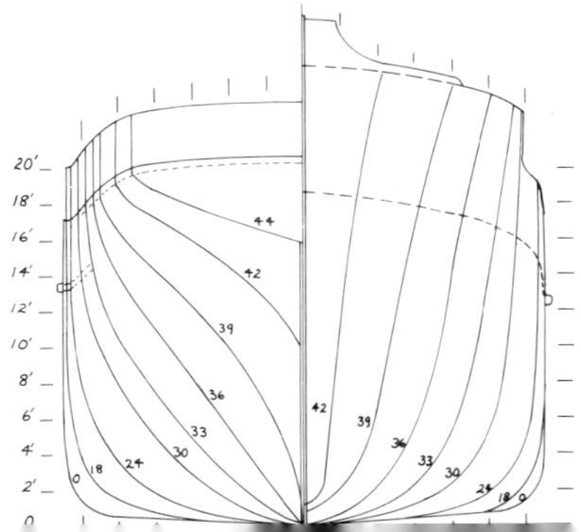
20'
18'
16'
14'
12'
10'
8'
6'
4'
2'
0
44
42
39
36
33
30
24
18
0
42
39
36
33
30
24
18
0

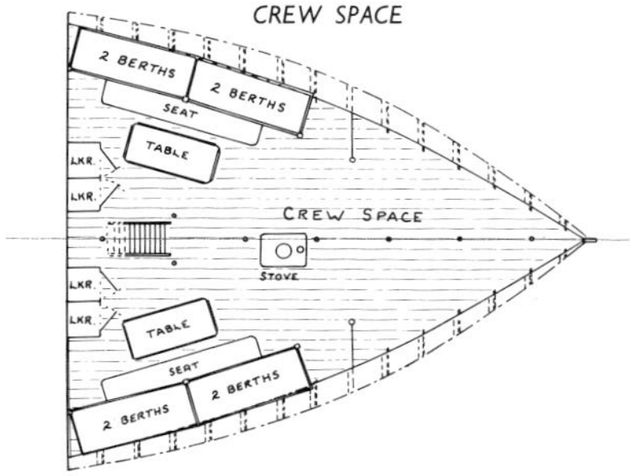
CREW SPACE
2 BERTHS
2 BERTHS
SEAT
TABLE
LKR.
LKR.
CREW SPACE
STOVE
LKR.
LKR.
TABLE
SEAT
2 BERTHS
2 BERTHS

Plate 26

Steam Coaster OPHIR

GENERAL ARRANGEMENT

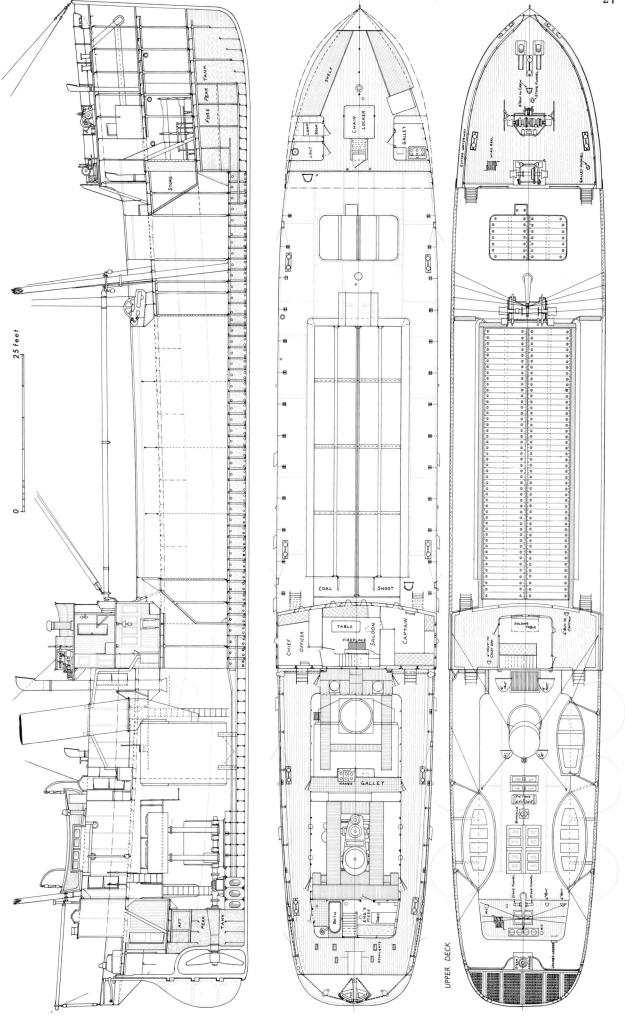

UPPER DECK

wooden deck. In the latter case, horizontal knees (brackets) or a deck stringer plate would be fitted along the sides to prevent twisting of the wooden deck in a rough sea. Hatch coamings also cause a loss of strength in decks, and to allow for this, a strong coaming round the opening spreads the load to beams at either end of the hatches which were specially strengthened and were often supported by pillars from the keelson. To eliminate these pillars, extra strong frames, known as web frames (22) were fitted at intervals and at ends of hatches. Pillars were usually retained under the bridge and forecastle. Bulkheads, walls of plating extending from side to side or lengthwise, were used to divide the ship into a number of watertight compartments, so reducing the danger from flooding in the event of a collision or grounding and to separate cargo from engine room and crew. The collision bulkhead, fitted in the bow was designed to prevent the hold flooding and this saved many coasters from a watery grave. Most coasters had solid bulwarks rather than open rails and they were essentially a continuation of the side plating supported by stanchions, which were usually placed on every third frame and in any case not more than six feet apart.

With the introduction of iron and later steel-shipbuilding in the 1880s, the shipwrights' work was considerably reduced. Most of their work was now done in the mould loft making the wooden templates, but they still faired the steelwork and maintained the shoring and staging as well as carrying out all the heavy timber work. They were thus mainly involved in laying wooden decks, fitting masts and spars, lifeboats and deck gear generally. Perhaps the most varied work was carried out by the Blacksmith's shop. This was equipped with various hearths for heating the iron and steel as well as large furnaces for heating components to be forged into shape under the steam hammer, such as the stern frame and stem bar. The blacksmiths made many other parts such as, boat davits, hold pillars, rails, stanchions and rudder fittings. It was also their job to make and repair all the cutting tools used by the ironworkers and engineers. The engineering shops carried out all necessary machining of components prepared by the blacksmith, such as rudder pintles, rudder quadrant and roller fairleads. They also did all the turning and fitting of brass bearing surfaces required. However their main work was in the engine room where they carried out all installation, testing and finally the running trials.

Though the well known London shipbuilder, Scott-Russell, launched at least one ship fully completed with steam up in the 1850s, it was normal to launch the vessel when the hull was complete and so reduce the weight that had to be supported by the launching ways. In later years the speed of the vessel on reaching the water was accurately calculated so that sufficient drag chains could be fitted to stop the vessel at the required position. Also the maximum dip of the stern on reaching the water was checked to make sure the water was deep enough to receive it. By 1900 the stability of the vessel was also checked to make sure it would float upright on entering the water. In earlier times several vessels capsized on launching. The preparation of the ship for launching was carried out by the shipwrights. On completion of the hull, two sets of ways were erected. The fixed ways, extending from the bow of the ship to about low tide mark, were built of heavy timbers about twenty-four inches square. The slope used varied from yard to yard, but most were given a slight camber down to the water. The sliding ways were fitted to a timber cradle which supported the ship. A day or so before the launch, the cradle was partly dismantled so that the ways could be greased with tallow followed by soft soap. The sliding ways were then reassembled and the 'dog shores' or 'daggers' fitted to prevent the sliding ways moving. Early on the morning of the launch (the highest tides occur around 12 a.m.), long thin wedges were driven under the cradle, raising it and transferring much of the weight of the ship to the cradle, so that the keel blocks could be knocked out. The fixed ways were then greased and all was ready for launching. At the moment of launching the dog shores were knocked out by a series of levers and the ship slid into the water accompanied by the cheers of those in the yard (29a). Celebrations following the launch usually took up the rest of the day.

Prior to the launch, owners deliberated on a name for the vessel. The Merchant Shipping Act of 1906 made it mandatory that only one vessel at a time could have a particular name under the British flag unless the vessel already registered was to be renamed. They were often named after girls in the family or a merchant's family with an eye to the proposed trade. Names were often repeated many times, though some owners would not repeat a name if the vessel was lost, in case the bad luck was transferred to the new ship. Fitting out was then begun by putting the engine and boiler aboard. In the case of the Dublin Dockyard the Harbour Board's one hundred ton crane was used. This yard did not make engines or boilers and subcontracted this work to specialist builders. The machinery arrived by sea and was unloaded by the crane. The new ship was then towed to the crane and the machinery put aboard. The casing aft could then be closed up and the galley fitted, which was usually over the boiler in coasters. Similarly masts and deck gear were lifted into place and positioned by the shipwrights. The rigging shop could begin the setting up of the shrouds and rigging for the derricks and sails. The sailmaker also made up the hatch tarpaulins, boat covers and weather cloths for the bridge. Meanwhile the cabins were fitted out by the joiner and cabinet maker generally, guided by detail drawings from the outfit draughtsman.

The rough notebook showing details for the outfitting of the steamer SPRAY built by Hall, Russell & Co, Aberdeen in 1872 has survived and some of the numerous sketches are shown (30). The first pages of the notebook show details for gingerbread-work at the bow and the stern decoration. The vessel was closely similar to WARKWORTH (51), with the addition of a small fore hatch between the forecastle and the foremast, and all decks of wood. Sketches for the smith-work show that the vessel had a yard on the foremast but apparently no gaffs. The SPRAY had a registered length of 181.1 feet and was built for Pyman, Watson & Co., of West Hartlepool. She was sold to Ellis & McHardy, the Aberdeen coal merchants, in 1887.

Launch of FLUOR from Scott's yard at Bowling (1898).

29

Dublin Dockyard Co; Two vessels on No.2 slip, the nearer belongs to Joseph Fisher of Newry.

She became something of an institution during her 45 years with them, and so it was not surprising that the order for a new SPRAY went to Hall, Russell. On delivery in 1932, the old SPRAY was sold to Monroe Brothers' Kyle Shipping Co. of Liverpool where she became the DUNVEGAN. She traded for them until 1943 when she passed to the Springfal S.S. Co. and was hulked in 1945. The drawings in the notebook show that the cowl vent was in use for the engine room while mushroom type vents were used for all other requirements. Details of the old type up-and-down action windlass are also shown. This had a handle on each side and was usually operated by two men. By about 1900 this had been completely superceded by the steam windlass for larger vessels or the hand-cranked windlass in smaller vessels (7). The chain stopper shown continued in general use for most of the steam era. While out-fitting was going on, the plumbers' shop completed the necessary pipework. The amount of pipework progressively increased over the years as steam deck machinery became general. However the greatest increase was brought about by central heating and the fitting of wash-basins throughout the officer's cabins after the second world war.

At some stage during the fitting out, the vessel was drydocked to attach the rudder and clear away the gear attached for launching. Final adjustments were made and at the Dublin Dockyard, while the vessel was empty, the stability was checked by moving a known weight across the deck through a measured distance and noting how much the vessel listed compared with that predicted by the drawing office. The draft of water fore and aft was also noted and the displacement calculated, this being equal to the actual weight of the ship. This was expected to be in close agreement with that predicted by the design department.

The vessel was then 'readied' for sea trials. At the trials, the shipbuilders, the engine builders and the owners would be represented, probably accompanied by their consultants. Trials light or laden were then carried out as agreed in the contract and sometimes trials in both conditions were carried out. Owners were usually interested in trials laden, and so a suitable full cargo offering near the yard would be loaded and the owners generally watched to see if the ship could load the full deadweight as specified in the contract. The ship was then taken out on the measured mile. This usually was a sheltered length of water on the adjacent shore of which there were marks one mile apart which could be observed from the ship. The tidal currents are also accurately known and usually eliminated from speed calculations by making runs first in one direction and then in the other, accurately timed by stopwatch. Graphs of propellor revolutions, propellor slip, and horse-power are plotted against the vessel's speed in knots and the fuel consumption determined by weighing the amount of coal used. Typical of the measurements taken in the engine room are those for the coaster MICKLEHAM recorded by the engine builders (31). The graphs are indicator diagrams and show how the steam pressure changed within the cylinder during a complete cycle, that is a down stroke followed by an up stroke. The top of the cylinder is indicated by 'T' and the bottom by 'B'. The upper diagram shows the pressure changes in the high pressure cylinder and the lower diagram in each case shows the pressure changes in the low pressure cylinder. The solid horizontal lines represent atmospheric pressure (about 14 lbs). In the upper diagrams, at 'T', steam is admitted at 130 lbs and the piston moves down, the motion causing the valve gear to close the admission valve, after which the pressure drops as the steam expands and the piston continues to move down until it reaches the bottom of the cylinder (below 'B'), where the exhaust valve opens and remains open for most of the up stroke, which is recorded by the lower line (now reading from right to left). When the valve closes there is a small rise in pressure as the steam remaining in the cylinder is compressed followed by the vertical rise back to 130 lbs as the inlet valve opens to begin the cycle again. Since the cylinders are double acting, the plot for the bottom cylinder appears as the mirror image of the cycle just described. The mean effective pressure (M. E. P.) is calculated for the complete cycle which acts on the piston, and the indicated horse power worked out. The steam, as can be seen from the tables below the diagrams, leaves the high pressure cylinder at between 24 and 26 lbs. So this is the pressure at which the steam is admitted to the low pressure cylinder in the lower diagrams. The solid horizontal line represents atmospheric pressure, but the pressure drops below this and shows how important the vacuum of the condenser is. Indicator diagrams are also used to check the condition of engines as they soon show if the valves are leaking or incorrectly set.

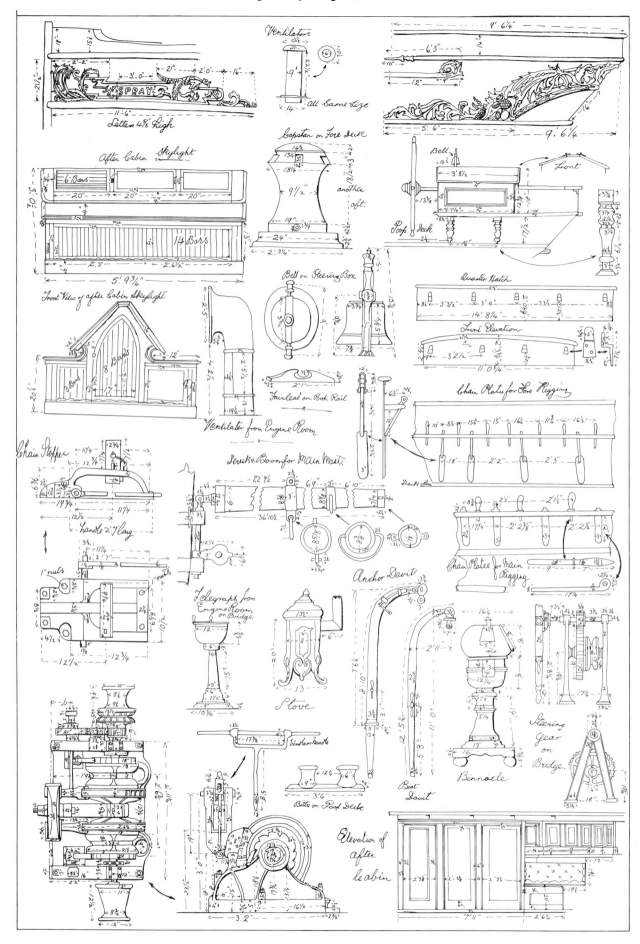

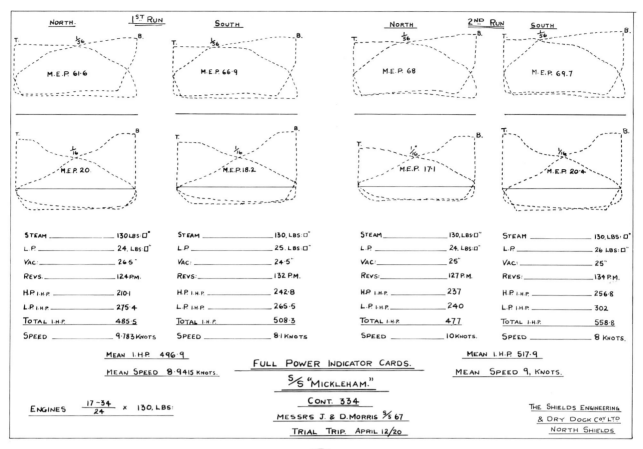

(31)

By the turn of the century it was unusual for vessels not to meet the terms of the contract as much experience had been gained in calculating weight of materials and displacement. In earlier times failures did occur and owners sometimes refused delivery. As soon as the loaded trials were completed successfully, the owners' crew took over and the ship sailed on her maiden voyage.

Repairing Steam Coasters

This was perhaps a better business proposition than building, for whereas owners could usually defer ordering new ships, repairs generally had to be put in hand as soon as the damage was sustained or noticed if it affected the vessel's seaworthiness or cargo carrying ability. This was required if the vessel was to remain classed with Lloyd's, or more seriously, the vessel could be prevented from sailing if considered unseaworthy. Many shipyards had their own repair departments and the Dublin Dockyard was no exception, indeed, vessels were built there as a means of keeping workers fully employed in between repair jobs. Dublin is well situated for the Irish Sea coasters as many regularly visited the port. The dockyard was adjacent to the Harbour Board's graving dock and the No. 2 graving slip was actually within the dockyard complex. The dock could be emptied in about 30 minutes while vessels weighing up to 1,000 tons could be hauled out on to the slip in about 20 minutes allowing emergency repairs to be quickly attended to. The commonest was rivets loosened in the bottom plating near the bow due to the ship plunging into the troughs of heavy seas, with the flat bottom plates taking the full force of the impact. The repair facilities were electrically lit so that work could go on round the clock. In addition, compressed air was available for riveting, drilling, caulking and sand blasting while water was on hand for testing and filling tanks and boilers. The slip was generally used for coaster repairs often with two coasters on the slip simultaneously (29b). It was sometimes necessary to slide or launch one of the vessels sideways in order to slip or unslip the other but the yard were practiced in this and it was easily carried out by them.

Usually the repair period for a coaster was the survey every five years for the renewal of the Loadline provided there was no serious damage to be repaired earlier. A loadline was a legal requirement and was issued by the Board of Trade and lasted for the period of five years. For the issue of the certificate, the ship had to be surveyed structurally in dry dock or on a slip. To ease the work on its survey staff, the Board of Trade agreed that these rules could be administered by an approved classification society such as Lloyd's, the British Corporation and certain foreign societies. The initials of the assigning authority are placed on each side of the mark. When the vessel had been placed in drydock or slipped, the surveyor was called in and, accompanied by representatives of the ship's owners and the repair yard, he would go round the bottom. If there was likely to be an insurance claim, the underwriters surveyor would be there also. The shell plating would be surveyed for any damaged or corroded plates. Damage is obvious, but for thin plates the surveyor's experi-

ence would guide him where to look. These were the days before ultrasonic thickness test-
ers and the surveyor's friend was his test hammer. By listening to the sound and feeling
the vibration with the fingers of the other hand an experienced surveyor could detect a thin
plate. Suspect plates would then be drilled and the thickness in way of the test hole gauged
by a plate gauge. Plates were measured in twentieths. Anything below four twentieths was
out immediately. A coaster's plating was usually more than three eights. On shell plans, the
thicknesses were denoted by weight very often, thus 10 lbs was a quarter inch thick plate.

Putting on a doubling plate was an accepted method of coping with the problem. It depended on how much of the plate was thin. It was not reasonable to demand an entire plate
renewal for a small area of thinning, but a doubler had to be big enough to ensure that it
was fastened to the frames. In terms of cost it was not cheap since rivets had to be removed so that it could be fastened and a big doubler could cost as much as a new plate.
One objection to a doubler was that if not carefully red-leaded, corrosion could go on between doubler and plate. The arrival of welding made things much simpler as it was possible
to cut out the bad part and weld in an insert, as long as these were reasonable in size and
not postage stamps. However, doublers could be taken too far; such as doublers on doublers!
As well as looking for thin plates, rivets were checked for worn down points. If a rivet head
was so worn down that the countersink was gone, its holding power would be badly reduced.
There could also be slack rivets which would cause leaks and could be detected by hammer
testing. Banged hard with a hammer while the other thumb felt the rivet, a shaky one would
be obvious.

The rudder would also be checked and wear on the pintles and gudgeons noted.   Worn
pintles were replaced or built up and the rudder braces were drilled out and bushed in the
case of the gudgeons. It was also advisable to check the lining up of the helm indicator on
the bridge. By this method, creeping twist in the rudder stock could be revealed.   Anchors
and cables were ranged on the bottom of the dock and checked for wear and if necessary
sent for annealing. Inside the ship the frames were checked and badly distorted or fractur-
ed frames (and beams) would require rectification. In most coasters there were generally a
number of distorted beam knees to deal with. Bulkhead plating and stiffeners had to be checked also. Double bottom tanks were always unpopular with surveyors, as on these small ships
they were cramped and generally damp and dirty. If the ship had done any bad grounding,
buckled floors would result and might need straightening. All tanks were subject to a pressure test. This could be achieved by filling the tank until the water was up the sounding
pipe to give a reasonable head. The deck was also tested for thickness and then there would be
the question of closure of deck openings. This meant checking ventilator coamings and seeing their closing plugs and similarly for the air pipes; seeing that all the doors were in good
condition and closing properly.   Hatches had to have sound coamings, proper beams, sound
wood covers, tarpaulins and proper means of lashing and wedging. Side scuttles had to be in
good order with deadlights which could be closed (the rubbers in these usually needed replacing).   There were no rules for accommodation for many years apart from minimum floor
space and head room as defined in the Merchant Shipping Acts of 1894 and 1906. In the
1920s, the Board of Trade instructed their surveyors to report on the standards they found
on the ships they visited. As a result of the poor conditions found, the Board finally issued
instructions regarding standards of accommodation in 1937. These were not statutory and
it was up to the Surveyor to try and get compliance. The only enforcing medium was the penal-
ty of disallowing the deduction of the spaces from the gross tonnage. It was not until 1953
that the first actual crew space rules were issued which had to be complied with. This is
why ships built after that date have more plumbing and wiring. It also meant more trials
since it was necessary to see that standards of heating, lighting, ventilation and sanitation
had been met. These rules eliminated forecastle accommodation, though old ships were not
expected to comply with this, they were expected to comply as far as practicable.

Typical of the sort of repair which surveyors were called to, was the repair of the coaster NEWRY which while on passage to Liverpool was hit by a smaller coaster, the latter's
bows slicing right through the forecastle of the NEWRY. Repairs carried out by the Dublin
Dockyard required all the plates and frames to be made good and new wood decks laid. As
this was proceeding the carpenters worked to replace the forecastle accommodation. The
vessel was able to limp to Dublin as the collision bulkhead held. However, most of the work
was of a more routine nature such as painting and putting coasters through their surveys.

Collisions were generally followed by an exchange of telegrams between the owners thus:
'To Zillah, Liverpool: 10.47 a.m. Your steamer Priscilla ran into my steamer Enid in Menai
Straits this morning. I hold you responsible for damage done will advise you later as to time
and place of survey'. This was the telegram sent on the 21st of November 1911 by the
manager of the Dinorwic Quarry ships, Mr. E. E. Neele, to Mr. W. A. Savage of the Zillah
Shipping & Carrying Co. of Liverpool who promptly wired back at 11.31 a.m. 'Your telegram
will attend survey without prejudice meanwhile hold you liable for damage done to our

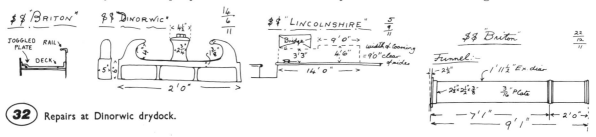

32 Repairs at Dinorwic drydock.

steamer_ Zillah.' It is interesting to examine the claim submitted against Zillah in the April following the incident:

To amount of repairs Houson & Co.	179.	0.	0.
To detention of vessel Nov. 22 - Dec. 12/11.			
viz:- 18 days @ £8 per day.	144.	0.	0.
To detention of vessel during trial.			
viz:- 2 days @ £8 per day.	16.	0.	0.
Paid Lloyd's agent for Certificate of Seaworthyness.		10.	6.
To paid Lloyd's survey fees before and after repair	8.	5.	0.
J. A. Rigley photos.		12.	0.
Superintendent Engineer.	10.	10.	0.
	Total £ 358.	17.	6.

As can be seen from the above figures, the cost of the repair from the shipowner's point of view is less than half the cost of the collision. Photographs were generally taken as part of the evidence as the claims were often settled long after the ship had been repaired.

The Dinorwic Quarry Company unlike most owners, did in fact have their own dry dock at Port Dinorwic which generally maintained the company ships and also undertook repairs for local owners from Connah's Quay and Liverpool. Their dry dock could accept coasters up to about 160 feet in length and Coppack's FARFIELD (80), was usually sent there for her overhauls and surveys. Mr. E. E. Neele, who managed the dry dock during the early part of the 20th century, kept a notebook which gives details of some of the repairs carried out such as the entry for the 14th of June 1911: 's. s. BRITON. New forward hatch fore and after, Double in way of hatch where wasted. Butt the doubling angle of the shear strake and joggle over the coaming angle. Renew defective carling, overhaul hatches and repair.Board of Trade survey.' This repair is fairly typical of the work carried out to meet Board of Trade requirements and illustrates doubling of a plate (32). Later, in December, she was in for a new funnel (32). On the same day the notebook records that the s. s. DINORWIC required a new fairlead and a dimensioned sketch (32), shows the pattern required. The company had its own foundry department so they could make up the appropriate wooden pattern and then make the casting. Fairleads and bollards tended to get broken when coasters were moored in exposed harbours and were ranging about at jetties open to the sea. The LINCOLNSHIRE needed rather more extensive repairs as the sketch (32), shows and included a 'new smoke-box, furnace fronts, (fire) bars etc., 2 bunker sides 12' long by 11'0" deep. 2 bunker ends.' The following year on the 8th of July 1912 she returned to have her boiler retubed, 62 plain tubes 3" in diameter by 6'2½" and 18 stay tubes. One of the main tasks in drydock is re-painting and he notes that the 145 feet long s. s. BANGOR belonging to the Anglesey Shipping Co. took the following; two coats black varnish (27 gallons used), while the boot-topping required 65 lbs for the first coat and 53 lbs for the second.

The company's own flagship ELIDIR began an overhaul on the 12th of February 1912 beginning with a new stern bush for the propellor shaft, and two new bilge discharge valves. Attention then turned to the boiler where a new main steam pipe was made and fitted in plus two new sludge doors for the boiler. The high pressure piston rod was taken out and trued up to '3 and 9/16 exact', replaced, and a new steam-tight packing fitted. A new M. P. piston was also apparently made. A similar notebook for 1920 reveals that a new 'scotch' boiler for s. s. PENRHYN measuring 13'0" by 10'0" with three furnaces, fittings and smokebox mountings was priced at £2,830 with delivery 6/7 months, reflecting the short-lived boom following the end of the first world war. It duly arrived and was fitted in April 1921. On the 18th of August, the old steamer PANMURE came in for a new propellor, another fairly common requirement, while the three year old TALACRE had her original 35' derrick replaced with one measuring 50'10", the original apparently not having a sufficient reach. The Dinorwic Drydock did not do major repairs, but when the ELIDIR was involved in a serious grounding the entire double bottom was rebuilt (see page 72).

From the crews' point of view drydocking was not popular as it generally meant being signed off or accepting half-pay and working aboard the cold ship and this tended to happen in winter when coasters, particularly in ballast, rode over the crest of a wave and repeatedly slammed down into the wave troughs and loosened rivets. Crews also made repairs a-float, such as applying a red-leaded canvas patch over a few leaking rivets often followed by a cement patch over the whole area. If there was a bad rivet in the fore-peak, for example, the rivet was punched out and then a cork on a string was pushed out to float to the surface where a bolt was quickly attached and pulled into the hole. A nut and washer were then fitted and tightened up. Cement boxes were an accepted first-aid treatment to tide vessels over to the next drydocking. In a big cement box, a few empty bottles were placed with their necks just breaking the surface of the cement to provide holes for crow-bars when it was time to remove the cement patch and make permanent repairs to the leak.

Repairs were also carried out by putting the coaster aground and digging underneath and so reaching the leaking seam. This was also a common method of painting the hull. If the vessel was put aground on one of the higher tides in an area where there was a considerable difference between springs and neaps, say 10 feet, during the neaps the tide would hardly reach the vessel and painting could go on practically uninterrupted. The area most prone to corrosion is around the waterline and this area could thus be effectively treated, but the bottom which could not usually be done in this way had to await drydocking.

The most frequent maintenance work for the crews was painting and this never ending task was undertaken whenever work and weather permitted, usually when the ship had to wait to load or discharge. The basic colour scheme was laid down by most owners, but the details were usually at the discretion of the mate who might ask permission to grain and panel the engine casing so that it looked like wood panelling, rather than paint it plain brown. Owners such as Kennaughs took particular pride in their grey hulled coasters but it meant more work for their crews, who also had to mix their own paint in the 1920s. Red lead for the boot-topping and undercoating elsewhere came in powdered form. To make this up, the powder was first soaked in soapy water (to prevent it swelling when applied). After the water had been drained off, the pigment was mixed with boiled oil (boiled linseed oil) and some 'driers' so that the paint would dry in a reasonable time. The grey paint arrived as a thick concentrated paste which was similarly made up by adding boiled oil and driers. The brown paint was so thick and stiff in winter that it had to be stood in a bucket of hot water to make it flow on the paint brush and so made painting the masts rather difficult in winter. As Kennaugh ships had a plain yellow funnel it required frequent painting if it was to be kept in good condition. Most coasters had four blocks permanently fitted to the funnel top to facilitate painting and when repainting was needed the mate or A. B. would go up the funnel ladder carrying a rope, climb up over the whistle and get a handhold on the rim of the funnel and then edge his way round the funnel to the first block precariously standing on the stiffening band to which the the funnel stays are attached. Having threaded the first block, he then used it to haul up the second and so on until all were threaded and bosun's chairs could be hauled up. This was usually the job for the day and as soon as it was finished, the rest of the day was their own. There would also be a general painting session whenever the ship was to visit the home port of Liverpool. The bridge decks were scrubbed and oiled, the brown paint inside the bulwarks touched up and the red hatch coamings looked over. Finally the brasswork would be given an extra polish.

The table of paint schemes below was compiled from notes kindly made available by Mr. I. W. Rooke who recorded coasters visiting Shoreham between 1936 and 1940. His early notes were not so detailed as later observations, hence the question marks. For ventilators the outside colour is given first followed by the inside colour. Usually only the colours for the main ventilators round the funnel is given, but where details for ventilators elsewhere has been recorded, it is given underneath the entry for the main ventilators. Ships observed plus extra or differing colour details are given in the right hand column.

COMPANIES having BLACK HULLS with RED BOOT-TOPPING.

Company	Superstructure	Boats	Masts	Ventilators (out/in)	Vessels observed, funnel colours and notes.
W. A. Andrew	Brown	?	Brown	?	Luffworth. Funnel; black, later buff, black top.
Anglo-Amer. Oil	Brown/White	White	?	Black/Red	Allegheny (black/green vents), Eastwick, Oneida, Caldergate, Southgate (company name on side, grey/white superstructure (1937). Funnel; red, black top.
E. P. Atkinson	Brown	Black	Brown	Black/Red Brown/Red	Faxfleet (yellow top line), Yokefleet (black derricks). Funnel; red, black top and two equally spaced black rings.
J. A. Billmeir	Brown	Black	?	?	Stangrove. Funnel; black, white band.
Brit. Isles Coasters	Brown	Brown	Brown	Black/Red Brown/Red	East Coaster (green boot-topping, black/black ventilators). South Coaster (mizzen topmast black). Funnel; buff, black top separated by a blue band.
Buchan & Hogg	Reddish Brown	White	Brown	Black/Red	Dungrange. Funnel; red, black top.
Bulk Oil S.S.	Brown/White	White	Brown	Black/Mauve (white edges)	Pass of Ballater, Pass of Balmaha, Pass of Leny, Pass of Melfort, White dividing line and hull line. Funnel; see Plate 23.
E. C. Burden	Brown	Green	?	?	Dunleith. Rigged with sails. Funnel; black, white band.
Cheesewright & Ford	Brown (grained)	White	Buff	Black, yellow tops/ Red	Foam Queen (brown masts and uppers), Jersey Queen (vents blue inside), Norman Queen (vents. black/blue). Funnel; buff with blue and white houseflag: white / blue
A. Chester	Buff	Brown	Buff	Brown/Red	Broomlands/Gorselands (buff a yellow shade). Southwick (brown derricks, cream masts, vent colour refers to this vessel only, others not recorded). Funnel; red, black top.
R. R. Clark	Brown	White	Brown	Black/Black (Westdale only)	Beeston, Edern, Halton, Overton, Westdale (grained masts), Weston (vents. black, brown tops/blue, others brown/white). Funnel buff with blue 'O'.
Stephenson Clarke	Brown	Brown	Brown	Black/Red	Eleanor Brooke, Henry Woodall, J. B. Paddon, Petworth, Pitwines, Portslade, Sylvia Beale. Pulborough (green boot-topping in 1938). Funnel: black with silver band.
Coast Lines	White/Brown	White	Brown	?	Anglian Coast, Cambrian Coast, Suffolk Coast (light brown boats and masts). White dividing line. Anglian Coast has black boot-topping. Funnel; black with white chevron continuous round funnel.
J. Constantine S.S.	White or Brown	White	Brown	Black/Red	Levenwood, Linwood (white hull line and topsides), Homewood. Funnel; red, black top and black ring, see Plate126.
W. Coombs	Brown	Black	Brown	Black/Black	Afon Dulais, Afon Towy (white boats, black/blue ventilators). Funnel; black with a narrow blue band.
Coppack Bros.	Brown (light)	White	Brown (dark)	Brown/Red Brown/Blue	Hove (black mizzen mast). Watergate (vents. and boats not recorded All have yellow top line. Funnel; buff, black top sometimes with 'c'.
Hugh Craig	Brown	Brown	Brown	?	Craigolive. Funnel; yellow, black top separated by broad red band.
Don David Coastal S.S.	White	Black	White	Black/Red	Efford (white dividing line), Continental Coaster (green boot-topping, no vent. colours noted). Funnel; black.
T. H. Donking	Brown	Brown	Brown	Black/Red	Trentwood, Whitetoft (blue boats). Teeswood (white boats and top line. See also grey hulls. Funnel; red with blue 'D' on white diamond, black top.
O. Dorey	Brown	Brown	Brown	Black/Red	Sarnia(black mast tops, white top line). Funnel; blue 'D' on white diamond superimposed on, and touching the sides of a red square itself superimposed on a narrower blue band on black.
F. T. Everard	Brown	White	Brown	Black/Red	Anonity(brown/red vents.), Asperity, Authority, Signality and Serenity (vents. buff/black). Ability (vents buff/buff). Aptity (vents. brown/red). Glen Mary (vents. not recorded). Agility (boats and vents not recorded). Funnel; black with flag: white / red
James Fisher	Brown/Red	Brown	Brown	Black/Pale Blue	Assurity and Annuity. ALL white top line.
	Brown/White	Varnish Brown		Yellow/Red	Arduity (white boats), Tirydail.
	Brown	White	Brown	Black/Red (yellow top)	Bay Fisher. Channel Fisher (buff masts/white tops, black/red vents). Loch Fisher (buff/blue vents., brown topsides). Torrington.
	Buff	White	Brown	Black/Black	Ford Fisher, Sound Fisher (no vents recorded). Funnel; buff, black top separated by white band with black 'F' and a thin black ring between buff and white band. All have yellow hull line.
Robert Gardner	Brown	White	Brown	Black/Red	Lancaster City, Mount Charles, Multistone (yellow topsides, vents black/black and brown/brown, varnished masts, mizzen black). Funnel; black, with black 'G' on white band.
Geo. Gibson	Light brown	Black	Buff	Black/Black Brown/red	Bowling (black mizzen mast). Funnel; black.
J. Gibson	Ochre	Black	Ochre	Black/Black Ochre/Ochre	Jim. Funnel; Black, with black 'G' on white band.

Company	Superstructure	Boats	Masts	Ventilators (out/in)	Vessels observed, funnel colours and notes.
Gillie & Blair	Brown	Brown	?	?	Cromarty Firth/Moray Firth (white dividing line), Northern Firth, Murrayfield. Funnel; black, white/thick blue/white bands.
Goole & Hull	Brown	Brown	Brown	Black/Black Brown/Brown	Goole (black mizzen), Dicky (black uppers, no vent details). Funnel; equal parts of black over white over red.
Hargreaves	Brown	White	Brown	Black/Red Brown/Red	Sanfry. Funnel; black with red band and four pointed white star with its points vertical and horizontal containing a black 'H'
Harris & Dixon	White	White	?	?	Horley, Dixley (dark buff uppers, brown boats). Funnel; buff with two narrow red bands.
P. Hawksfield	Brown	Brown	?	?	Peter Hawksfield. Funnel; buff with black top and red band with a white 'H' within the band.
John Hay	Light Brown	Brown	Brown	Black/Black Black/Red	The Viceroy. The Duchess (varnished boats, vents. black/red). The Marquis (varnished boats, vents. elsewhere;brown/red). Funnel; pink with a black top, see plate 6.
Henry & MacGregor	Brown	White	Brown	Black/Red	Kinnaird Head, Marwick Head. Rattray Head (brown boats, masts and vents not noted). Funnel; black with two narrow white bands.
Hook S.S.	Brown	Brown	Brown	Black/Black	Kaluna (black mast tops). Funnel; red, black top separated by a fairly broad white band.
Hudson S.S.	Brown	Black	Brown	Black/Black	Brasted. Funnel; black, red band white 'H' touching the edges.
R. Hughes	Brown	White	Brown	Black/Red Brown/Red	Brier Rose, Cornish Rose, Dorrien Rose (brown/red uppers), Fowey Rose, Guelder Rose, Joffre Rose, Jellicoe Rose, Pink Rose, Sturdee Rose, Welsh Rose, Moss Rose. Most;black mizzens. masts. Funnel; black with fairly narrow red band see Plate104.
W. J. Ireland	Brown	White	Cream	Black/Red	Porthleven (black mizzen and black tips to derricks). Funnel; buff with black top separated by white over red bands.
James & Emanuel	Brown	Brown	?	?	Archmor. Funnel; red, black top and two black rings.
John Kelly	Brown	Black	Varnish	Black/Black Brown/Black	Clapham. Crossgar (white boats), Cushendall (the latter two have brown masts). All have black mizzen masts and pink boot-topping. Funnel;black with red over white over blue bands and a black letter 'K' contained within the white band.
C. Longstaff	Brown and/or White	Black	Brown	Black/Red	Wintown (black mizzen). Westown (white boats, vents;black, yellow tops/black). Williamstown (white uppers, brown/red vents and white top line. Woodtown (white dividing line, brown/brown vents except round funnel. Funnel; black with red band or plus white letters 'CL'. Woodtown white band with red letters.
Monroe Bros.	Brown/White Brown	Black White	Brown ?	Black/Red ?	Kylebay (black mizzen, white dividing line). Kylegorm. Kyle Prince (boats not recorded, black/black vents). Kyle Queen (brown boats). Test. Funnel;black, red over white bands.
Moray S.S.	Brown	Black	?	Black/Black	Spey. Funnel; pinkish red with a black top.
National Benzole	Brown White	Brown White	Brown Brown	Brown/Red ?	Ben Read. Funnel: Ben Olliver, Ben Johnson (white,black top/black; buff vents elsewhere). Also noted with black, silver/red vents. Camroux I. Funnel; black with a red burgee containing a white diamond on which there is a red 'C'. *(funnel diagram labelled: black, yellow, white, yellow, black, yellow; NATIONAL BENZOLE MIXTURE)*
Newcastle Coal	White	?	White	Brown/Red Grey/Red	Crossbill (white top line). Funnel; red, black top.
R. & W. Paul	Buff Brown	White ?	? ?	Black/Red ?	Firecrest (white dividing line), Oxbird (white top line).
J. M. Piggins	Brown	Brown	Brown	?	Belford. Funnel; black, white 'P' and narrow white rings above and below separated from the letter by about the ring thickness.
Rainham S.S.	Brown	White	Brown	Black/Red	Surreybrook (white top line). Funnel; black with silver band.
R. Rix & Sons	Brown/White	White	Brown	Black/Red Brown/Red	Ebbrix, Errnrix, Pegrix, Robrix, Lesrix (brown boats). Funnel see Plate 83.
Wm. Robertson	Brown/White Grey/White	Black Black	Brown Brown	Black/Red Black/Red Brown/Red Brown/Red	Cameo, Coral, Essonite, Gem, Jade, Nephrite, Olivine, Sphene, Topaz and Turquoise. All have short white line below bridge. Axinite, Fluor, Girasol, Jargoon, Obsidian. Nugget, Pebble and Emerald have white uppers. Funnel; black.
C. Rowbotham	White	White	Brown	Brown/Red	Guidesman (white vents at bridge front). Steersman (yellow top line, blue boats and white topsides). Rudderman, Tillerman and Wheelsman (no vent colours noted for these three vessels). Funnel; buff with red 'R' near the top and black band.
Shell Mex & B.P.	White	White	White	Black/Black	Shellbrit 2, Energie (no boats, masts or vents noted). Funnel: black with yellow flag on which there is a green cross. The upper canton of the hoist has the red 'shell' emblem while the lower canton of the fly has black letters 'BP' on white shield.
Shield S.S.	Brown/White	White	Brown	?	Balfron. White, black top separated by red band.
Shipping & Coal	Light Brown	Lt.Brn.	Brown	Black/Black Brown/Brown	Waterland. Funnel; black, white band with blue diamond.
Shoreham Sg.	Brown	Brown	Brown	Black/Blue	Betswood, Phylwood. Funnel; black, white band and black monogram arranged thus:
A. J. Smith	Brown	?	?	Black/Red	Tanny. Collin (white boats, vents not recorded). Funnel; black with a red band.
John Stewart	Brown	White	Brown	Black/Blue	Yewcroft, Yewglen (black/black vents), Yewtree (vents not noted). Funnel; see Plate 92.
Stone & Rolfe	Brown	Brown	Brown	Black/Red	Eskwood, Monkstone (boats not recorded), Presto (white boats), Runnelstone (boats, masts and vents not recorded). Funnel; black with a deep red band.
Matt. Taylor	Brown	Buff	Cream/ Black	Black/Red	Methil Hill, Sojourner (brown boats, masts not noted). Black funnel with a yellow band.
O. H. Thomas	Brown	Black	Brown	?	Miriam Thomas (white dividing line). Funnel;black, with a red band containing a black 'T',separated from the black by narrow white bands top and bottom.
T. W. Ward	Brown(grained) Grey	White Black	? Brown	? Black/Red	Endcliffe. Rivelin. Funnel; buff, black top separated by a white band on which there is contained a red letter 'W'.
R. Williamson	Brown	Brown	Brown	Black/Red	Corinia (masts black), Ravonia (vents black/black). Funnel; Plate 6.
Wm. A. Wilson	Brown	White	Buff	Black,yellow tops/ Red	Ngarua (white top line, cream derricks), Ngatira (vents yellow, brown tops/red, other vents brown/red). Funnel; buff, black top.
Zillah	Brown	White	Brown	Brown/Red Brown/Blue	Briarfield, Broomfield (mast tops white, mizzen black). Aquilla (buff vents). All have a yellow top line. Funnel; buff with black top.

COMPANIES having GREY HULLS.

Company	Superstructure	Boats	Masts	Ventilators (out/in)	Vessels observed, funnel colours and notes.
Ald Shipping	Brown	?	Brown	Yellow/Black Black/Black	Castle Combe. Haptree Combe (vent colours not recorded). Funnel; buff with red 'A' on upper part, black top.
Brighton Corp.	Grey	Grey	Grey	Black/Blue	Arthur Wright, Henry Moon. Both have green boot-topping. Funnel; blue with black top separated by white band with black:
T. H. Donking	Brown	Brown	Brown	Black/Red	Moortoft (vents and boats not recorded). Funnel as above.
F. W. Horlock	Brown Brown	White Brown	Brown Brown	Brown/Red Brown,yellow top/Red	Jolly Days, Jolly Girls (brown boats, vents not recorded). Ipswich Trader. Funnel; buff, blue pennant with white maltese '+'.
C. Longstaff	White	White	Brown	Buff/Red	Petertown (white topsides). Arthurtown (masts not recorded). Black funnel with red band. See also black hulls above.
W. S. Kennaugh	Brown	White	Brown	Brown/Red	Birker Force, Dalegarth Force, Eden Force, Stanley Force, Stock Force. Most have white dividing line. Funnel; pale yellow.
P. MacCallum	Grey	Grey	Grey	Black/Red	Ardgryfe, Ardgantock. Ardgarvel (varnished masts, black boats, vents brown/green, brown front to poop deck. Funnel; red with black top and two black rings.
Stone & Rolfe	White	White	Buff	Buff/Red	Lottie R. (hull greenish grey). Funnel; as above.
Western Coasters	Dark brown	White	Varnish	Brn,grey tops/ Blue	Western Hill (hull bluish grey). Funnel; yellow, two blue bands.

3.

The
Engine
Room

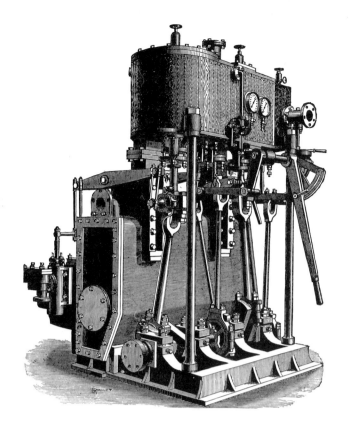

36 Compound engine of 25 nominal h. p. by Ross & Duncan of Glasgow circa 1880.

The engine room has seen the greatest changes over the years. Whereas the captain of the 1850s would find the wheel and compass familiar, a hundred years later, the Victorian engineer would have been completely baffled by the engine room of a motor coaster. The engines used in the 1850s had to be large to develop sufficient power from the low pressure boilers then available. Pressures of twelve to thirty pounds per square inch were usual and thirty pounds was about the maximum possible for the box shaped boilers of the early colliers. Boilers were constructed of wrought iron or copper for longer life. The furnaces were fitted inside the lower part of the boiler and the hot gases made to pass the full length of the boiler along the furnace, and then back again along nests of tubes above the furnaces, before passing out up the funnel. The earliest boilers were not of this return-tube type and the funnels often became red-hot with flames from the furnaces passing directly to the funnel. During the 1850s a great variety of engines were in use, but the majority were simple engines, that is, the steam expanded in the cylinder and then passed directly to the condenser. Many of the engines at this time had oscillating cylinders, in which the piston rod was connected directly to the crank on the propellor shaft. If the cylinders were placed at right angles, only one crank was needed. The oscillating engine is very compact and needs no valve gear, as the movement of the cylinders themselves covers and uncovers the inlets and exhausts. The steam reached the cylinders via the central pivots and sealing these joints was not too difficult at low pressures, but was more difficult in screw vessels where higher shaft speeds were needed. In addition the oscillating cylinders also caused vibration. A speed of 20 r. p. m. was ideal for paddle wheels, but efficient propulsion by screw needed at least 60 r. p. m. These early engines served the early colliers well, but they had a high fuel consumption and most were replaced by more modern machinery in the 1870s. In the early engines the steam passed from the cylinders to a condenser where sea water was sprayed on to the steam to condense it. The condensation of the steam produced a partial vacuum, which was maintained by an engine driven vacuum pump. This pump removed air and water from the condenser. The great advantage of condensing the steam is that air pressure is also harnessed for driving the engine. Thus if the steam starts 20 lbs. above air pressure and finishes about 12 lbs. below air pressure, the effective pressure acting on the piston is 32 lbs. per square inch. In the simple oscillating engine, steam pressure pushes the piston down while at the same time the suction of the vacuum is acting on the other side of the piston. The 'V' arrangement fitted neatly into the stern of the coasters while larger ships often had horizontal engines.

The inverted engine, so called because unlike engines in common use the cylinders were placed above the shaft, was in use by the 1860s, but still had to be fully developed. Because of the high fuel consumption of the simple engine, cargo space was lost to bunkers and so there was considerable interest in the development of more efficient engines. One way of achieving greater efficiency lay in higher boiler pressures, but this led to new problems. Cylinders had to be made much stronger to withstand the high initial pressure which then fell sharply as the steam expanded giving a very uneven push to the crank. To overcome this the compound engine was introduced. In this type of engine a small high pressure cylinder absorbs the initial energy of the steam which is then led to a larger low pressure cylinder where the remaining expansion of the steam takes place. The cooling effect of the condenser was now confined to the low pressure cylinder, allowing the high pressure cylinder to run hotter and so reducing heat losses. Compounds of the type shown in (36) came into general use for coasters during the 1870s and used steam at pressures ranging from 70 to 100 lbs. per square inch. This design remained unchanged for all further small steam coasters built during the next fifty years. The compound engines showed a fuel saving of about 12% compared with the simple engines. The final development was the triple expansion engine which gave a further 20% saving, working at steam pressures of 160 lbs. per square inch. By the 1890s the triple expansion had become standard for the larger coasters, though the compound continued to be used for coasters under about one hundred and forty feet in length because it was lighter and shorter in length. Also the lower pressures meant that the boiler could also be of lighter construction. The main development of the marine steam engine was now complete, but there was a further step, the introduction of the superheater. This consists of a nest of tubes as close as possible to the fire, through which the steam passes on its way from the boiler proper to the engine. In this way all the moisture is removed from the 'wet' steam leaving the boiler and the temperature of the steam is also increased. Superheating was first tried in the 1850s when it was shown that a saving of about 20% could be obtained when the temperature of the steam was raised by 100ºF. However it was soon abandoned in favour of compound engines because the tallow then used to lubricate the piston rod and piston, was reduced to a charred mass at temperatures above 450ºF and pistons tended to seize up. As better mineral oils were developed, the problem was overcome and large vessels were successfully using superheaters by 1900. They first began to appear on the larger coasters during the 1920s. The advantage of superheating stems from the fact that the boiler converts heat energy from coal into a form that the engine can use and so a smaller quantity of hotter steam can be used to obtain the same power from a smaller engine. There is also much less danger of condensation occurring.

As both the compound and triple-expansion engines used for coasters after the 1870s had fixed cylinders, various types of valve gear were needed to control the steam inlet and exhaust. The commonest is the link motion invented by Stephenson, two eccentrics are fitted to the shaft (38A), one set to give the correct opening to the valve for forward motion and the other for reverse. The top ends of the eccentric rods are joined by a sliding link so that either rod may be used to control the valve opening. By using intermediate settings, partial motion from both eccentrics can be used to cut off steam when the piston has only moved a short distance and so obtain power by expansion of the steam. Joy's valve gear was also used on some engines and here the motion of the valve gear is derived from the connecting rod (38B). The final development, also confined to larger vessels, was the triple expansion reheat engine built by North Eastern Marine introduced in the 1930s. In these engines a steam jacket was used to reheat the exhaust steam from the high pressure cylinder so that it entered the intermediate pressure cylinder at the most favourable temperature. All the large steam colliers built in later years had this type of machinery.

Boiler development also continued and the most important change was the introduction of steel and improved alloys for boiler plates and tubes which allowed the construction of the higher pressure boilers needed by triple expansion engines. Corrugated furnaces were also used to handle the higher pressures. The low pressure boilers of the 1850s used salt water and this had to be periodically run off ("blown down") by opening valves at the bottom of the boiler, to prevent the salt from becoming so concentrated that it was deposited inside the boiler. Sea water had to be used, because the steam was condensed with a sea water spray and so the condensate could not be kept separate. It was also contaminated with some of the tallow lubricant used for the cylinders. These problems were eliminated with the introduction of the surface condenser. In this, sea water is pumped through nests of tubes and the steam is admitted to the spaces between the tubes (Plate 45). The steam then condenses on the cold surfaces of the tubes. The tubes were usually made of brass enclosed in a strong casing, often cast as part of the engine itself. The condenser of the Ross and Duncan engine (36) was incorporated into the engine bed plate while the upper part supports the cylinders. The casing has to be strong enough not to collapse under the considerable air pressure acting on the outside, since inside there is a vacuum produced by condensation of the steam and maintained by the vacuum pump. At first, difficulty was experienced sealing the tube ends into the tube plate to prevent sea water leaking into the condensed steam. Eventually a good seal was obtained by expanding the tube ends into the plate. Oil contamination was tackled with canvas filters which gave water suitable for re-use in the boiler. However, as soon as this was done, the corrosion of boilers became severe, since the protective layer of salt deposits in the old type boilers had been eliminated. Corrosion was eventually controlled by fitting zinc plates inside the boilers. These were attacked by the water in preference to the steel. A great variety of water treatments were devised over the years but none entirely eliminated corrosion. The round drum 'Scotch' type boiler was introduced about 1862 and was soon in general use for the higher pressures needed by compound engines. The cylindrical casing could withstand the higher pressures without the need for so many stays and the tube plates at each end were supported by some of the tubes themselves which acted as stays also, Plate 40. Forced draught systems were introduced by 1880 for ocean going vessels, but were not used even for the larger coasters until the 1920s, and the smaller coasters never had them.

The usual arrangement of the engine room for a steam coaster with engines aft is illustrated by Plate 42. The aft peak ballast tank, holding a reserve of fresh water for the boiler is in the extremity of the stern; next, is the main engine and auxiliary machinery and finally boiler and stokehold. In larger vessels, two boilers side by side, were usual while in smaller vessels the single boiler was sometimes fitted the other way round so that the engineers could act as firemen also. In larger vessels stoking needs the full attention of a fireman. The main engine is dependent to a large extent on the auxiliary steam engines which drive

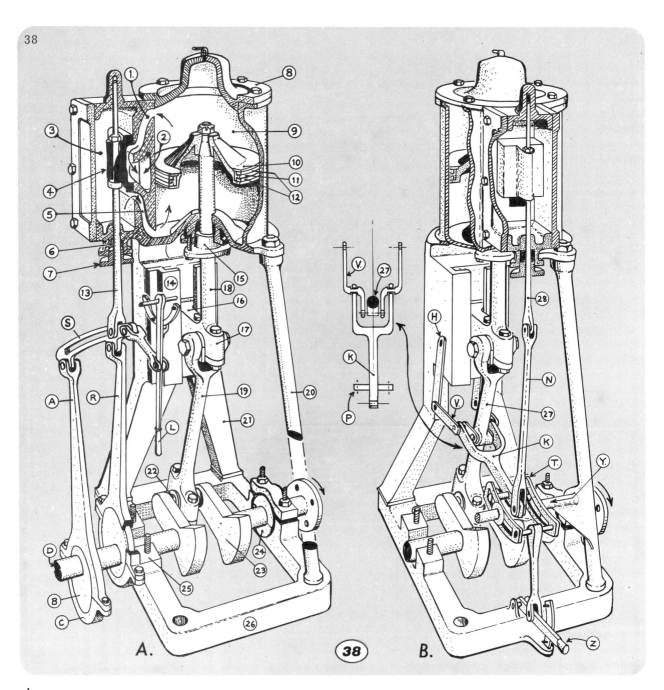

A. B.

(38)

A. STEPHENSON'S LINK MOTION. In this valve gear, two eccentric sheaves (B) are fitted to the crank shaft (D) and attached to eccentric rods (A) and (R) by straps (C). The two sheaves would normally be in contact but are shown slid apart for clarity here. The ahead eccentric rod (A) and the reverse eccentric rod (R), are joined by the link (S), so that by means of the lever (L) either may be brought into line with the valve rod (13) to operate it. Intermediate settings between (A) and (B) can be used to control the amount of steam (or "Cut-off").

B. JOY'S VALVE GEAR. Here eccentrics are not used and the motion of the valve rod is obtained from the connecting rod. The vibrating link (V) is attached to the connecting rod (27) at one end and the radius rod (H) at the other. The rod (K) takes its motion from a point some distance along the vibrating link (V). Near the other end of forked rod (K) is fitted a pin (P) which is free to move back and forth in the sectors (T). A rod (N) joins the end of rod (K) to the valve rod (28). Ahead or reverse is obtained by tilting the sectors clockwise or anticlockwise about their mid-point (Y) using lever (Z). When the sectors are horizontal 'mid-gear' is obtained. One of the advantages of this type of gear is that it is placed on the side of the cylinders rather than between them and so allows a triple expansion engine with this gear to be shorter than one with Stephenson's link motion.

Key to the other parts: (1) Top steam port. (2) Exhaust port. (3) Valve chest. (4) Slide valve. (5) Bottom steam port. (6) Valve rod stuffing box. (7) Valve rod gland. (8) Cylinder cover. (9) Cylinder. (10) Junk ring. The origin of this name may be traced back to the time before metal piston rings were used and pistons were kept steam-tight with a hemp gasket (Junk Packing) and the ring was used to keep this packing in place. (11) Restriction ring; this is used to hold the packing rings (12) in place. The rings shown are those for a high pressure cylinder. (13) Valve rod. (14) Slipper guide. (15) Piston rod gland. (16) Slipper. (17) Crosshead. (18). Piston rod. (19) Connecting rod. (20,21) Columns. (22) Crank pin. (23) Crank web with balance weights. (24) Main bearing and (25) with bearing shells removed. (26) Engine bed.

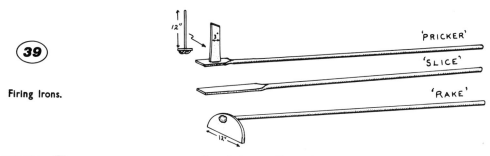

39

Firing Irons.

various pumps. Three pumps are usually driven directly from the crosshead of one of the cylinders. Most important of these was the vacuum pump, Plate 42, with pumps 32* and 33*, which removed any air and the water from the condensed steam, which was discharged to the hot well or feed tank, formed by the double bottom under the engine room in many vessels. The was water passed through grease-removing filters before entering the tank. Adjacent to the vacuum pump is a feed pump (34*, 35*, 36*) which continually returns water to the boiler. In addition, there was a bilge pump on the other side of the vacuum pump in most cases, to discharge overside any water seeping into the ship (37*, 38*, 39*, 40*). As will be seen from this engine room plan, twin feed and bilge pumps were fitted to this engine. In addition, the cooling water pump for the condenser is also run from this main engine (29*, 30*, 31*). A separate steam-driven feed pump is available when the main engine is stopped, to replace steam used by other machinery (42*-50*). Weir's feed or donkey pumps were commonly used in coasters. This pump has two vertical cylinders one above the other and the pistons are joined by a common piston rod, Plate 45a. Steam pushing the piston up and down pumps water in the lower cylinder which forms a double acting water pump. Since the whole stroke usually needs full steam pressure, the valve gear is of a special shuttle type. A small auxiliary valve admits steam to the main shuttle valve which is thus blown across to give full steam admission immediately. This produces a sharp "knock", and the regular toc---toc---toc--- beat of the feed pump was one of the most characteristic sounds of the steam coaster. The engineer always paid particular attention to the feed pumps to see that the boiler water was maintained at the correct level on the gauge glass. If the boiler needed topping up rapidly, the injector could be used but was rather wasteful of steam. If the water was allowed to rise too high, there was a danger of some carrying over in the steam to the main engine. Since water is almost incompressible, it can cause considerable damage if caught between piston and cylinder head. However, relief valves are fitted to prevent damage occurring as far as possible in this case. If on the other hand, the water level falls too low, then the tubes or even the crowns of the furnaces will be exposed, overheat, soften and collapse under the pressure of the steam. Finally there was the ballast pump, the main duty of which was to empty and fill the water ballast tanks of the ship, but like the donkey pump it was arranged with a great variety of connections (51*-68*) so that it could be used for other duties as well. Its most important secondary role was to supply cooling water to the condenser when the ship was not under way. There are a number of other connections completing the layout as the plan shows. Among these is the exhaust tank to which the auxiliaries are connected. As the exhaust pipes are not lagged on the deck machinery, much of the exhaust steam is already condensed and this is collected in the exhaust tank.

Raising steam from cold was usually done over about twenty-four hours. The fireman selected coals around three to six inches in diameter and laid them evenly on the firebars. The cast-iron firebars ran along the length of the cylindrical furnaces which were usually about three feet in diameter and around six feet in length. The bars were kept about one inch apart by bulges at the ends and centres so that air could get to the fire from underneath. Coal at the front of one of the furnaces was then covered with wood-shavings, firewood and oily waste. A further layer of coal was added on top, the fire lit and the ash pit door closed, but the furnace door was left open to draw the fire back over the coals. Lighting one furnace helped to get the water circulating and warm the boiler evenly to reduce uneven expansion leading to stress and leaks. If steam was needed in a hurry, the fire was regularly topped up and the second furnace lit after three hours or so. In this way steam could be raised in as little as eight hours. However, the more usual procedure was to bank up the fire with small coal, close the dampers and leave overnight. By morning the boiler was thoroughly warmed through and the fires could be allowed to burn more freely. Meanwhile, the chief engineer had turned on the steam valve slightly and opened all the drain cocks to remove any steam condensing in the pipes and it also allowed any air trapped in the boiler to escape. The fires were then spread so that they burned evenly throughout the whole length of the furnaces. The draft on the furnaces was carefully adjusted so that there was a full head of steam by sailing time. As the time for departure approached, the engineer opened the main steam valve to the engine, allowing steam to pass through the engine and warm up the cylinders. Finally the engines were allowed to turn over slowly to check that all was ready to start. If the engine happened to stop with the high pressure cylinder on dead-center, a little high pressure steam was passed to one of the other cylinders to start it. The compound and triple expansion engines of coasters were very reliable and often gave seventy or more years service. Piston rings were usually renewed every four or five years, when the vessel was surveyed. The slide valves were reground by the engineers as required. After twenty or thirty years service the cylinders were usually re-bored. The slow running nature of the engines (60 to 150 r.p.m.) caused little wear on the bearings as long as routine lubrication was carefully carried out. Indicator tests, page 31, were used for 'tuning' the engine.

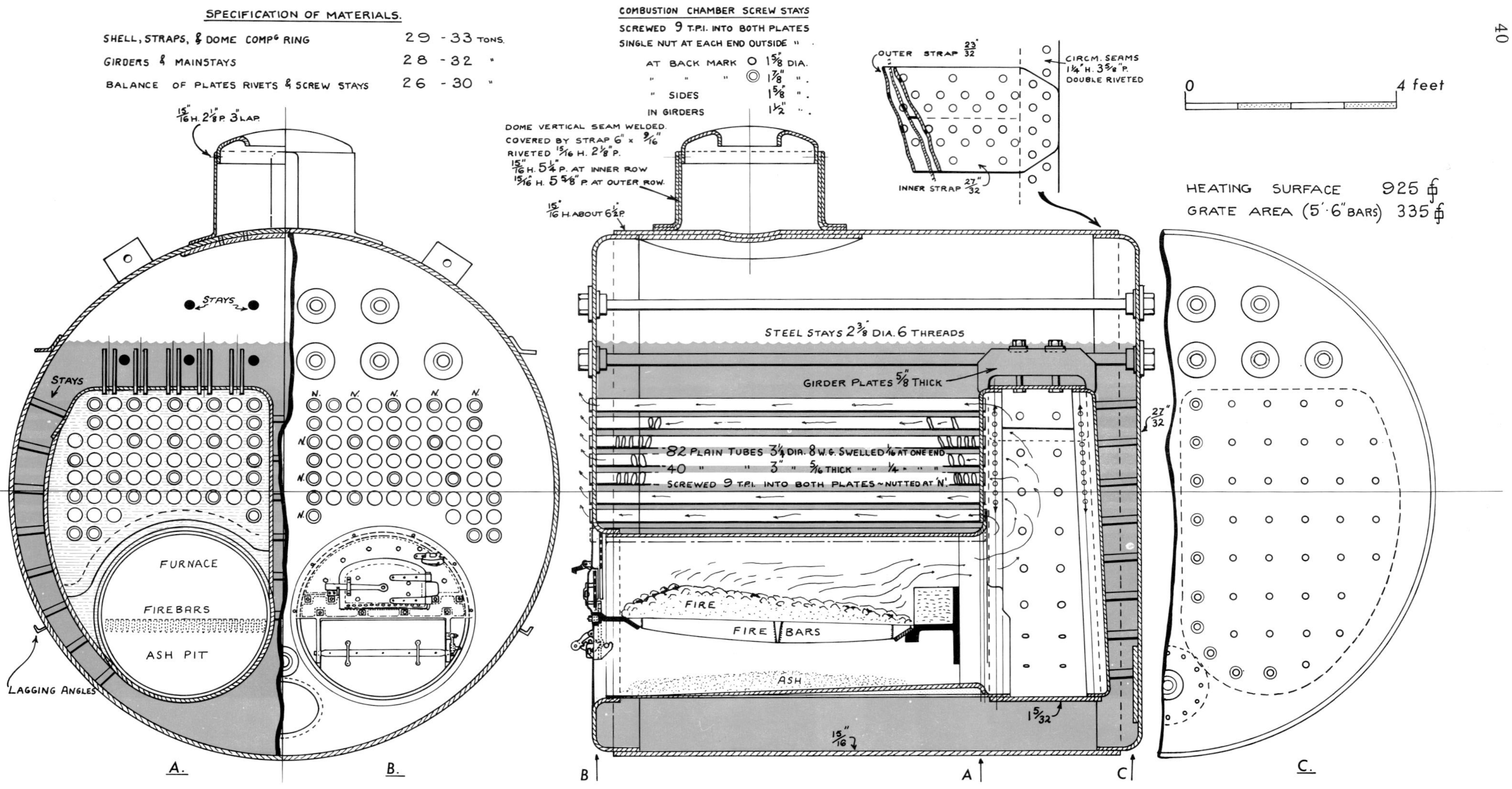
SPECIFICATION OF MATERIALS.
SHELL, STRAPS, & DOME COMPG RING 29 - 33 TONS.
GIRDERS & MAINSTAYS 28 - 32 "
BALANCE OF PLATES RIVETS & SCREW STAYS 26 - 30 "
COMBUSTION CHAMBER SCREW STAYS
SCREWED 9 T.P.I. INTO BOTH PLATES
SINGLE NUT AT EACH END OUTSIDE "
AT BACK MARK ○ 1 5/8" DIA.
" " " ◎ 1 7/8" " .
" SIDES 1 5/8" " .
IN GIRDERS 1 1/2" " .
DOME VERTICAL SEAM WELDED.
COVERED BY STRAP 6" x 9/16"
RIVETED 15/16 H. 2 1/8" P.
15/16" H. 5 1/4" P. AT INNER ROW
15/16 H. 5 5/8" P. AT OUTER ROW.
15/16" H. ABOUT 6 1/2" P.
15/16" H. 2 1/8" P. 3" LAP.
OUTER STRAP 23/32"
INNER STRAP 27/32"
CIRCM. SEAMS
1 1/4" H. 3 5/8" P.
DOUBLE RIVETED
0
4 feet
HEATING SURFACE 925 ft²
GRATE AREA (5'·6" BARS) 335 ft²
STAYS
STAYS
N.
FURNACE
FIREBARS
ASH PIT
LAGGING ANGLES
STEEL STAYS 2 3/8" DIA. 6 THREADS
GIRDER PLATES 5/8" THICK
82 PLAIN TUBES 3 1/4" DIA. 8 W.G. SWELLED 1/16 AT ONE END
40 " " 3" " 5/16 THICK " " 1/4 " " "
SCREWED 9 T.P.I. INTO BOTH PLATES ~ NUTTED AT 'N'.
FIRE
FIRE BARS
ASH
27/32"
1 5/32"
15/16"
A.
B.
C.
B
A
C

Plate 40 Cut-away of a 'Scotch' boiler similar to that shown in (41).

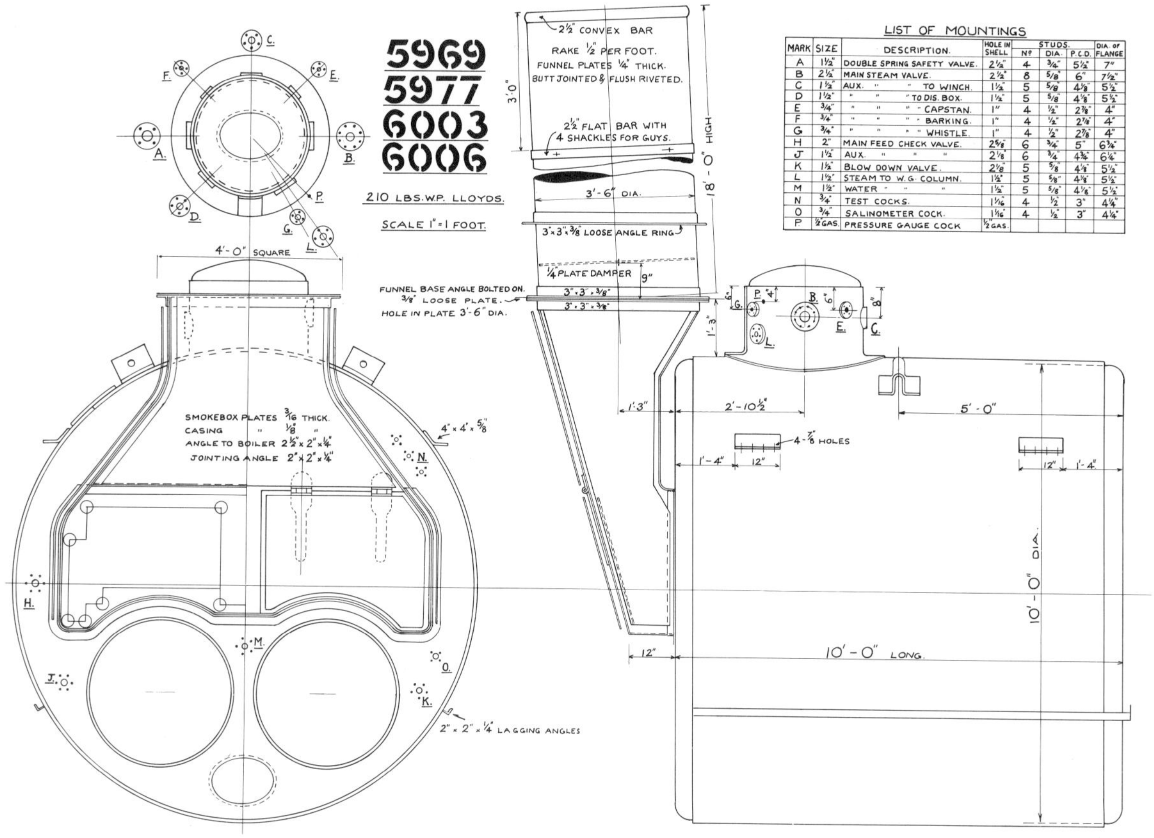
5969
5977
6003
6006
210 LBS.W.P. LLOYDS.
SCALE 1" = 1 FOOT.
2½" CONVEX BAR
RAKE ½" PER FOOT.
FUNNEL PLATES ¼" THICK.
BUTT JOINTED & FLUSH RIVETED.
2½" FLAT BAR WITH 4 SHACKLES FOR GUYS.
3'-6" DIA.
3"x3"x⅜" LOOSE ANGLE RING.
¼ PLATE DAMPER
FUNNEL BASE ANGLE BOLTED ON.
⅜" LOOSE PLATE.
HOLE IN PLATE 3'-6" DIA.
18'-0" HIGH
4'-0" SQUARE
SMOKEBOX PLATES 3/16 THICK.
CASING " ⅛ "
ANGLE TO BOILER 2½"x2"x¼"
JOINTING ANGLE 2"x2"x¼"
4"x4"x⅝"
2"x2"x¼" LAGGING ANGLES
4-⅞ HOLES
10'-0" LONG.
10'-0" DIA.
5'-0"
2'-10½"

LIST OF MOUNTINGS

MARK	SIZE	DESCRIPTION.	HOLE IN SHELL	STUDS. Nº	STUDS. DIA.	STUDS. P.C.D.	DIA. OF FLANGE
A	1½"	DOUBLE SPRING SAFETY VALVE.	2½"	4	¾"	5½"	7"
B	2½"	MAIN STEAM VALVE.	2½"	8	⅝"	6"	7½"
C	1½"	AUX. " " TO WINCH.	1½"	5	⅝"	4⅛"	5½"
D	1½"	" " " TO DIS. BOX.	1½"	5	⅝"	4⅛"	5½"
E	¾"	" " " " CAPSTAN.	1"	4	½"	2⅞"	4"
F	¾"	" " " " BARKING.	1"	4	½"	2⅞"	4"
G	¾"	" " " " WHISTLE.	1"	4	½"	2⅞"	4"
H	2"	MAIN FEED CHECK VALVE.	2⅝"	6	¾"	5"	6¾"
J	1½"	AUX. " " "	2⅛"	6	¾"	4¾"	6¼"
K	1½"	BLOW DOWN VALVE.	2⅛"	5	⅝"	4⅛"	5½"
L	1½"	STEAM TO W.G. COLUMN.	1½"	5	⅝"	4⅛"	5½"
M	1½"	WATER " " "	1½"	5	⅝"	4⅛"	5½"
N	¾"	TEST COCKS.	1 1/16"	4	½"	3"	4¼"
O	¾"	SALINOMETER COCK.	1 1/16"	4	½"	3"	4¼"
P	½" GAS.	PRESSURE GAUGE COCK	½" GAS.				

(41) External details of a 'Scotch' boiler made by Ridley Boilers, Stockton-on-Tees, for the coaster COLLIN.

The engine's performance at sea depended largely on the skill of the fireman at maintaining good fires and hence a good head of steam on the boiler. The air for the fire mostly entered via the ash pit below the firebars, so it was important for the fireman to keep the fire spread over the whole area of the firebars or cold air entered the furnace and cooled the boiler. The good fireman was always watching out for this and looked under the firebars for the tell-tale dull red patches where the fire was burning thinly and soon put matters right with a well aimed shovel full of coal. Firemen had differing methods of firing, but one of the best was to keep the fire deepest near the door and keep the bars just covered at the back. With good bunker coal, the fire continued to burn well for several hours, but slowly clinker built up on the firebars and the fire began to take on a dull appearance; the time had come for the fire to be cleaned. With a two furnace boiler, one furnace was usually cleaned once per watch of four hours. The furnace to be cleaned was allowed to burn down as much as possible without losing steam pressure. Then the slice, a long iron bar with a flattened end, was taken and used to lever the burning coals over to one side. Then another long bar with a blade at rightangles to the end, the pricker (39), was taken and used to lever up the clinker on the firebars. Finally the red-hot clinker was raked out on to the furnace plates. In a rough sea this became a rather hazardous operation as the fireman had to dodge the hot clinker sliding about under foot. However, a bucket of sea water was always kept handy under the ashcock and used to dowse the ashes as soon as possible. As soon as this was done, the fire was spread back over the cleaned area with the slice and stoked up. If the boiler was maintaining steam, then the other half could be cleaned, otherwise it would be left until pressure had built up again. Good firebars lasted about six weeks before they finally burned away. Sometimes this hapepned at sea and replacing the firebars in a hot furnace could be a tricky operation, especially if the bars had distorted. The boiler tubes were swept out with a long handled wire brush about once a week. If in port for a few days, the opportunity was taken to draw the fires so that the fireman could crawl through the furnace and clean the tube plate at the back. When cleaning the tubes the fireman always looked for any tell-tale white salt deposits left behind where water from a leaking tube had evaporated. The engineers put this right by tightening the tube with a tube expander, and the tube would be inspected again at the next cleaning, for any signs of leaks. If the tube itself had burnt through and was leaking, then it could be blanked off with plugs in each end, held in place by a long bolt running the length of the tube. Bad leaks at sea usually meant the ship limping into the nearest port or shelter where the engineers would begin repairs on the boiler while still hot, working for a few minutes at a time in the intense heat. This problem was eliminated in larger vessels by having a small auxiliary donkey boiler or twin boilers so that one could be shut down under way to make repairs. In port the donkey boiler was often used to provide steam for the winches rather than keep the main boiler in steam.

Many coasters were kept going on old boilers by the careful maintenance of their engineers and some even used to retube the boilers themselves. They often saw to it that any unburnt coal in the ash was saved and used to keep enough steam on the boilers for working winches in port. Engineers also took care not to waste fresh water. The boiler water level

GENERAL ARRANGEMENT OF MACHINERY IN SHIP AND PIPING PLAN

ENGINE Nº 448 $\frac{14''\text{-}22''\text{-}38''}{24''}$

PIPE LIST

Nº	DIA.	L.S.G.	MAT.	PURPOSE
1	3¾	8	C	MAIN STEAM
2	1¼	13	-	AUXILIARY STEAM TO M.P. CYLINDER
3	1¼	13	-	" " " L.P. "
4	¾	15	-	STEAM TO REVERSING ENGINE.
5	2"	11	-	" " REDUCING VALVE.
6	2"	11	-	" " DECK AUXILIARIES FROM REDUCING VALVE.
7	1¼"	13	-	" " AFTER CAPSTAN " " "
8	1¼"	13	-	" " WHISTLE
9	1½"	12	-	" " INJECTOR AND BILGE EJECTOR
10	1½"	/	G.M.	" " INJECTOR.
11	1"	1"	"	" " BILGE EJECTOR.
12	1"	14	C	" " BALLAST PUMP.
13	1¼"	13	"	" " DONKEY AND ELECTRIC ENGINE.
14	1"	14	"	" " ELECTRIC ENGINE
15	¾"	15	"	" " DONKEY PUMP
16	10½	/	C.I.	EXHAUST FROM MAIN ENGINES TO CONDENSER
17	2"	15	C	EXHAUST RANGE TO EXHAUST TANK.
18	2"	15	"	" " " CONDENSER.
19	1"	16	"	" FROM ELECTRIC ENG. TO EXT RANGE.
20	1¼"	16	"	" " DONKEY " " " "
21	1½"	16	"	" " STEERING ENG. " " "
22	1½"	16	"	" " BALLAST PUMP " "
23	2½"	.	"	" " DECK MACHINERY " " TANK.
24	1½"	16	"	" " CAPSTAN " " "
25	¾"	17	"	" " REVERSING ENG. TO CONDENSER.
26	2¾"	15	"	" " EXT TANK TO WASTE STEAM PIPE.
27	1¼"	16	"	DRAIN FROM SAFETY VALVE TO EXHAUST TANK.
28	4"	14	"	WASTE STEAM PIPE.
29	5½"	12	"	CIRCULATING PUMP SUCTION FROM SEA.
30	5½"	12	"	" " DELIVERY TO CONDENSER.
31	5½"	12	"	" " DISCHARGE OVERBOARD.
32	4"	13	"	AIR PUMP SUCTION FROM CONDENSER.
33	3"	"	C.I.	" " AIR DISCHARGE TO BILGES.
34	2¼"	14	C.	FORE & AFT FEED PUMP SUCTIONS FROM HOTWELL.
35	2¼"	9	"	" " " " DELIVERIES TO Y PIECE.
36	2½"	9	"	MAIN FEED RANGE TO BOILER
37	2¼"	"	G.I.	FORD BILGE PUMP SUCTION FROM BILGE SUCT BOX.
38	2¼"	"	"	" " " " " E.R. BILGE.
39	2¼"	"	"	AFT. " " " " "
40	2¼	"	"	" " " DISCHARGE OVERBOARD.
41	2¼	"	"	FORD " " " "
42	1½"	11	C	DONKEY PUMP SUCTION FROM BOILER.
43	2"	14	"	" " " " SUCTION BOX.
44	2"	"	G.I.	" " " " HOTWELL THRO' BOX.
45	2"	"	"	" " " " AFT PEAK TANKS " "
46	1½"	"	"	" " " " EXHAUST TANK " "
47	2"	14	C	" " " " SEA " "
48	1¾	10	"	" " DELIVERY TO BOILER.
49	2"	"	G.I.	" " DISCHARGE OVERBOARD.
50	2"	"	"	" " DELIVERY TO DECK.
51	3½"	13	C	BALLAST PUMP SUCTION FROM SEA
52	3"	✓	G.I.	" " " " BILGE SUCTION BOX.
53	3½"	✓	"	" " " " BALLAST TANK.
54	2½"	✓	"	" " " " E.R. BILGE (SPECIAL).
*55	2½"	✓	G.I.	" " " " AFT. PEAK.
56	2½"	✓	G.I.	" " " " HOLD (FORD) THRO. BOX.
57	2½"	✓	"	" " " " " (STARD AFT) " "
58	2½"	✓	"	" " " " " (PORT AFT) " "
59	2½"	✓	"	" " " " S'HOLD. BILGE " "
60	2½"	✓	"	" " " " FORE PEAK " "
61	2½"	✓	"	" " " AND DELIVERY TO FORE PEAK.
62	2½"	✓	"	" " " " " " AFT. PEAKS.
62A	2½"	✓	"	" " " " " " " " (UPPER)
63	3½"	✓	"	" " " " " " BALLAST TANK.
64	3½"	13	C	" " DISCHARGE OVERBOARD.
65	3½"	✓	G.I.	" " DELIVERY TO BALLAST TANK.
66	2¼"	✓	"	" " " " CONDENSER.
67	2½"	14	C	" " " " AFT. PEAKS.
68	2½"	✓	G.I.	" " " " FORE PEAK.
69	2"	14	C.	HAND PUMP SUCTION FROM SEA AND BILGE SUCTION BOX.
70	2"	✓	G.I.	" " " BILGE BOX (THRO' SWITCH COCK).
71	2"	✓	"	" " DELIVERY TO DECK
72	2"	14	C	" " DISCHARGE OVERBOARD
73	1½"	11	G.I.	INJECTOR SUCTION FROM SEA OR TANK
74	1½"	11	"	" " " AFT PEAK TANKS (THRO' SWITCH COCK).
75	1½"	11	C.	" DELIVERY TO BOILER.
76	1½	11	"	BOILER SURFACE BLOW DOWN.
77	1½"	11	"	" BOTTOM " " TO SEA.
78	3½	11	G.I.	BILGE INJECTION.
79	1¼"	11	"	WATER SERVICE TO ASHCOCK IN STOKEHOLD.
80	¾	16	C.	DRAINS FROM L.P. CYL. & CHEST TO CONDENSER.
81	1½"	11	"	WATER GAUGE PIPES.
82	½"	16	"	SUPPLEMENTARY FEED FROM DONKEY SUCTION BOX.
83	2½"	✓	G.I.	BILGE EJECTOR SUCTION FROM HOLD.
84	2½"	✓	"	" " " " STOKEHOLD.
85	2½	✓	"	" " DISCHARGE OVERBOARD.
86	1½"	✓	"	EXHAUST TANK OVERFLOW PIPE.

* Not shown on plan.

VIEW OF BALLAST PUMP

LOOKING TO STARD.

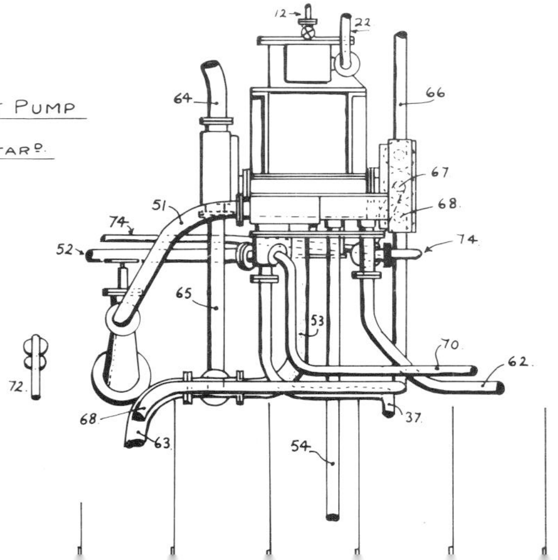

Plate 42

Engine Room of the coaster BEECHFIELD.

See page 37.

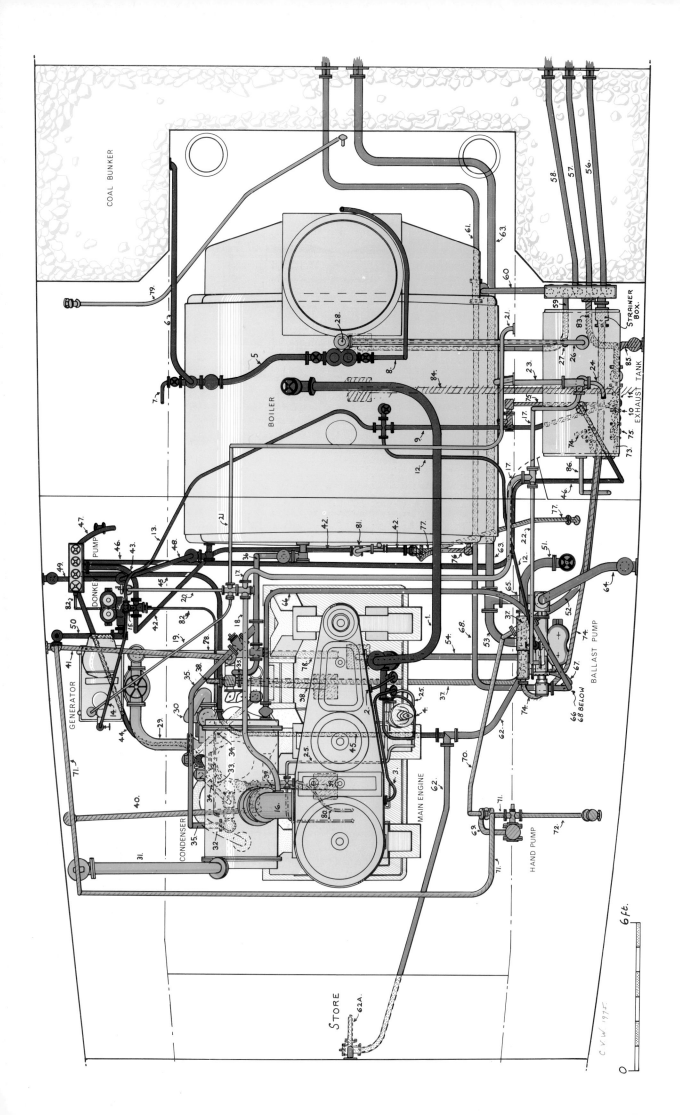

COAL BUNKER

BOILER

STRAINER BOX.

EXHAUST TANK

DONKEY PUMP

GENERATOR

CONDENSER

MAIN ENGINE

BALLAST PUMP

HAND PUMP

STORE

C.V.W. 1975

6 ft.

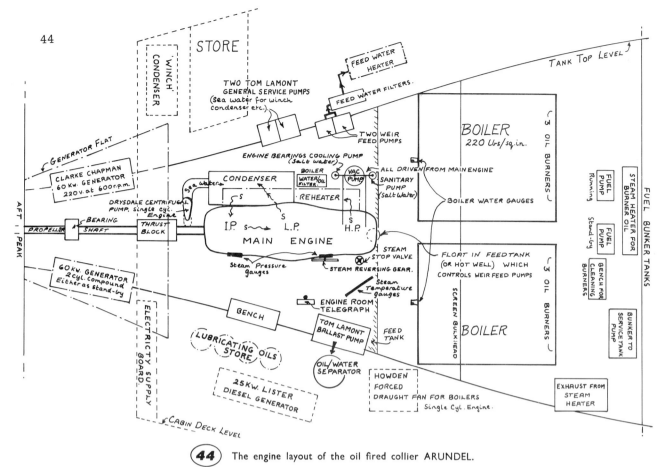

(44) The engine layout of the oil fired collier ARUNDEL.

was allowed to drop approaching harbour so that when the main engine was stopped, the feed pump could be turned on full and the cool feed water used to absorb heat from the fires while they were banked and closed up. In this way water was not lost as steam blowing off from the safety valve. Most also found time to polish the steelwork and keep the pipe lagging spotlessly white.

Naturally the engine rooms of the big East Coast colliers were much more complex with their twin boilers, superheaters and, in the last vessels oil firing, as the sketch plan (44) of ARUNDEL's engine room shows. The twin boilers each have three furnaces fitted with oil burners. At the beginning of each four hour watch, the steam fuel bunker pump, similar to a feed pump, was started and the starboard settling tank topped up. This tank held about 10 tons of fuel oil and the ship used between 2.4 and 2.7 tons during each watch at sea. The engineer always kept a careful check on the gauge because the overflow poured black boiler oil all over the boat deck. The similar port settling tank was kept in reserve. The bunker tanks were fitted with steam heating coils to make the oil flow freely through the pumps. The fuel was drawn from the settling tanks by one of the burner feed pumps and the oil under a pressure of 175 lbs. per square inch passed through a heater which raised the temperature to 250°F so that it readily burnt on reaching the spray nozzles in the furnaces. All the main fuel and steam valves had extensions up to the deck above, so that they could be shut off in the event of an engine room fire. For day service in port, the central furnaces only were lit and the spray nozzles changed by the fireman to suit steam requirements. This provided sufficient steam for the steam generator which was run during the day, mainly to provide enough power for the electric galley range and any deck gear used. The steam plant was shut down at night and an automatically governed diesel generator in the top of the engine room, by the switch board, was sufficient for lighting. The boiler water was drawn from the feed tank under the main engine by twin Weir feed pumps (one running, one stand-by) and passed to the boilers via high pressure filters and the feed water heater which used exhaust steam from the auxiliaries. The twin boilers had quite individual characteristics and one boiler always required more water than the other, but careful adjustment of the splitting valve took care of this. The feed pumps were automatically controlled by a float in the hot well. As the water was returned to the hot well from the condenser, the level rose and lifted the float controlling the steam valve on the pumps. The engineers still had to keep a careful eye on the gauge glasses and make adjustments from time to time. Steam drawn off from the boilers passed down to the superheaters at the back of the furnaces, which raised the steam temperature to about 700°F. This had to be reduced to about 570°F by adding some unsuperheated steam, before it entered the triple expansion reheat engine, to prevent the lubricating oil burning. Steam entered the high pressure cylinder at about 190 lbs. per square inch and passed on to the intermediate cylinder at about 74 lbs. Finally the combined pressure and vacuum was about 10 lbs. on entering the low pressure cylinder. The auxiliaries used steam at 150 lbs. per square inch which was saturated, a pressure reducing valve was fitted for the purpose. The main condenser needed a considerable volume of cooling water which was supplied by a centrifugal pump as they are ideal for supplying large quantities of water at low pressure, Plate 45c. A steam driven fan supplied the forced draft for the boilers. There was a second condenser used for the auxiliaries in port, especially the generators. It was usually known as a winch condenser as its main purpose was condensing steam from the winches in most vessels.

Plate 45

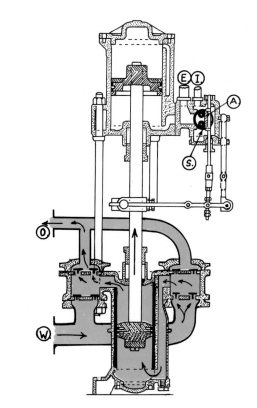

Weir - Type Double Acting Pump.

Steam enters the valve chest at (I) and the auxiliary slide valve (A) admits steam to the main shuttle valve (S) which is blown fully open immediately to give full steam admission to the cylinder. This is maintained until the valve is again blown across to give full admission to the top of the piston for the down stroke. Exhaust steam leaves via (E). Water enters at (W) and leaves at (O).

Surface Condenser.

Cool sea water enters the condenser at (C) and then passes through nests of tubes, cooling them. This sea water leaves via (D) and is returned to the sea. Steam from the engine enters at (A) and is condensed on the cold tubes. The water produced by condensation is drawn off at (B) by a vacuum pump and this also removes any air from the system.

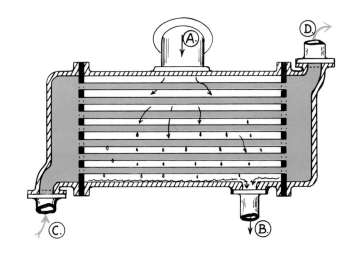

Centrifugal Pump.

This consists of an impellor which revolves inside a casing (B). The impellor has a central web (A) with two side plates (C, C) which are angled towards each other and nearest at the tips. Between the side plates are a series of curved vanes (D) between the boss and the circumference. Water enters at the centre (E) and is flung outwards round the casing to emerge at (F). The impellor is driven by a single cylinder steam engine.

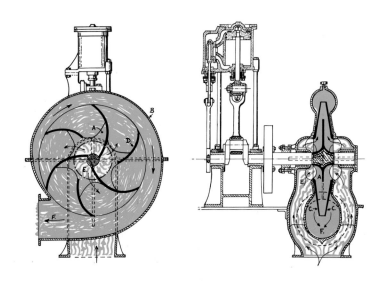

4.

Early

Steam

Coasters

(46) COLLIER, built 1848 and still retaining wood bulwarks in the 1890's.

The first steam vessels which operated successfully at the beginning of the 19th century were all paddle driven and much more expensive to build and operate compared with sailing vessels. Because of this, they were at first almost exclusively used for passenger services where the regular services the vessels could offer justified the high capital outlay. Later the vessels began to carry more cargo, especially high value goods and perishables needing prompt delivery, but most continued to carry at least some passengers. Even by 1850 only 3% of the vessels in the coasting and continental trades were steam powered, according to the Mercantile Navy List and the majority were tugs and passenger vessels. Bulk cargoes such as coal were still the preserve of the sailing vessel. The first true steam coasters were expressly designed to regulate the North East coal trade to London. Their development went hand in hand with the development of the screw propeller. Francis Smith took out his first patent in 1836 for a propellor placed at the stern of a vessel. After successful experiments with a small vessel on the Thames, he established the ship propellor company which had the 239 ton ARCHIMEDES built at Millwall by Henry Wimshurst. Completed in 1839, she was immediately so successful that Brunel changed the GREAT BRITAIN, then building at Bristol, from paddle to screw propulsion. The Admiralty also carried out numerous trials and by 1845 were convinced of their superiority. Meanwhile, the Bedlington Coal Company had decided that steam was the answer for their shipments of coal from Blyth. The iron screw collier BEDLINGTON was built at South Shields for them and entered service in 1842. Screw machinery was much lighter than paddle machinery and so steam became a possibility for the London coal trade. Though the BEDLINGTON traded successfully, other owners were more cautious. At first the steam machinery was an auxiliary to sails, with the intention of helping vessels over calms or against adverse winds. One such vessel, the barque Q.E.D. of 127 tons was built in 1844 by the Tyneside shipbuilder and collier owner, Mr. Coates. The machinery was of just 20 h.p. and the funnel also acted as a mizzen mast. Unfortunately the experiment was short lived as the vessel was wrecked on the French coast soon after entering service. However, the screw steamer had shown its paces and further vessels were soon built. The fire risks involved in fitting steam machinery to wooden vessels encouraged the use of iron for the construction of steam vessels. Iron also had the advantage that a lighter and stronger vessel could be built, especially when used for larger vessels. The iron screw vessel built at Port Glasgow in 1848 was appropriately named COLLIER. She changed hands a number of times in her early years and in 1855 was even prepared for a voyage to Australia. The project was eventually abandoned and she went on to have a long life in the coasting trade. Even when 50 years old she was active (46) carrying coal and other cargoes for Pockett's Bristol Channel S.P. Co.

When built, COLLIER was probably very similar to the vessel shown in (47). This vessel is featured in J. Scott Russell's treatise on Naval Architecture, published in 1864. As can be seen from the plan, the vessel closely resembles a schooner in appearance. Though the hull is of iron, the main deck and hatches are of wood supported by iron deck beams while the decks in the accommodation are entirely of wood. The shipbuilders found it hard to give up using wood and so these ships had an inherent weakness. The wood of the deck was more flexible than the iron sides, so that the iron topside plating tended to take all the strain, and in some of these early vessels the topside plates actually cracked in rough seas. This was prevented by fitting iron margin plates to the decks. However, the bulwarks were largely of wood until the 1870s. The collier shown in (47) was propelled by a two cylinder oscillating engine supplied with steam from a low-pressure box-like boiler. In later years many of these vessels were re-engined with conventional compound machinery as their iron hulls were still

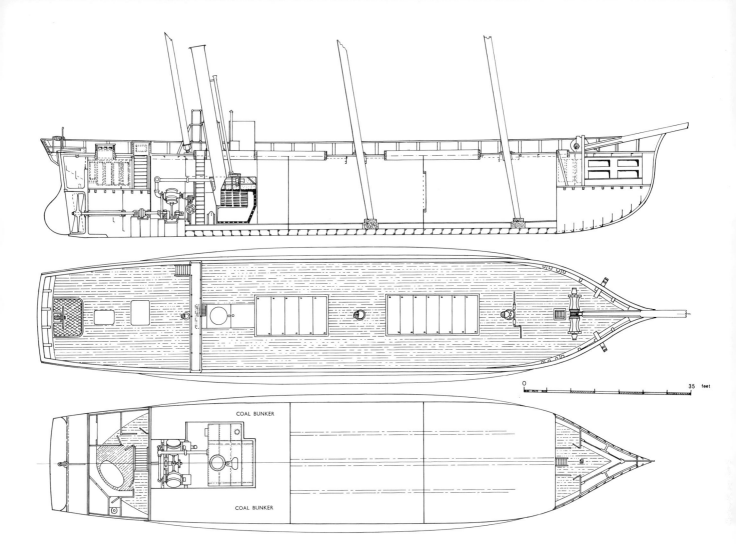

 GENERAL ARRANGEMENT of a screw collier built 1852. Length 125 feet, breadth 28 feet, and depth at side 16 feet 2 inches. She carried 333 tons on a draft of 12 feet corresponding with a displacement of 692 tons. Gross tonnage was 403. The 60 h.p. angular oscillating engine had two cylinders 24 inches in diameter by 27 inches stroke. Lines were similar to EAGLE with less parallel mid-body.

in excellent condition. The officers were berthed in the after part of the vessel, as in schooners and brigs of the period, and had a comfortable saloon and toilet facilities. The remainder of the crew had eight bunks forward, built along the sides of the ship, ahead of the sail locker and bosun's store. Entering or leaving the small accommodation hatch must have been rather difficult if seas were coming over the bows as the hatchway has only a low coaming. The steering position was aft as in sailing vessels, but a very simple bridge, hardly more than a plank surmounted by rails, was fitted to give the officer in charge a better view forwards. The galley was sited just forward of the funnel in this vessel. A wood hand-operated windlass was fitted to handle the stocked anchors, which were suspended from catheads as in the schooners of the period.

This little steamer was so successful that she was followed by the larger EAGLE, built the following year, (48). She had virtually the same machinery and dimensions except that an extra 24 feet was added amidships, increasing the length to 149 feet. The heating area of the boiler furnaces was increased slightly, but the extra length reduced the service speed from nine to eight knots with a propellor speed of about 85 r.p.m. As can be seen from the plan, the high coal consumption of these early vessels meant that every corner of space around the engine had to be used for coal bunkers. Perhaps best remembered of these early colliers is the JOHN BOWES built by one of the Tyne's leading builders, Charles Palmer, for the influential colliery owners John Bowes and Partners, attracting the attention of the Illustrated London News. Her design was not particularly revolutionary and she carried a deadweight of 650 tons on dimensions very similar to those of EAGLE. Her machinery came from R. Stephenson's works and gave her a speed of eight knots. On her maiden voyage from the Tyne to London with a full cargo of coal, she took 48 hours, was discharged in a day and arrived back in the Tyne 48 hours later. She and the other steam colliers were able to maintain this sort of timetable for much of the year and so justified their high cost of around £10,000 as well as the cost of bunkers. She was fitted with larger engines in 1864 and a new compound engine and higher pressure boiler in 1883 by which time the bowsprit had been discarded. She traded on the coast until 1898 when she was sold first to Scandinavian and later Spanish owners. She was lost in heavy weather off the coast of Spain in the Autumn of 1933 after 81 years service.

Steam and sailing colliers of the period, had to load ballast of some form if a good passage northwards was to be made. That meant loading some sand, shingle or chalk in those days. Chalk was often loaded as it could be sold for a few shillings on arrival in the Tyne.

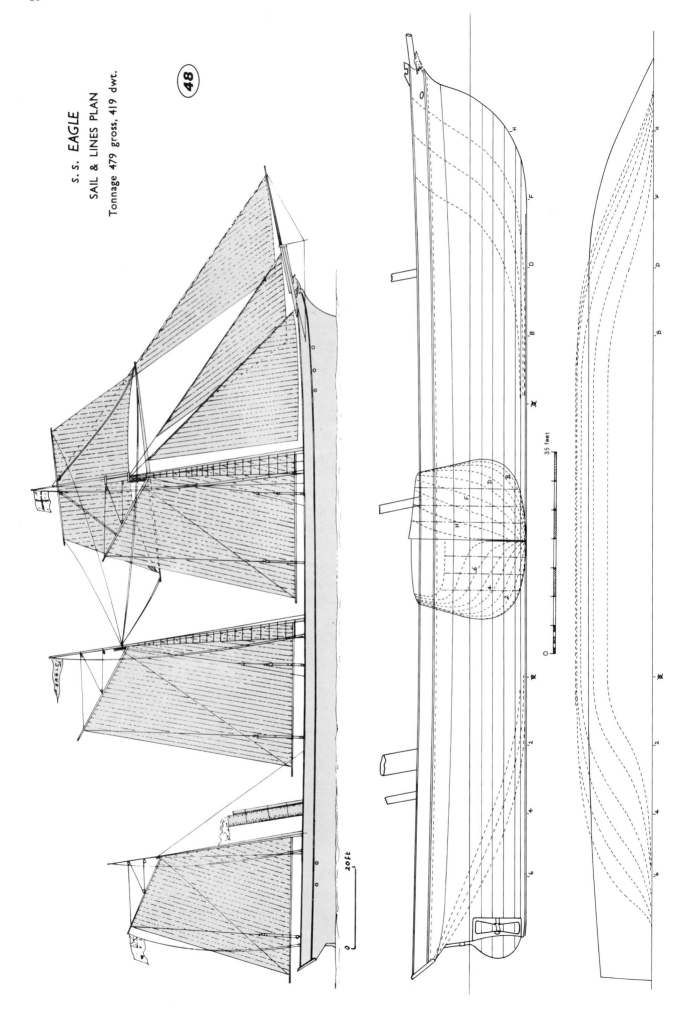

s.s. *EAGLE*
SAIL & LINES PLAN
Tonnage 479 gross, 419 dwt.

48

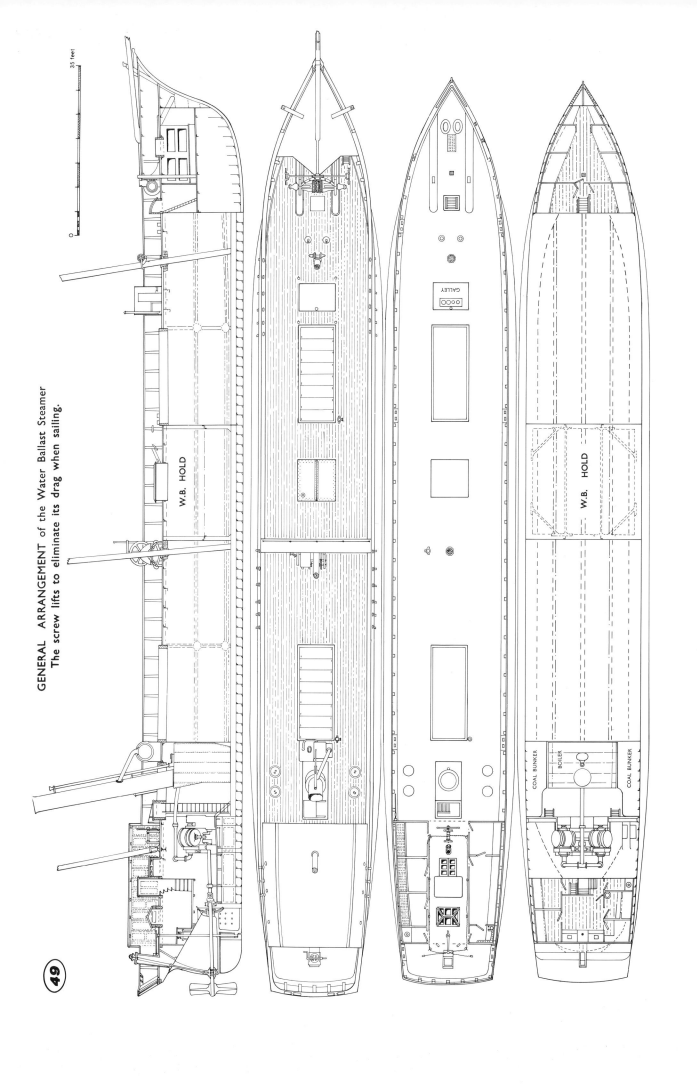

GENERAL ARRANGEMENT of the Water Ballast Steamer
The screw lifts to eliminate its drag when sailing.

49

35 feet

W.B. HOLD

GALLEY

W.B. HOLD

COAL BUNKER

BOILER

COAL BUNKER

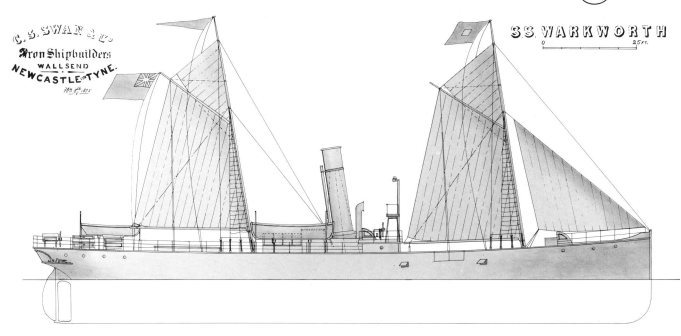

C.S.SWAN & Cⁱˢ
Iron Shipbuilders
WALLSEND
NEWCASTLE ᵒⁿ TYNE.

S.S. WARKWORTH

However loading and unloading this ballast delayed the loading of more profitable coal car-goes. The problem was tackled by the then novel method of fitting ballast tanks, as the water could be quickly and easily discharged while loading was taking place. The hold of some ships was divided up with watertight iron bulkheads so that part of the hold could be directly filled with water. The forecastle deck (49) made a tentative appearance in this design and provides a convenient stowage for the large stocked anchors. The entrance to the forecastle became a more substantial structure and the galley was placed just aft of the fore mast. A small auxiliary (donkey) boiler was sometimes fitted aft on deck. The accommodation in this vessel for the officers and engineers aft is more substantial also in this design. TANFIELD (53) probably presented a similar appearance when built in 1865. Water ballast holds caused a number of difficulties. Firstly, the bulkheads needed considerable strength, especially at the bottom to stand the weight of water and secondly the hold was wet on arrival and could only be used for certain cargoes. In addition, unless carefully filled, water surging back and forth could cause damage. John McIntyre, who was manager of Palmer's shipyard on the Tyne, tried another approach. He fitted shallow tanks along the bottom of the holds. They were soon generally adopted and became known as McIntyre tanks. The transverse floors were constructed in the ordinary way and then longitudinal girders were placed on top and the ceiling was laid on these longitudinals as shown in the cross-section of WARKWORTH (51).

Effective ventilators were not developed until the 1860s and up to that time only gratings were fitted over the stokeholds to provide air for the fires. With gratings there was always the danger of water cascading down on to the firemen below in heavy seas and flooding the stokehold. This was solved by the introduction of the cowl ventilator which could be turned to face the wind and so give a good draught for the fires. Naval architects of the period, such as Scott Russell, felt that the lines should be fine at the bows which meant that the

50b SAIL PLAN

Water Ballast Steamer

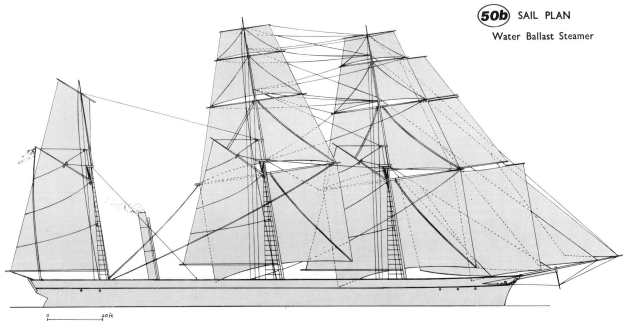

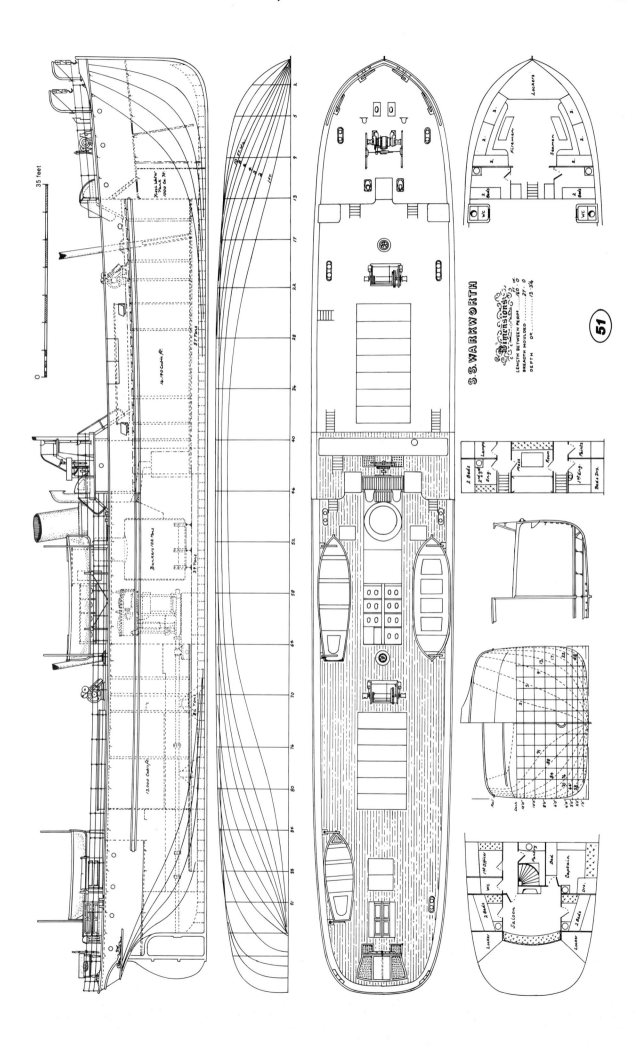

S.S. WARKWORTH

51

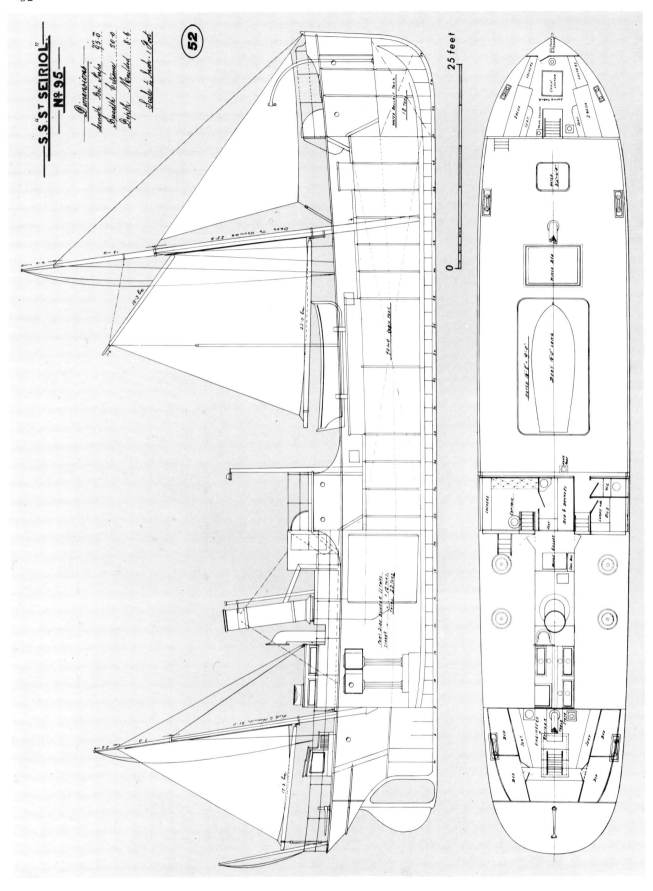

vessels tended to sail through waves and so were soon awash in moderate head seas. To prevent these seas sweeping the decks, a strongly cambered iron deck was fitted, generally known as a hurricane deck. At first they were confined to the fore deck, but proved so effective that they were extended the whole length of some passenger vessels. It was also applied to passenger cargo vessels such as STOCKTON (5), built for the Stockton & London Screw S.S. Co., leaving breaks for access to the hatches. It was later replaced by more conventional forecastle, bridge and engine casing, but bridges continued to have curved sides for many years. The stern was often covered by a 'whaleback' which protected the after emergency steering gear as seen in ROBIN (143).

Perhaps the greatest advances in coasting vessels were made in the 1870s and during this decade the three basic designs were established which were to remain in use for the next 100 years. One of these was the screw steamer with engines amidships (51). WARKWORTH was built by C.S. Swan, Newcastle for H. Andrews, in 1874, who was connected with the Broomhill Coal Co. She shows several advances compared with earlier designs particularly in the lines. It is now known that if the angle of the water flow to the line of the keel aft, exceeds about 18º, the flow of water to the propellor is liable to be turbulent, increasing drag. EAGLE's lines aft are steeper than this, while those of WARKWORTH are much more satisfactory and compare favourably with those of the ANNAGHMORE built almost 50 years later. The only major difference is the greater 'flare' on the latter's bows (indicated by sections curving outwards on the body plan) to help her ride over head seas. WARKWORTH also has a full forecastle deck, and the foredeck is now wholly iron, but the bridge is still a rather flimsy structure. However, the steering position is now placed beneath it, immediately in front of the engine casing. Cowl ventilators give a good draught and the stokehold grating, which allows hot air to escape, is well protected. The raised quarter deck is still of wood and officers' accommodation still aft. The engine room is of modern appearance with conventional compound engine and 'Scotch' boiler. There is also a donkey boiler and extensive ballast tanks, including a McIntyre tank. When built, many of these steamers had yards on the foremast and could set square sails, as was the case with SPRAY built in 1872 (see page 28), but they were soon discarded leaving a fore-and-aft rig as seen in WARKWORTH (50a) and GLENMORE (front endpaper) built in 1869. This latter vessel also has her donkey boiler on deck whereas WARKWORTH has hers in the boiler room which became the general practice. The type eventually developed into the large four hatch collier.

Two other designs were then developed from 'TANFIELD' type vessels by varying the length of the raised quarter deck. Most of the smaller vessels had a short raised quarter deck with all their hatches in the well deck (52). ST. SEIRIOL was built for Lewis & Co., of Bangor, North Wales, in 1887 for the general cargo trade. Many of these early vessels had open rails round the stern and it was not until the end of the 1890s that solid bulwarks were general. Similarly the open passage through the bridge was eliminated to prevent lamp room and W.C. being flooded by heavy seas.

The second type was created by extending the raised quarter deck forward to the bridge, which was then placed approximately amidships, with at least one hatch on the raised quarter deck. This design was used for coasters over about 130 feet in length, as in smaller vessels there was insufficient room to fit two hatches of a reasonable size, one on the well deck in front of the bridge and the other on the raised quarter deck aft of the bridge as seen in ASTERIA (title page).

 TANFIELD was built in 1865 by Palmer Bros' yard on the Tyne for Richard Cory & Co. Registered dimensions were 202.5' x 28.0' x 17.4.' Gross tonnage was 734. She is shown as running circa 1900. However, the shortened topmasts and wooden quarter deck rails indicate a veteran of the coal trade.

5.

54 SPARTAN at Tyree.

Clyde 'Puffers'

These little vessels sixty to ninety feet in length are confined to sheltered waters for the most part, but the largest vessels are suitable for coasting voyages over longer distances. The most important group were the small vessels built to serve the Clyde, In the mid-19th century, the upper part of the Clyde was shallow and sea going vessels had to discharge at Port Glasgow. The cargo was then carried onwards in small vessels. In contrast, the Forth had deep water and so the Forth & Clyde Canal was built to connect Glasgow with the deep water port of Leith. This canal saw the first effective use of steam, when the paddle steamer CHARLOTTE DUNDAS was built in 1802 for towing barges along the canal. However, it was felt that the wash from the paddle would damage the banks and the project was abandoned. Horses then continued to pull the scows, which carried 50 to 70 tons. In 1856 one was converted into a screw steamer to operate a regular service between Port Dundas and Falkirk and proved very successful and more were soon built. These vessels were flush decked, had no bulwarks and were steered by tiller. As the water in the canal was fresh, no condensers were fitted and so steam puffed out of the funnels as they went along, hence the name 'puffer'. To increase their sphere of operations, they were made more seaworthy by fitting continuous bulwarks and a raised quarter deck in later vessels. Engines received condensers and wheel steering was fitted to many vessels. In this way the most successful of the small steam coasters was created. Many vessels were fitted with compound rather than simple engines to reduce coal consumption. The single mast was fitted with a strong derrick and could also be used to set a trysail. The first canal vessels had no real crew accommodation, but it was provided on all vessels for regular use outside the canal.

The length was limited to a little over 66 feet by the locks on the canal and breadth to 18 feet. About 6 feet of water was usually available in the canal and this led to the development of two types. Shallower drafted vessels carrying 85 to 100 tons particularly for canal use, and deeper vessels able to carry 120 tons, which could pass through the canal only with a reduced load, but were suited for the trade through the Crinan Canal which accepted vessels drawing up to 9'6", and the coasting trade to Ireland. Examples of the two types from J. & J. Hay's fleet were TURK of 65 gross tons which had the dimensions 66.3 x 16.7 x 6.7 feet, designed for the canal, while the DRUID of 89 gross measuring 66.5 x 17.9 x 8.5 feet was an example of the deeper type intended for coasting. Such then was the picture on the Clyde, but it was quite different on the Thames where the sailing barge was firmly established as the local cargo carrier. In addition, numerous dumb barges were available worked by tugs. By the time a more efficient service was demanded from the Thames barge, paraffin and oil engines were available to power them, adding many years to their working lives.

In the Bristol Channel the local trade was largely handled by the numerous West Country schooners and ketches, also the railway network was well established by the time the small steam coaster became economic. However, some were built for the local trades, particularly in Welsh steam and household coal. On the Mersey and Humber numerous small steamers were built, mainly for use within river limits and so will not be considered in detail here. The Mersey originally had sailing barges 70 to 90 feet in length known as 'flats'. Many of these were fitted with steam engines and eventually oil engines, while others were not converted until later years and received oil engines directly. They traded on the Mersey, Weaver and Manchester Ship canal with occasional short coasting voyages. The iron sailing barges of the Humber, known as 'keels', were soon replaced by steam keels and latterly by large fleets of motor barges.

The arrangement of earlier 'puffers' is conveniently illustrated by GARMOYLE and AILSA which were built in 1904 by Denny Bros., at Dumbarton for A. McG. Leslie, Glasgow (59). Though most 'puffers' being built by this time had wheel steering, the tiller and steering platform were often rigged when working in the Forth & Clyde Canal, especially when light in order to give the helmsman a better view. By about 1910 the wheel and engine controls were fitted on top of the engine casing which improved visibility and kept the skipper's feet dry in choppy waters. It was not until 1925 that this became general and the small enclosed wheelhouse behind the funnel became such a characteristic feature. Denny's yard usually built

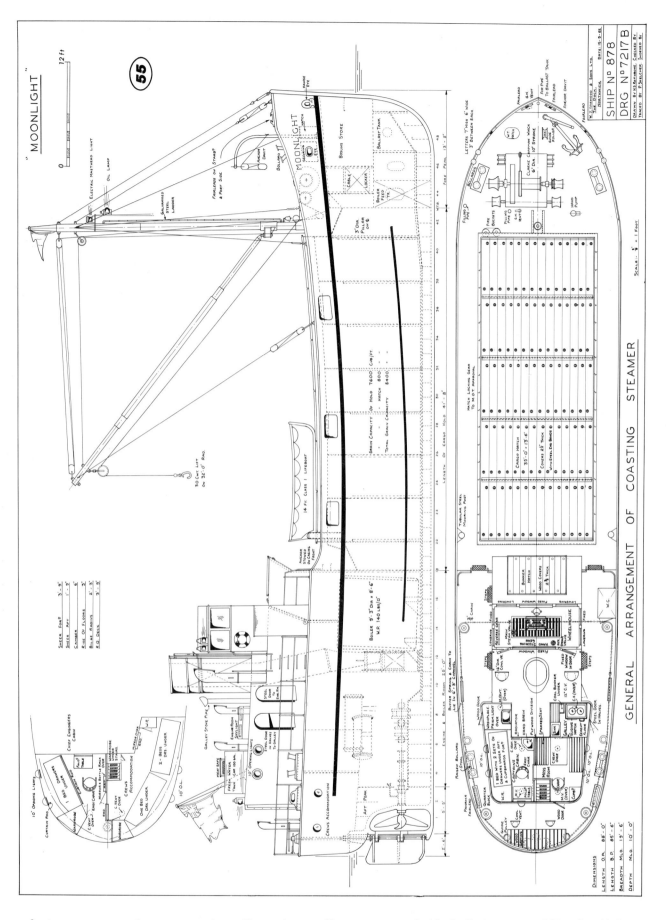

GENERAL ARRANGEMENT OF COASTING STEAMER

fast passenger steamers and so these two puffers were probably built because of Mr. Leslie's connections with the firm. He sold them after three years to A.F. Henry & MacGregor of Leith, the AILSA costing them £1,600. They were employed on local cargo services ranging from Montrose to Berwick-on-Tweed. By the 1920s this trade had declined so much that both vessels were sold. GARMOYLE passed to the Dundee, Perth & London Shipping Co., for their service between Dundee, Perth and Leith, while AILSA was sold to Ross & Marshall of Glasgow. GARMOYLE was renamed NORTH INCH by her new owners and fitted with an open bridge ahead of the funnel. Their local trade also soon declined and she was sold a year later to Colin McPhail of Glasgow and renamed STRONSHIRA. An enclosed wheelhouse was eventually fitted. In 1946 she was sold to the Arran Sea Transport and Supply Co., Ltd., and was renamed ARRAN ROSE. In 1953 she passed to J. A. White of North Queensferry, Fife.

The next stage in 'puffer' development was the building of larger vessels for the longer voyages, such as those to the Western Isles. At first the 66 feet long vessels were lengthened. This was done with STORMLIGHT built in 1888 which was lengthened to 86.3 feet in 1891 and SEALIGHT which was lengthened to 85.9 feet in 1911, near the limit for the Crinan Canal. This canal which can accept vessels up to 88' x 20', cuts through the Mull of Kintyre at Lochgilphead and takes some 150 miles off voyages to the Hebridean Isles and nearby mainland. It also allows the vessels to avoid the exposed coast of the Mull of Kintyre. The lengthened vessels were successful and further vessels of this size were built for Ross & Marshall. MOONLIGHT (55) illustrates this larger type and was one of the few to be built outside Scotland. She was completed in April 1952 by W.J. Yarwood at Northwich, Cheshire. As can be seen, all the accommodation is aft in this post-war vessel, which had such improvements as a wash place and radiators. Cargo capacity was 188 tons, but up to 25 tons of this was taken up by bunker coal. She traded until 1966 when the increasing costs of running a coal burner caused her to be sold to Mr. A.H. Turner who renamed her HURST. However, no work was found for her and she was sold to the West of Scotland Shipbreaking Co., in 1970 and broken up. A further steamer, STORMLIGHT, was built for the firm in 1957, but the trend was now in favour of motor vessels which by this time could show considerable savings over steam. Typical of these vessels was RAYLIGHT (60a) completed in 1963 by Scott's yard at Greenock. As can be seen from the profile, the compact machinery leaves considerably more crew space. In addition only 8 tons of bunkers are needed for the oil engine which gave a speed of nine knots in strong contrast to MOONLIGHT with a speed of seven and a half knots and 25 tons of bunkers, Plate 58.

Small motor vessels were not new on the Clyde and the earliest vessels appeared before the First World War. The first owner to put his faith in motor ships was John M. Paton who left Paton & Hendry to found the Coasting Motor Shipping Co., just prior to the First World War. Though the vessels could carry more cargo than steamers of the same size, their hot-bulb engines proved unreliable except in the hands of expert motor engineers who were difficult to find. Because of this the project failed and the vessels were sold. One of the vessels to leave the Clyde was the INNISHOWEN which was purchased by another pioneer motor ship owner, John Summers Steel Works on the Dee. The Dee is shallow and so motorships with their ability to carry more cargo on less draft were soon taken up. Of course, the Steel Company had the necessary engineering resources to keep the ships going and were not quite so concerned about running costs, as they were not competing with other shipping companies for cargoes. Their first vessel, OGARITA of 95 gross was purchased in 1912 and several larger vessels were ordered at the same time. These were found satisfactory and various second hand vessels were purchased including INNISHOWEN which was lengthened from 74.7 feet to 88.7 feet in 1925 and could carry 195 tons on a draft of 8'6". Though the INNISHOWEN was often employed in carrying her owners' steel products to Liverpool, returning with raw materials, she also made coasting voyages as far as Belfast. Coal was carried from the Point of Ayr Colliery to the Isle of Man and Lancaster, pig iron from Liverpool and Workington to the company's wharf, and basic slag from the wharf to Solway Firth ports. The freight rate for basic slag was about 4/6d per ton in 1936.

'Puffers' were built in large numbers and the Mercantile Navy List for 1910 lists 130 vessels of this type, the vast majority belonging to owners in the Clyde area. Owners were numerous as the price of second hand vessels was not beyond the means of a small business man. The position for purchase had been rather different in earlier times as shown by the accounts of William Robertson of Glasgow, which gives prices for two vessels built in the 1860s. The shallow drafted JASPER was built by J. & R. Swan at Maryhill for £906, while the deeper drafted DIAMOND cost £1,270 and could carry 95 tons of cargo. The price of £1,270 included £783 for the hull, £387 for the compound engine and £100 for outfitting and sails. Both vessels were used in the local coal trade, but JASPER also carried stone from Arran for the construction of Troon Harbour. William Robertson sold both vessels after a short time to concentrate on the coasting trades. Ross & Marshall were established in 1872 and from early days adopted names ending in 'light', which reflected the name of the owning company, the Light Shipping Co., Ltd.

J. & J. Hay was the style used for the 'puffer' interests of the Hay family, while the coaster interests were operated by J. Hay & Sons, but both used names of races, creeds or tribes such as 'Spartan'. The coal trade to the Western Isles was largely handled by 'puffers', but the total trade was made up of a large variety of cargoes. For example, when a house was built at Glenmore Bay on Loch Sunart in 1953, the SPARTAN was chartered by the builders. Bricks, timber, window frames, doors, in fact all the materials needed for construction were loaded in Glasgow. SPARTAN then sailed for Ardrishaig where she entered the Crinan Canal to reach Loch Linnhe. She then steamed through the sound of Mull and into Loch Sunart. On arrival at Glenmore Bay, a smooth part of the beach was selected at low tide and a stake driven in to mark the spot. Then at high tide, SPARTAN steamed up to the stake and waited for the tide to recede. Carts were then brought alongside so discharging could begin.

Coal cargoes were usually loaded at Glasgow, Greenock or Troon and then taken to the small stone jetties of the Western coast or isles or beaches if no jetty was available. The cargoes were either delivered to local merchants or perhaps the 'big house' would order a

57
'Puffer' in the Crinan Canal.

cargo about once a year. The 'puffer' would then duly arrive and beach herself if necessary. Meanwhile the local farm carts and even wheelbarrows would be mustered, day or night, to unload the ship as quickly as possible, for there could be extra to pay if the ship was unduly delayed discharging. Later the cargo was divided up among the local people. The 'puffer' would then move on to the next quay or beach until all the cargo of perhaps 120 tons had been distributed. Bunker coal was carried to coaling hulks at Stornoway for use by the fishing fleet. Bunker coal was also carried to Port Ellen and Portree for MacBrayne's passenger and cargo steamers, often in Hay's 'puffers'. Hay's also had the contract to supply the local lighthouses and deliveries of coal were made to them twice a year. Some of the largest single customers were the whisky distilleries which required coal, malt, barley and empty barrels. The 'puffers' often returned laden with whisky for export and distribution from Glasgow. The whisky distillers often owned 'puffers' themselves. Other large coal users were the gas works at Millport, Campbeltown and Rothesay which were supplied with gas coal, the vessels returning with coke for distribution to various users.

Coal and other cargoes such as refined salt from Carrickfergus were also moved through the Forth & Clyde canal. The 'puffers' often carried salt to Methil where they also loaded coal which they carried as far as Fraserburgh in the summer months. Scandinavian timber brought to Grangemouth was taken through to Glasgow and beyond, but this trade was lost to the railways by the 1940s. Other cargoes from Northern Ireland were fertiliser and limestone. The limestone was for Nairn's linoleum factory at Kirkcaldy as well as agricultural users. 'Puffers' also carried stone and macadam as required.

'Puffers' were also used to carry materials and prefabricated units between the various Clyde yards. One such item often carried by Hay's vessels was boilers from Rowan's works and the 'puffers' even ventured as far south as Newcastle carrying these, after passing through the Forth & Clyde Canal. The general pattern of trade in later years for these vessels is well illustrated by looking at one day's movements for the 18 vessels in Hay's fleet.

The Positions of Hay's Steamers for Friday 2nd November 1956

Name	Activity	(Progress or Next Voyage)
TURK	Barge work.	
SLAVE	Barge work.	
GAEL	On Kirkintilloch Slip.	
CUBAN	Discharges gas coal, Rothesay.	(Monday: Troon to load coal)
TEXAN	On hire to Grand, Sutcliffe & Gell.	
INCA	Discharging coal, Tighnabruaich.	(Saturday: Troon to load coal for Ardrishaig for Bell)
CRETAN	Loads gravel, Bowling for Rothesay.	(Queen's Dock: Boiler cleaning)
BOER	Discharging coal at Ardrishaig for Bell.	
CHINDIT	Discharging coal, "Devon Doubles", Dunoon.	(Rothesay Dock, Clydebank to load for Rothesay)
MOOR	?	
SERB	Discharging bricks at Port Ellen.	
ANZAC	Discharging timber at Dumbarton.	
LASCAR	Discharging coal at Whiting Bay for S.D. & S.	
KAFFIR	Due Irvine to load bricks for Stornoway.	(Loading by 1 p.m.)
SPARTAN	Discharging coal at Dunvegan for Dis.W.B.	(Loch Ailort/Girvan)
DANE	At Kirkintilloch.	
CELT	Loads coal and coke at Troon for Peterfort.	(Sailed 11.20 a.m.)
SIR JAMES	On way Port Ellen with casks.	(Cleared Crinan Canal 1 p.m.)

Hay's built many 'puffers' in their own yard at Kirkintilloch on the canal and also repaired them there. The Hamilton family also built a 'puffer', their first, at Brodick, Isle of Arran in 1895. They later moved to Glasgow and changed to motor vessels, beginning with the GLENSHIRA in 1953. The only major owners outside Glasgow were the Leith, Hull and Hamburg S.P. Co., Ltd., whose vessels were identified by letters of the alphabet. 'A' was built in 1873 while 'Z' appeared in 1889. The Carron Company of Falkirk had vessels identified by numbers written in full, mainly for canal work, though only NUMBER TWELVE

58

Steam Coaster AILSA
DIMENSIONS: 66′6″x 18′4″x 8′10″
Tonnage 100 gross.

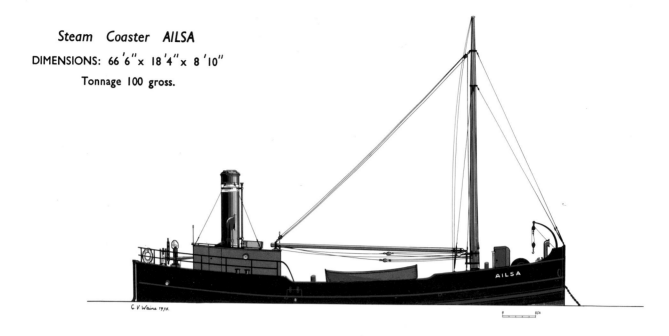

Steam Coaster MOONLIGHT
DIMENSIONS: 85′6″x 19′6″x 10′0″
Tonnage 164 gross.

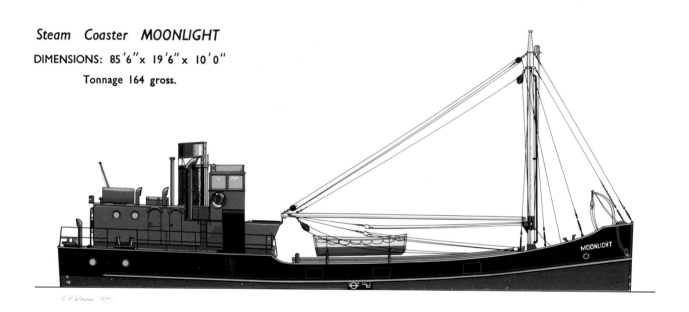

Plate 58

remained by 1908. Some 'puffers' were sold to owners outside Scotland. ADELAIDE went to Cork, GLENIFFER to Gillingham, Kent and the RUSHLIGHT ended up carrying coal from Barry to the paper mill at Watchet. Further North, BRITON which had been built as the ROSLIN GLEN in 1893, carried coal from the Mersey to destinations along the North Wales coast for her owner, Mr. Davies who owned a shop in Nevin, Caernarvonshire. At Nevin, BRITON was beached under a gantry which had buckets on cables for discharging. Elsewhere she was beached in bays such as Cemlyn, Anglesey and unloaded by horse and cart as in Scotland. Much of this local trade was in the hands of the small schooners and ketches of North Wales. Screw steamers, slightly larger than 'puffers', appeared on the Irish Sea in the latter part of the 19th century, the forerunners of the true Irish Sea coasters, they were slightly larger and more suitable for Irish Sea conditions in winter. One such early vessel was the WILD ROSE (front endpaper) of Coppack, Carter & Co., Ltd., Connah's Quay, North Wales. She measured 100.9′ x 18.0′ x 8.8′ and was mainly employed carrying bricks and coal to Ireland. She soon became popular with the Dublin coal merchants.

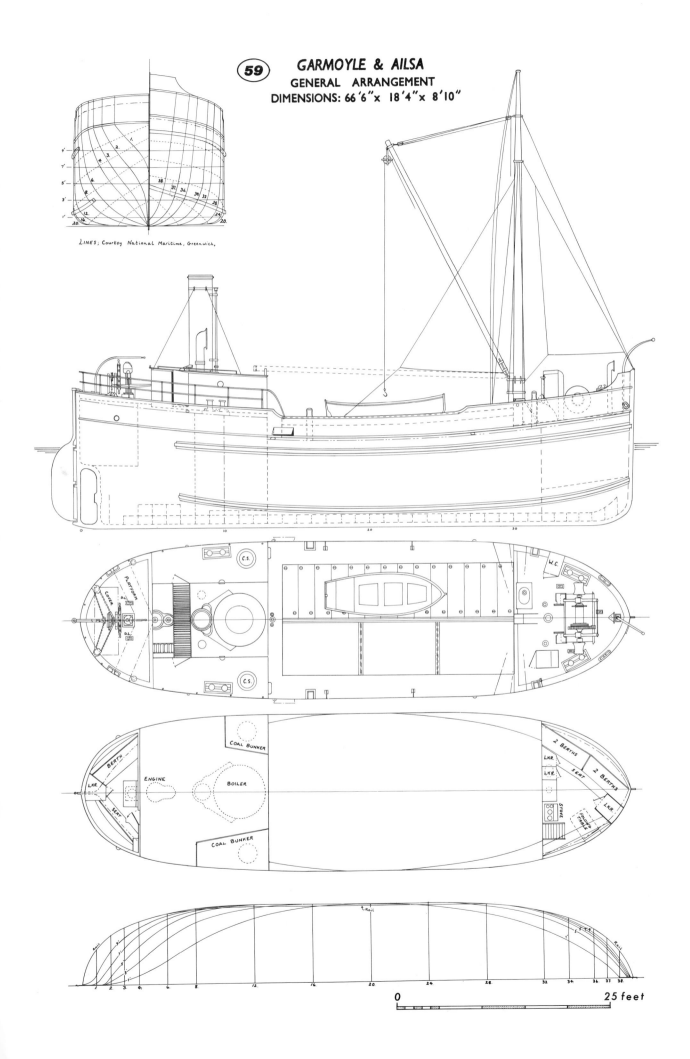

(59) GARMOYLE & AILSA
GENERAL ARRANGEMENT
DIMENSIONS: 66'6"x 18'4"x 8'10"

LINES; Courtesy National Maritime, Greenwich.

COAL BUNKER

2 BERTHS

2 BERTHS

LKR.

SEAT

BERTH

ENGINE

BOILER

LKR.

STOVE

LKR.

SEAT

COAL BUNKER

0   25 feet

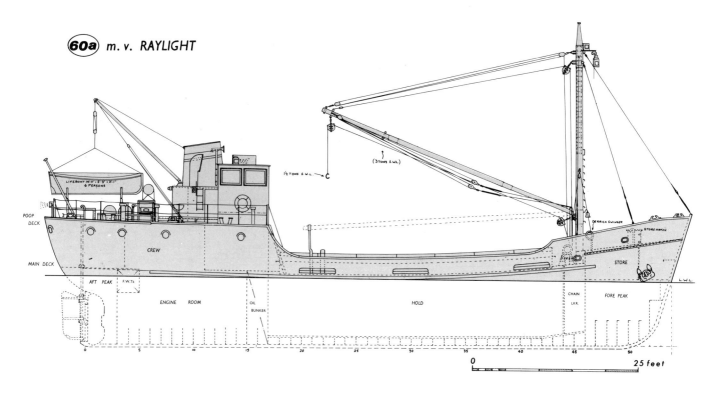

60a *m. v.* RAYLIGHT

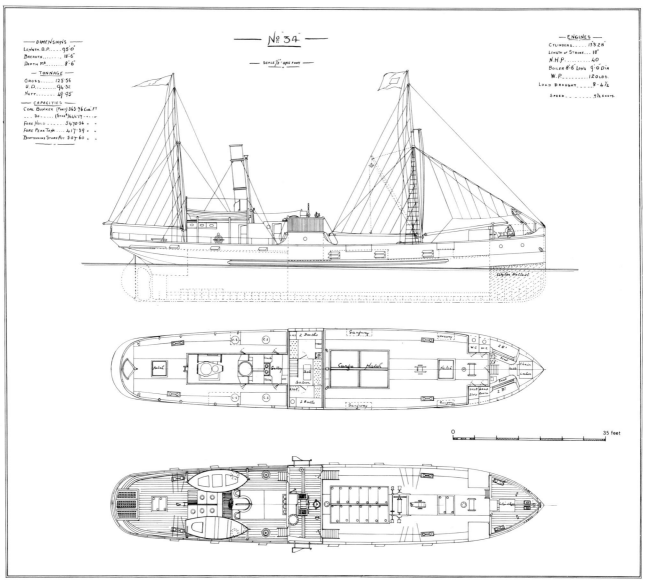

No. 34

60b VELINHELI built in 1892 by S. McKnight & Co., Ayr, was typical of the trim little coasters built in the 1890's. For most of her life, a single dinghy replaced the two boats shown here on the original plan.

6.

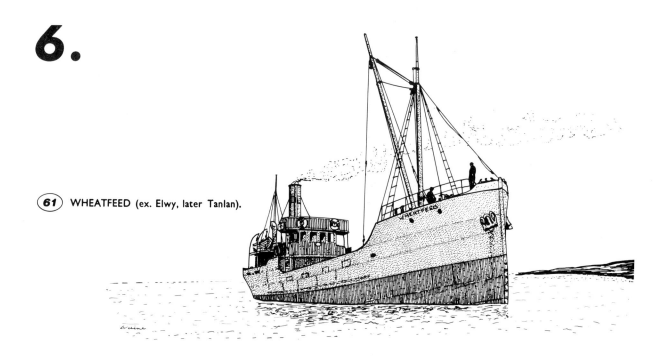

(61) WHEATFEED (ex. Elwy, later Tanlan).

Short Raised Quarter Deck Coasters

These vessels are essentially larger versions of the 'puffers' already described and ranged from 90 to 150 feet in length for the most part. Bridge and engines were aft, associated with the raised quarter deck. A forecastle deck also extended a short distance from the bows, leaving a long well deck amidships (61). This was protected in most vessels by bulwarks at least three feet in height. The earliest vessels often had two small hatches with the mast between them. This design was retained for the larger vessels in many cases, but many later vessels were often fitted with one long hatch and a single mast placed on the forecastle with one long derrick. To improve the efficiency of discharging with the ships gear, a second mast or king post, was fitted at the after end of the hold in some vessels as seen in the steamer SPURNPOINT (front endpapers). These coasters were well suited to the more exposed waters around the coast and included the smallest vessels making the longer coasting voyages. The larger vessels in the group often made long voyages around the coast or to the Continent.

VELINHELI (60b), built for the Dinorwic Quarry Company, illustrates one of the smallest vessels. She was built for carrying the Dinorwic slates from the quarry in Caernarvonshire to depots at Preston and Liverpool, as well as discharging directly into ocean ships at the latter port. She also made trips to near Irish ports. She usually managed three trips per week from the Company's own harbour at Port Dinorwic on the Menai Straits. Her registered dimensions were 95.0 x 18.5 x 7.5 feet, similar to a 'puffer' but some 30 feet longer. This more streamlined shape, together with a compound engine of 40 r.h.p., gave a speed of nine and a half knots, which was fast for a small coaster when she was built in 1892. Deeper, fuller, bluff bowed vessels like EDITH (63a) were the more usual type in the main tramp fleets, but they were slower at around eight knots. However they were good cargo carriers able to take over twice as much as VELINHELI. Some of these vessels such as EDITH were built without a raised quarter deck, but otherwise the layout was the same as those with raised quarter decks. The layout of VELINHELI is typical of small vessels of the period, with two firemen and two seamen sharing the forecastle, while captain, mate and two engineers had accommodation below the bridge. A small galley is fitted in behind the bridge but there is no room for more accommodation further aft because of the fine lines of the hull terminated by the graceful counter stern. The cargo hatches are both small following schooner practice making speedy loading and discharging difficult. However, as better steel structural design was developed, sufficiently strong large hatches were soon introduced. The fore and aft sails had several uses. Firstly, they reduced rolling in heavy seas. Secondly, many of the captains began their sea service in the local schooners and so could put the sails to good use. Finally, in the event of a boiler leak or engine trouble, the sails could be used to keep the ship under way or hove to in a storm until repairs were completed. In later years, VELINHELI like many other two hatch vessels of this type, was fitted with one large hatch and the mast moved forward. Small steamers like VELINHELI were in many ways steam replacements for the schooners, where the need for regular deliveries made the increased cost acceptable, Plate 123.

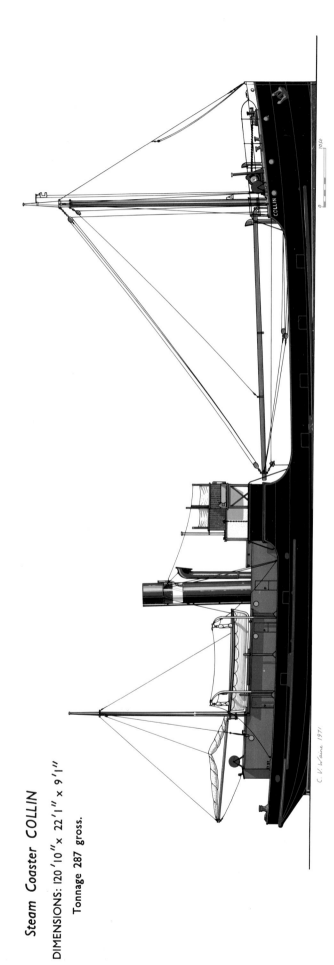

Steam Coaster COLLIN

DIMENSIONS: 120'10" x 22'1" x 9'1"

Tonnage 287 gross.

Plate 62

Steam Coaster BEN SEYR

DIMENSIONS: 120'0" x 22'1" x 9'0"

Tonnage 265 gross.

(63a) EDITH of Monroe Bros., Liverpool was originally built for Joseph Monks, Liverpool in 1900 by Scott & Sons, Bowling. Registered dimensions were 100.0' x 23.1' x 10.8' and tonnages were 229 gross, 298 deadweight.

These little steamers were mostly built between 1860 and 1900. One of the last was the LUCENA, built for Joseph Monks of Liverpool in 1913. She was essentially a rather more advanced version of EDITH built 13 years earlier, the length having crept up to 114 feet. However, her life was much shorter than EDITH's as the LUCENA was sunk by a German submarine on the 27th of June 1915. Joseph Monks commenced business in Warrington with steam flats which were soon making voyages outside the river. The business prospered and he went on to build a number of similar sized coasters for the local trades such as coal to near Irish ports and stone from North Wales quarries. LUCENA was designed to give a good cargo capacity with the minimum of wasted space, the bunkers being placed on either side of the boiler and the mast well forward to give maximum hold length. The carrying capacity was aided by the broad beam and she makes an interesting contrast with the fine lined VELINHELI. The LUCENA was built by Hawthorns & Co Ltd, Leith and the drawing shows a feature which was common on many drawings from this yard, that is the depicting of the cargo battens on the inboard profile on the general arrangement. Cargo battens are wooden battens spaced several inches apart running along the sides of the hold and secured to the frames. They are fitted to protect the plating from damage by the cargo. Like many small coasters, she was fired from the engine room side of the boiler. Coasters with this arrangement can generally be identified at a glance because the largest ventilators, those to the stokehold, are slightly behind the funnel. An unusual feature of the design is the built-up steering position on the bridge to give a better view over the forecastle. A minor detail of

(63b) *Motor Coaster INDORITA*
DIMENSIONS: 108'7" x 22'1" x 10'6" MLD.

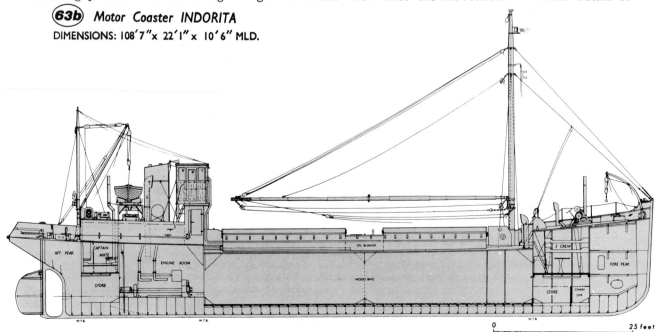

0   25 feet

note is the stiffening of the hatch sides with brackets rather than angled stanchions. Later vessels had the stanchions capped by a heavy horizontal angle just below the hatch batten hooks to reduce the tendency of heavy seas sweeping up under the edge of the hatch tarpaulin and loosening it. This arrangement can clearly be seen on the midship section of BELFORD (74) and can be discerned on the plan of DORIS THOMAS (66). In the 1920s they had strong competition from the schooners and ketches fitted with oil engines. These early engines were small with one or two cylinders giving the schooners a speed of about 5 knots on power alone. Progressively more powerful engines were fitted so that they became motor vessels with auxiliary sail. One such vessel was the schooner KATHLEEN & MAY which had a Crossley engine giving her a speed of 8 knots by the 1950s.

Steamers able to carry 250 to 300 tons showed considerable savings over the smaller vessels and were built in some numbers prior to the First World War. They were around 120 feet in length and few were built in later years as cargoes tended to increase in size. Some of the early motor vessels also appeared in this size range. Many of these were designed by Pollocks of Faversham, often for building in other yards. One such yard to build to a design from Pollocks was Abdela & Mitchell at Queensferry near Chester. For example, INDORITA (63b) was one of several vessels built for John Summers Steel Works. This vessel was designed about 1913 and laid down at the yard about 1915. She was then taken over on the stocks by the Admiralty and the design slightly modified. However, construction proceeded only slowly as the yard was occupied with more urgent war work. When construction was resumed, both the shipyard manager and head foreman had left. The remaining staff were left to finish the hull which was launched on the 7th of February 1920 without the side keelsons and some deck beams. However, these faults were corrected before she entered service in 1921. Her usual cargoes for them were pig iron from Workington to their wharf on the Dee with outward cargoes of steel sheets or basic slag. During the Second World War she worked for the Admiralty as a tender on the Clyde. On return to John Summers in 1946 she was reconditioned on Cubbin's slip at Birkenhead and sold to Coppack Bros., Connah's Quay, for their local coasting trades.

Her old 2-cylinder Bolinders engine soldiered on but was by this time rather worn and difficult to start. The engine would be primed and compressed air for starting applied sev-

(64) JAMES TENNANT built by Wood, Skinner's yard at Newcastle in 1893. Registered dimensions were 120.0′ x 20.1′ x 9.0′ and tonnages were 203 gross, 230 deadweight.

eral times before the engine would start. On one occasion in Birkenhead, after several such attempts, the engine started, but the unburnt mixture from the earlier attempts exploded blowing a hole in the front of the funnel and the back of the wheelhouse, blowing out all the windows and the top skywards. The result was a new funnel and a few years later in 1958, a new Crossley engine of 240 b.h.p. This gave a speed of nine knots and extended her working life until 1970.

By far the most popular size for these coasters was between 120 and 130 feet in length and this size featured in all the main fleets engaged in the shorter coasting voyages and carriage of the smaller cargoes. Leading owners were Robinson, Brown of Newcastle, J.G. Frew (Home Trade Steam Carrying Co.) and J. & A. Gardner both of Glasgow. They were particularly popular for the Irish Sea trades to the smaller harbours and were the largest vessels that many of them could safely accept.

AGATE (67) was built of iron for William Robertson as early as 1878 for the Irish Sea coasting trade and cost £5,100. The 35 r.h.p. compound engine and boiler by W.King & Co, cost £1,580. Many vessels of this type were built by Scott & Sons, Bowling, Wood, Skinner of Newcastle and John Fullerton of Paisley. The last building CLINT (8) in 1896. Though the plan of AGATE shows no hatches, they were probably similar to those shown on the plan of CLINT. The JAMES TENNANT (64) was built in 1893 for 'T' Steam Coasters and managed by Robinson, Brown of Newcastle. She shows an interesting combination of old and new feat-

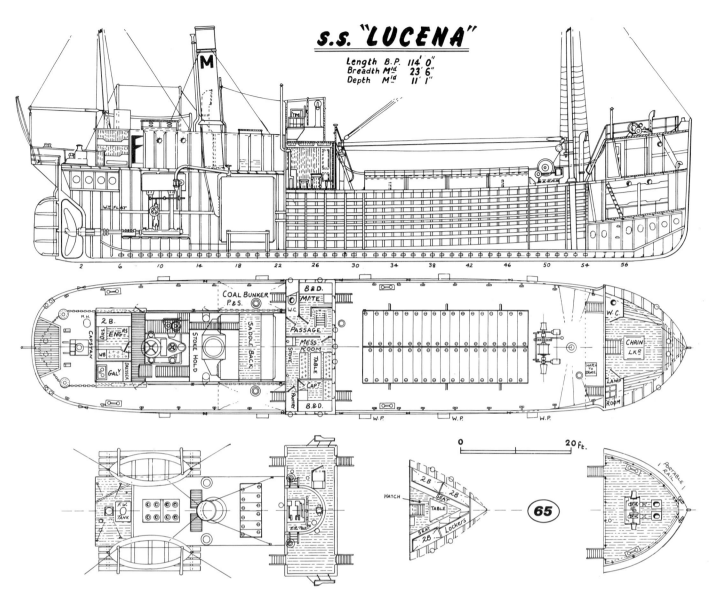

S.S. "LUCENA"

Length B.P. 114' 0"
Breadth M'ld 23' 6"
Depth M'ld 11' 1"

65

ures. She has the older type forecastle which was longer and lower and is fully rigged with
a main sail supported by a gaff. In strong contrast to these features is the enclosed wheelhouse which did not become general for another 20 years. The more usual open bridge is
seen in SAINT MODAN built by Scott & Sons, Bowling for J. & A. Gardner of Glasgow in 1910
(69). The low forecastle is also retained but the main mast has been moved forward to make
way for a single hatch. She also has a full complement of steam deck machinery. These
steamers had little flare on the bows and tended to steam through waves rather than over
them. This made for a more pleasant motion and allowed the ship to maintain speed but they
were soon awash in a rough sea and access to the crew accommodation forward was difficult
to say the least. A further danger was the well deck filling with water in particularly heavy
seas. If this had not drained off before following seas arrived, there was a danger of the
vessel foundering. This was counteracted by the man on watch rushing to the engine room
telegraph and pulling it up to 'stop' to give the ship a chance to ride up and shed the water,
rather than plunge headlong into the next wave. The problem was reduced by adding more
flare to the bows and a full height forecastle such as that seen in CALATUM (68). This
vessel was designed some 10 years later than the JAMES TENNANT and shows the trend to
less sail area and the larger single hatch. The vessel was designed in 1903 and was not
completed until 1908. She was built by Williamsons of Workington for their own account. She
worked in the coasting trade until 1913 when she was sold to Spanish owners. J. G. Frew of
Glasgow had a number of similar coasters built at Paisley by J. MacArthur's yard.

Accommodation in the forecastle above the main deck was much more airy and lighter.
COLLIN, Plate 62, of 1915 has such accommodation as indicated by the row of portholes vis-
ible just below the forecastle rails. In some vessels the forecastle was of iron or steel, but
in most it was wood laid on iron or steel deck beams and these decks often leaked in older
vessels, making conditions rather damp for the luckless seamen and firmen below who re-
taliated by taking a hot poker from the bogey stove and applying it to the seam suspected of
leaking and hoping the pitch thus melted would seal the leak. The W. C. and lamp room under the forecastle deck in earlier designs were displaced to positions either side of the fore
mast. The final development is seen in the DORIS THOMAS (66), built for Thomas Bros. of
Liverpool. She was one of four sisterships built for local owners by the Manchester Dry
Docks Co. Ltd., Ellesmere Port, beginning with BEN SEYR in 1920 (Plate 62) and ending in
1926 with PENSTONE. DORIS THOMAS was the third vessel in the series and was completed
in 1924. As can be seen from the plan, she was fitted with a true enclosed wheelhouse with

S.S. Nº 73.
GENERAL ARRANGEMENT

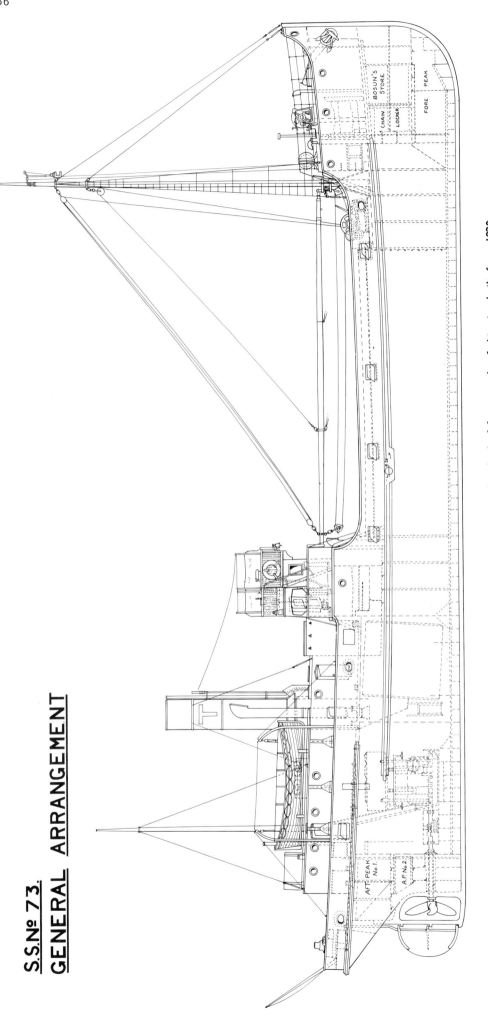

66 DORIS THOMAS (profile above, decks below) was the third of four vessels of this size built from 1920 to 1926. Registered dimensions were 120.0' x 22.1' x 9.1' and tonnages were 266 gross, 270 deadweight. She was sold to A. F. Henry & MacGregor of Leith and renamed DENNIS HEAD. Sold again two years later, she became BEN AIN of the Ramsey S.S. Co., Ltd., Isle of Man until scrapped in 1963.

67 AGATE (profile, below) was built in 1878 by T. B. Seath's yard, Rutherglen. She was the same length as DORIS THOMAS built 46 years later, and so makes an interesting comparison. The most obvious differences are the open bridge and low forecastle. Registered dimensions were 120.6' x 20.1' x 9.6' and tonnages were 178 gross, 210 dwt. She traded for Wm. Robertson, Glasgow stranding in the Kenmare River Ireland in 1911. She had two hatches (19'11" x 7'11" and 6'7" x 6'11") and was probably like CLINT.

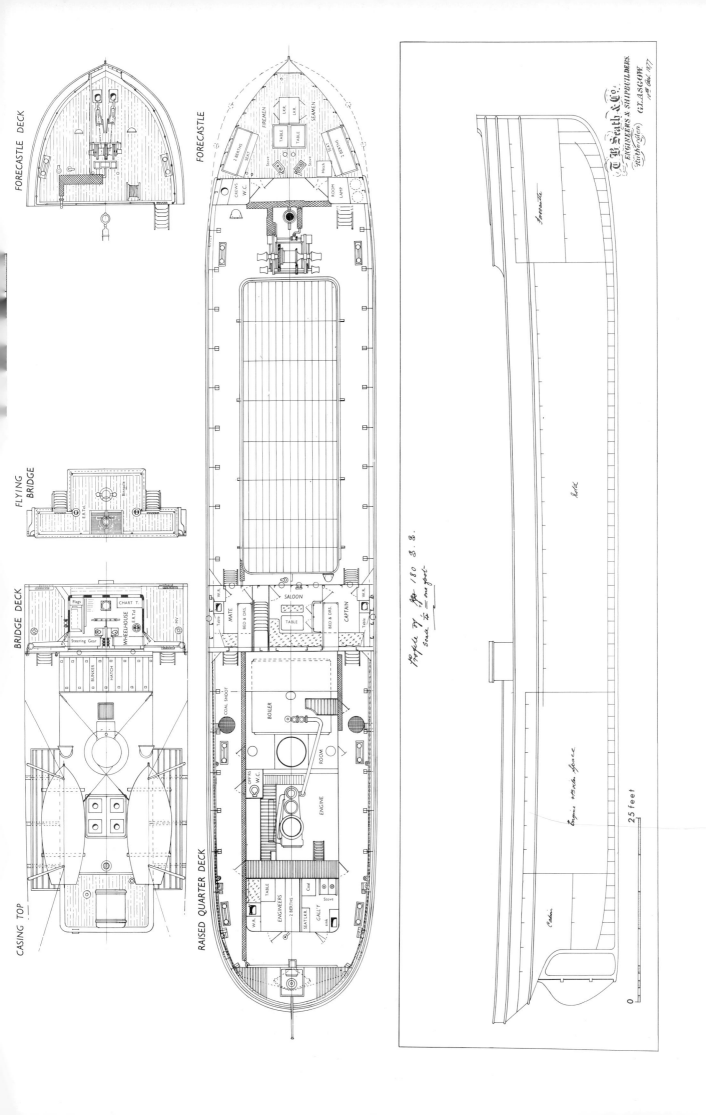

FORECASTLE DECK

FORECASTLE

FLYING
BRIDGE

BRIDGE DECK

CASING TOP

RAISED QUARTER DECK

FIREMEN   SEAMEN

2 BERTHS   TABLE TABLE   2 BERTHS   SEAT

Stove   Stove   Hatch   SEAT

CREWS   W.C.   LAMP ROOM

LKR.   LKR.

W.R.   SALOON   W.R.

Table   MATE   BED & DRS.   TABLE   BED & DRS.   CAPTAIN   Table

COAL SHOOT   BOILER   ROOM

OFF RS   W.C.   ENGINE

W.R.   ENGINEERS   SEAT   GALLY   Stove   Coal   Table
LKR   sink   2 BERTHS

Flags   CHART T.
E.R.Tel.   M.V.
Steering Gear   WHEELHOUSE
BUNKER   HATCH

E.R.Tel.   Binnacle

Profile of Ship 180 g.g.
Scale ¼ = one foot

Forecastle

hold

Engine +Boiler Space

Cabin

25 feet

0

T.B. Seath & Co.
ENGINEERS & SHIPBUILDERS
Rutherglen
GLASGOW
14th Oct. 1877

an open flying bridge above, used for inshore navigation. They were designed for local Irish Sea trades were some cargoes around 250 tons were still the order of the day.

Few further steamers of this size were built, the reasons can be seen by comparing the DORIS THOMAS with the motor coaster AFFARIC, built in 1934. This motor vessel was able to carry over 87 tons more cargo on 1'2" less draft at a higher speed with much better crew accommodation. Most of the steamers built after 1910 were in the 130-140 foot range and were able to carry between 300 and 450 tons. They were popular with Liverpool owners and were also a feature of fleets managed by Gillie & Blair, Newcastle. They were the largest size for many harbours and this was the case at the Point of Ayr Colliery jetty. This colliery is situated at the mouth of the Dee, North Wales almost at the waters' edge and so was ideally placed to export coal to Ireland. The colliery owned two vessels of this size and one a little smaller for many years, as they could sail fully loaded on most tides without the need for extensive dredging. However, the amount of water in the long gutter was strongly dependent on the direction of the wind. On occasion, TALACRE, Plate 2, or one of the other vessels would set off on the morning tide only to stick fast in the mud some yards from the jetty and be left high and dry until the evening tide came to set her free. Barnacles had a rough time on the bottoms of these ships.

TALACRE had a single hold and derrick which was usual in later vessels, but the earlier vessels often had two hatches with the mast between them, this arrangement continued to be used for these larger vessels for some time after it had been discarded for smaller coasters. Typical of the larger vessels was SHOTTON (71, 79), built for Thomas Coppack & Co of Connah's Quay. He had successfully chartered his 120-130 foot coasters for the fruit and vegetable trade from France for a number of years. He then decided to build a somewhat larger coaster with this trade in mind and SHOTTON was the result completed in 1909. Her compound machinery of 62 r.h.p. gave a maximum speed of about $9\frac{1}{2}$ knots fully loaded. To attain this speed, the builders gave her rather finer lines than expected and she could not carry 330 tons of cargo as intended with full bunkers, indeed with full bunkers of 41 tons, the cargo capacity was reduced to 289 tons. Speed was essential for the fresh fruit and vegetable shipments if they were to arrive in good condition and markets were to be caught. In this trade with light vegetable cargoes, speeds up to 11 knots were obtained, but of course it meant pushing engine and boiler to the maximum. This was done to be sure the ship's charterer caught the best of the market and in any case they paid for all the coal used. But at the end of the fruit and vegetable season, she had to work in the coal trade for the most part, and her lack of carrying capacity for her crew and fuel requirements very much reduced her profitability. Since she was fired from a separate stokehold, she had to carry extra firemen compared with other vessels in the fleet which were fired from the engine room allowing combined engineer/firemen to be used except for the chief who did not fire. She was a well built ship but not a profitable one and this is probably why she had no less than

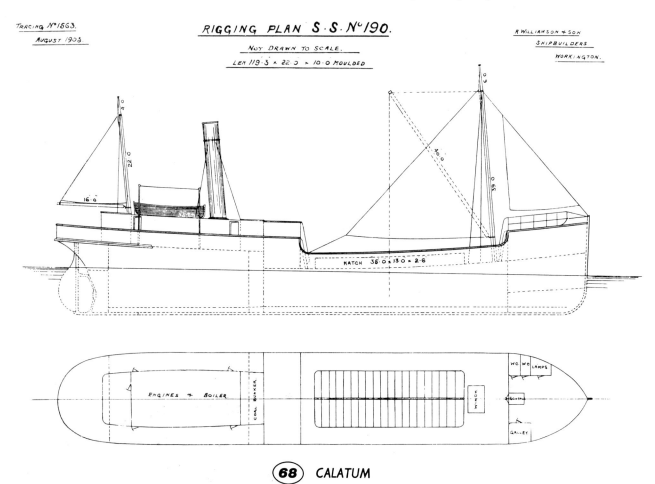

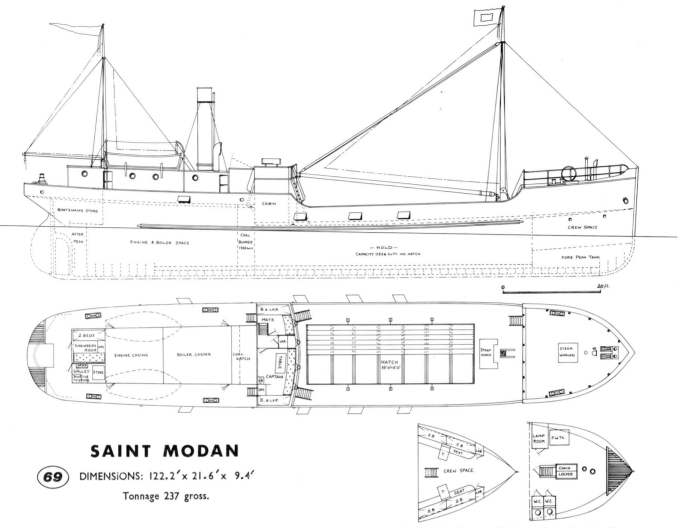

SAINT MODAN

(69) DIMENSIONS: 122.2' x 21.6' x 9.4'

Tonnage 237 gross.

eight owners in her 40 years existence. Thomas Coppack decided to sell her after just three years trading. Her end came in 1949 when, on the 14th of April, she went ashore at Irvine Harbour with a cargo of carbide. Seawater penetrated the cargo producing acetylene gas which exploded and she was destroyed by fire.

Coppack's vessels often carried explosives but because of the small weight of explosives usually constituting a cargo, extra ballast capacity was preferable. Also it was preferable to have a fully insulated hold, because of the need for these special features, many of the explosives companies had their own ships. FLORENCE COOKE was built by Hepples (1919) Ltd for Cooke's Explosives Ltd (later Cooke's Explosives Shipping Co) in 1923. She had two holds, the after hold being specially insulated (70). Fore peak capacity was 36 tons and that of the aft peak was 19 tons, but in addition there was a trimming tank which gave another 56 tons of ballast when carrying the small explosives cargoes. She traded for the company until the late 1950s, latterly under the management of Antony & Bainbridge, Newcastle. She was probably built with two hatches because of the intended trade, however, the most usual design in the 1920s had a single hatch though still retaining two derricks for rapid discharge of the long unobstructed hatch. This was achieved by fitting a second mast or king-post at the after end of the hold as seen in BELFORD (6, 74), one of seven similar vessels built by J. & D. Morris Ltd, Newcastle between 1918 and 1921. They were a particular feature of the Walford fleet which had three of them for a time around the 1930s. The same design was also a feature of the Rix and Robinson, Brown fleets.

The trend to larger cargoes meant that few further ships of this size were built after the 1920s and when replacements for existing vessels were needed, the motor ship was the obvious choice as they could carry more on less draft. However, they continued to hold their own, particularly in the coal trade as it was cheap and easy to bunker at coal loading ports. Also the bunker hatches of some coasters were incorporated in the after end of the main hatch. This sometimes made bunkering a little too convenient; as one shipper remarked, "it was surprising how much coal intended for the cargo fell down the ever open bunker hatches". One of the last steam colliers of this size to be built was the MOUNT BATTOCK, completed in 1939. She was employed carrying bunker coal for the Aberdeen fishing fleet, especially in her earlier years. As the number of coal-fired trawlers dwindled, she was often used for other cargoes in the local coasting trades. As can be seen (4), she had a modern type cruiser stern replacing the counter stern of earlier designs. A wheelhouse was also fitted and the fore mast was placed well forward on the forecastle, clear of grabs used to discharge the cargo. Discharge was also facilitated by the single large hatch.

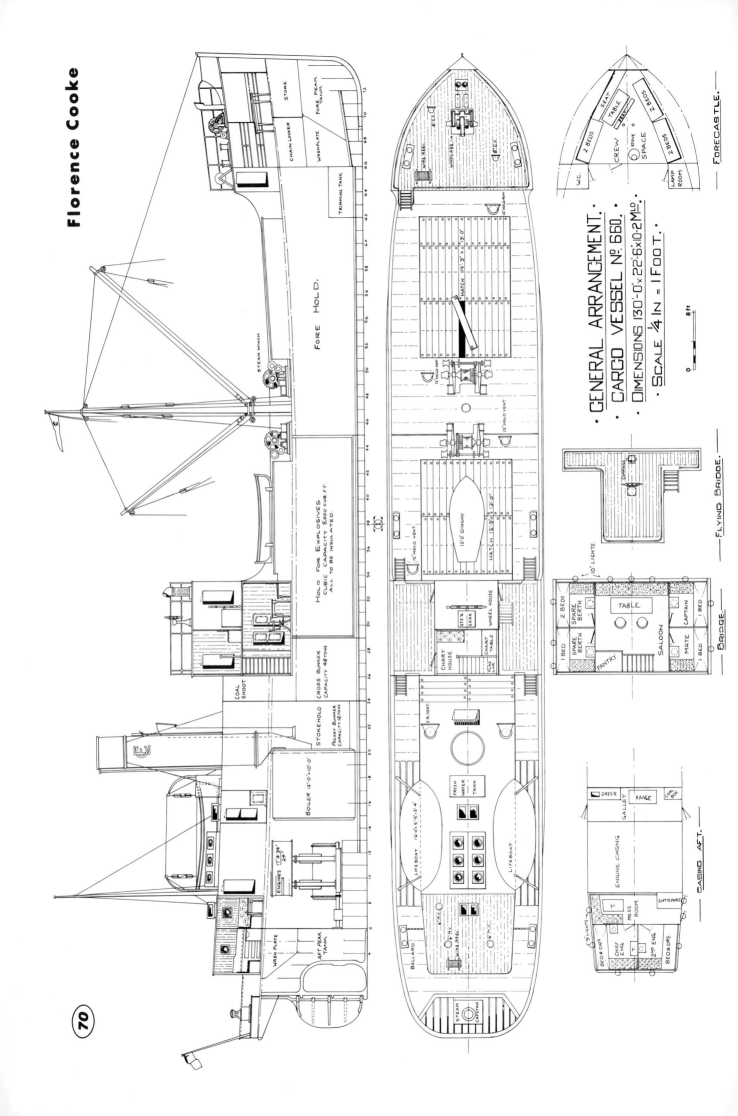

Florence Cooke

70

FORE HOLD.

STORE

CHAIN LOCKER

FORE PEAK TANK

WASHPLATE

TRIMMING TANK

STEAM WINCH

HOLD FOR EXPLOSIVES
CUBIC CAPACITY 5,000 CUB. FT.
ALL TO BE INSULATED.

COAL SHOOT

CROSS BUNKER
CAPACITY 48 TONS

STOKEHOLD

POCKET BUNKER
CAPACITY 12 TONS

BOILER 12'-0"×10'-0"

ENGINES 17"&34"
24"

WASH PLATE

AFT PEAK TANK

WHEEL REEL

WINDLASS

8"×2"

8"C.Y.

12" HOLD VENT

HATCH 119'-3" × 3'-0"

3'-0"

12" HOLD VENT

12" HOLD VENT

12" HOLD VENT

12" HOLD VENT

12'-0" DINGHY

HATCH 15'-9"× 13'-0"

STEG. GEAR

WHEEL HOUSE

CHART HOUSE

CHART TABLE

FLAG LKR.

E.R. VENT

FRESH WATER TANK

LIFEBOAT 16'-0"×5'-5"×2'-4"

LIFEBOAT

BOLLARD

W.V.

W.V.

WISE REEL

STEAM CAPSTAN

GENERAL ARRANGEMENT.
CARGO VESSEL N°. 660.
DIMENSIONS 130'-0"× 22'-6"×10'-2"MLD.
SCALE ¼IN = 1FOOT.

0   8ft

FORECASTLE.

W.C.

2 BEDS

SEAT

TABLE

CREW

STOVE

SPACE

2 BEDS

LAMP ROOM

FLYING BRIDGE.

COMPASS

10" LIGHTS

2 BEDS

SPARE BERTH

TABLE

1 BED

CAPTAIN

1 BED

SPARE BERTH

PANTRY

SALOON

MATE

1 BED

BRIDGE.

DRES'R

GALLEY

RANGE

COAL BOX

ENGINE CASING

6"LIGHTS

6"LIGHTS

BED & DR'S

CHIEF ENG

MESS ROOM

ENTRANCE

2ND ENG

BED & DR'S

T

T

CASING AFT.

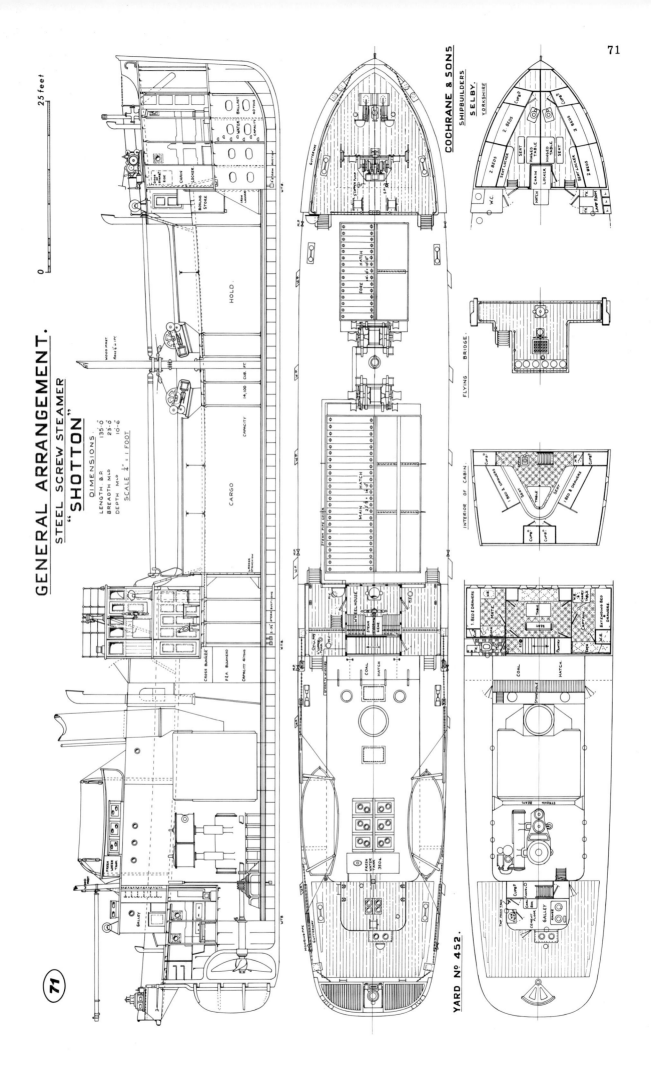

GENERAL ARRANGEMENT.

STEEL SCREW STEAMER
"SHOTTON"

DIMENSIONS

LENGTH B.P.   135·0
BREADTH MLD   23·0
DEPTH MLD   10·6

SCALE ¼" = 1 FOOT

COCHRANE & SONS
SHIPBUILDERS.
SELBY.
YORKSHIRE

FLYING BRIDGE.

INTERIOR OF CABIN.

YARD Nº 452.

25 feet

0

71

(72)   SODIUM of 1923 (left) and BARIUM of 1918 (right) were built for the United Alkali Co.

Steam coasters over 150 feet in length with a long well deck were not so numerous, though they were a feature of some Liverpool based fleets, particularly W. A. Savage's Zillah Shipping & Carrying Co., and J. H. Monks. There were two main designs. The design favoured by Savages had a small trimming hatch between the foremast and the forecastle as for example OPHIR, Plate 26 and 27, built by the Ailsa Shipbuilding Co., in 1908. The other type, favoured by Captain Rowland, had one long unobstructed hatch and so was particularly suited to loading such cargoes as 60 foot long rails which were a common outward cargo from Workington for the various railways. They were mainly built between 1890 and 1920 and for the most part had long lives in the Irish Sea trades. Both types were used by the North Wales slate quarries. The ELIDIR, built for the Dinorwic Quarry Company in 1903, Plate 123, is closely similar to OPHIR and both were built by the Ailsa Shipbuilding Company then of Ayr. ELIDIR had a longer raised quarter deck with the bunker hatch behind the bridge rather than ahead of the bridge as in OPHIR. Particular care was taken with the design of the ELIDIR to insure that the hold would twist as little as possible in heavy seas. This was very important because slates were loaded in bulk, by stowing them on edge in rows across the ship, each layer was then covered with straw and a further layer added. The more usual long raised quarter deck coaster with bridge amidships, built to Lloyd's requirements, was often too flexible for slate carrying. This was clearly demonstrated on one occasion when the ELIDIR and the HARLAW PLAIN, a long raised quarter deck coaster, both sailed North-about on the same day. Even though it was summer, bad weather was encountered and so the captain of the HARLAW PLAIN decided to go via the Caledonian Canal. Meanwhile the ELIDIR battled on round Cape Wrath and then on through the Pentland Firth, giving the lighthouse keepers at Duncansby Head a friendly blast on her whistle as she passed. On arrival at Aberdeen, about 10% of the slates carried by HARLAW PLAIN were found to be broken and useless whereas ELIDIR arrived with her cargo virtually intact even though she had passed through the worst of the weather, and had saved her owners paying canal dues.

ELIDIR's voyages were usually uneventful, but on one occasion, in dense fog she stranded at Cairnbulg, near Fraserburgh. She refloated herself, but as the forepeak and double bottom were leaking badly, she made for Aberdeen. After inspection by a surveyor at Aberdeen she was allowed to proceed to Kirkcaldy and discharge her cargo of slates. She then slowly made her way back to Dinorwic via the Caledonian Canal. She was drydocked in the Company's own drydock for repair at Port Dinorwic. The damage was found to be very extensive stretching from the bows all the way back to the engine room bulkhead. In addition, the floors were in many cases very badly buckled and the rocks had even penetrated to the tank top in the forward part of the hold. As the Company did not normally undertake such major repairs, estimated from repair yards were sought. All the estimates received were well over £10,000. Lloyd's decided she was a constructive total loss and paid out the market value of the ship, about £3,000. Mr. Williams, the yard manager at Port Dinorwic thought he and his men could repair her for £10,000. The owner of Dinorwic Quarries, the Hon. W. W. Vivian was keen to keep her, but felt that Mr. Williams had perhaps underestimated the cost. The problem was discussed for some weeks. Finally it was agreed that repairs should commence. It was going to be a difficult job, as much of the bottom, the backbone of the ship, would have to be removed. ELIDIR would need very careful shoring up if she was not to collapse or buckle when all the damaged bottom was cut away. She was carefully placed in the drydock and angle lugs were welded on to the sheerstrake and the sides extensively shored up (73a). After the damaged bottom and floors had been cleared away, the buckled tank top plates were taken off, faired and put back in place. This done, any of the floors which could be straightened, together with any bottom plates which could be used again, were refitted. The remaining new floors and bottom plates were then made in the workshops. Finally the work was completed; it had cost a fraction over £10,000.

ELIDIR was loaded down to her marks with a slate cargo when the hold directly below the main hatch was filled and so the small trimming hatch forward did not obstruct the loading. Of course the smaller main hatch and greater deck area all helped reduce twisting in a seaway. It was essential that the slate cargo was not placed too far forwards, otherwise the vessel would trim by the head and would be difficult to steer. Also too much weight forward would make the vessel sluggish lifting herself free of heavy seas and so it was usual to trim these coasters slightly aft. When carrying cargoes such as coal, especially when grab discharge was to be used, they were at a disadvantage, so to extend their useful

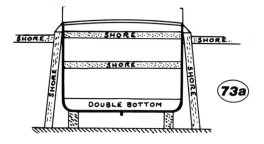

Repairing ELIDIR. Keel blocks removed for access.

working lives, the mast was moved forwards and the main hatch lengthened. This was done with the ELIDIR after she had passed to Coppack Bros. of Connah's Quay. This was in 1942 and she was immediately taken over by the Government for commando training. She did not begin coasting for them until after the war was over. When she was overhauled by Scotts of Bowling after her war service, the opportunity was taken to lengthen the hatch.

Vessels of this type exceeding 160 feet were rarely built. However, three 180 foot long vessels were built for the United Alkali Company of Liverpool. BARIUM and CALCIUM were built in 1918 and were followed by SODIUM in 1923. Their distinctive appearance was enhanced by their grey hulls. They were designed to carry limestone from the Company's quarry in North Wales and later became part of the Imperial Chemical Industries fleet (72).

Some of the earliest vessels of this size with short raised quarter decks, had two hatches with the bridge placed between them, on the well deck, such as DERWENT (9). In other vessels the bridge was placed aft but two hatches, each with a mast at the forward end, were fitted as seen in WANS FELL (73b). As can be seen, the after deck of these early vessels was kept clear for handling the mizzen sail which can be seen furled in the photograph. The illustration is from a sale leaflet issued by James Kell, Sunderland, who was a ship sale and purchase broker. Matt. Taylor of Methil found the larger ships in the Mediterranean trades more profitable and decided to sell his smaller coasters in the 1920s. Meanwhile, before WANS FELL could be sold, she collided with the drifter GIRL PATRICIA off Hartlepool on the 2nd of October 1929 and was beached to save her sinking. However, she was abandoned as a total loss and later broken up for scrap.

S.S. "WANS FELL."

S.S. WANS FELL

Built of **Iron, 5/1882** by H. M'Intyre & Co., Paisley.

Dimensions:—145 × 22 × 10.1/11-ft. moulded.

Classed *100 A 1. Lloyds. Special Survey No. 3. 1/1921.

Tonnage:—Gross 300 tons, net 118 tons.

About **320** tons Deadweight on **10-ft. 6-ins.** mean draft.

Cubic capacity about 15,000 cubic feet.

Bunker capacity about 45 tons.

One Deck (Iron) part new 1907, Rqd. 49-ft. Focle 22-ft.

Two Hatches (19-ft. 2-in. × 13-ft.; 19-ft. 4-in. × 10-ft.

Two Steam Winches.

Water Ballast in Fore Peak Tank 13 tons.

Wood Belting.

C.S.C. Engines by Kincaid & Co., placed Aft.

Cylinders 17¼-in. and 38-in. by 27-in. stroke.

One Single Ended Boiler **new 5/1896,** 100-lbs. working pressure.

Speed about 8½ knots for about 5/6 tons consumption.

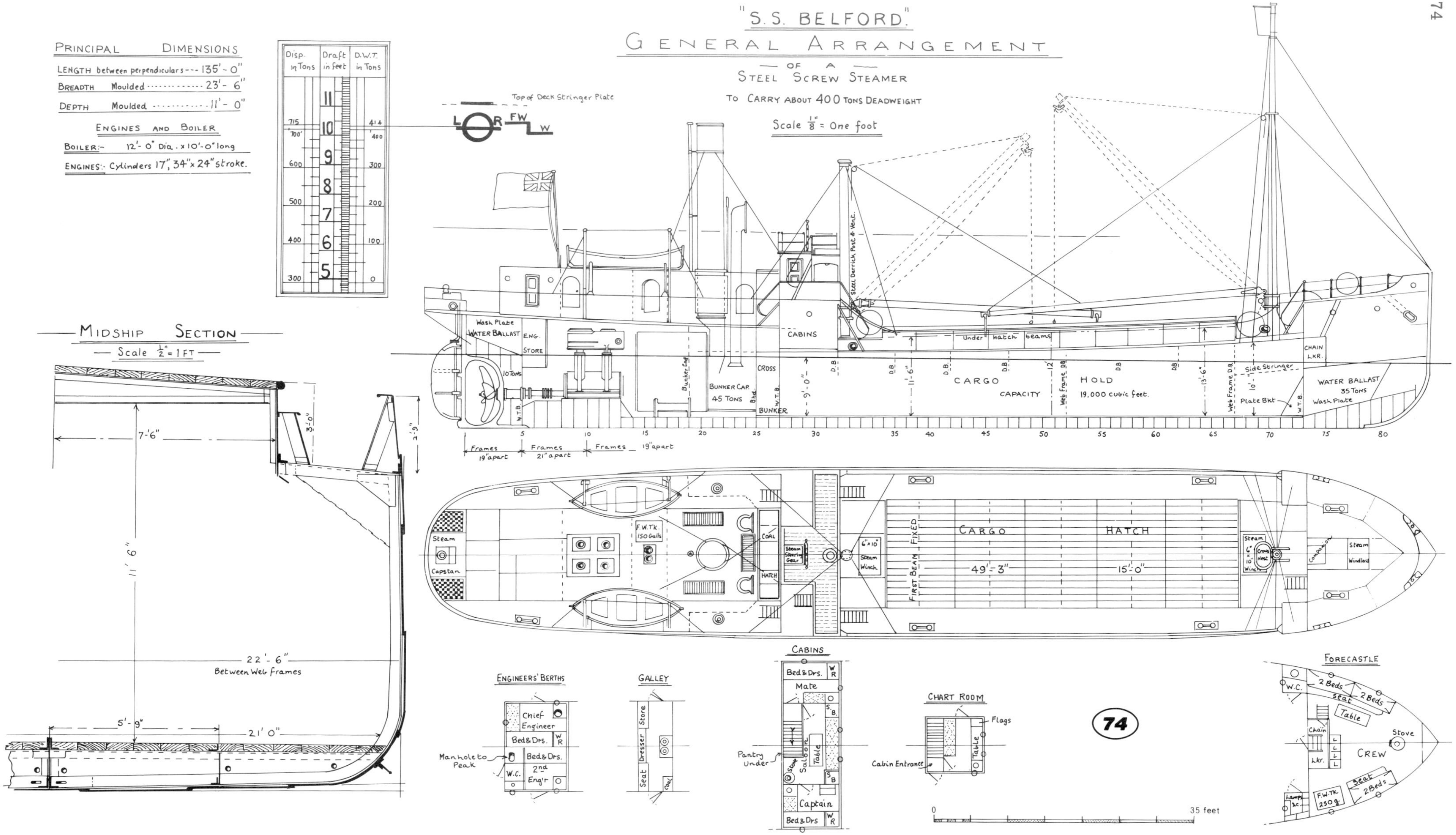

"S.S. BELFORD".

GENERAL ARRANGEMENT

OF A
Steel Screw Steamer

To Carry About 400 Tons Deadweight

Scale $\frac{1}{8}$" = One foot

PRINCIPAL DIMENSIONS

LENGTH between perpendiculars ---- 135'-0"
BREADTH Moulded -------- 23'-6"
DEPTH Moulded -------- 11'-0"

ENGINES AND BOILER

BOILER:- 12'-0" Dia. x 10'-0" long
ENGINES:- Cylinders 17", 34" x 24" stroke.

MIDSHIP SECTION

Scale $\frac{1}{2}$" = 1 FT

22'-6" Between Web Frames
21'-0"
7'-6"
11'-6"
5'-9"

FORECASTLE

CREW

2 Beds, 2 Beds, Table, Seat
W.C. Chain Lkr. Stove
Fw.Tk. 250 g.

35 feet

(74)

CHART ROOM

Flags, Table, Cabin Entrance

CABINS

Mate, Bed & Drs., W.C., S.B., Toilet, S.B., Captain, Bed & Drs., Pantry Under

GALLEY

Seat, Dresser, Store, Coal

ENGINEERS' BERTHS

Chief Engineer, Bed & Drs., W.C., Beds & Drs., 2nd Engr., Manhole to Peak

---

WATER BALLAST 35 Tons
Wash Plate
CHAIN LKR
Side Stringer
Plate Bkt.
Web Frame D.B.
W.T.B.
HOLD 19,000 cubic feet
CARGO CAPACITY
Under Hatch Beams
Web Frame D.B.
13'-6"
9'-11"
CABINS
6'-0"
CROSS
BUNKER
BUNKER CAP. 45 Tons
Bunker Fd.
WATER BALLAST ENG. Store
Wash Plate
10 Tons
Top of Deck Stringer Plate
LR FW W

Steam, Windlass
Steam
Foundation
Steam Control Fan
12 x 9
HATCH 15'-0"
CARGO 49'-3"
FIRST BEAM FIXED
Steam Winch 6 x 10
COAL, HATCH
Steam Cargo Gear
Fw.Tk. 150 galls.
Steam, Capstan

DISP. in Tons / Draft in Feet / D.W.T. in Tons

715, 800, 600, 500, 400, 300
11, 10, 9, 8, 7, 6, 5
414, 400, 300, 200, 100

75 SPRAYVILLE (ex. Hazelfield), was the last steam coaster built at Lytham and reverted to the bridge amidships design. Registered dimensions were 178.4'x 28.9'x 11.4'and tonnages 692 gross, 851 dwt.

Long Raised Quarter Deck Coasters

These vessels with their bridge amidships and engines aft, typify the British steam coaster. They were built in large numbers as can be seen from page 11. They were represented in most of the great coasting fleets and the last steam coasters built were also of this design. They formed the backbone of such leading fleets as that of Gillie and Blair of Newcastle, James Fisher of Barrow, Joseph Fisher of Newry, Richard Hughes of Liverpool, Monks of Liverpool and William Robertson of Glasgow. The design was developed during the 1870s and was well established by 1880; the basic hull form then remained virtually unchanged throughout the steam era.

The smallest vessels of this type were around 130 feet in length, though the little steamer FAIRY was only 120 feet long. Most of these smaller vessels were built prior to 1910. As page 11 shows, there is a distinct peak in the numner of vessels between 140 and 150 feet in length and in fact most of these vessels have a registered length of approximately 142 feet. This size was popular with owners working in the Irish Sea Trades because it was the largest size for vessels using the Ringsend Dock in Dublin, the main dock for the coal trade. Larger vessels could not be accommodated in the entrance lock. The type is represented in the fleet of W. A. Savage of Liverpool, Robertsons of Glasgow and the leading Irish owned fleets, such as Kellys of Belfast and Joseph Fisher of Newry. The designs of the yards became fairly standard and were often used, with slight modification, to produce a series of ships for various owners over several years.

Perhaps the most important group was that built by the Lytham Shipbuilding and Engineering Company between 1914 and 1925. The first three were completed at the beginning of World War I and differed from the later six built after the war, in minor details. Two were built for the Alliance & Dublin Gas Consumers Co., and the remaining seven for the fleet of the Zillah Shipping and Carrying Co. Ltd., which was managed by W. A. Savage of Liverpool and was closely connected with the Lytham yard for many years. The vessels were considered well appointed when the lead ship, ASHFIELD appeared in the Autumn of 1914, Plate 79. Many vessels built in earlier years had compound machinery whereas these vessels had triple expansion engines. They also had extensive ballast facilities with a generous aft peak, fore peak and forward deep tank, making for easier passages in ballast. One interesting feature is the collision bulkhead at the forward part of the crew accommodation in the forecastle, this must have been reassuring to the crews when the ships were feeling their way through fog, with the chance of a collision ever present. This plan (78 & 82) shows the BRIARFIELD, one of the later series built in the 1920s. The main changes in the later vessels were the straight fronted bridges, slightly longer forecastles and lower sterns with less sheer aft. They were among the best proportioned coasters built, but of the two series, the earlier vessels had the rather more attractive bow-fronted bridges. See also Plate 42.

In the designs of the 1920s it was usual for the crew to be accommodated in a full height forecastle and the whole of the space below the main deck in the bows was then used as a store. This is seen in the plans of the CORNISH TRADER and CORNISH MERCHANT (77), built by Abdela & Mitchell at Queensferry, near Chester for Cornish Traders Ltd. of Falmouth. CORNISH TRADER was completed in 1920, followed by the CORNISH MERCHANT in 1923. Both were sold after a few years trading to Richard Hughes of Liverpool becoming CORNISH ROSE and FOWEY ROSE respectively. As can be seen from the plan, the shorter compound machinery allows the engineers to have a mess room in these ships. The forecastle shows the other popular layout, with seamen's and firemen's bunks arranged along the centre line. The seamen are separated from the firemen by a bulkhead and have separate entrances, which was the usual arrangement in most ships built in later years. The first of the more advanced versions was represented by ROWANFIELD of 495 gross tons, built for Savages in 1938. Her dimensions were 142.5 x 27.2 x 11.4 with a summer draught of 12'9$\frac{3}{4}$'' and corresponding deadweight of 535 tons. The last steamers to be built of this size were the BALSA and EBONY completed for Joseph Fisher in 1947.

Vessels between 143 feet and 160 feet were fewer in number. They operated in a variety of trades and were often employed in the East Coast coal trade to the smaller South Coast ports, as for example HOVE of Stephenson Clarke's fleet. In the 1920s a series was built for Irish Sea owners. Most went to the Overton S.S. Co., managed by R.R. Clark of Liverpool, which had five built and one each went to R. Neill & Sons, Bangor, County Down, the Northwich Carrying Co., Ltd., Samuel Lockington of Dundalk and Thos. Coppack of Connah's Quay. Certainly Thomas Coppack purchased his vessel. FARFIELD after the original purchaser failed to take up the vessel on completion, owing to the slump in shipping. The original inflated price was about £38,000 but Thomas Coppack's offer of about £12,000 was eventually reluctantly accepted by the builders who were Cook, Welton & Gemmell for this particular ship. Design and construction of the others was the work of Cochrane and Sons Ltd., of Selby. They were similar in layout to CORNISH TRADER, though a little larger, carrying 530 tons on a draft of 11'10", but were fitted with triple expansion engines (80).

FARFIELD (76), carried a great variety of cargoes, but was particularly active in the fruit and vegetable trade from Northern France and the Channel Islands. At other times she carried china clay for Grimsby to Peter Dixon's paper mills and then moved to a coal loading port for a return cargo of coal to one of the Cornish ports. This contract for china clay shipments was carried out for many years, but required constant vigilance on the part of the owners, captain and crew to ensure that any coal remaining in the hold was carefully cleaned out before the china clay was loaded, otherwise there would be black specks in the paper and the contract to carry the clay lost.

Two hatch coasters 160 to 170 feet in length were also very popular, as can be seen from page 11. They were similar to those just described, but were better suited for much longer voyages around the British Isles and Continent. In summer they sometimes traded to the Baltic for timber. William Robertson of Glasgow had vessels of this size running regularly to the Baltic and operating on the East coast of the U.S.A. in the 1890s. William Robertson, to a large extent, led the way in developing these larger coasters for general trading, and his fleet was approaching 40 vessels of this type by 1900. CITRINE (later BRONZITE) was built for the Robertson fleet in 1894 by Scott & Sons, Bowling, Plates 23 & 137. She could carry 735 tons on a draft of 13'3" and is typical of the early vessels of this size and type. The triple expansion engine was a standard feature of these larger coasters. The long open forecastle is a prominent feature of these early vessels and in this vessel has been extended to accommodate the forward steam winch. At this time it was usual to fit a manually operated anchor windlass which could be chain driven by the forward steam winch, so placing this winch on the forecastle simplified this. In the earliest vessels such as ASTERIA of 1891 (3), the mast was placed on the after side of the small trimming hatch. Even though the mast had been moved to the forecastle in the later design, the small trimming hatch was retained. Though having two hatches undoubtedly strengthened the deck, it made loading long railway lines a work of art for the stevedores especially in the smaller vessels. The crew were in a lower forecastle below the main deck, as was usual in the 1890s. The engineers' accommodation is fitted into the stern below the raised quarter deck leaving no room for a ballast tank. The vessel does have a double bottom which is an early design in which only alternate floors reach to the ceiling top (bottom of hold). One of the most interesting features is the whale-back cabin over the emergency steering gear on the stern and also incorporates a wash place and W.C.

CITRINE traded for William Robertson until 1899 when a favourable offer was made by M. Langlands & Sons, also of Glasgow, who urgently needed a ship for their general cargo-liner service around the British Isles. They renamed her PRINCESS THYRA and she then traded in their colours for the next five years. Then she became surplus to their requirements and was offered for sale through John Stewart & Co., one of Glasgow's leading sale and purchase brokers. Mr. Stewart approached Mr. Robertson to see if the latter would like her back. On inspection she was found to be in good condition and so she rejoined the Robert-

76 FARFIELD off Barry.

C. V. Waine. 1968.

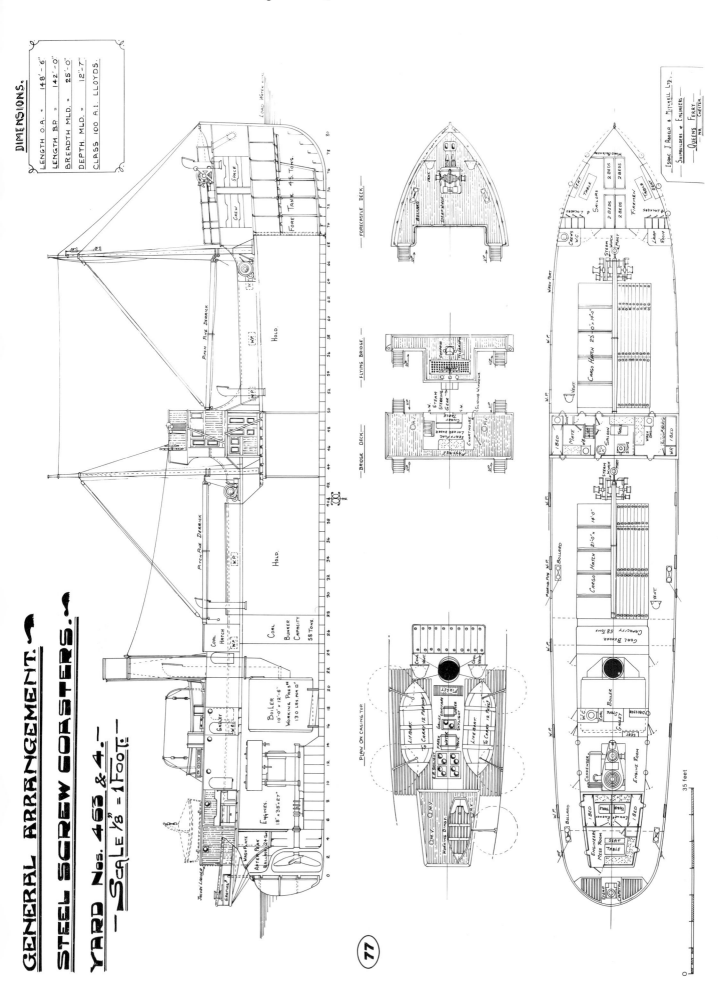

GENERAL ARRANGEMENT.

STEEL SCREW COASTERS.

YARD Nos. 463 & 4.

Scale 1/8" = 1 Foot.

DIMENSIONS.

LENGTH O.A. =	148'-6"
LENGTH B.P. =	142'-0"
BREADTH MLD. =	25'-0"
DEPTH MLD. =	12'-7"
CLASS 100 A.1. LLOYDS.	

Isaac J. Abdela & Mitchell Ltd.
SHIPBUILDERS & ENGINEERS
Queens Ferry
Nr. CHESTER.

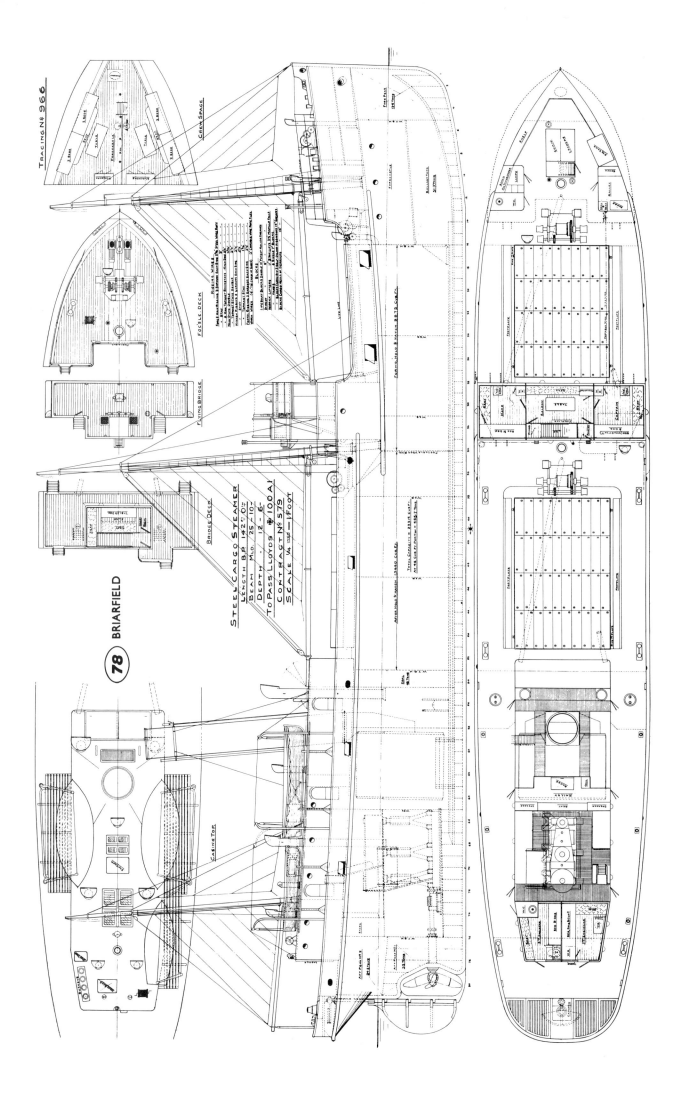

78 BRIARFIELD

STEEL CARGO STEAMER

LENGTH B.P 142'-0"
BEAM MLD 25'-10"
DEPTH " 12'-6"
TO PASS LLOYDS ✠100 A1
CONTRACT Nº 579
SCALE ¼ INCH — 1 FOOT

TRACING Nº 966

Steam Coaster ASHFIELD

DIMENSIONS: 142'6" x 26'0" x 11'6"

Tonnage 426 gross.

Plate 79

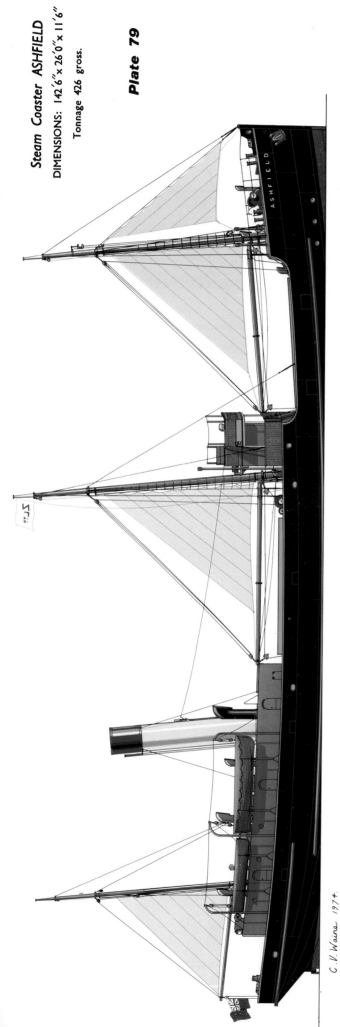

C. V. Waine 1974.

35 feet

0

Steam Coaster SHOTTON

DIMENSIONS: 135'0" x 23'1" x 9'4"

Tonnage 300 gross.

C. V. Waine 1972.

s.s. *FARFIELD*
DIMENSIONS: 152.0′ x 25.2′ x 10.8′

80

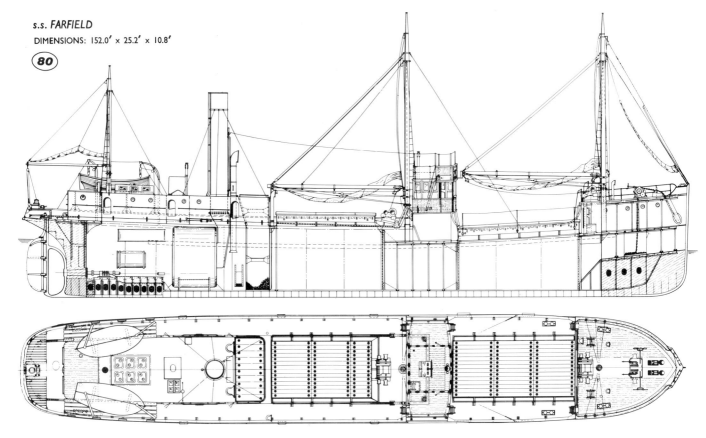

son fleet.

All the early steamers tended to have quite long well decks in comparison with later steamers in which it was progressively shortened. In HELMSMAN, built in 1903 for Christopher Rowbotham of London, the long well deck has been retained (81). At this time Rowbothams specialised in the carriage of guns, steam pinnaces and other large items of naval equipment, hence the need for a large hatch. A typical cargo recorded in Christopher Rowbotham's note book for her is: '29/5/09. Quoted Naval Stores Officer, Portsmouth £35 (for a) 40 ft. steam launch Portsmouth to London Dock, transhipped at Woolwich per HELMSMAN - accepted!' The terms, proving satisfactory, another 40 foot launch was conveyed from Portsmouth to London by HELMSMAN on the 1st of September. With the decline in the Navy following the end of the First World War, the Rowbothams progressively sold off their ships and looked to other trades. HELMSMAN was sold in 1920 to the Tyne-Tees Steam Shipping Company Ltd., becoming CRAIGSIDE and was sold for breaking up after a further 15 years service.

John Lewis of Aberdeen built many coasters in this size range beginning with the coaster WYNDHURST in 1917. The design was then slightly altered for the series which began with the HADRIX completed in February 1919 as yard No. 54, for Rix management. The design proved particularly attractive to West Coast owners and two were managed by J. W. Fisher, Liverpool (FREELAND and TARNWATER), two for D. R. Llewellyn, Merrett & Price Ltd, of Cardiff (RIVER DEE and RIVER USK), one for the Allied S. N. Co. Ltd of Hull (COLLOONEY, later TOPAZ of William Robertson) and four (ANNAGHER, ANNAGHMORE, DONAGHMORE, and CARRICKMORE) were built for John Kelly, Belfast. The last of the 10 vessel series was completed in 1925. As can be seen from the lines plan (13), Rix preferred the more elegant canted out stern while John Kelly preferred the plumb stern as it was less liable to damage. The layouts of the vessels were all similar, but differed in some details, for example, COLLOONEY had the positions of her dinghy and lifeboats reversed as compared with ANNAGHMORE (85). The design shows the trend towards more flared bows to help her lift over heavy seas and so make for a drier ship. Other features of note are the foremast and windlass placed on the forecastle which became fairly general practice from the 1920s, but some owners had it on the well deck as seen in the NORRIX (Plate 83), where it was usually canted up on the sloping hatch end, the latter feature helping to make the hatch more nearly self-trimming. NORRIX was one of several coasters of about this size built for Rix around 1920. She was some 10 feet shorter but otherwise very similar to the 175′ series vessels ERNRIX, KENRIX, LESRIX and MALRIX which soon proved their worth on the East Coast coal trade to wharves on the Thames and South coast where there were restrictions on size. Accommodation was good for the period and the forecastle crew had Hoskins patent iron beds with spring mattresses as original fittings and a bath alongside the galley. An unusual feature of the forecastle accommodation is the elimination of all portholes which are replaced by a number of large decklights. Portholes tended to get broken when coming into berths and sometimes at sea, and this effectively eliminated the problem (back endpaper).

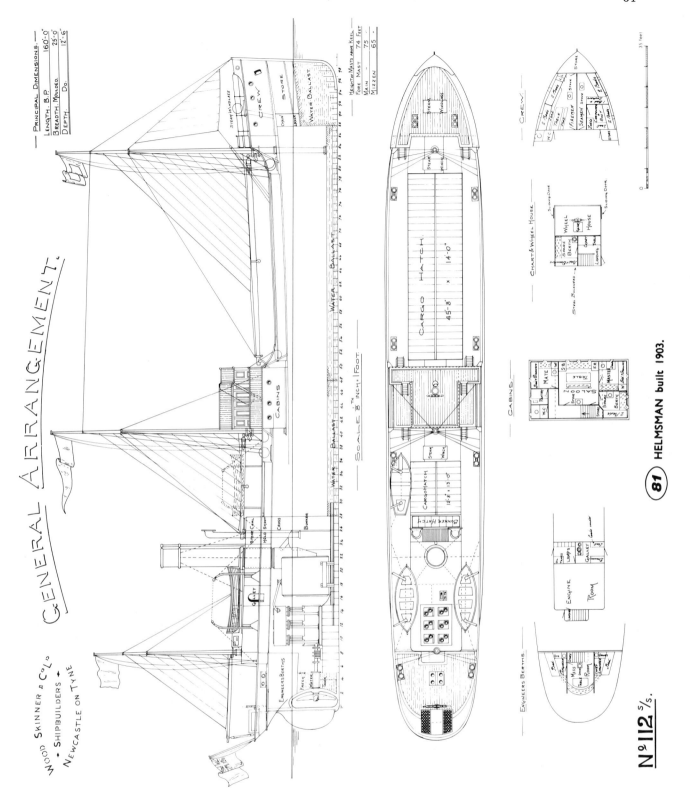

GENERAL ARRANGEMENT.

WOOD SKINNER & CO.
— SHIPBUILDERS —
NEWCASTLE ON TYNE

PRINCIPAL DIMENSIONS:-
LENGTH B.P. ...... 160'-0"
BREADTH MOULDED. ...... 25'-0"
DEPTH Do. ...... 12'-6"

HEIGHTS MASTS ABOVE KEEL
FORE MAST ...... 74 FEET
MAIN " ...... 75 "
MIZZEN " ...... 65 "

SCALE 1/8 TH INCH I FOOT.

No. 112 S/S.

81 HELMSMAN built 1903.

The counter stern was replaced by the cruiser stern and it is interesting to contrast the lines of the Hadrix series with those of the DEEMOUNT which was built in 1933. She illustrates the trend to the all-aft design which was also tried at this period. She was built for G. T. Gillie & Blair management and mainly intended for an Aberdeen coal contract. Renamed OLNA FIRTH in 1946, she was sold two years later to William Robertson of Glasgow and renamed TOURMALINE. She was converted to an oil burner in 1950 for a charter in African waters and was sold to Coe of Liverpool in 1955 becoming BANNPRINCE (13).

SLIGO, built by the Dublin Dockyard Company in 1913, appears at first, not to have a well deck (82). The well deck is present, but flanked by particularly high bulwarks which conceal it. They are not a desirable feature as, although they keep out the smaller seas, a large sea filling the well could endanger the stability of the ship. This arrangement never became popular, possibly for this reason. By 1910 most vessels were fitted with an aft peak ballast tank to improve the ship's handling in ballast. It was often used by the engineers to store fresh water for the boiler.

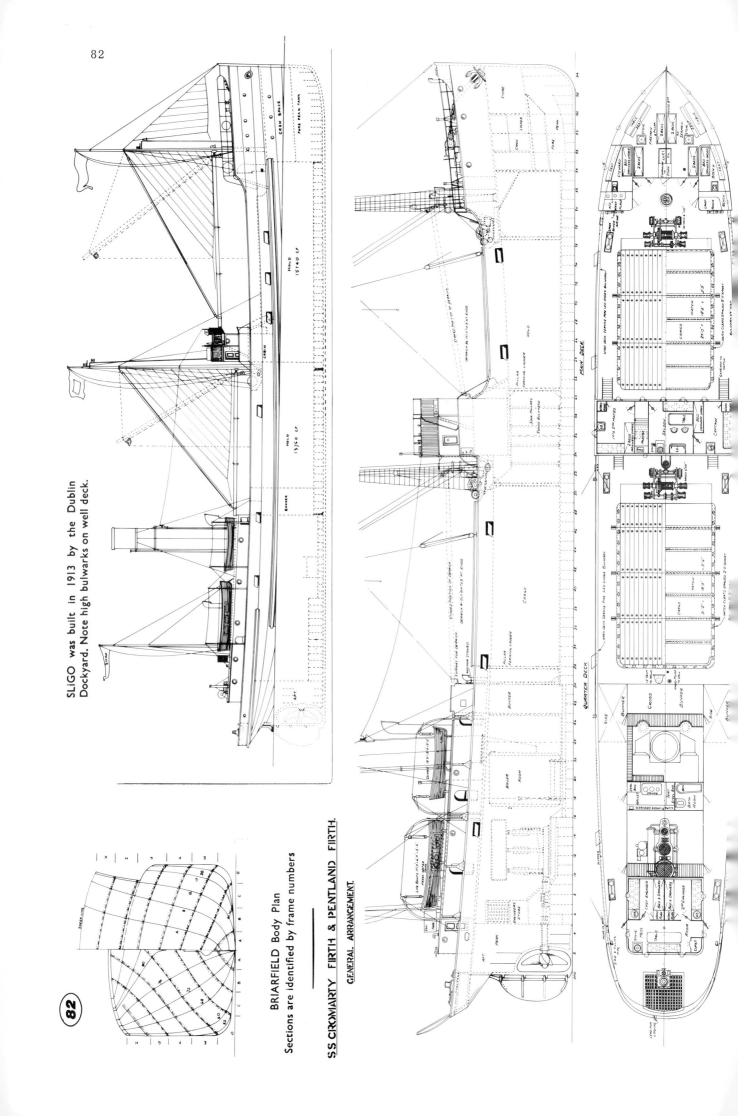

SLiGO was built in 1913 by the Dublin Dockyard. Note high bulwarks on well deck.

BRIARFIELD Body Plan
Sections are identified by frame numbers

S.S. CROMARTY FIRTH & PENTLAND FIRTH.
GENERAL ARRANGEMENT.

Steam Coaster PENTLAND FIRTH

DIMENSIONS: 175'5'' x 28'4'' x 10' 1''

Tonnage 638 gross.

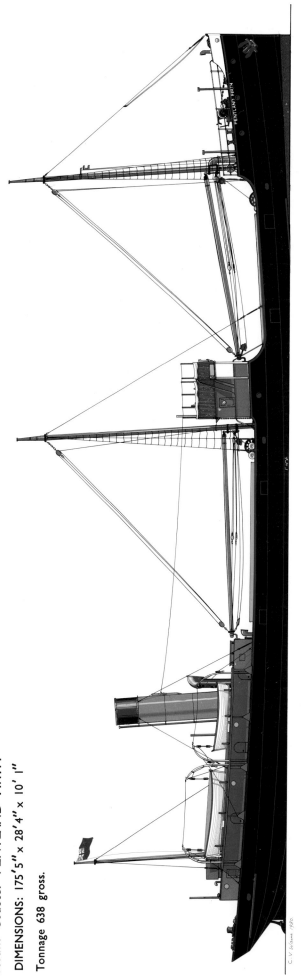

C. V. Waine 1920

Steam Coaster NORRIX

DIMENSIONS: 165'0'' x 27'0'' x 11'0''

Tonnage 576 gross.

Plate 83

C. V. Waine 1975

Design of accommodation took a distinct leap forward in the 1920s and this is well illustrated by the CROMARTY FIRTH and PENTLAND FIRTH built for the Border Shipping Company of Glasgow, which was managed by Gillie and Blair of Newcastle. The two vessels were delivered by the Ardrossan Drydock & Shipbuilding Company in 1919 and 1920 respectively. They were good sea boats and were specially designed for the longer continental voyages and made a number of long voyages when favourable cargoes offered. Coal was carried from the Clyde to Iceland where cargoes of dried fish were loaded for Bilbao or Barcelona. At other times they traded to the Baltic and made some voyages to Leningrad. They could carry 770 tons on a draft of 12'6" and so were a distinct improvement on the CITRINE built 25 years previously. Because they were intended for longer voyages, particular attention was paid to the crew accommodation. Separate cabins were provided for the bosun and a new addition to the crew, the steward, who cooked for the officers and sometimes the crew. These cabins were made by dividing off part of the forecastle from the seamen and firemen as can be seen on the plan (82). The officers' accommodation was little changed, but the engineers have their cabins completely separated from the engine room, entered by a separate door in the side of the casing. In most steam coasters, there are three doors in the side of the casing aft, giving access to the stokehold, galley and nearest the stern, the engine room, off which, the engineers' cabins often opened. In this vessel there is a fourth door giving access to a large mess room. In addition, the galley has been reduced in size to make room for a W.C. and bath. PENTLAND FIRTH is seen in Border Shipping Co's colours in Plate 83.

The CROMARTY FIRTH and her sister PENTLAND FIRTH were soon sold in the slump, the CROMARTY FIRTH passing to William Robertson for just £13,000. The good accommodation attracted the attention of the General Steam Navigation Co., who purchased the PENTLAND FIRTH for rather less in 1924, and renamed her ALOUETTE. She was renamed DUNVEGAN HEAD in 1936 when sold to A.F. Henry & MacGregor of Leith. Ironically both ships were lost at the Normandy landings in 1944. The vessels have quite a strong sheer aft, which was something of a feature of vessels built by the Ardrossan yard.

Towards the end of the First World War most owners were expecting an upsurge in trade and ordered these larger sized coasters to cater for the larger cargoes expected. Among these were Richard Hughes of Liverpool and two newcomers, E. T. Lindley and H. Harrison (Shipping) Ltd., both of London, John Lewis of Aberdeen built a number of these larger coasters as did Hall, Russell. The THRIFT came from the latter yard and illustrates the trend to the steel enclosed wheelhouse (145) which became general in the 1930s together with a raked stem. She was completed in 1931 to replace an earlier ship of the same name also owned by the Northern Co-operative Society of Aberdeen dating from 1904. The vessel was operated by the coal department of the Society and carried coal from Blyth, Seaham and Methil to Aberdeen throughout her working life. By the time she was scrapped in September 1968, she was the last of the true coal burning steam coasters trading on that coast.

A further change in the 1930s was the appearance of cruiser sterns as, for example on DEEMOUNT already mentioned and PYROPE, Robertson's last steamship built in 1936. Probably the most advanced design to appear in the 1930s came from the Lytham Shipbuilding & Engineering in 1938. Two ships, BRACKENFIELD and BROOMFIELD were built (6, 86), for the Zillah Shipping & Carrying Co., Ltd., Liverpool which was managed by W.A. Savage. As can be seen, they contrast strongly with those already described. A poop deck has been added on the raised quarter deck to provide accommodation aft for all the crew. The mate has a large room next to the saloon, while the captain has a cabin alongside the chart room directly below the enclosed wheelhouse which is also aft in this vessel. However the seamen and firemen had rather cramped quarters and no steward was provided for. The aft peak tank was large in this design, holding 47 tons. The forecastle was open to reduce tonnage. The ship also had improvements in the engine room with the boiler working at 200 lbs. pressure, and a forced draft fan was fitted. The last steamer to be built at Lytham was the HAZELFIELD, completed with oil firing in 1948, again for the Zillah fleet. Unlike the two vessels just described, the bridge was sited amidships, between the two hatches. She was sold after eleven years, in 1959, as the change to motor ships took place. She was purchased by J.S. Monks Ltd. and renamed SPRAYVILLE (●), but the high operating costs of steamers led to her sale four years later, to Greek owners, the fate of many British coasters.

The change to motor ships began later for these larger vessels, partly because reliable engines for a suitable power were slower in becoming available. The change to motor was led by Everards of London followed by Robertsons in Glasgow and Rix in Hull. Everards' first vessels, built in the early 1930s were less than 160 feet in length, but by the 1940s larger vessels were being built for the fleet. They mostly came from the yards of George Brown at Greenock and later, from Fellows at Great Yarmouth, the latter yard having close ties with Everards. The whole series of vessels presented a rather low profile which was quite characteristic of the Everard fleet at this time. The last to be built in the series were SONORITY and SEVERITY of 1952 (Back end paper).

It is interesting to compare the vessels just described in this chapter, for example, BRONZITE was 5 feet longer and 10 inches greater beam than CROMARTY FIRTH, but she carried 35 tons less cargo on a greater draft. The steamships also had higher boiler pressures in later years allowing the engines to be smaller for the same power. However the most interesting comparison is between BROOMFIELD and the motor ship JACINTH of Robertsons, built within a year of each other. The motor ship was seven feet longer but one inch less in beam and of the same moulded depth. At the same draft of 13'0" the motor ship was able to carry almost 150 tons more cargo and it was hard facts like these which caused most owners to stop building steamers of this size in the 1930s. However the motor shipowners had higher bunker costs (marine diesel) and maintenance costs.

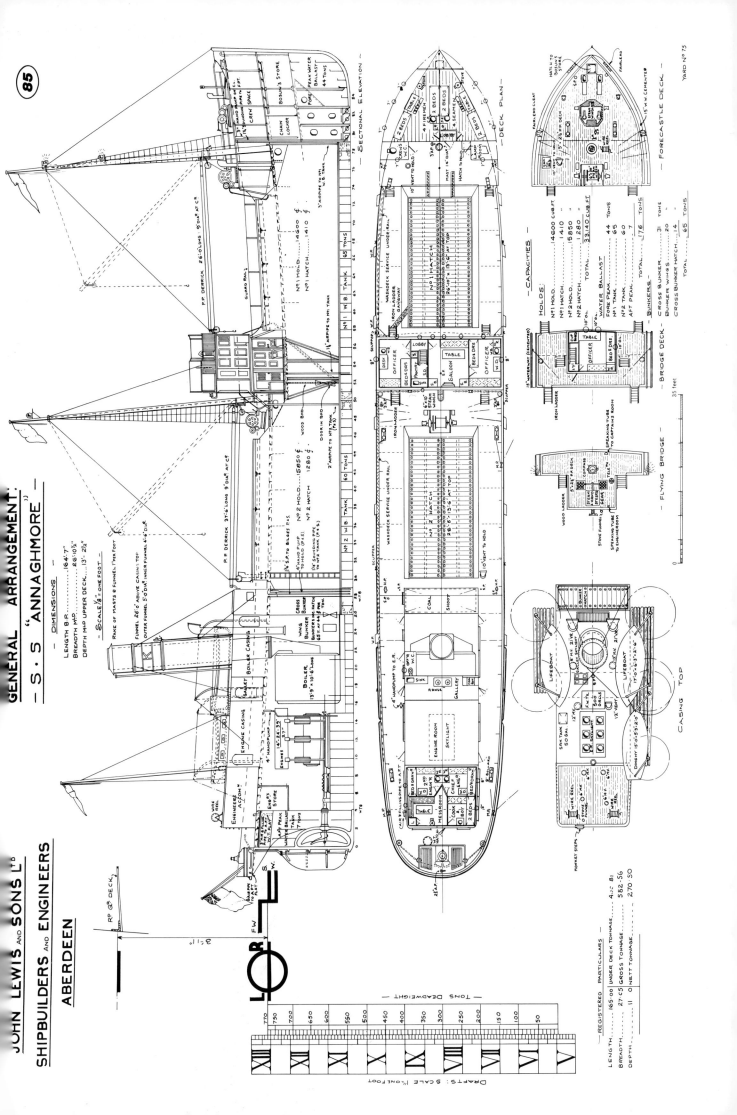

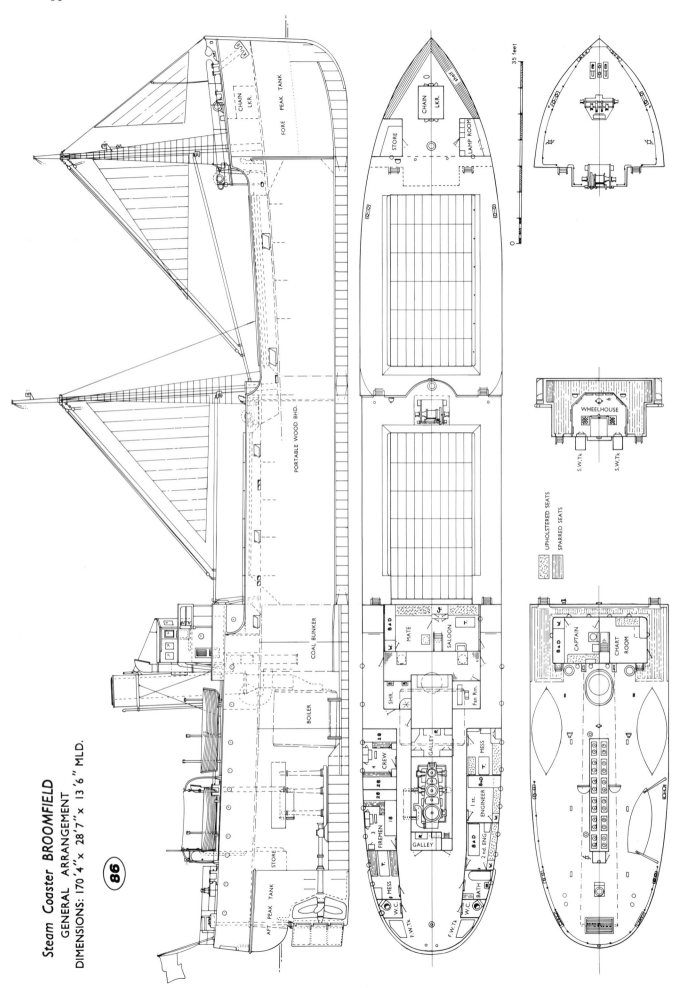

Steam Coaster BROOMFIELD
GENERAL ARRANGEMENT
DIMENSIONS: 170'4" x 28'7" x 13'6" MLD.

86

8.

Larger Coasters

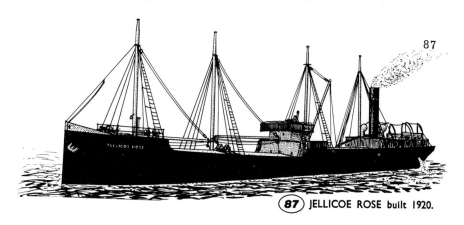

87 JELLICOE ROSE built 1920.

with Long Raised Quarter Decks

These vessels were often employed on voyages to the continent of Europe and were the true steam short sea traders. They had two or sometimes three hatches. At times they went outside the home trade limits of Elbe and Brest. East Coast owners used them for coal to the harbours and jetties with draft restrictions while the West Coast owners developed the type for more general trading. By 1927 there were about 90 vessels of this type in service with British owners. Most were around 195' in length and could carry about 1,000 tons on a draft of a little under 14 feet in most cases. Some of the earliest vessels were built for William Robertson of Glasgow and were larger editions of BRONZITE already described. One of these early vessels was PEARL, built by John Shearer & Sons, Glasgow, at yard No. 19 at a cost of £8,605 (20, 21, 22). The price included a triple expansion engine which was usual even in the earliest vessels of this type. The main difference from BRONZITE was the crew accommodation on the main deck and the extra bunks fitted in a separate lower cabin for the extra hands needed for voyages outside home trade limits. She was delivered in 1896.Another interesting feature is the gangway between the bridge and the forecastle, which was fitted to a number of vessels at this time, but discarded in later years. Further vessels of progressively improved design were added to the Robertson fleet over the years culminating in the FLUOR of 1925. The awkward trimming hatch of PEARL was eliminated by extending the fore hatch in 1933 and she was also fitted with a wheelhouse at this time. These improvements extended her useful life until 1950 when she was sold for breaking up at Llanelly, after 55 years under the Robertson flag.

In larger vessels such as YEWMOUNT (149), the well deck was too long to be spanned by a single derrick and so the mast was placed between the two hatches. She was built for D. W. Willey of Southampton as HAMPSHIRE, later passing to Hill (Southampton) Ltd, who were coal merchants. She could carry about 1,000 tons and this was about the largest coaster able to reach Goole. Thus the design often featured in the fleets of Goole owners and the graceful KNOTTINGLEY (10), was built for Wetherall's in 1907. Later she passed to Wadsworth who also operated from Goole.

However, the two hatch arrangement was simpler and was preferred by most owners and builders such as Williamsons shipyard which was at Workington. Unlike most builders, this yard built coasters for their own coasting fleet and so knew at first hand what was needed to make a good coaster. Their ships were looked upon by owners and crews alike as well built, reliable vessels. For example, the hatches were built with curved sides and ends, a more expensive form of construction, but giving added strength and facilitating the trimming of bulk cargoes (91). The early vessels in the series such as SEAGULL which was built for the Shoreham Shipping Co. in 1902, were around 183' long, but later vessels were about 186' in length. As can be seen from the plan of STEPNEY (89) large hatches were fitted. In addition the raised quarter deck has been extended further forward in this design when compared with PEARL built 20 years previously. STEPNEY was built for the Commercial Gas Co. of London in 1916. Her regular arrival at their wharf was ensured by fitting twin boilers, which was sometimes done in these larger vessels so that they could proceed at a reduced speed on one boiler should a tube burn through or start leaking in the other. The design soon proved popular in the east coast coal trades and Constantines of Middlesbrough purchased vessels such as EDENWOOD, LEVENWOOD and HOMEWOOD. They had a single boiler as the extra expense of twin boilers was not considered necessary for general trading, but a donkey boiler was fitted for working winches in port. Williamsons only built a few vessels in the 1920s and 1930s and with the death of Mr. Williamson, the founder's son, in 1938 the shipyard was closed down. The last vessel in this series was still under construction at the time and was bought on the stocks by Everards who had it towed round to Goole for completion by the Goole Shipbuilding & Repairing Co., as the motor ship SODALITY. Her steamship origins were always betrayed by the small screw suited to her diesel engine sitting in the large propellor aperture designed for a big slow turning propellor associated with steam machinery.

Perhaps the greatest compliment to the design was paid by Ellerman's Wilson Line. They purchased one of the series in 1920 and named it DYNAMO, when she was disposed of in 1946 they purchased a younger ship from the same series which was renamed DYNAMO and operated for them until 1956. The vessel purchased was the KYLEBROOK, built in 1927 as the HOMEWOOD (91). Most of the series had two derricks to work the main hatch and so differed from STEPNEY who served her original owners until 1944. In that year she was sold to Comben Longstaff & Co, becoming KYLEBROOK of Monroes in 1952, being broken

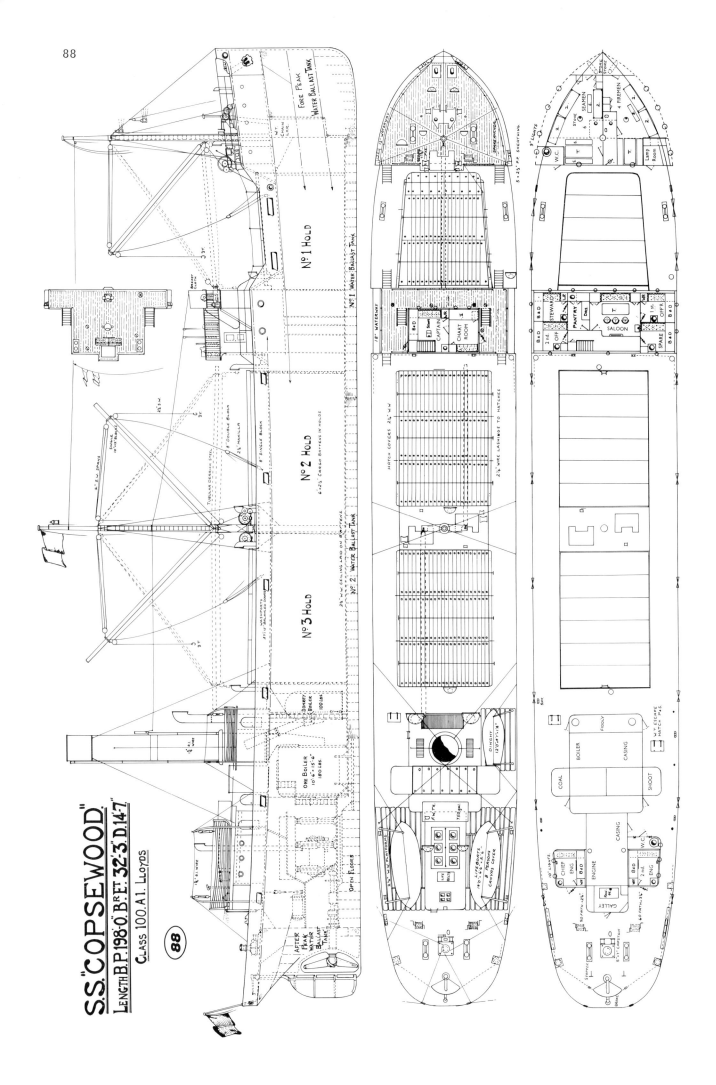

S.S. "COPSEWOOD."
LENGTH B.P. 198'·0" BR'T 32'·3" D.14'·7"
CLASS 100.A1. LLOYDS

88

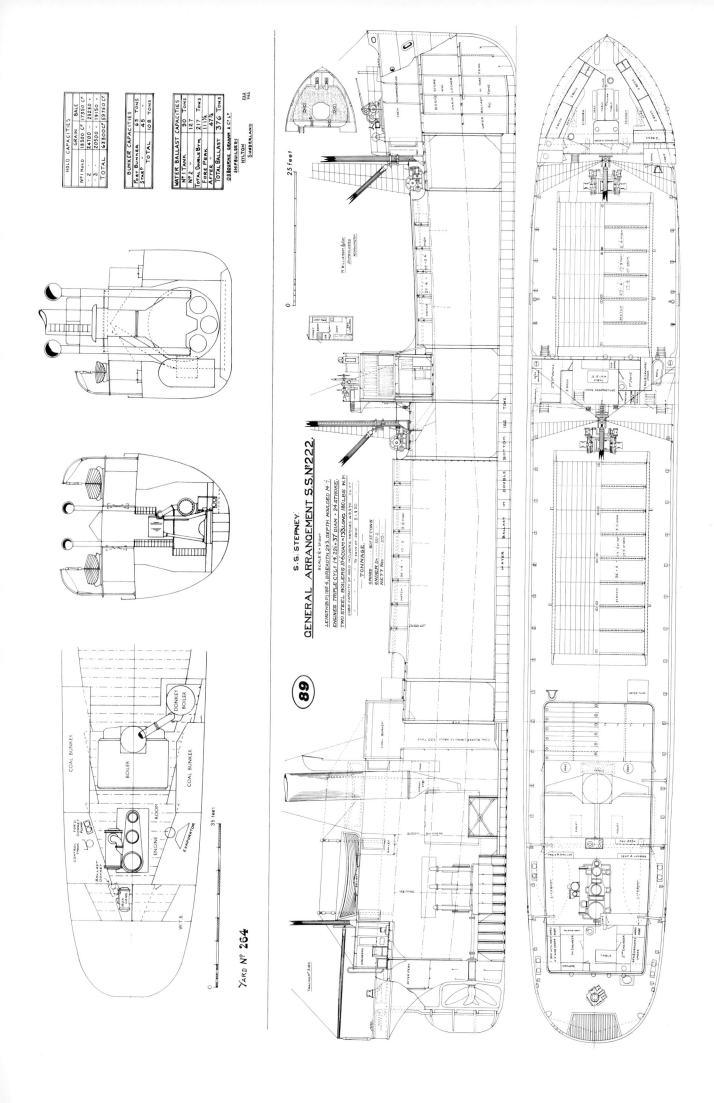

HOLD CAPACITIES		
	GRAIN	BALE
Nº 1 HOLD	18300 C.F	17350 C.F
" 2 "	24700 "	23250 "
" 3 "	20500 "	19150 "
TOTAL	63300 C.F	59750 C.F

BUNKER CAPACITIES	
PORT BUNKER	63 TONS
STARᴰ "	45 "
TOTAL	108 TONS

WATER BALLAST CAPACITIES	
Nº 1 TANK	90 TONS
Nº 2 "	127 "
TOTAL DOUBLE BᵀᵀM.	217 TONS
FORE PEAK	11½ "
AFTER "	47½ "
TOTAL BALLAST	376 TONS

OSBOURNE GRAHAM & Cº Lᵀᴰ
SHIPBUILDERS
HYLTON SUNDERLAND

YARD Nº 264

25 feet

0

35 feet

CONTROL TANK
FORᴅ DONKEY
BALLAST DONKEY
AUX. COND.
W.T.B.
COAL BUNKER
BOILER
COAL BUNKER
ENGINE ROOM
EVAPORATOR
DONKEY BOILER

89

S.S. STEPNEY

GENERAL ARRANGEMENT S.S. Nº 222.

SCALE ¼ = 1 FOOT

LENGTH(B.P.)185·4. BREADTH 29·3. DEPTH MOULDED 14·7.
ENGINES TRIPLE CYL.I 14·22i. 37 DIAM × 24-STROKE.
TWO STEEL BOILERS 10·6DIAM ×13·6 LONG 180 LBS W.P.
CUBIC CAPACITY OF HOLD INCLUDING HATCHES 49,170 CUFT.
TO RAILS OF SHIP

TONNAGE.	
GROSS	1071·55 TONS
UNDER DɪNɢ	551·2
NETT REᴳ	675

R. WILLIAMSON & SON
DUNBARTON

FORE PEAK
CHAIN LOCKER
BOSNS STORE
WATER BALLAST 40

WATER BALLAST IN DOUBLE BOTTOM 162 TONS

OFFICERS ROOM

COAL BUNKER
COAL BUNKER CAPACITY ABOUT 100 TONS

GALLEY
LIFEBOAT
LIFEBOAT
TABLE
1ˢᵀ ENGINEER
2ᴺᴰ ENGINEER
REFRᴳ ENGR.

up in 1957. John Hay of Glasgow had a number of coasters of this size from 1890s but in the 1920s he began to build this size exclusively. The first two vessels to be completed were THE MARCHIONESS and THE DUCHESS which came from C. Rennoldson's yard in 1924. Unlike the Williamson ships, the forecastle deck was extended aft to support the winch and the increased covered space below was used to provide mess rooms for the seamen and the firemen separate from the sleeping accommodation (94). The vessel apparently proved satisfactory, for Rennoldsons also completed THE MARQUIS to the same design in 1924. Several similar ships came from the Ailsa Shipbuilding Co., until the early 1930s. However the biggest single order for this size of ship was that placed by John Kelly with John Lewis of Aberdeen. The lead ship was ROSAPENNA (197.7' x 30.7' x 12.1') and she was followed by a further 9 sisters during the 1930s.

Another large order for this type of steamer was placed in the latter part of the 1920s by John Stewart & Co., Glagsow. Mr. Stewart was a sale and purchase broker, as well as a shipowner, and had purchased a number of war surplus triple expansion engines of around 90 registered horsepower. He had expected to sell them for use in tugs, but as no sales had been concluded for six of the engines, he decided to take advantage of the low building prices brought about by the slump, and have six coasters built round them. Scotts of Bowling submitted the most favourable tender and so six useful ships, able to carry 1,150 tons on 13'7", were completed between 1928 and 1931, Plate 93 & (92). Their size made them useful for the East Coast coal trade to the smaller Thameside wharves. The accommodation is typical of the period, but features to note are the improved engineers' cabins and mess room aft, together with a berth for a steward. There is also a spare berth in the chart room. They proved efficient vessels in service using about 9 tons of coal per day for a speed of 9 knots. They could do up to ten knots, but at this speed, consumption went up to eleven tons per day and so the extra speed was used only when it was important to catch the tide. Bunker capacity at 100 tons was very good, giving them about eleven days steaming. Under favourable weather conditions this could give a range of about 2,000 miles. Of course, bunker requirements were always carefully planned because every extra ton of coal could reduce the weight of cargo that could be carried, by a ton. The amount of bunker coal was carefully calculated so that there was just sufficient to bring the ship back to a port where bunker coal was cheap. When, for example, the ships were carrying Scottish coal their holds were full when about 900 tons had been loaded and so they could take full bunkers as well, leaving the ship not quite down to her marks. This contrasted with the heavier Durham coal where they were down to their marks before the holds were full, consequently on this run, the bunkers were filled with just sufficient coal for the round voyage. The total water ballast in these vessels was about 300 tons and this gave a draft of about 5 feet forward and 10 feet aft. In winter it helped to have the bunkers full to get the stern down to about 12 feet 6 inches and so reduce the danger of the screw coming out of the water in rough seas.

Some designers progressively extended the raised quarter deck so that by the 1920s, vessels with a very short well deck were being built. There was now space for two hatches on the raised quarter deck as shown in the plan of COPSEWOOD, (88) & Plate 126, built for the Joseph Constantine S.S. Line Ltd., Middlesbrough. Completed in 1925, she was the second of two ships built for the company by Osbourne, Graham & Co., Ltd. The raised quarter deck is 133 feet in length, some 23 feet longer than that of YEWTREE. The bluff bow and stern lines contrast strongly with the finer lines of YEWTREE which was the faster vessel. However, the bluff bow of the COPSEWOOD allows more space for the crew accommodation and fore peak ballast tank. The bridge is also longer so that there is space for four berths below, including one for a steward. Above, the captain's cabin is next to the chart room. In this vessel side bunkers are fitted, fed by a central shoot from a coal hatch behind the funnel. The chief and second engineers have their cabins on opposite side of the engine casing and the cabin tops also serve as a platform for the lifeboats. The work boat is carried on a separate platform in this ship. In many ships it was placed adjacent to one of the lifeboats so that one of the davits could serve both boats. Unlike most general arrangement drawings, a plan of the engine room and two sections are shown. At the forward end of the boiler room, a vertical donkey boiler is fitted to provide steam for the capstan and winches in port, so that the main boiler could be shut down. An evaporator was fitted so that a good supply of fresh water was always available for the boilers and an auxiliary condenser was fitted in the stern for the steam winches or other steam machinery used in port.

One of the last vessels with two hatches forward of the bridge was BUSIRIS completed in 1929 for J. & P. Hutchinson, Glasgow. The company engaged some of their ships in tramping as well as running regular services to France, Spain and Portugal. For the latter trade, the BUSIRIS incorporating a number of refinements as compared with colliers and tramps, such as the twin derricks available at all except the fore hold, capable of good lifts of four and five tons. Double derricks are commonly fitted to vessels for the liner trades, so that a union purchase can be used for rapid discharge of cargo. In this system, one derrick of the pair is arranged over the quay, and the two hooks shackled together. The derrick over the hold is used to hoist the load up from the hold while the other derrick's wire is left slack. As soon as the load is clear of the hatchway, this slack is taken up and the wire on the first derrick slacked away until the load is suspended from the second derrick over the quay. This second derrick is now used to lower the load on to the quay, road or railway wagon. Accommodation is provided for seven firemen and five seamen in the forecastle. The sides of the forecastle have considerable flare as revealed by the marked difference in outline between the main deck and the forecastle deck. While the accommodation has such refinements as a hospital cabin, it is surprising to find the ship has an open bridge. Unlike most

S.S. "KYLEBROOK"

GENERAL ARRANGEMENT S.S. No. 240

OWNERS:- MESSRS NORTH WEST SHIPPING Cº LTD

WORKINGTON

ENGINE PARTICULARS	
BUILDERS:- Wᵐ BEARDMORE & Cᴼ LTᴰ	GOVAN, GLASGOW
SIZE OF ENGINE	14", 24", 40" X 27"
SIZE OF BOILER	14'-6" DIA X 10'-6"
WORKING PRESSURE	200 LBS/☐"
GRATE AREA	55 ☐'
HEATING SURFACE	1952 ☐'
DONKEY BOILER	6'-0" DIA X 12'-6"
WORKING PRESSURE	100 LBS/☐"
MAIN CONDENSER	750 SQ FT COOLING SURFACE
SURFACE FEED HEATER	20 SQ FT ANDREW CAMERON
STEERING ENGINE	TREED, PAISLEY
FEED FILTER	DAVY & HORNE
EVAPORATOR	50 TONS CAPACITY ANDREW CAMERON
WINCH CONDENSER	200 SQ FT COOLING SURFACE Wᵐ BEARDMORE & Cᴼ LTᴰ
AUXILIARY FEED DONKEY	LAMONT, 5"X 3½" X 6"
GENERAL SERVICE DONKEY	Dᴼ Dᴼ
BALLAST DONKEY	Dᴼ 6" X 8" X 8"

DISPLACEMENT SCALE

SALT WATER
(1025 OZS)

DRAFT	CARGO	DISPLACEMENT	TONS PER INCH
XIV		1700	11·45
	1100	1600	11·375
XIII	1000	1500	11·30
	900	1400	
XII	800	1300	11·105
	700	1200	
XI	600	1100	10·91
	500	1000	
X	400	900	10·80
IX	300	800	10·69
VIII	200	700	10·50
VII	100	600	10·31
VI			
V			

CUBIC CAPACITIES

CAPACITY OF HOLD TO SKIN OF SHIP & LOW SIDE DECKS, INCLUDING HATCHES	54,687 CUBIC FEET.
CAPACITY OF HOLD TO INSIDE CARGO BATTENS & LOW SIDE OF BEAMS, INCLUDING HATCHES,	51,010 CUBIC FEET.
CAPACITY OF BUNKER	4,732 CUBIC FEET.

APPROXIMATE DEADWEIGHT OF COALS THAT CAN BE CARRIED IN Nº 1 & 2 HOLDS WITH FULL BUNKERS	
Nº 1 HOLD	423 TONS
Nº 2 HOLD	635 TONS
LIABLE TO ADJUSTMENT.	

WATER BALLAST

DOUBLE BOTTOM	177	TONS
FORE PEAK TANK	44	TONS
TOTAL	221	TONS

CUBIC FEET PER TON OF HOLD SPACE AVAILABLE FOR CARGO AFTER DEDUCTING BUNKERS FROM DEADWEIGHT ON SUMMER & WINTER LOAD MARKS.

	SUMMER 51·68	WINTER 52·68
107 BUNKERS		
100 "	51·54	52·48
90 "	50·67	51·98
80 "	50·4	51·49
70 "	49·94	51·01
60 "	49·49	50·54
50 "	49·04	50·07

TRIM OF VESSEL NOT TAKEN INTO CONSIDERATION.

HULL PARTICULARS

LLOYDS DIMENSIONS	
LENGTH (B.P.)	188'-2"
BREADTH (MLD)	30'-0"
DEPTH (MLD)	14'-7"
DEADWEIGHT, TONS, ABOUT	1165
LLOYDS CLASS	100 A1
LOADED SUMMER DRAFT, SALT WATER	14'-1½"
BLOCK COEFFICIENT TO LOAD LINE	·765
TONNAGE:- GROSS TONS	869·65
NETT TONS	426·26
WINCHES:- 3, ROGER, STOCKTON	6" X 10"
WINDLASS:- CLARK, CHAPMAN	6" X 9"
LIFTING CAPACITY OF DERRICKS	30 CWTS.
CABLE SIZE	1⁵⁄₁₆"

R. WILLIAMSON & SON LTD.
SHIPBUILDERS
WORKINGTON
TRACING Nº 3,567

THE ABOVE PARTICULARS ARE BELIEVED TO BE CORRECT, BUT ARE NOT GUARANTEED.

LONGITUDINAL SECTION

MAIN DECK

FORECASTLE DECK

RAISED QUARTER DECK

BOAT DECK

CAPTAINS ROOM & CHART ROOM

MIDSHIP SECTION

64 ft

91

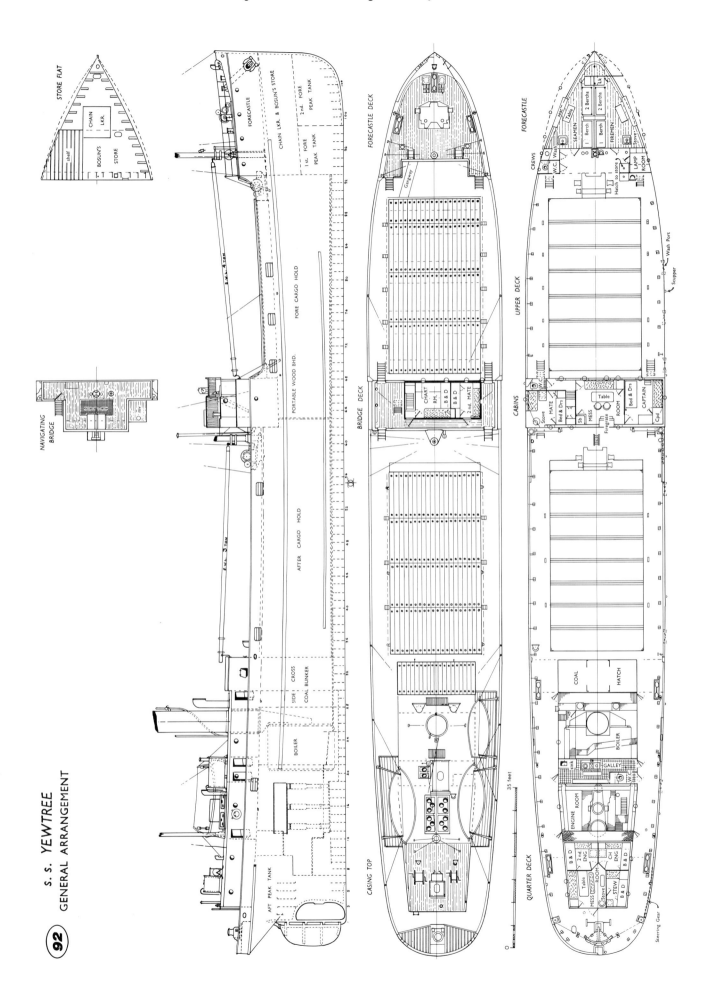

S.S. YEWTREE
GENERAL ARRANGEMENT

92

Steam Coaster YEWPARK

DIMENSIONS: 195'0" x 31'1" x 14'0"

Tonnage 827 gross.

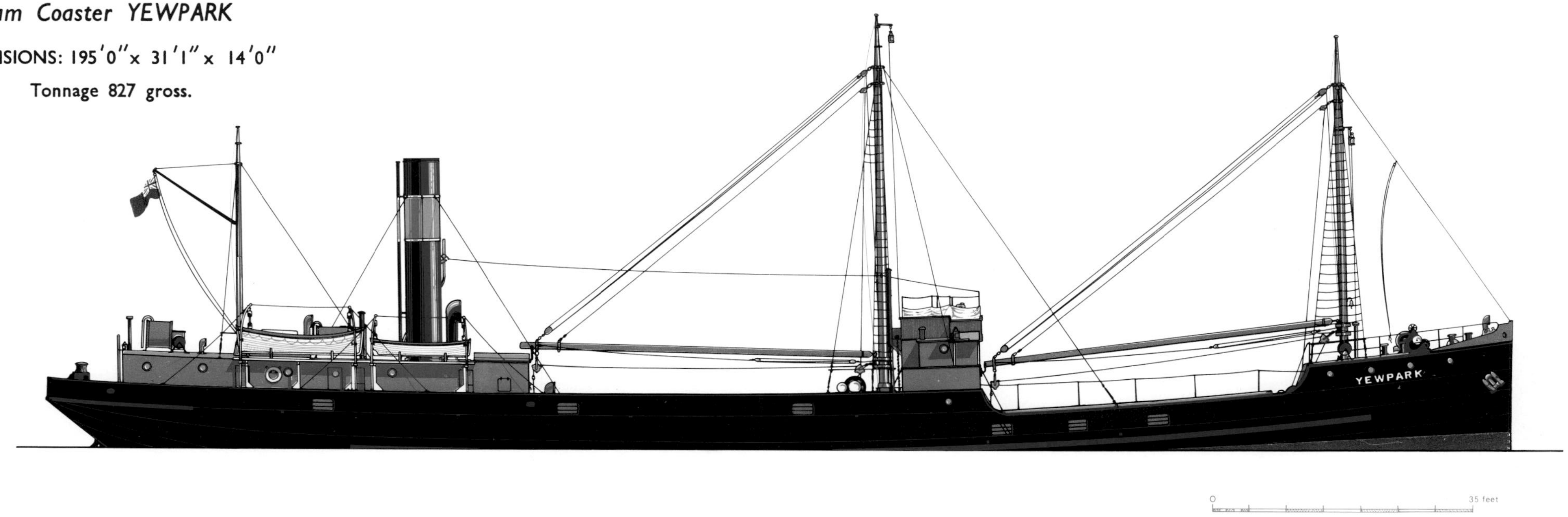

YEWPARK

35 feet

Motor Tanker ARDUITY

DIMENSIONS: 193'0" x 34'1" x 14'8"

Tonnage 959 gross.

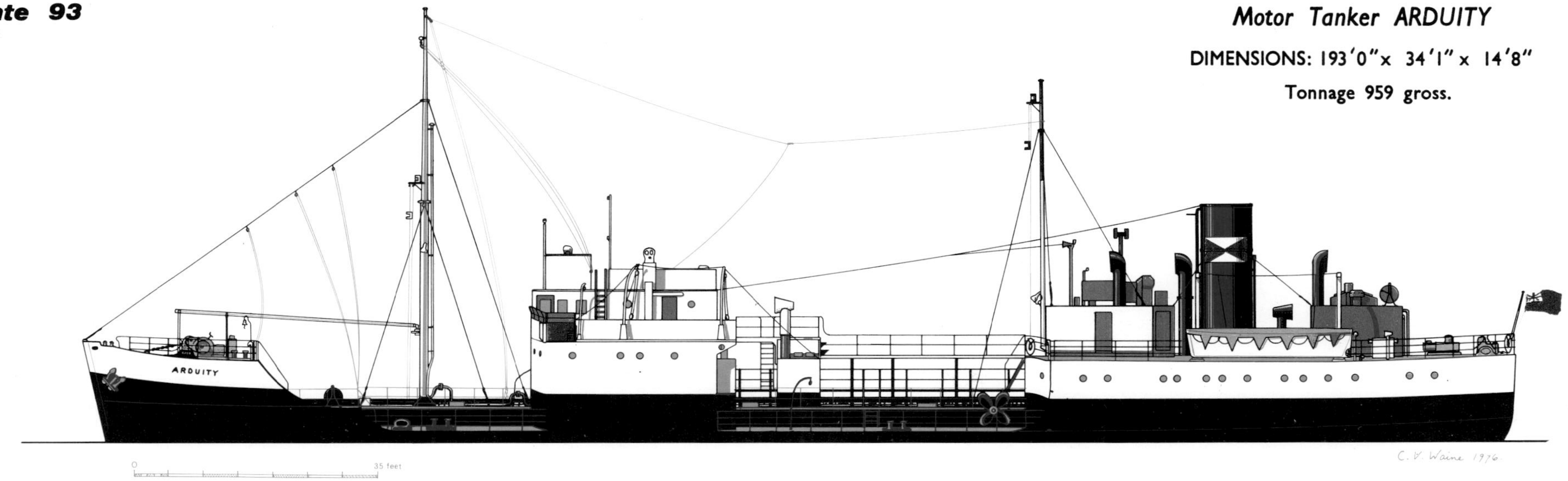

ARDUITY

35 feet

C. V. Waine 1976

Plate 93

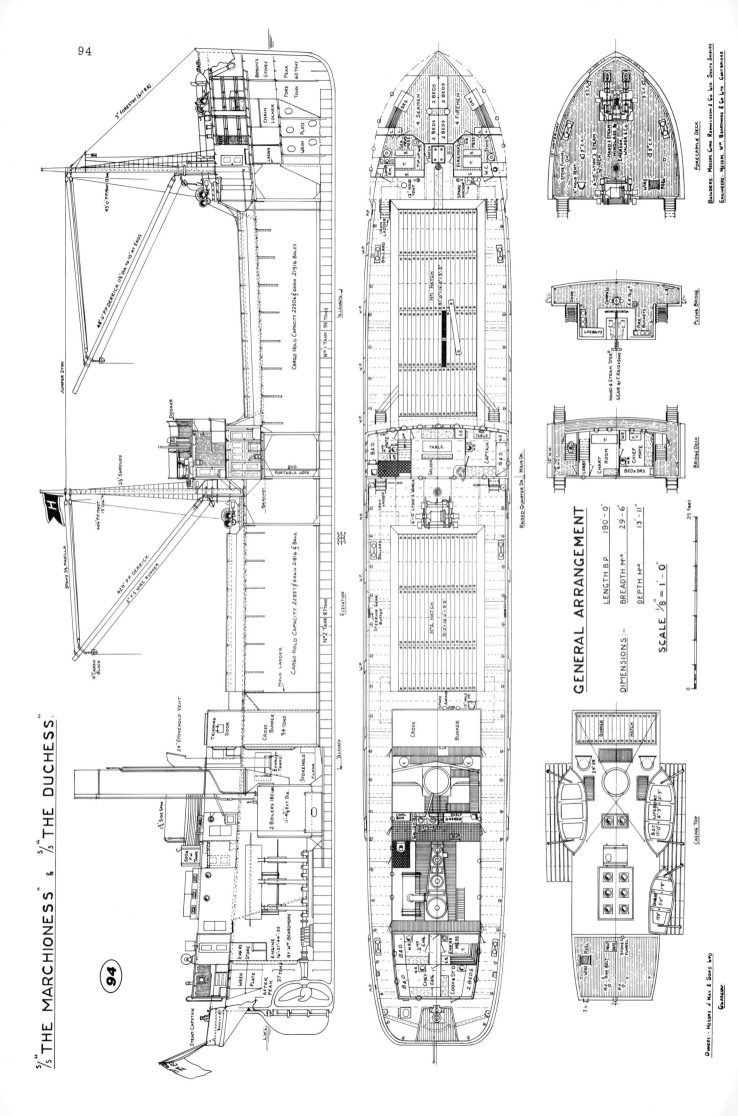

S/S "THE MARCHIONESS" & S/S "THE DUCHESS".

94

GENERAL ARRANGEMENT

DIMENSIONS :-	LENGTH B.P.	190'-0"
	BREADTH. M.LD	29'-6"
	DEPTH. M.LD	13'-11"

SCALE 1/8" = 1'-0"

0   35 feet

FORECASTLE DECK

FLYING BRIDGE

BRIDGE DECK

CASING TOP

Builders:- Messrs. Chas. Rennoldson & Co. Ltd. South Shields
Engineers:- Messrs. Wm. Beardmore & Co. Ltd. Coatbridge
Owners:- Messrs. J. May & Sons Ltd. Glasgow.

ships, the chief and second officers have their cabins aft with the engineers. The aftermost part of the casing houses two apprentices and the cook. The steam steering gear is fitted between this accommodation and that of the officers but the creaks and groans of this could hardly have made for a good night's rest at sea (96).

During World War Two, BUSIRIS was employed in the home trade and along with other coasters to survive, could list several lucky escapes. At the beginning of May 1941 she was in Liverpool and the engineers had partly dismantled the main engine to make some repairs. These repairs had still not been completed when an air raid took place on the night of the third and fourth. Incendiary bombs blanketed the docks and several fell on the BUSIRIS. The skeleton crew aboard successfully put them out and then attended to those on the quayside. They then realised that the adjacent ship which was loaded with explosives, had caught fire and so it became imperative to move the BUSIRIS. As the main engines were out of action, this presented the mate with a difficult problem. However, the second engineer managed to raise enough steam for the capstan and windlass to be used. With the aid of these, the ship was slowly moved away to the remotest part of the dock. This had successfully been carried out when the burning steamer exploded, showering the BUSIRIS with debris. Fortunately she was not seriously damaged and was soon back dodging the shells of the German guns in the Dover Straits. On another occasion, sailing independently of the convoys on a voyage from Maryport to Plymouth, a German bomber attacked her. The first bomb missed and exploded in the water on the port side and the second fell on the deck and lodged in the steering gear aft, failing to explode, but it jammed the steering gear. The bomb had to be moved. It was decided that it would be best to throw it overboard, and this was safely accomplished. The ship then managed to reach Penzance where temporary repairs to the steering gear were made. As soon as these were completed they pressed on for Plymouth.

BUSIRIS continued in the coasting trade after the war, as she was purchased by Monroe Bros., Liverpool, who renamed her KYLEGLEN. By this time coal was moving in much larger consignments on the Irish Sea and she was purchased with this trade in mind. However, as was the case with most coasters a variety of other cargoes were fitted in, particularly in summer, and she loaded stone on occasion at Carreg-y-llam on the Lleyn Peninsula, for Liverpool. As she was built for the liner trades she was faster than most coasters of her size and could manage eleven and a half knots. At this speed coal consumption went up to around 15 tons per day. However, if it meant catching the tide when coming to Liverpool with South Wales coal and in so doing reducing the voyage from 36 hours to 24 hours, it was worth the extra cost. Though a well built ship she was not designed for coal cargoes and needed more attention from the coal trimmers than COPSEWOOD which joined the Monroe fleet as KYLEBANK in 1939, KYLEGLEN was scrapped in 1958 followed by the KYLEBANK in 1959, which was broken up in Holland.

Some vessels with two hatches in the well deck were also built for the fleet of Richard Hughes of Liverpool, who went in for larger vessels at the end of the First World War. His vessels were recognisable at a considerable distance as they had two masts in the well deck one placed at the forward end of each hatch, as seen in JELLICOE ROSE (87). By 1930 the tendency was towards vessels with long clear holds to expedite loading and discharging. To assist in trimming bulk cargoes, the hatch ends were angled off beneath the steam winches as seen in HOLME FORCE (97). Also the hold is free of stanchions which assists stowage generally. HOLME FORCE was completed in 1930 for W.S. Kennaugh & Co.'s West Coast S.S. Co., Liverpool for their coastal and near continental trades. Unlike most coasters of the period the coasters were painted grey, but had the usual red boot-topping and white dividing line, as can be seen in Plate 126. The Kennaugh brothers took a considerable interest in the appearance of their ships and often when inspecting one of their vessels, would run their fingers along the underside of the steel bulwark rail to check if it had been properly scaled and painted as well as the parts that showed. Improvements in the accommodation include a bath as can be seen on the plan (97). Another feature is the central wheelhouse, flanked by two separate cabhouses placed on the bridge-wings. Unlike most coasters of the period, a mizzen mast is still retained. Like many coasters, she was a war victim falling prey to a German motor torpedo boat eight miles off Newhaven, on the 8th of August 1940, while on a voyage from Tynemouth to Devonport.

To make good war losses such as this, a series of 12 vessels were built between 1944 and 1946 to Admiralty account. The design was similar to the TUDOR QUEEN built for the Queenship Navigation Co in 1941, but had a number of detail differences. The plan (98) is of the EMPIRE KEW which was built by John Lewis, Aberdeen who also built four others in the series. The basic design is similar to COPSEWOOD, but has improved crew facilities such as the elimination of the forecastle accommodation. This has been achieved by adding a short poop deck on the stern which provides room aft for the extra accommodation needed. The war-time gun crew were housed in a small cabin separate from the main facilities. At the end of the war they were purchased by a number of owners. EMPIRE KEW passed to Constants (South Wales) Ltd as BELTINGE in 1947 and during 1950 became the MONKTON COOMBE of the Ald Shipping Co. The others in the series became respectively SALTFLEET, NORDIC QUEEN, ROMAN QUEEN, LEVENWOOD, HUMBERGATE, PULBOROUGH, YEWFOREST, THE MONARCH and THE EMPEROR and most were disposed of by 1960.

By the 1930s reliable diesels were available for these coasters. One of the owners who took the step into larger motor coasters was William Robertson who had the CAMEO delivered in 1937. She had long unobstructed hatches and all-aft crew accommodation and was very much ahead of her time in this respect. Most of the motor vessels of this size tended to follow the steam tradition with the bridge amidships.

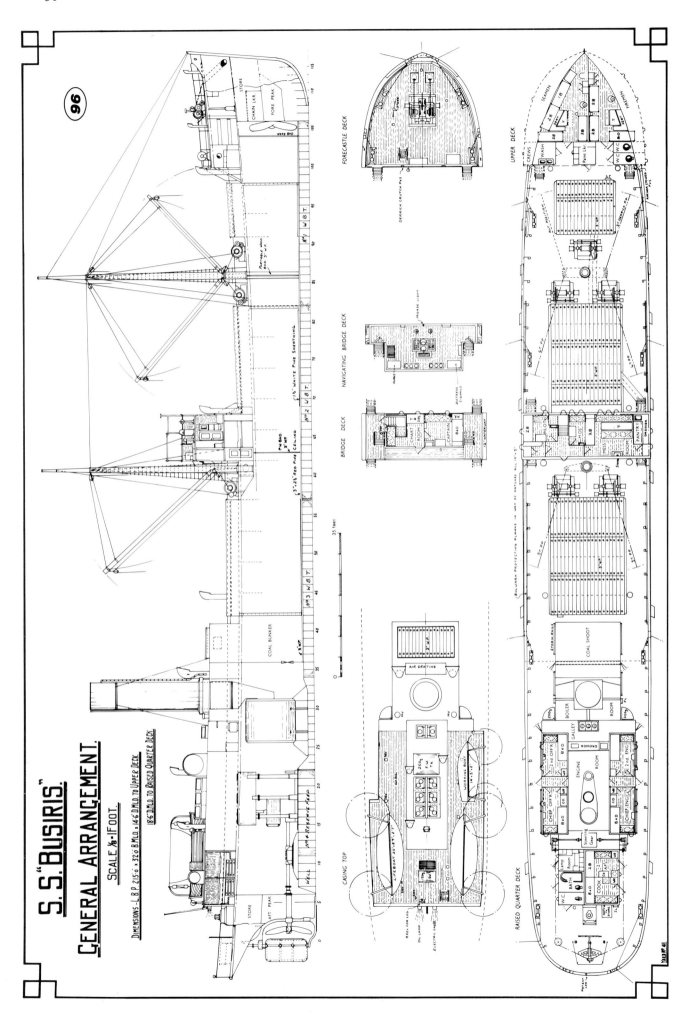

S.S. "BUSIRIS".

GENERAL ARRANGEMENT.

SCALE ⅛·IFOOT.

DIMENSIONS — L.B.P. 215'·0 × 32'·0 B.MLD × 14'·6 D.MLD. TO UPPER DECK
18'·6 D.MLD. TO RAISED QUARTER DECK

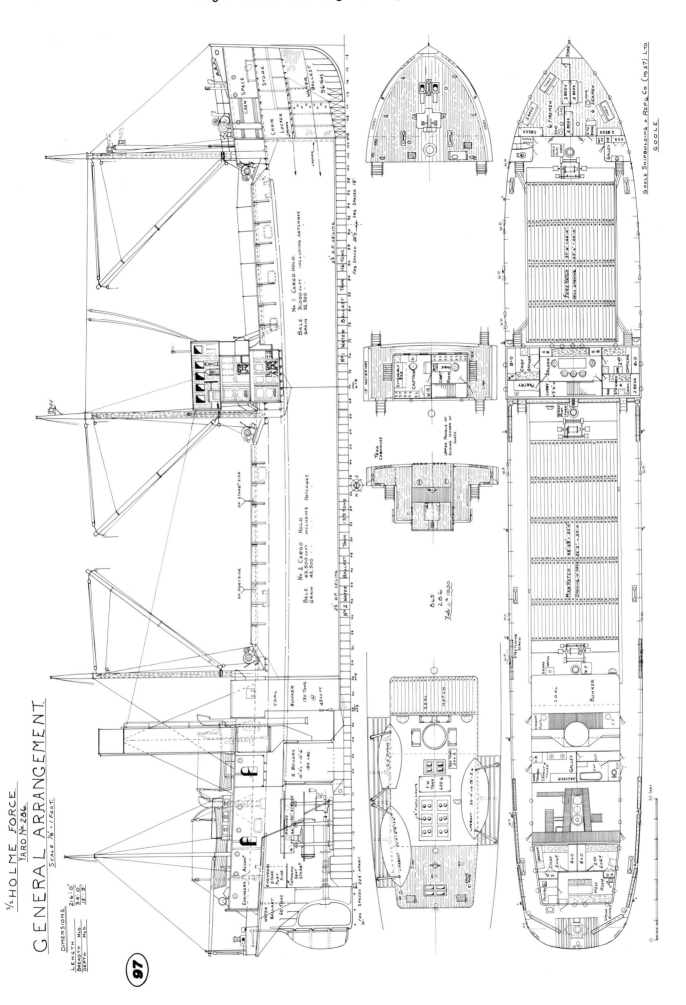

S/S HOLME FORCE.
YARD Nº 286.

GENERAL ARRANGEMENT.

SCALE 1/16" = 1 FOOT.

DIMENSIONS.

LENGTH	MLD.	216'·0"
BREADTH	MLD.	34'·0"
DEPTH	MLD.	15'·9"

97

GOOLE SHIPBUILDING & REPG. Cº (1927) LTD.
GOOLE.

No. 1 CARGO HOLD.
INCLUDING HATCHWAY
BALE 31,000 CU.FT.
GRAIN 32,500

No. 2 CARGO HOLD.
INCLUDING HATCHWAY
BALE 43,500 CU.FT.
GRAIN 45,500

845
Feb 11th 1930

35 feet

98

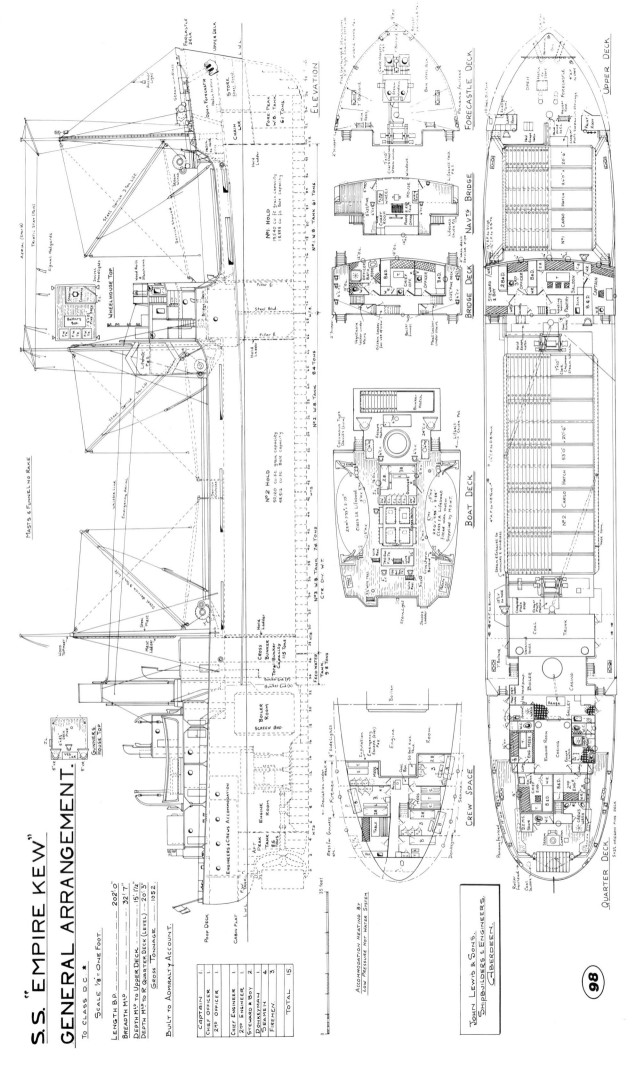

S.S. "EMPIRE KEW"
GENERAL ARRANGEMENT.

TO CLASS D.C. *

SCALE ⅛ = ONE FOOT.

LENGTH B.P. ———— 202'0"
BREADTH M.LD ———— 32'7"
DEPTH M.LD TO UPPER DECK. —— 15'11½"
DEPTH M.LD TO R.QUARTER DECK (LEVEL) — 20'3"
GROSS TONNAGE. —————— 1052.

BUILT TO ADMIRALTY ACCOUNT.

CAPTAIN	1
CHIEF OFFICER	1
2ND OFFICER	1
CHIEF ENGINEER	1
2ND ENGINEER	1
STEWARD & BOY	2
DONKEYMAN	1
SEAMEN	4
FIREMEN	3
TOTAL	15

ACCOMMODATION HEATING BY
LOW PRESSURE HOT WATER SYSTEM

JOHN LEWIS & SONS,
SHIPBUILDERS & ENGINEERS,
ABERDEEN.

98

ELEVATION

FORECASTLE DECK
NAVIG BRIDGE
BRIDGE DECK
BOAT DECK
CREW SPACE

UPPER DECK
QUARTER DECK

9.

Engines Amidships

For vessels more than about 225 feet in length, builders recommended placing the engines amidships, because of trim, stability and weight distribution problems that they encountered when designing vessels of this size with engines aft. As the size of coal cargoes continued to grow, the collier with engines amidships began to appear in the 1870s on the East Coast. These vessels were developed from designs such as WARKWORTH already described, and resulted in vessels such as MEDWAY (99), which was built by Austin & Hunter, Sunderland for Lambert Brothers' coasting collier fleet. The design closely follows WARKWORTH, but differs in mast layout. In MEDWAY the main mast is placed at the forward end of the hatch on the raised quarter deck with a mizzen mast used for carrying sail only, at the after end of the hatch. Also, in this larger vessel, there are two hatches on the well deck with the foremast placed between them. As can be seen from the sketch, the rig had been considerably reduced by 1900 and the fore-topmast is little more than a stump, but the gaff is retained. The crews, used to the more pleasant motion of sailing ships, invariably set the fore and aft sails at sea. MEDWAY measured 226.3x31x13.5 feet and had a gross tonnage of 944. She passed into the Cory fleet in 1896, when the collier fleet of Lambert Brothers was amalgamated with the Cory fleet.

The sketch of NORTHWOOD shows that the profile had changed little by 1889 (100a), though her hatch arrangement was superior to many colliers subsequently built. The three hatches were as large as possible so that she was practically self trimming. That is, the coal hardly needed to be shovelled under the hatch coamings by the coal trimmers and they just levelled off, so that the covers could be put on. Her excellent design was the work of Palmer's yard on the Tyne. She was built for H.C. Pelly of London, which merged with Wm. France & Co., to become Wm. France, Fenwick & Co. The vessel often traded to Goole because of her shallow draft. She was sold after 35 years service, to foreign owners and broken up 10 years later. The rig was less cumbersome by 1889 and just two masts were fitted, though fidded topmasts and gaffs were still in use, and a good spread of canvas still possible. Gaffs were often retained in vessels for cargo working, after gaff sails had been dispensed with.

The usual speed of these colliers was around nine knots and this was quite satisfactory for the North East coal trade. However, in 1896, Steam Colliers Ltd, which was managed by H.C. Pelly, placed an order with J. Blumer of Sunderland for two colliers of 1143 gross tons, which became LOCKWOOD and ROOKWOOD. They were designed for a service speed of twelve and a half to thirteen knots with the idea of making the passage from South Wales to London in four tides rather than five. Their fuel consumption proved to be enormous at between 25 and 30 tons per day. Even though the price of bunker coal was only 7/6d a ton at the time, they could not show a saving at the higher speed. Because of this, they were usually restricted to a speed of nine and a half knots. However, if they looked like missing the tide, they always had some reserve power in hand which could be put to good use on these occasions, but the experiment of higher speed ships was not repeated. Unlike most colliers built at that time, they were not fitted with any cargo gear as they were intended for the coal trade exclusively where discharge would be by shore cranes. Because of their higher power, they were chartered by Wm. Cory for many years, on the condition that they were fitted with towing hooks. Cory's had a large seagoing barge, the SNARK, which could carry 1000 tons of coal and these two colliers, because of their higher power, were ideally suited to towing the SNARK, and when towing, France, Fenwick received £20 to £25 extra per voyage, depending on the distance. Several barges had been built for the trade from Goole, but all had been sold except for SNARK which was sold after a few more years, because of the time wasted picking up the barge from tugs and dropping it off on arrival in the Thames.

The three or two hatch raised quarter deck design was also used for general cargo liner vessels and a number of these such as ISLAND QUEEN, built for the London & Channel Islands S.S. Co., Ltd., London, by Swan, Hunter and Wigham Richardson, Wallsend, found their way into the tramp trade. After trading to the Channel Islands, she was sold in 1934 to Monroe Bros. of Liverpool and renamed KYLE QUEEN. She was used for a short time tramping on the Irish Sea and then sold to Egyptian owners (100b).

Perhaps the two ships best remembered for their bunker arrangements were the HAWKWOOD, built 1900 and her sister MONKWOOD. They had side bunkers, one of which had more than twice the capacity of the other, because of the space taken up by the donker boiler on one side. As the bunker coal was consumed, the ship would develop a list. Masters did their best to reduce the effect by loading the cargo so that the vessel, started with a slight list the other way, came upright and arrived with a slight list the opposite way. The self trimming type of collier, like NORTHWOOD with large hatches to facilitate discharge, was progressively increased in size and had reached about 1,600 tons deadweight by 1900, which was about the maximum that coal merchants could handle in the distribution trades at that time. The lower freight rate made possible by larger cargoes had pushed this figure up to about 3,000 tons by the 1920s for the London market and Near Continental Ports (Bordeaux to

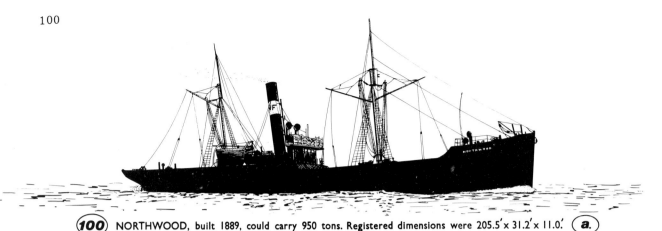

100 NORTHWOOD, built 1889, could carry 950 tons. Registered dimensions were 205.5' x 31.2' x 11.0'. **a.**

Copenhagen range). Typical of the smaller vessels with engines amidships being built for the trade in the 1920s was the ISLINGTON (101). She was completed in 1924 by Swan, Hunter and Wigham Richardson for H. Harrison (Shipping) Ltd., London, who ordered a number of ships at the end of World War One. As can be seen from the plan she was a single deck 'three-island' collier, where the islands are the forecastle, bridge-deck and poop. By the 1920s, it was usual to have the crew aft and the accommodation for the officers and engineers amidships, leaving the forecastle for use as a store, which usually had tonnage openings. The poop in ISLINGTON has space for six seamen and four firemen. In addition, there is a seperate two berth cabin for the donkeyman and bosun. Amidships, the officers' mess is placed under the bridge and flanked by cabins for the captain, steward and chief officer. The pantry and captain's bath room are placed either side of the coal trunk. The tween deck bunkers then occupy the central part of the space below the bridge deck. Aft of this, alongside the engine casing, was the accommodation for the second officer and the second engineer on the port side and the chief engineer and engineers' mess on the starboard side. The galley was placed on the bridge deck above, over the boilers. A chart room was fitted below the wheelhouse. As can be seen, the hatches were as large as possible and the steam winches were offset on either side of the mast to reduce the inaccessible area between the hatches.

The three-island type suffers a distinct defect. As already noted, the propellor shaft tunnel significantly reduces hold space aft and so, although the fore and after hold are the same length, the after hold has 8,097 cubic feet less space and so loaded with a full cargo of coal, there would be about 185 tons more coal in the forward hold and this difference was probably enough to make ISLINGTON trim by the head if a full cargo was loaded. In addition to this there was only about 44 cubic feet of hold space allowed per ton. This is satisfactory for the heavy coals, but lighter washed coals stow at about 50 cubic feet per ton so she would not be able to load a full deadweight of these cargoes. A somewhat different approach to the three-island layout is shown in a vessel built for R. H. Penney & Sons of Brighton (102), who were active in the south coast coal trade. She was originally named ALGOL when completed in 1924 by Dobson's yard on the Tyne, but was sold to Monroe Brothers of Liverpool in 1941. Because of war-time restrictions, she was not renamed KYLEBROOK until 1949. In this vessel the crew accommodation was in the forecastle and the poop structure eliminated. This reduced both construction costs and steel weight. Also the vessel has rather better bunker arrangements compared with ISLINGTON with a large bunker hatch just in front of the bridge. Ballast capacity is also much more satisfactory, with an aft peak tank capacity of 117 tons, compared with the 19 tons of ISLINGTON and must have given much better screw immersion in ballast. The design of the double bottom also indicates that careful thought has been given to ballast passages. The frame spacing has been arranged at 30 inches throughout most of the ship, except in the forward part where it is reduced to 27 inches and finally to 24 inches in the peak ballast tanks. As can be seen from the plan, like all cargo

100 ISLAND QUEEN (later Kyle Queen) had a deadweight of 910 tons on a draft of 13 feet 5 inches. **b.**

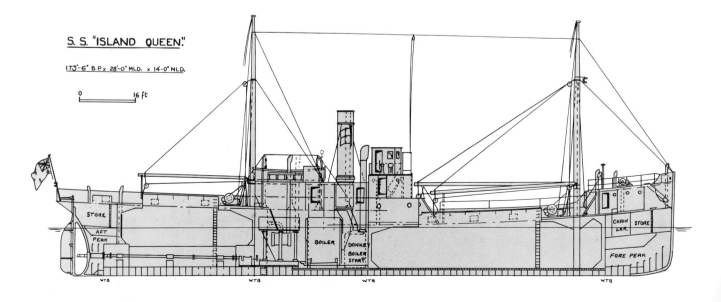

S. S. "ISLAND QUEEN."

173'-6" B.P. x 28'-0" MLD. x 14'-0" MLD.

0   16 ft

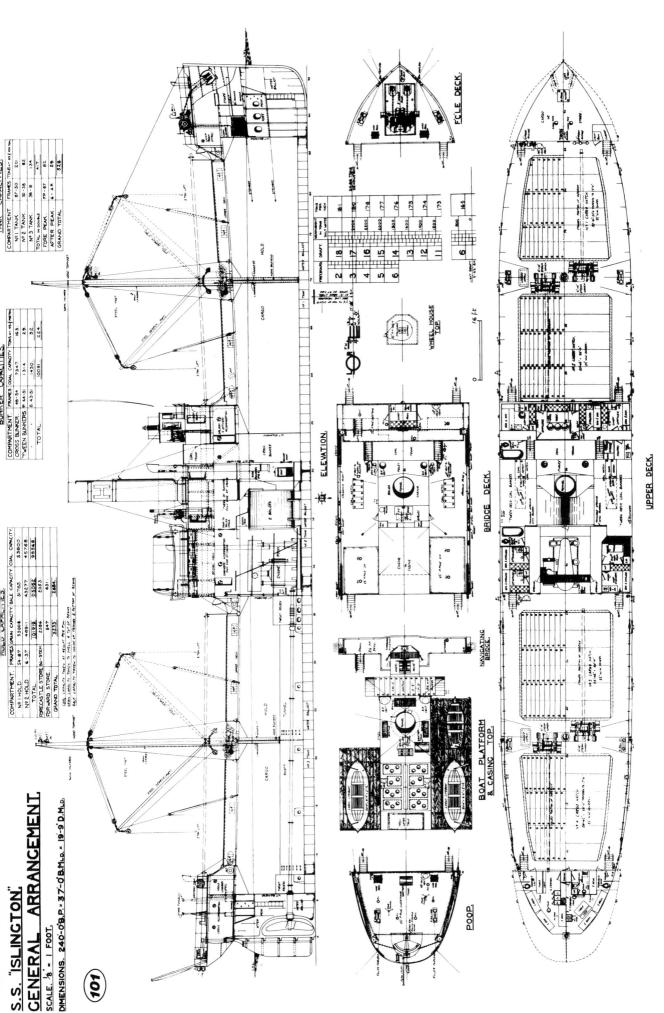

S.S. "ISLINGTON"
GENERAL ARRANGEMENT.
SCALE. ⅛" = 1 FOOT.
DIMENSIONS. 240'-0"B.P. x 37'-0"B.MLD. x 19'-9"D.MLD.

101

SWAN, HUNTER & WIGHAM RICHARDSON LTD.   SHIPBUILDERS & ENGINEERS.   WALLSEND SHIPYARD.   WALLSEND-ON-TYNE.

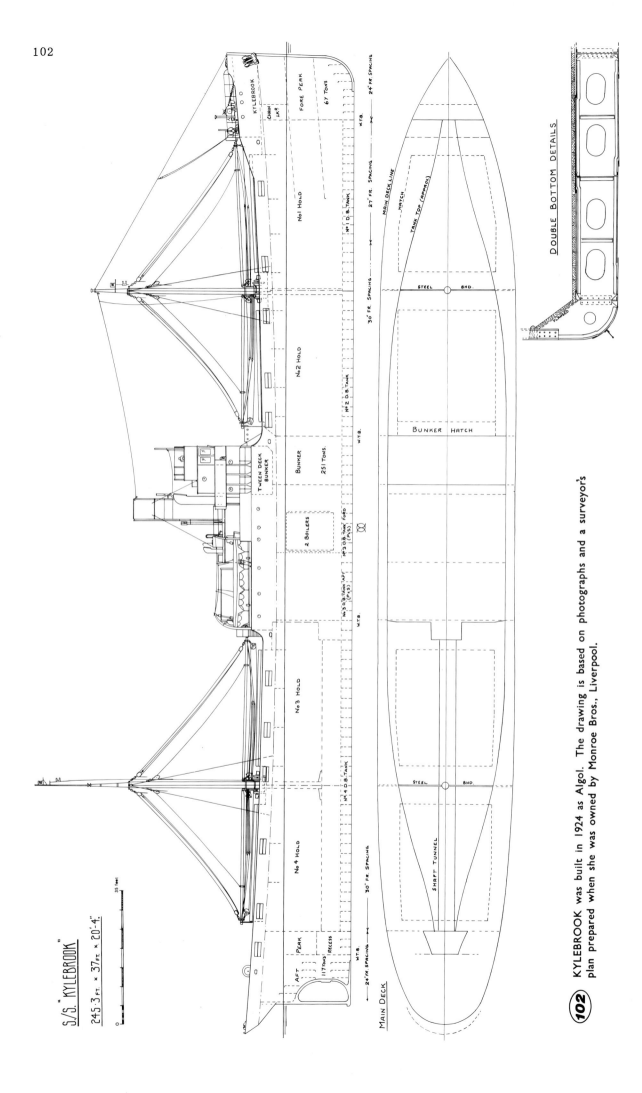

S/S "KYLEBROOK"

245.3 FT × 37 FT × 20'4".

35 feet

DOUBLE BOTTOM DETAILS

KYLEBROOK

CHAIN LKR

FORE PEAK

67 TONS

No1 HOLD

No1 D.B. TANK

24" FR. SPACING

W.T.B.

27" FR. SPACING

No2 HOLD

No2 D.B. TANK

30" FR. SPACING

W.T.B.

TWEEN DECK BUNKER

BUNKER

251 TONS.

2 BOILERS

No3 D.B. TANK FORD (P.S.S.)

No3 D.B. TANK AFT (P.L.S.)

W.T.B.

No3 HOLD

No4 D.B. TANK

30" FR. SPACING

No4 HOLD

RECESS

117 TONS

AFT PEAK

W.T.B.

24" FR. SPACING

MAIN DECK

MAIN DECK LINE

HATCH

TANK TOP (APPROX)

STEEL BHD.

BUNKER HATCH

STEEL BHD.

SHAFT TUNNEL

FLANGE

102 KYLEBROOK was built in 1924 as Algol. The drawing is based on photographs and a surveyor's plan prepared when she was owned by Monroe Bros., Liverpool.

vessels, the bottom is virtually flat throughout most of the length, and this flat bottom is prone to "slamming" in rough seas. This generally occurs when the bows lift out of the water on a large wave and then slam down into the succeeding trough. The force of the impact can often dent the bottom plates and so, to reduce the danger of this happening, the frames are placed closer together. The officer on watch will endeavour to adjust the speed of the ship so that slamming is avoided as much as possible, but in confused seas it cannot be eliminated when making passages in ballast and so the closer spacing of the frames helped to stiffen the bottom plating and reduce the possibility of damage. The portable wood bulkheads used to divide the forward and after holds in two, have been replaced by steel bulkheads in KYLEBROOK. These bulkheads were particularly important in colliers as they often carried different grades of coal in each compartment of the hold.

Design shortcomings in the 'three-island' type colliers were largely the result of the way in which owners ordered their ships. In many cases, even as late as 1900, it was common practice to invite tenders from 10 or more yards for a 'self-trimming' collier of a certain deadweight, draft and speed', with perhaps a few more details such as cargo gear. Since builders knew the order would generally go to the yard offering the lowest price, margins were cut to the minimum and the three-island type was usually offered because it was the cheapest and easiest to construct. For the same reason the hold volume was kept down and so was ballast capacity. This resulted in some vessels which were very unsatisfactory in service and in this respect it is interesting to compare two vessels which were built for France, Fenwick.

Name	Year	Reg. dimensions	Deadweight	Grain Capacity	Ballast (tons)	
NEEDWOOD (Three island type)	1906	279.5 x 40.1 x 18.1	3,363 tons	155,000 cu.ft. (46 cu.ft/ton)	Double Btm	458t.
					Aft Peak Tk	29t.
						487t.
CORNWOOD (Raised quarter deck type)	1911	287.0 x 41.0 x 17.2	3,100 tons	160,000 cu.ft. (51.5 cu.ft/ton)	Double Btm	602t.
					Fore Peak T.	46t.
					Aft Peak Tk.	112t.
						760t.

As can be seen from these figures, the NEEDWOOD type has quite adequate stowage at 46 cubic feet per ton. However, the water ballast of only 487 tons, with an aft peak of just 29 tons proved inadequate in service and she could make little or no progress in ballast, against strong head winds. Sometimes she was blown off course and on several occasions had lucky escapes from lee shores. In the CORNWOOD the ballast was increased and the vessel given a raised quarter deck, giving a more satisfactory hold capacity. As can be seen, the extra volume gives a stowage rate of over 51 cubic feet per ton, but the extra steel weight has reduced the deadweight. The raised quarter deck design was already common in the fleets of Cory and Stephenson Clarke.

Vessels with a deadweight of more than about 1,800 tons were not self-trimmers and had proportionally smaller hatches. This was because owners and builders felt that if the hatch size was increased, there was a danger that the deck remaining would be too weak to stand the stresses and strains of a rough sea. As it was, plates sometimes cracked, particularly at the corners of hatches. These non-self-trimmers worked in the coal trade during the winter and then, with the fall in coal demand with the arrival of Spring, they went to the Baltic with coal, returning with sawn wood cargoes. Another popular cargo was iron ore from Spain and so these vessels were also short sea traders.

By the 1920s, raised quarter deck self trimmers had cautiously been increased in size until vessels the size of CORDENE (105), Plate 104, were built for the London coal trade. She was completed in 1924 for Cory Colliers Ltd., by Swan Hunter and Wigham Richardson, Wallsend. The accommodation was similar to ISLINGTON, but a wireless operator and wireless room were placed next to the chart room. The raised quarter deck design means that the accommodation can be better arranged, with the galley on the same deck as the mess and more cabins amidships. Steam steering gear was fitted and also, because of her size, the ship is equipped with wire compressors, as mooring wires rather than ropes were used. Rollers were carefully arranged on the forecastle and poop so that the steam winches could be used to handle the wires. A sister ship, CORDUFF was completed in 1923 and both ran regularly in the London coal trade. Both were sunk off Cromer. CORDUFF was first to be lost when she was torpedoed by a German E-boat on the 7th of March 1941 while bound North in ballast. CORDENE was bombed and sunk a few months later, on the 9th of August, on a voyage from Rochester to Blyth in ballast. Though vessels of the 1920s were a great advance on those built 20 years previously, they still suffered from two defects. Firstly the shaft tunnel was always suffering grab damage. To eliminate this, France, Fenwick had the collier HELMWOOD built, with deep tanks on either side of the shaft tunnel, thus giving a level bottom to the hold. The stability had not been checked, and she proved so tender with a full coal cargo over the empty tanks that they had to be removed at considerable cost. Secondly, the prime area suitable for cargo was taken up by machinery and so no more colliers were built with engines amidships after the late 1920s. However, this type of collier continued in service until the late 1950s and their final demise was particularly noticed by their captains and chief engineers. As, in heavy weather when the screw came out of the water, the weight of the long propellor shaft reduced the tendency of the engine to race, they often made better progress than the new engines-aft colliers, in which the engineers often had to stand by the steam valve and cut off steam to the engine to stop it racing dangerously.

Plate 104

Steam Collier CORDENE

DIMENSIONS: 284'5" x 42'1" x 19'6"

Tonnage 2,345 gross.

CORDENE was one of the last colliers to be built with engines amidships for William Cory & Son Ltd., the well known London owners. Of the later, raised quarter deck type, she was completed in 1924 by Swan, Hunter & Wigham Richardson, Newcastle. She was bombed and sunk off Cromer on a voyage from Rochester to Blyth in ballast in August 1941.

Steam Ship LOUIE ROSE

DIMENSIONS: 250'6" x 37'1" x 16'5"

Tonnage 1,596 gross.

LOUIE ROSE was completed in 1924 by John Fullerton of Paisley for Richard Hughes of Liverpool. She was mainly employed in the South Wales and East Coast coal trade. Later vessels all had the bridge placed at the end of the well deck which reduced the nett tonnage abd hence harbour dues. She was sold to foreign owners in 1936 for conversion into a wine carrier.

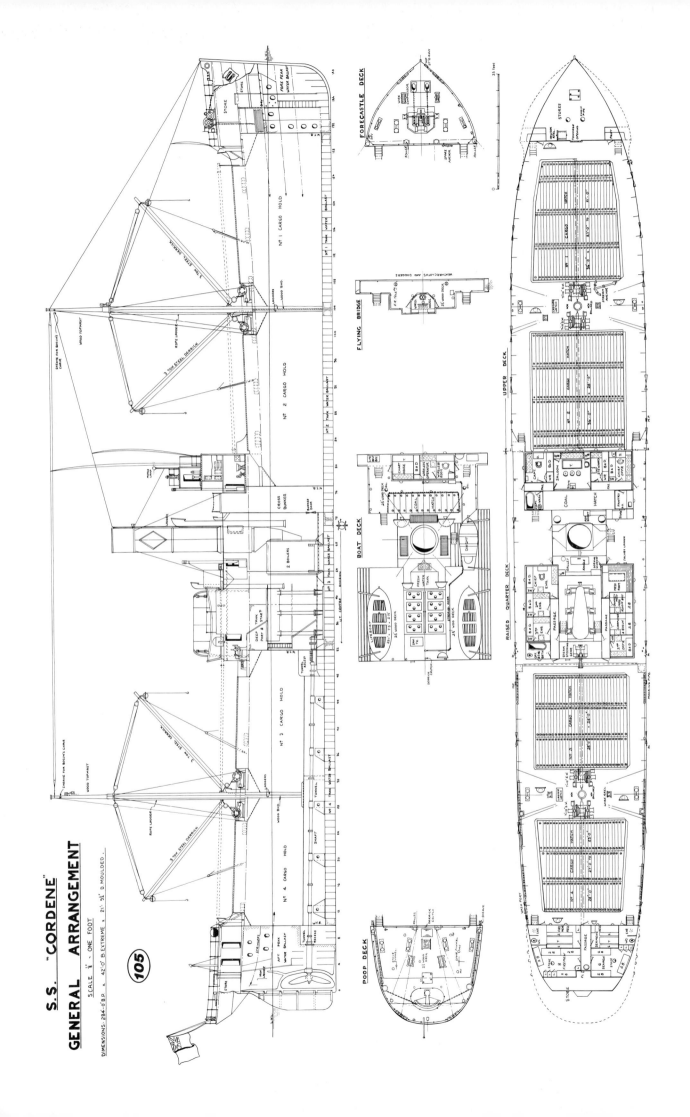

S.S. "CORDENE"
GENERAL ARRANGEMENT

SCALE ⅛" = ONE FOOT

DIMENSIONS 284'-0" B.P. × 42'-0" B.EXTREME × 21'-5½" D.MOULDED.

105

FORECASTLE DECK

FLYING BRIDGE

BOAT DECK

POOP DECK

UPPER DECK

RAISED QUARTER DECK

35 feet

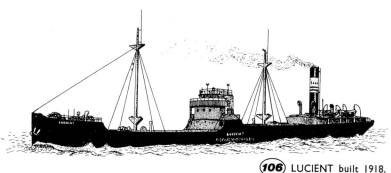

Big Engines-Aft Colliers

The collier owners never entirely deserted the engines-aft vessel, for, throughout the period during which colliers with engines amidships were built, one group of vessels was always constructed with engines aft. These were the special colliers designed to pass under the low fixed bridges of the River Thames. The bridge and engine casing were made as low as possible, while taller structures, the mast and funnel, were arranged to fold flat on to the deck. The mast was of light construction as it was required for navigation lights only. Originally the gas works, such as that at Wandsworth, sited on the riverside above the low bridges of the Thames, obtained their coal supplies in barges. Conventional colliers brought the coal from the North East and anchored in the Pool of London. The vessels then discharged into barges, which were then towed up river to the Gas Company's wharf. This transhipment was slow and expensive. To avoid this, the construction of special colliers was proposed. The suggestion seems to have come from the London Collier owners T. & C. Nicholls in the latter part of the 1870s. The construction of the vessels was carried out by Palmer's yard on the Tyne, after careful studies to determine the clearances needed for the bridges. This resulted in plans for vessels with a registered length of 220 feet, breadth of 32.2 feet and depth of 13.8 feet. VAUXHALL and WESTMINSTER were completed in 1878 and were then followed shortly afterwards by the slightly larger LAMBETH which was based on the operating experience obtained with the first two vessels. The colliers proved very successful, as the LAMBETH, for example, could carry 1,050 tons on a draft of 12 feet and deliver it directly to the Company's wharf. Their strange low profiles, broken only by a tall thin funnel immediately attracted attention and they were soon dubbed 'flat-irons'. These early 'flat-irons' were little bigger than the two or three hatch steam coasters already described. There was little change in their size or design during the next 30 years or so and the ETHYLENE (108), built for the Gas, Light and Coke Company, was almost the same size as LAMBETH. However steelwork and design improvements increased her deadweight to 1,320 tons. Further power stations were built and old ones expanded as the demand for electricity rose and these also needed 'flat-irons'. One such project was the building of a new power station in the 1930s for Fulham Borough Council. After careful studies, three vessels were ordered from the Burntisland Shipbuilding Company, to supply the plant. Each was able to carry 2,390 tons on a draft of 16'8". As will be seen from the plan of the FULHAM (107), the wheelhouse is low and protected by bulwarks, Similarly, the remainder of the profile is also low. The funnel is lowered and raised with the aid of the steam warping capstan aft and is arranged to lower into a recess provided in the top of the engine casing. To keep this area clear, the engine room skylight has been divided into two portions which are placed on either side of the recess. The work boat and lifeboat davits are also made as low as possible because of the even more limited headroom at the sides. For quick discharge on arrival, the hold is fitted with hopper side tanks. These cause the coal to flow into the area open to the hatch and so within reach of the discharging grabs. The vessel was usually discharged in about six and a half hours and so was able to go down river on the next tide. The wedge shaped ballast tank below the bridge, was fitted to make trimming practically unnecessary when loading. The forecastle has to be kept low in order to improve the visibility from the wheelhouse and this made the ships rather wet in winter. All the accommodation was aft in the FULHAM and the vessels proved efficient in service. As they had not proved awkward to handle, the larger FULHAM IV was constructed in 1939, which could carry 2,440 tons on a draft of 16'9". All were powered by a 950 indicated h.p. triple expansion engine made by North Eastern Marine, Sunderland. This gave a service speed of ten knots. The three furnace 'Scotch' boiler working at 220 lbs. per square inch had a forced draft fan and an auxiliary donkey boiler was fitted as a stand-by.

Similar vessels were built for the other undertakings such as the Gas, Light and Coke Co., Ltd. In earlier days the Company used to charter their colliers. For many years, the Nine Elms gas works was supplied by vessels chartered from the River Steam Colliers Company. The BATTERSEA, which was the largest vessel serving the Nine Elms wharf, just above Vauxhall Bridge, could carry 1,250 tons. This vessel was purchased in 1915, but it was not until the 1920s that new vessels such as the ETHYLENE (108) were built. Usually all went well on the voyages under the bridges, but occasionally vessels did get stuck.

Some vessels were built during the Second World War to replace war losses, but it was not until the end of the war that a large rebuilding programme was started. Two of the first vessels to be completed were the SIR JOSEPH SWAN in 1945 and the SIR ALEXANDER KENNEDY, completed in 1946 for the London Power Co., Ltd. The vessels were some 14 feet longer than those previously built and became the forerunners of the post-war series of 'flat-irons'. Registered dimensions were 260.0 x 39.6 x 16.6 feet, with a draft of 16'9" and these were the largest vessels of this type to be built. Before any more vessels were delivered,

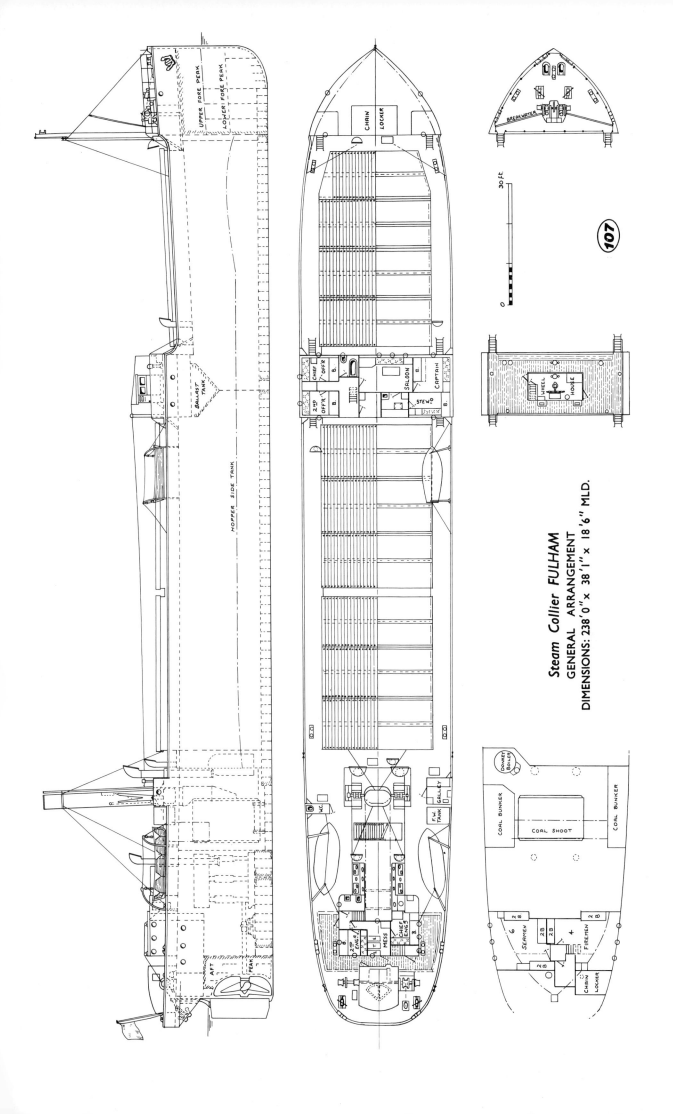

Steam Collier *FULHAM*
GENERAL ARRANGEMENT
DIMENSIONS: 238'0" x 38'1" x 18'6" MLD.

107

30 ft.

0

UPPER FORE PEAK
LOWER FORE PEAK
BALLAST TANK
HOPPER SIDE TANK
AFT PEAK
PEAK

CHAIN LOCKER

CHIEF OFF'R
2ND OFF'R
SALOON
CAPTAIN
STEW'D

W.C.
GALLEY
F.W. TANK
MESS
2ND ENG'R
CHIEF ENG'R

BREAKWATER

WHEEL HOUSE

DONKEY BOILER
COAL BUNKER
COAL SHOOT
COAL BUNKER

SEAMEN
FIREMEN
CHAIN LOCKER

the gas and electricity undertakings were nationalised, that of the electricity companies coming into effect on the first of April 1948. The British Electricity Authority, as the new body was called, increased the orders of up-river colliers already placed before nationalisation and a series of eight vessels of similar design to the SIR ALEXANDER KENNEDY was ordered. One of the steam powered vessels in the series was the BRIMSDOWN, completed in May 1951 by the Burntisland Shipbuilding Co., Ltd., Dundee. She had a deadweight of 2,680 tons on a draft of 17'2". The basic outline of the new vessels was little different from the pre-war FULHAM, but below decks there was quite a considerable improvement. All crew members now had separate cabins and there were additional messes for the seamen and the firemen (6). The steamers had a donkey boiler and a single 'Scotch' boiler supplying steam to a North Eastern Marine triple expansion engine. This gave a service speed of about ten knots. The motor vessels, also based on the same hull, were rather faster with a service speed of about eleven knots. The hatch covers of these vessels were all MacGregor single-pull type steel covers which could be opened and closed in a few minutes.

Nationalisation of the gas industry took place on the first of May 1949 and by this time the Gas, Light & Coke Co., Ltd., were already well advanced with their programme of up-river colliers, all of which were motor vessels. They were based on a hull closely similar to BRIMSDOWN. One advantage of the motor vessel was that a fixed squat funnel proved quite adequate for the exhaust. Most of the 'flat-irons' had long lives, serving their owners until lost or finally scrapped. However, a few were sold to Greek and other owners for trading in the Mediterranean and elsewhere. Some even made Atlantic voyages for their new owners, attracting curious glances from dockers far removed from London's river.

Though owners such as France, Fenwick, Pelton S.S. Co., and Cory, were mainly building vessels with engines amidships, a few owners remained much more faithful to the engines aft configuration. These owners, such as Stepehnson Clarke and the Gas, Light & Coke Company, were able to build vessels with engines aft because they had to work to a restricted draft. The first of the larger engines-aft colliers to be constructed for Stephenson Clarke was the ABBAS, completed in 1911 by S.P. Austin. She measured 240.0 x 36.0 x 15.6 feet and could carry 2,150 tons on a draft of 16'6". She had a single main boiler backed up by a donkey boiler. By the time ABBAS was delivered, the slightly larger KINGSWEAR (109), had been in service with the Dartmouth collier owners and coal merchants, Renwick, Wilton & Co., for over two and a half years. As can be seen, she had a short raised quarter deck with four hatches on the well deck and the bridge placed between hatches two and three. ABBAS and nearly all 4 hatch colliers built at this time and later, had the raised quarter deck extending to the bridge amidships to give better cubic capacity and trim. The next significant advance was the completion of FLAMMA and a sister-ship LUCIENT (106). The vessels had been ordered from Wood, Skinner's yard on the Tyne by the Gas, Light & Coke Company in an effort to replace war losses. FLAMMA was completed in June 1917 and could carry 2,880 tons on a draft of 18'3". She measured 270.6 x 38.2 x 18.0 feet and so the big engines-aft collier had arrived. Almost immediately FLAMMA was a war casualty when she was seriously damaged by an under-water explosion off Seaham. Fortunately, she was successfully beached at Seaham, but was so badly damaged there seemed little chance of saving her. However, she was carefully cut in two and the relatively undamaged portion towed back to Wood, Skinner's yard. There she was repaired with plates intended for her sistership LUCIENT. In this way the FLAMMA was soon back in service helping to maintain vital coal supplies to the gas undertakings.

Vessels such as FLAMMA were defensively armed with machine guns and perhaps up to a two and a half pounder in later years during both World Wars. However, in the First World War, a number of coasters were selected by the Admiralty to take a more active part. These were the 'mystery' or Q-ships, cargo vessels fitted with concealed guns. The vessels cruised the Irish Sea and English Channel inviting a submarine attack. This often meant weeks of waiting only to be blown to pieces by a torpedo and so for these missions special volunteers, from all branches of the Navy, formed the crews. The first German submarines were as fast as coasters only on the surface and could not manage more than six and a half knots submerged. They were fitted with guns which they often utilised for a surface attack, rather than use expensive torpedoes on coasters. When the submarine fired on a coaster, out of range of the coasters guns, the crew usually abandoned ship whereupon the submarine closed in to finish her off with more shells or put out a boarding party to sink her with explosive charges. The Q-ship took advantage of this method of attack. Up to four-inch guns were fitted, carefully concealed by false bulwarks which folded down, fake lifebelt lockers, or even a ship's boat carefully sawn in half which could fold away from the guns when they were brought into action.

One coaster taken up by the Royal Navy as a Q-ship was the PENSHURST. She was smaller then the LUCIENT and had been built by the London & Montrose Shipbuilding Co., Ltd., for the Power S.S. Co., of London. She had a long raised quarter deck with two hatches on it, bridge amidships, and two more hatches forward. She was armed and began cruising the English Channel in 1915, but it was a year before she saw any action. PENSHURST was south of Start Point, Devon, Steaming at a steady eight knots South-West down the English

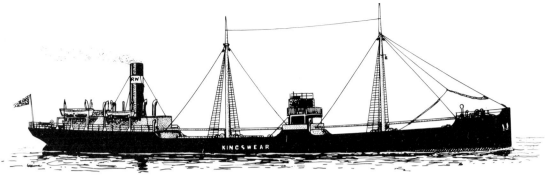

109 KINGSWEAR measured 245.3' x 36.5' x 16.6' and carried 2,180 tons on a draft of 16'7".

Channel at dawn on the 29th of November 1916 (110). A sailing vessel had been sunk in a similar position the day before and all the crew were hoping that the submarine was still in the area and that there would be some action. At 7.45 a.m. a look-out spotted a small object to the South-East. Further identification was prevented by the rising sun, but the flash of gunfire confirmed that it was a submarine approaching from the South-East. The first shell fell short, but a second passed over the ship. The PENSHURST slowed and altered course to the North-West, tempting the submarine to close in. However, the submarine commander had spotted a larger cargo vessel which was rapidly approaching on a North-Easterly course. Fortunately, Commander Grenfell of the PENSHURST was able to get between the cargo vessel and the submarine. As the PENSHURST closed with the submarine again, a third shot fell short of the ship. Selected members of the crew, dressed in old clothes such as those worn by merchant seamen, got ready to "abandon ship". They rushed about and lowered the lifeboats as erratically as they could to waste time and lure the submarine nearer. By this time the ship had practically stopped and the submarine lay silhouetted against the sun making it difficult to judge the range. After a while Commander Grenfell decided it was not approaching any closer and so the PENSHURST's gunners were ordered to open fire, as soon as the white battle ensign had replaced the merchant flag. The glare from the low sun made aiming difficult and no definite hits were recorded before the submarine dived. The action had been inconclusive and to make matters worse their description would soon be passed to other submarines in the area, so it was time for a change of appearance. The usual method was to fill in the well with false bulwarks, erect false deck houses and add or remove the mizzen mast. In addition the ship could be repainted in a different livery. The following day the ship picked up a radio message from the Weymouth-Guernsey packet IBEX that a submarine had been spotted 20 miles South-West of the Casquets.

PENSHURST soon arrived in the area and at 1.50 p.m. a submarine was sighted on the surface about five miles to the South, but after a short time it turned East and dived. At about the same time a sea plane arrived and attacked the submarine with bombs which missed. The ship was readied for an attack using depth charges and the seaplane signalled, with the object of using it to spot the submarine for them. As it was calm, the sea plane landed alongside and arrangements were agreed for the pilot to guide them to where the submarine was thought to be. However, this was not to be, for as the seaplane took off, the engine apparently failed and it crashed into the sea. The crew were picked up in the ship's gig and one of the cargo derricks rigged to pick up the seaplane. While the crew were thus occupied, the submarine had surfaced about three and a half miles away and opened fire. Recovery of the seaplane was hastily abandoned and the PENSHURST turned away to port while the crew rushed to action stations. The gig was still in the water and so it had to be towed alongside. The submarine dived, but soon surfaced astern and so the PENSHURST turned further to port. The submarine closed slowly, firing intermittently. The ship then stopped and the usual mock "abandon ship" was enacted. Thus, two boat loads of men, the "panic party" pulled away from the ship on the starboard side. Meanwhile the gun crews were ready to open fire at a moment's notice. The submarine having spotted the boats, went across to them to get the ship's papers from the "captain". The "panic party" had this carefully rehearsed and had a full set of false papers. It worked so well that the submarine came within 250 yards of the ship without even bothering to man their guns. At that moment all the PENSHURST's guns opened fire. Large portions of the conning tower were blown away and the hull riddled with shells. After a few minutes the submarine sank, bows first. PENSHURST's boats then picked up sixteen of the German crew and learned that the submarine was UB 19 which had sailed from Zeebrugge on the 22nd of November.

After landing her prisoners, the PENSHURST was readied for another mission and was soon steaming for the Casquets area once more. On January the 14th, 1917, a submarine was spotted on the surface closing in, under two miles away. The "panic party" took their places in the lifebpats and pulled away from the now stationary PENSHURST, while the gun crews went to action stations. The submarine stopped about seven hundred yards away on the starboard bow and opened fire. The first shell did superficial damage, but one exploded among the 6-pounder gun crew which killed the gunlayer and the loader and seriously wounded two others. The other gun crews were then given the order to open fire. A shot from the 12-pounder struck the submarine's conning tower setting off some ammunition, followed by other hits which soon sank the submarine, identified as UB 37. As soon as the "panic party" were aboard, the ship headed for Portland at full speed to land the dead and wounded. The ship was soon repaired and resumed cruising in the English Channel and engaged another submarine a month later, but it escaped. At 11.34 a.m. on the 22nd of February they spotted a submarine shadowing them. The PENSHURST turned towards the submarine now known to

PENSHURST in
the Channel.

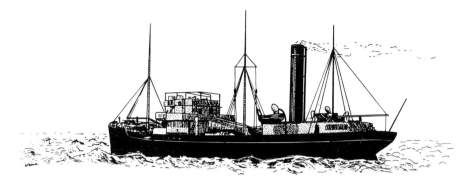

have been UB 84, but it was soon out of sight. A few minutes later an open boat was sighted and beyond, the upturned hull of the barque INVERCAULD. At the same time periscopes were observed at a short distance and the track of a torpedo. The ship was turned hard to starboard and it just missed. The submarine then surfaced and began firing and so the "panic party" pulled away while the submarine dived and made a careful inspection. The submarine then surfaced and one of the German officers ordered the lifeboats alongside. Eventually it was agreed to bring the lifeboats to the stern, thus giving the PENSHURST's gunners a clear shot. As soon as the ship opened fire, the submarine dived and then came up again with jammed hydroplanes and made off on the surface, pursued by other naval vessels attracted by firing. PENSHURST had another two indecisive engagements in July and August and in the latter was badly damaged by a torpedo and had to be towed to Portsmouth for repairs. She was ready for sea on Christmas Eve 1917 and sailed for the Irish Sea. About mid-day the lookout observed a submarine ahead, following the usual approach tactics. It then submerged and fired a torpedo which struck aft, in the engine room, bringing the PENSHURST to an immediate stop. The "panic party" were soon away in one remaining boat and liferafts. Surprisingly the submarine surfaced about 250 yards away and opened fire. Most commanders had been warned that any ship could be a Q-ship, ready to send them to the bottom. However, the PENSHURST was soon so much down by the stern that the guns could not bear on the submarine properly and few hits were scored. A patrol boat was attracted by the firing and the submarine dived. It was clear that this time the PENSHURST was doomed and so the remainder of the crew were taken off by the patrol boat. The PENSHURST sank later that evening having accounted for several enemy submarines damaged or sunk.

By the end of the First World War, LUCIENT and FLAMMA had shown themselves to be very efficient in the coal trade, so a similar, but deeper drafted vessel, was ordered from J. Crown & Sons to carry 3,020 tons on a draft of 18'10". She was named CHARTERED by the Gas, Light and Coke Company, as it had been incorporated under a Royal Charter and was often referred to as the chartered company to distinguish it more clearly from other gas companies with similar names. The vessels were under the management of Stephenson Clarke and so it was not surprising that they ordered similar vessels for their own fleet and, in particular, that of the new Normandy Shipping Company, formed in association with Powell Duffryn, to ship coal to North France.

Meanwhile Richard Hughes of Liverpool felt that there was scope for this size of vessel in the coasting and short sea trades. He began with a series of vessels of 210' and 220' in length such as the JELLICOE ROSE already mentioned. These proving successful, they were followed by the 250' long FULLERTON ROSE and LOUIE ROSE. Though the hulls were similar LOUIE ROSE (113a), had her bridge placed on the raised quarter deck rather than at the end of the well deck as was usual. As can be seen from the plan, the seamen and firemen had their accommodation aft, built out to the sides of the ship. This distinctive feature was retained in the series of four similar ships built by D. & W. Henderson & Co., Glasgow for the company beginning in 1929 with DOROTHY ROSE. The bridges in these vessels reverted to the usual position on the well deck and so presented a rather low profile.

During the early 1920s, most collier owners continued to place their faith in vessels with engines amidships and it was not until the later 1920s that France, Fenwick looked seriously at the possibility of building large colliers of around 4,000 tons deadweight with engines aft. It was generally considered by Naval Architects that to build such vessels would present both trim and strength problems. However, the Company drew up a detailed specification for an experimental ship. Contrary to previous practice, a builder was selected, approached and a price of £42,500 agreed for construction. The vessel was named CHELWOOD and delivered in 1928 by S. P. Austin and Son and had a deadweight of 4,190 tons. Hold capacity was 199,000 cubic feet giving a rate of stowage of about 50 cubic feet per ton with bunkers about three-quarters full, and so was ideal for carrying washed coal. Other owners were also moving in the same direction and Cory's first large engines-aft collier, the CORGLEN of 4,300 tons deadweight was completed in 1929 by the Cowpen Drydock and Shipbuilding Co., Ltd., Blyth.

Smaller engines-aft colliers were also built for the distributive trades where the cargoes were around 3,000 tons. By far the most numerous series of this size were built for the Cory fleet, beginning with the CORFIRTH in 1934. They had dimensions of 257.0 x 39.5 x 16.7 feet and could carry 2,650 tons on a draft of 17'4". The design proved very satisfactory and a further nine vessels were built by various yards for the Cory fleet during the next ten years. Perhaps the best known of these colliers was the series begun by ICE MAID, completed in 1936 for the Gas, Light & Coke Company. The design was adopted for the standard war built colliers of 2,900 deadweight built throughout the Second World War, to replace those lost to enemy action. The last 2,900 ton steam collier to be built was the LADY CHARRINGTON completed for the well known coal merchants, Charringtons, in 1952, (111). The crew had much improved accommodation compared with earlier vessels of the size, but the machinery in all the vessels was the well known North Eastern Marine triple expansion reheat engine.

The 4,000 ton deadweight collier was also built throughout the 1930s, particularly for supplying the needs of the gas and electricity undertakings. An example of a collier of this size was MR. THERM of 4,610 tons deadweight, completed in 1936 for the Gas, Light and Coke Co. A series of eight vessels was built between 1940 and 1941 by William Gray's yard at West Hartlepool, to help replace war losses. In the post-war rebuilding period, a series of 4,500 ton colliers was built between 1945 and 1956. Twenty eight vessels were constructed for various owners, which varied in length from 320 to 325 feet measured between perpendiculars. The first vessel delivered was the HUDSON STRAIT, completed in 1946 for the Hudson S.S. Co., followed by the HUDSON FIRTH in 1949. Most of the vessels were built for the British Electricity Authority, formed in 1948. The red funnel with a black top was adopted from the London Power Co., but the letters LPC were replaced by the letters BEA. The style was soon changed to CEA for Central Electricity Authority, but when the title was changed further to Central Electricity Generating Board, the letters were omitted from the funnels.

The lead vessel was the CLIFF QUAY, delivered by Austin & Pickergill in June 1950 and followed by five sisterships in less than a year. They presented a very modern profile and were designed from the outset to carry coal to the Lower Thames power stations and that at Ipswich. For this purpose, all cargo gear was eliminated and steel hatch covers were fitted. All had triple expansion reheat engines with the cylinders of 19", 31" and 54" in diameter and a stroke of 39". All used superheated steam at 750°F amd 220 lbs. pressure. This gave an indicated horse power of about 1,450 and a speed of about ten and a half knots. A further five vessels of slightly differing appearance and dimensions were built between 1954 and 1955, four of which had a narrower beam and lower deadweight of 3,640 tons and the higher service speed of eleven and a quarter knots, for serving Shoreham.

First of the 325 foot vessels was the BORDE, delivered to Stephenson Clarke in 1953 to be followed by two for the North Thames Gas Board who also took three of the 320 foot type. Two were also built for France, Fenwick and four more joined the Cory fleet, two of which were motor vessels, CORSEA and CORSTAR. Though the hulls were all built to the same basic model, the superstructure differed in design and masts were fitted in different positions, to suit the different owners. The BORDE was the only vessel in the series designed with full cargo gear of two derricks per hatch, but in service only had one per hatch, which was usually stowed vertically without being rigged. Four cargo winches were grouped round each mast and they proved very useful for discharging her cargo into 'puffers' when she ran aground in the Clyde on one occasion. A sistership, ARUNDEL (124,133), the last steam ship in the series, was completed in November 1956 for Stephenson Clarke, who had arranged a long term charter for her to the Central Electricity Authority. ARUNDEL is also illustrated as running on her last cargo-carrying voyage for Stephenson Clarke in 1972 (6). The main additions were the various aerials, including those for television for the crew. It will also be noted that the funnel design was changed after the general arrangement drawing (124) was completed and the lifeboats were also fitted a few inches further aft. The accommodation was however, as shown on the plan and may be taken as typical of these large post-war colliers. The officers had a lounge with settee, tables, chairs, T.V. and a rug on the lino floor. On the forward bulkhead a picture of Mrs. Eccles was hung. She had launched the ARUNDEL on the 25th of July 1956. The bulkheads were all lined with wood-grained plastic. All officers' cabins had running water piped to the hand basins, a later addition, not shown on the plans. The engineers' accommodation was similar, with hard wearing plastic matting on the floor which was also used for the passageways in the officers' accommodation. A liberal supply of doormats at entrances helped keep coal dust out. Crew cabins were also lined, but floors

(111) *s.s. LADY CHARRINGTON*

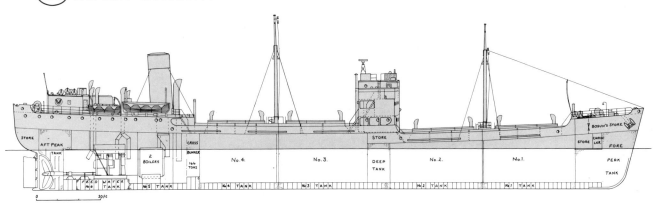

were cement with a covering of red rubber composition. As bedding was provided by the company, the blue and white bedspreads appropriately had the company monogram 'S.C.' worked into them. The ARUNDEL's last cargo-carrying voyages for Stepehnson Clarke may be taken as typical for these large colliers.

It is the morning of the 5th of June 1972 and the ARUNDEL is approaching the Tyne from Dagenham. There is a cargo suitable for her at Harton Staiths, but back in the London office of Stephenson Clarke, the continental fixture for STORRINGTON is still not finalised and if it falls through, then STORRINGTON will take the coal cargo and the ARUNDEL will be laid up in the Tyne. However, by the time ARUNDEL picks up the Tyne pilot, STORRINGTON's continental voyage is assured and ARUNDEL goes to Harton Buoys to await loading. Here she is secured to buoys fore and aft, parallel with Harton Staiths, alongside the collier SIR WILLIAM WALKER. By the following evening the ASHINGTON, which has been loading at the staiths, is almost full. The work boats of the two colliers moored to the buoys, ferry those going ashore for a drink, to the quay. In ARUNDEL the mate is in charge of the watch aboard, with the second engineer. Most of the crew are local and the crew is roughly divided into two watches and they take it in turns to go ashore and so they get home every other voyage, apart from the usual leave. The work boats pick up those ashore about 10 p.m. The following day, the ASHINGTON leaves and the SIR WILLIAM WALKER is warped across to begin loading. Meanwhile the mate of the ARUNDEL has gone ashore to find out when the ship will be loading. It is a fine day with a gentle breeze and there will be no problem warping the ARUNDEL across to the staiths. At 2.30 p.m. warping wires are run out to the staith and great care is taken to ensure that the forward wire is on the bottom as the SIR WILLIAM WALKER will pass over it on sailing. She does so at 4.00 p.m. as soon as her hatches are closed up. ARUNDEL starts to haul in on her wires about 15 minutes later. The mate, assisted by two of the crew, handles the forward wire on the forecastle, using the warping ends of the anchor windlass. Aft, the bosun is assisted by an A.B. with the after wire. Hauling in on the wires starts as soon as the boatman has released the mooring wires, which secure the ship to the buoys. As she is bows on to the tide, the boatman releases the stern wire first. He then moves round to the bows and unscrews that shackle, but although the wire has been released from the wire compressor, there is still some tension on it and the shackle pin is yanked out of the boatman's hand and is lost. It takes about 15 minutes for the ARUNDEL to be hauled over to the quay. The tug NORTHSIDER returns from turning the SIR WILLIAM WALKER and gives the bows of the ARUNDEL a friendly nudge in towards the quay, and then ties up ahead of her. Other wires are now run out along the staith so that the ship can be moved along to suit the coal shoots. After a few minutes, loading begins and small coal in which there is much slack, pours into holds two and four. After a while the ship is moved so that coal can be put into holds one and three. At about 6.00 p.m. the mate goes round and says the ship will be sailing at 10.00 a.m. the following day. The captain and the remainder of the crew come aboard the following morning while the loading has been in full swing again, since 6.00 a.m.

As the water rises towards the load line, the mate watches the marks carefully. The third hold is now full and the hatch is closed by the seamen as loading of hold number one continues and the mate watches the stem marks. He then asks for more to be loaded into number four hold and this is loaded while the mate watches the load line amidships. The coal trimmers level off the coal in the forward holds and shovel the spillage from the shoots off the deck. As soon as this is done, the seamen close the hatches, but first they sweep any remaining coal from the coamings so that the steel hatches will roll into place properly. Meanwhile the last coal for number four hold is loaded and the hatch closed up while the mate goes ashore to find out how many tons have been taken on. Meanwhile the pilot has come aboard and the captain, who has changed out of his suit into a sweater and slacks, joins the pilot on the bridge and at 11.15 p.m. the mooring lines are cast off. Prior to this a towing wire had been passed to the tug KING GEORGE V. The mate, on the forecastle, then supervises casting off. The tug pulls the tow off the quay and moves slowly ahead and round in an arc to turn ARUNDEL for the voyage down river. The pilot rings slow ahead on the engine room telegraph. As soon as the ship is clear of the next collier waiting to load, the pilot calls to the tug 'let go your tow' and the wire is cast off to be recovered by the mate and A.B. on the forecastle. Full speed ahead is then rung up on the engine room telegraph and the pilot boat comes out to meet the ship. After carefully adjusting its speed to that of

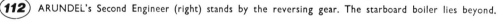

112 ARUNDEL's Second Engineer (right) stands by the reversing gear. The starboard boiler lies beyond.

s.s. "LOUIE ROSE."

a.

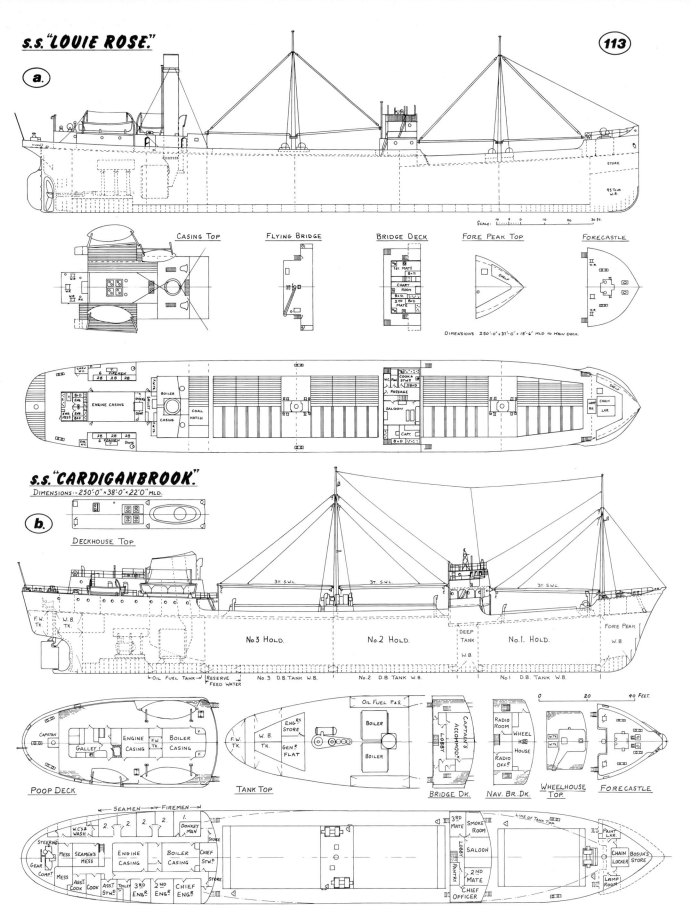

CASING TOP   FLYING BRIDGE   BRIDGE DECK   FORE PEAK TOP   FORECASTLE

DIMENSIONS 250'-0" x 37'-0" x 18'-6" MLD TO MAIN DECK.

s.s. "CARDIGANBROOK"

DIMENSIONS :- 250'-0" x 38'-0" x 22'0" MLD.

b.

DECKHOUSE TOP

POOP DECK   TANK TOP   BRIDGE DK.   NAV. BR. DK.   WHEELHOUSE TOP.   FORECASTLE

the ship, it bumps gently against the side and the pilot steps on to it. ARUNDEL passes between the Tyne piers at 11.45 a.m. out into a calm hazy North Sea. This is recorded in the
ship's log as 'steering course 114°, wind SW force 1, sea SE, temp 54°F, visibility fine/
hazy'. Up till now an A.B. has been at the wheel, but the autopilot is now set to 114°, but
the ship fails to hold the course, so the engineers are told this and they inspect the electro-
hydraulic steering gear. A relief A.B. takes the wheel at 12.00 and remarks that it does not
feel quite the same as usual. Meanwhile the steward has rung the bell for lunch. The captain
takes the head of the table and the second mate is left in charge on the bridge. By now, the
engineers have located a loose bolt in the steering and corrected the fault. The breeze
freshens and a few thundery showers are met before ARUNDEL passes Flamborough Head

at 6.40 p.m. At 11.45 p.m. ARUNDEL passes Dowsing Light vessel and as she does so the WILMINGTON overtakes, bound for Dagenham also. By the time ARUNDEL reaches Haiseborough Sand, it is overcast and the breeze is freshening from the South West with frequent showers. The wind is against the tide and some of the larger waves send a plume of spray over the forecastle. ARUNDEL heads for Barrow Deep Channel as the tide will give sufficient water for her. At 1.45 p.m. the mate calls Tilbury Radio for orders. They reply that the ship is to proceed to Erith Buoys. The weather improves and at 3.00 p.m. the mate calls the bosun to clear the anchors. The bosun goes on to the forecastle and takes the claws, stops and covers off the hawse pipes. At 4.15 p.m. ARUNDEL passes Southend and reports her position to Southend Radio. By 6.00 p.m. ARUNDEL is off Gravesend and the river pilot boards to take her up to Erith where she arrives an hour later. By this time she has overtaken the tide which is still on the ebb at Erith. However, it will turn in a few minutes and so the pilot decides to swing ARUNDEL so that she will be facing the incoming tide during mooring operations. As the current runs fastest on the outside of the bend, the ship is brought up on the inside of the bend and the bows turned into the faster flowing water which helps to turn the ship, but on this occasion it was not to be. The pilot, having arrived at the turning point, stepped out on to the bridge wing, looked to see if the 'D' ring on the end of the wire was actually connected to the whistle and then pulled on it five times to warn other shipping of the impending manoeuvre. He then stepped back into the wheelhouse and ordered the turn to port to begin. ARUNDEL responds and comes to lie across the river, meanwhile full astern is rung on the engine room telegraph. The ship shudders to a stop and begins to go astern. This is repeated a number of times, but by now the tide has turned and it is soon clear that she is not coming round any further. Reluctantly, the anchor is let go and the ship slowly swings round it to face the incoming tide. The anchor is then hauled up and the ARUNDEL moves slowly up to the mooring buoy at the bow, just stemming the tide, and the mate on the forecastle passes the mooring wire down to the waiting boatman who shackles it to the buoy. This done, the stern wire is made fast. The operation is complete when two wires have been made fast to both bow and stern. The signal 'finished with engines' is particularly welcome down below, as they have been hard pressed to keep up with the string of engine orders, each of which has to be entered in the engine room log with the time. This is done by the chief engineer while the second engineer hauls away on the reversing gear and the donkeyman looks to anything else needing attention (112).

By now it is 7.50 p.m. and the boatman takes the pilot and members of the crew going ashore. Saturday is a calm fine day and at 10.15 the bunkering barge BATSMAN comes up river and crosses over to the ARUNDEL. One of the crew jumps aboard, makes fast, and then connects up the pipe. The order is for 50 tons of boiler oil and bunkering is completed by 11.15 a.m. At about 12.45 the boatman arrives to take off-duty crew members ashore. At 1.45 p.m. a second bunkering barge arrives with the gas oil needed for the diesel generator. By this time the chief, second and third engineers have completed overhauling the port generator and it is now running with the starboard generator on stand-by. At 6.00 p.m. the donkeyman starts the diesel generator, stops the steam generator, shuts down the boiler furnaces for the night and closes up the engine room to keep the heat in and so reduce heat losses from the boilers. The safety valve blows off a little, some time after shutting down, which does not please anyone as the ship is low on water already. Sunday is fine with a light breeze and at 6.00 a.m. the ship's night watchman goes off duty. At 9.00 a.m. the mate calls Tilbury Radio and asks them to call Fords at Dagenham to find out when the ARUNDEL will be going alongside to discharge. The message comes back that they will be ready at about 2.30 p.m. By 3.30 p.m. the pilot is aboard and the moorings are singled up, at 3.45 p.m. the moorings are cast off and by 4.30 the ship is alongside at Dagenham. The vessel is ready for immediate discharge as the hatches were opened on arrival off Erith. Grab discharge begins about 15 minutes after arrival. The crane driver is careful and so there is unlikely to be any damage for the foreman and mate to agree on. All damage due to grab discharge is traditionally the responsibility of the receiver, in this case Fords. Clumsy crane drivers have knocked mast tops off occasionally.

All the colliers built for the London coal trade after 1956 were motor vessels such as the CORSEA. This collier, built by the Burntisland Shipbuilding Company was very similar to the ARUNDEL but had five holds, three of which were on the raised quarter deck. Bulwarks were dispensed with and replaced by open rails. The main engine was a Sulzer 2-stroke unit of 1,430 b.h.p. giving a service speed of 10 knots. They were fitted for more general trading and had awning supports for use in hot climates for example. CORSTAR was the first large motor collier to join the Cory fleet and their first collier to cross the Atlantic, sailing for Philadelphia on the 9th of December 1956. In the latter part of the 1940s most of the smaller colliers were built for Stephenson Clarke who favoured motor vessels.

However, some owners were still not convinced that motor ships were the answer and in 1952 Comben Longstaff took delivery of the CARDIFFBROOK and CARDIGANBROOK (113b). The hulls were identical, but the former was a motor vessel. The steamer carried 4 tons less cargo, giving it a deadweight of 2,268 tons on the summer draft of 16'11", and so not significantly different, but the extra space needed for the boilers reduced the cubic capacity of the after hold by 2,620 cubic feet. John Lewis, the builders, provided the triple expansion engine of 1,150 i.h.p., which gave a service speed of 11½ knots. One further steamship was built for Longstaff's in 1954, but thereafter the change over to motor ships was rapid. It is interesting to contrast the streamlined CARDIGANBROOK with the LOUIE ROSE built 27 years earlier and of the same length (113). Hughes themselves had the slightly smaller RAMBLER ROSE built by John Lewis in 1954 to a similar streamlined design but she was a motorship.

11.

(115) Steam Tanker ONEIDA.

Coastal Tankers

Coastal tankers were a later specialised development of the steam coaster and did not become significant in the coasting trades until the 1920s. The first tankers were all ocean-going vessels built to carry refined oil products from the oil fields of North America and the Black Sea area, to Europe, in the latter part of the 19th Century. Originally the oil was carried in barrels, mainly in sailing ships, because of the fire risks associated with steam. However, this was costly and there were always problems with leaking barrels. To overcome this difficulty, large tanks were fitted in the holds. This also made loading and unloading much simpler, as the cargo could be quickly pumped in and out. Finally the ship's hull itself was used for the cargo tank and the first tank steamers were built during the 1880s. Their construction necessitated a very high standard of riveting, if oil and explosive gases given off by the cargo were not to find their way into the boiler room and cause an explosion. To prevent this happening, the cargo tanks were separated from other parts of the ship by narrow void spaces, known as coffer dams, at least two frame spaces wide (118). Because the ships were riveted there was always the danger of leaks, especially if the vessels were subjected to stresses in heavy seas. The cofferdams were either filled with water, which tends to force the oil back into the tanks, or left empty so that any seepage could be more immediately observed. In either case the cofferdams were frequently inspected for leaks and if the amount was significant, it was pumped back into the cargo tanks.

Another problem encountered in early tankers was that of stability when filling the tanks. If the ship took a slight list when a tank had been partly filled, the oil flowed in the direction of the list and could capsize the vessel if the tanks were not divided to minimise the effect. This is why an oil-tight central bulkhead is always fitted. Also it was essential to fill the tanks completely or the oil could surge about damaging the sides of the tanks. However this was not practical, as oil expands on a hot day and allowance for this must be made. The extra capacity for this expansion is often provided in a trunk above the main deck of the ship (116). As liquid cargoes exert more pressure on the sides of the hull than dry cargoes, their construction is different from that of dry cargo ships. Instead of vertical framing, horizontal framing is used in the tanks and is referred to as the Isherwood system after the inventor, Isherwood. One of the earliest coastal and short sea steam tankers appears to have been ALCYHMIST, completed in 1895 by W. Dobson & Co., Newcastle with the dimensions 147.5' x 24.1' x 12.8'. She had five tanks with a small dry cargo hold forward and could carry a total of about 480 tons of cargo. The triple expansion engine gave about nine knots on a consumption of about 5/6 tons of coal a day. The tanker, designed to carry tar in bulk, and so was fitted with steam heating coils to keep the cargo liquid, was built for London owners Burt, Boulton & Haywood. By this time, tar had become an important by-product of the London gas works. In service, she carried various cargoes and ventured outside home trade limits.

The most important derivatives of mineral oil carried at this time were paraffin and lubricating oils. Lighter fractions, such as petroleum, were just coming into use for the internal combustion engine. During the next 20 years, the development of the motor car completely changed the picture. Petroleum was needed in all parts of the country in increasing amounts. Ocean-going tankers brought in refined products for the most part to tank farms set up near the main ports. Much of the distribution was by rail, but demand soon became sufficient to make it more economical to use small coasting tankers to supply the smaller ports. One of the first coasting tankers built for this work was the ONEIDA (115), completed in 1908 by the Grangemouth Dockyard for the Anglo-American Oil Company, now known as ESSO. She had a deadweight of 741 tons on a draft of 12'1", part of the deadweight being taken up by bunker coal which was still cheaper than oil as a fuel. All the early steam tankers were coal fired and it was not until the 1920s that a change was made to oil firing. One of ONEIDA's runs was to the oil depot at Caernarvon opened just prior to the First World War. During the First World War, the internal combustion engine made great strides, particularly in aircraft. Though much of the fuel was imported, the National Benzole Company utilised the light fractions produced as a by-product in the production of coal gas. To distribute these fuel products, two tankers were completed for the Company in 1923, the larger of which, BEN READ was built by Charles Hill of Bristol. Both were fitted to use oil fuel rather than coal and so reduce the danger of sparks. One interesting feature of BEN READ (116a) was the

116a BEN READ Registered dimensions were 159.0' x 27.6' x 12.1'.

extension of the well deck aft, on either side of the bridge structure, protected by bulwarks. In 1919 the ALCHYMIST was purchased by F. T. Everard and Sons Ltd., with a view to entering the fish and vegetable oil trades. Her tanks were specially prepared and steam heating coils in the tanks made it possible to carry edible oils at a temperature suitable for easy pumping in and out. ALCHYMIST proved so successful that four new tankers were built for the trade during the 1920s. The most important cargo for the ships was whale oil imported from Norway. The demand for coastal tankers rose quite rapidly during the 1920s and one way to meet this demand was converting existing dry cargo ships. This method was employed by both the oil companies themselves and other shipowners attracted by the favourable freight rates being obtained by tankers in the coasting and short sea trades.

One such vessel converted was the steam coaster EASTWICK (116b) which had been built in 1920 by Swan, Hunter & Wigham Richardson for the Anglo-American Oil Co., Ltd. The arrangement of the tanks was sketched on the original drawing, from which the illustration is taken. A variety of tank sizes have been arranged between the pump room and the small cargo hold forward so that a number of different parcels of oil can be carried. The dry cargo hold forward is left empty when the ship is to carry a full oil cargo as the vessel would be down to her marks with the tanks full. One of the shipowners attracted by the favourable rates offered to tankers was the London firm C. Rowbotham & Sons, at the end of the First World War, who were looking to other trades with the rapid falling off in Admiralty work in which they had specialised. The small 20 year old steamer LOCHSIDE was purchased and, in 1927, converted into a tanker by Clelands yard on the Tyne. Unfortunately she was lost soon after entering the tanker trades, on a voyage from the Medway to Stockton, in one of the worst storms for many years. No trace of the ship or her crew was ever found. However, the conversion had been successful and the larger steamer CLYDEBURN, 594 gross, was purchased in 1928, converted and renamed STEERSMAN. This was so successful that the first new tanker TILLERMAN, a motor vessel, was built in Holland for the company in 1931. The only coastal liner company to become interested in tankers was the Dundee, Perth & London Shipping company who had the coaster BROUGHTY fitted with large tanks amidships in the 1920s, so that she was half tanker and half dry cargo. She then carried batching oil, a spindle oil used in the jute mills of Dundee, from the Thames where it was loaded from barges after her general cargo had been loaded. On her southward runs, she carried 'basis material' from Briggs' in Dundee for making up into printing ink on arrival in London. This was possible as the tanks had steam heating coils. Two large Weir-type steam pumps salvaged from the German battleships scuttled at Scapa flow were fitted on deck to handle the cargo. The thump of these could be heard all over the docks when the BROUGHTY was discharging.

Another company to enter the oil trades in the 1920s was J. W. Cook & Co., of London, who formed the Bulk Oil S.S. at this time. Their first tanker, PASS OF BRANDER was a

116b EASTWICK
Coaster to Tanker Conversion.

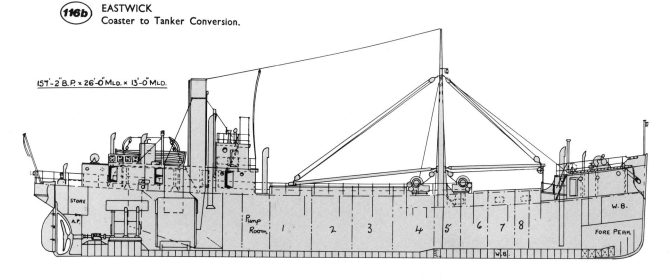

157'-2" B.P. x 26'-0" MLD. x 13'-0" MLD.

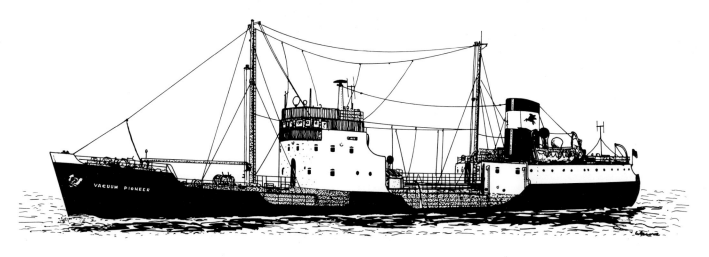

(117) VACUUM PIONEER measured 245'0"x 40'0"x 16'6" moulded.

coaster converted to carry lubricating or heavy fuel oils. This ship was successful and a new clean products tanker (petrol, etc.) was completed by the Blythswood Shipbuilding Co., Ltd. of Glasgow in 1926. This was the trunk decked steam tanker PASS OF MELFORT which could carry 840 tons on a draft of 13 feet. The funnel was fitted with a fine wire mesh spark arrester as she was a coal burner (23). The design was very satisfactory and further vessels of the same design, each a little larger than the previous vessel, joined the fleet. The last vessel in the series, PASS OF BALMAHA measuring 192.2'x 30.4'x 13.9', was chosen as the prototype for one group of tankers built during the Second World War. In all, 23 vessels were built based on the design, between 1941 and 1945. All had what was by then the rather old fashioned counter stern and triple expansion steam machinery giving a speed of $9\frac{1}{2}$ knots. However, in war-time the triple expansion machinery was easier to make and maintain than diesel machinery.

By far the most numerous of the coasting tankers were the Chant type of which 43 were built during the Second World War. They were all completed during 1944 to take part in the Normandy landings and most passed to foreign owners at the end of the War. As the European war drew to a close, more of the construction work in the shipyards was directed towards the Japanese theatre of operations. A special series of tankers, based on the dimensions of the Pass of Balmaha type was constructed. They were very different in appearance as they were built without sheer and had a massive bridge structure straddling the trunk deck amidships and were intended to have a large Asian crew, hence the extra accommodation. The Japanese surrender came before the 20 tankers saw more than a few months service at best and some were still incomplete when offered for sale. By far the largest number were taken up by Everards. Two types had been built, the TED (Tanker, Eastern, Diesel) and the TES (Tanker, Eastern, Steam). Everards owned 8 of the diesel type eventually (133), Plate 93. One, launched as the EMPIRE TEDSON was awaiting fitting out at the Grangemouth Dockyard. She was completed, with modifications for Everards and when fitted out for the smaller European crew, it was possible for all to have single berth cabins. All the vessels had steam heating coils fitted to the cargo tanks which were supplied with steam by twin oil-fired 'Scotch' boilers. The main engine was a British Polar two stroke unit of 640 b.h.p. The vessels were well suited to Everards' interests in the edible oil trades and AMITY carried the first cargo of edible lard from Brussels to Liverpool, in the post-war period.

Other owners to take up war-built vessels, included the Bulk Oil S.S. Co., Shell-Mex and British Petroleum. Though a number of smaller oil-engined tankers had been built in the war years, apart from the Chants, some owners preferred to have tankers specially built to suit their trades. One such owner was the National Benzole Company for whom the BEN HEBDEN was completed in November 1947 (119a). The vessel, built by the Rowhedge Ironworks Co., Ltd., was a slightly larger version of the BEN HENSHAW, which the yard had produced in 1933. She was fitted to carry a cargo of 340 tons of petroleum in eight tanks. A bunker capacity of 38 tons was provided for the British Polar engine which developed 560 b.h.p. at 375 r.p.m. For cargo handling, a Worthington-Simpson duplex pimp was fitted in the pump room. The pump was driven by one of the auxiliary diesels in the engine room by means of a shaft passing through the bunker tank. In this respect the steam tank vessel was at an advantage, for steam could easily be piped to the pump room to drive the pumps and was ideal where a fire risk was involved. Pipes connecting the pump room to the tanks are usually run along the deck close to the center line. The piping and pumping arrangements depend on how many different products requiring to be kept apart are carried at the same time.

Almost the last of the British steam coastal tankers to be built was the VACUUM PIONEER (117). She was completed in 1953 by the Grangemouth Dockyard Co., Ltd., for the Vacuum Oil Company which later became Mobil Oil. She had steam heating coils and was built mainly to carry lubricating oils from the Mobil Refinery at Purfleet on the Thames, to various distribution centres round the coast, such as that at Birkenhead. She was managed by Stephenson Clarke for seventeen years and, ironically, was lost in collision with one of their own colliers, WORTHING, off Haiseborough Sand on the 13th of November 1970. She

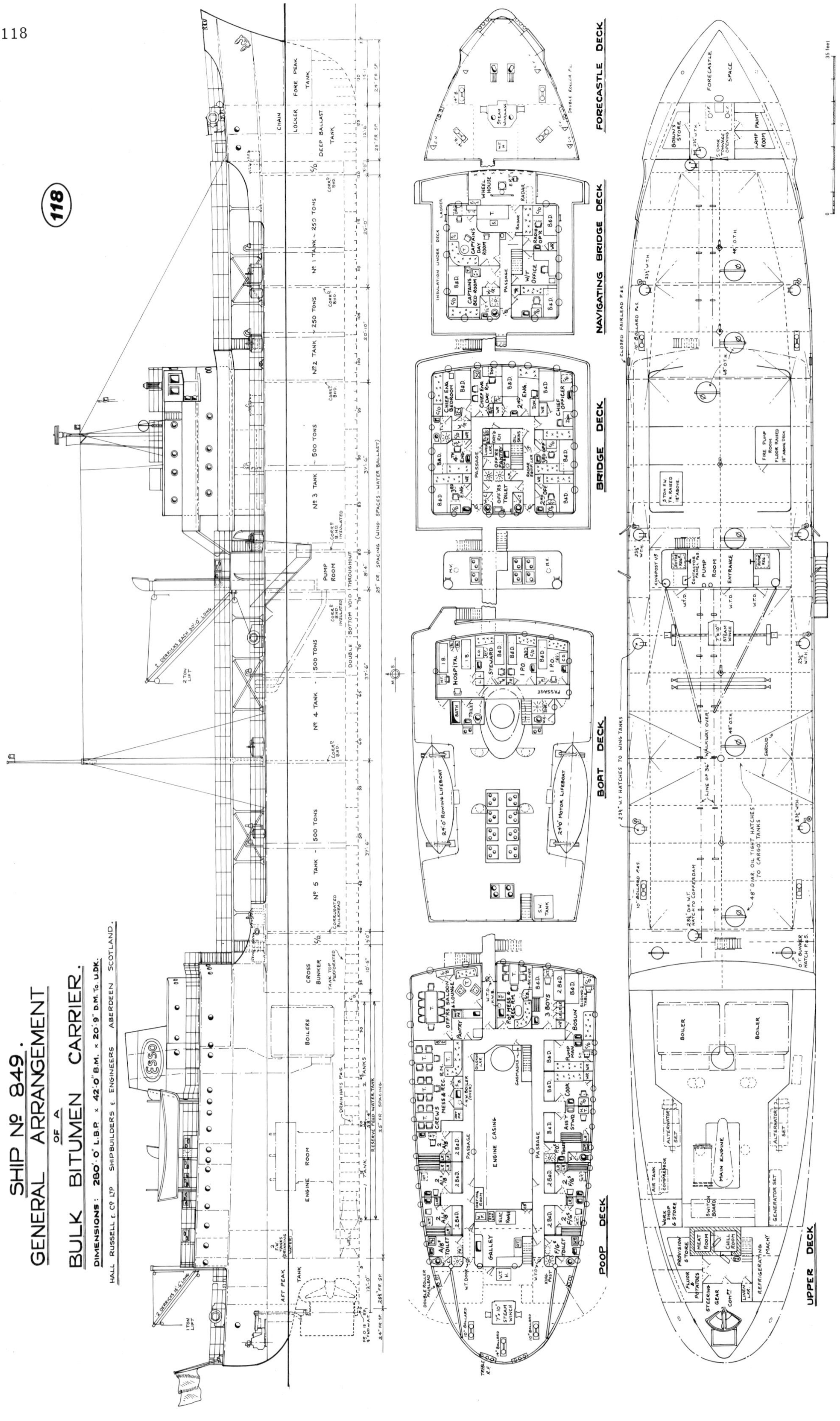

SHIP Nº 849.
GENERAL ARRANGEMENT
OF A
BULK BITUMEN CARRIER.

DIMENSIONS: 280'0" L.B.P. x 42'0" B.M. x 20'9" D.M. TO U.DK.

HALL RUSSELL & Cº LTD SHIPBUILDERS & ENGINEERS ABERDEEN SCOTLAND.

118

FORECASTLE DECK

NAVIGATING BRIDGE DECK

BRIDGE DECK

BOAT DECK

POOP DECK

UPPER DECK

Motor Tanker BEN HEBDEN
DIMS: 135'0"x 25'0"x 12'0" MLD.

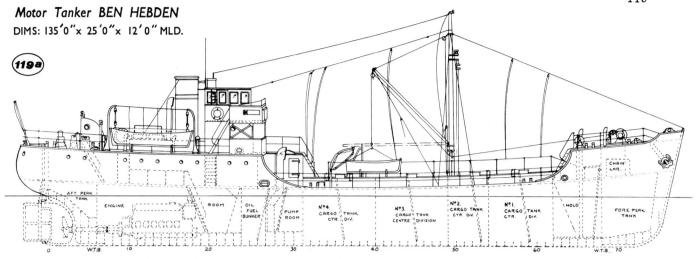

119a

was a constructive total loss and she arrived at Blyth a few days later to be broken up. The last to be built was the ESSO PRESTON, completed in 1956 by Hall, Russell & Co., Ltd. of Aberdeen. She was specially built to carry bitumen cargoes from the ESSO refinery at Milford Haven to Preston docks for use in the manufacture of road surfacing materials. Since bitumen needs to be kept hot and steam heating coils and their associated boilers were essential, a simpler engine room layout is possible using a steam main engine. As can be seen from the plan (118), the cargo tanks are separated from the sides by narrow wing tanks which can be used for water ballast. Unlike many tankers, a double bottom is incorporated and is not used. However, when carrying cargo, this void space in the double bottom and the wing tanks empty of ballast form an effective insulating air gap between the hot cargo and the much cooler sea. The accommodation follows a similar style to that seen in the colliers except that the messes for the officers, engineers and crew are all arranged aft making the serving of meals much easier than the colliers where the food had to be taken along the open deck to the officers' saloon amidships. The engineers were not so lucky as they had the open catwalk to traverse in order to reach their cabins amidships. ESSO PRESTON carried 2,790 tons on a maximum draught of 17'4¼" at a service speed of 10½ knots.

119b MAGGIE on her trials, 1907.

12.

Owners & Trades

Coasting owners usually originated from three sources, Merchants, Shipping Agents or Sea Captains. In each case they were well aware of the potential cargoes available for ships. Where a Merchant had regular cargoes to be moved, it was logical to own the ship and similarly Shipping Agents who had a variety of cargoes notified to them, often found it good business to have ships available to carry them. While Newcastle and London owners mainly controled the larger vessels in the coasting trade, Liverpool became the centre for the smaller steamers used in the Irish Sea Trades. Towards the latter part of the 19th century, Liverpool was firmly established in the ocean trades with America, from which raw cotton and tobacco were imported, while trade with Africa was on the increase. The ocean vessels carried a great variety of manufactured goods outwards and these were often delivered to the steamers by coasters. Similarly, cargoes of grain arriving at Liverpool were loaded into coasting vessels for delivery to mills adjacent to the smaller harbours around the Irish Sea. As Ireland has virtually no coal, steam coasters found ready employment taking coal from England, Wales and Scotalnd to Ireland. However, the sailing schooner was not easily displaced by steam coasters which were initially very much more expensive to build. At first the steam coasters were largely confined to numerous local regular liner-type services operated by equally numerous owners, which slowly came together to form Coast Lines in later years. Their services were largely aimed at livestock, general cargo of a manufactured nature and sometimes passengers as well. Though by the latter part of the 19th century passenger vessels were usually specially built for the passenger trade. One of the first men to see the advantage of steam for the bulk trades to Liverpool was Richard Hughes whose first steamer was the PANSY built in 1885. In the short space of 15 years a further 9 vessels were added to the fleet, largest of which was a new PANSY of 750 tons deadweight built in 1898. The smaller vessels were employed in the local stone and coal trade and the larger vessels carried china clay from Cornwall to Runcorn. The company advertised a regular steam service to Plymouth and Fowey for any cargoes offering for the return voyage southwards. By 1918 the fleet had grown to 14 ships and was jokingly referred to as the 'Welsh Navy', which was given more substance by the fact that many of the crews came from Anglesey. By this time, the china clay trade was so important for the company that they had an office in Fowey. Mr. Hughes was among those convinced that at the end of the First World War cargoes would be larger and ordered larger ships, at the high prices then prevailing. The entire fleet, excluding the new ships, was sold in March 1920 to a group led by Owen Donnelly, a coal merchant of Dublin and H. Leeson of John Edwards & Co., Liverpool, who had owned the old coaster KEMPOCK. They were financed by Irish Banks, but they were soon in difficulties and the fleet was sold back to Hughes, and Donnelly returned to operating a few small old coasters on the Dublin coal run. Between 1920 and 1925 eight large coasters were delivered, the last of which was the FULLERTON ROSE of 2,500 deadweight. He was now faced with making the ships pay for themselves on freight rates which had slumped to levels undreamed of a few years earlier. Stores were strictly controlled and crews had to make every drop of paint count. However, LOUIE ROSE, (104) 2,500 deadweight, was chartered for a regular steel contract, running Ghent to Bristol Channel Ports or Birkenhead, then coal from Bristol Channel to Continent. Smaller vessels such as WILD ROSE 873/21 were carrying coal to France and returning with flintstones from Treport to Weston Point for example, for use in glass making. China clay was also shipped to the Continent. By 1929 the company had reached a low ebb and was taken over by Martin's Bank. As prices for second hand ships were very low, the Bank continued to trade them under the management of Mr. Tom Tierney, the company later being reconstructed as R. Hughes & Co. (Liverpool) Ltd. in 1935. Because building prices had dropped, the company had ordered further large ships just prior to its collapse and these six vessels were delivered, the last of which was completed in 1931. By careful management, the Bank was paid off and Mr. Tierney took over the fleet himself, before selling out to Swansea owners in 1952. In later years names ending in 'rose' were usual, the ships built after the First World War commemorated various Admirals, while others were named after places in North Wales such as AMLWCH ROSE. Anglesey had long provided sailors for the coasting trades and it was normal for captains and mates to find places for boys from their own villages and in this way the whole crew sometimes came from one locality. There was little work in Anglesey at that time and tales of sea voyages soon interested the boys in a seafaring life. Conditions were hard in the 1920s and an Able Seaman got about £2-16-0 a week out of which he provided his own food and bedding, often a sack of straw from a local farm. Food was usually anything that could be quickly cooked in a frying pan. Two or three men often put money into a food kitty and took it in turns to buy rations when in port.

Perhaps the most meteoric rise on the Liverpool coasting scene was that of the Rowland family, who, commencing with the little steamer LADY KATE 131/81 in 1886, had no less than 13 ships by 1899 while Alfred Rowland had acquired 9 ships. Williams' ships mostly had girls' names such as GERTIE. His larger single hatch, long well deck coasters were designed to load gravel alongside dredgers and some were fitted with simple steam jet operated water ejectors to dump overside the water draining out of the gravel. The gravel was used in such projects as the construction of Brombrough dock. Alfred's coasters were named after such well known sea marks as BELL ROCK 368/93 and BISHOP ROCK 495/95, each owned by a 'single ship company'. Alfred's larger coasters soon established themselves in the important salt trade from Weston Point to East Coast fishing ports. After discharging salt, outward cargoes such as flour, grain and cattle food were loaded. All the coasters were sold during the First World War including those of William Rowland which had passed to Alfred some years before. A few larger coasters were operated during and after the war, but all were sold by the mid-1920s. The dispersal of Rowlands' coasters was taken advantage of by other local owners such as Joseph Monks, another master mariner, who resided at Warrington at the head of the Mersey estuary. The construction of the Manchester Ship canal meant a considerable increase in trading prospects for such local owners. The first ship in which Captain Monks held an interest was HELVETIA 189/92, built for Monks, Hall & Co., Atherton Quay. The principal of this Warrington firm was Frederick Monks, but they were not closely related. Joseph Monks held 16 of the 64 shares (into which all ships were still divided at this time). He sold his interest in January 1894 in order to purchase the iron steam flat IRIS and start his own fleet. He soon sold a half share in this ship to Tom Pierpoint, his son-in-law. The new venture prospered and the similar PERU was acquired in 1897. Weaver flats such as these were not usually traded outside river limits, but under Captain Monks they made short coasting voyages. PERU foundered in July 1899 on one such voyage from Fleetwood to Liverpool with gravel. It was suggested that the 200 tons of gravel she had loaded was too much for her. The first news of the loss came when the crew struggled into Lytham in the ship's boat. In 1897 also, members of the families, Monks, Pierpoint, Tanner and Tilling decided to form a shipowning company, Joseph Monks & Co., Ltd. They concentrated on the local stone trade and coal to smaller Irish ports, owning 14 steamers by 1908. The usual pattern was coal to Ireland and then in ballast to the quarry jetties of North Wales such as Nant or Carreg-y-llam on the Lleyn Peninsula. The stone was taken to Liverpool, Manchester, Preston or Glasson Dock (near Lancaster). The new company ordered 4 coasters from Scott & Sons which were launched in 1899 and given girls' names. They were little bigger than flats but were better sea boats. Soon well established in the local trades, slightly larger vessels followed such as DAISY 297/04 which could carry 350 tons. In 1919 this company was sold to Monroe Bros, but the Monks continued to be connected with the local coasting trade as a second company had been formed by two of Joseph's sons in 1907. Family and friends subscribed the £20,000 capital for J.H. Monks (Preston) Ltd. as construction of the first coaster was put in hand by Scott's yard and launched as the MAGGIE (119b). After two years in Preston the brothers returned to Liverpool and expanded steadily and had 11 ships by 1917, though the MAGGIE had been lost on a voyage from Youghal to Fleetwood in ballast. Another loss was J.H. Monks who died leaving his brother J.S. Monks at the 'helm' and this is why the company changed to J.S. Monks Ltd. in 1923. During the First World War their coaster SUZETTA was among vessels requisitioned for the Dardenelles campaign. When the evacuation took place, she loaded stores, guns and 300 Turkish prisoners bound for Port Said. Unfortunately a wire caught in the propellor, but although under enemy fire, the chief engineer jumped into the water armed with a crowbar and managed to free it sufficiently for her to get away and reach Port Said. The machinery had been badly strained and she had to limp on to Bombay where she was finally drydocked, the remaining wire removed and the machinery repaired. Prior to the war, the important contract for carrying for the Workington Iron & Steel Co. had been secured, but during the war had been suspended. However, it was regained in 1919 and remained with the company until it was wound up in 1963. Like all coasting companies they had their share of losses, which often as not happened in fog, especially before the days of radar. By an odd chance two vessels were lost in separate collisions on the 31st August of 1931. Their largest steamer, SHOREHAM 805/14, bound from Cardiff to Rouen with coal and CLARETTA 519/96 from Port Talbot to Honfleur, also with coal, were both sunk off Trevose Head, Cornwall; the former by ANNIK and the latter by BORDERLAND in thick fog. Apart from these losses the company were able to weather the slump and the fleet was increased slowly, reaching 19 vessels by 1938. Apart from the coal trade the company also accepted grain overside from ocean steamers for delivery within home trade limits and handled gravel supplies from Fleetwood, a trade in which they had begun. In the post-war period coal and steel kept the fleet occupied which had been reduced to 8 ships by 1958 as the older vessels were scrapped and by 1963 the falling freight rates and rising bunker costs made the last steamers uneconomic and the company went into liquidation. Returning now to Joseph Monks' fleet which was offered for sale in 1919, Mr. Monroe, who had sold his interest in Monroe, Rutherford & Co., to join the Army in the First World War, had returned to Cardiff and on hearing of the sale promptly travelled to Liverpool and purchased the company. At first the fleet was managed from Monroe Bros'., office in Cardiff until a Liverpool office could be opened. Monroes' first coasters were small and worked in the Irish coal trade and the North Wales stone trade. Approaches to these ports were often difficult and groundings inevitably occurred. The little steamer ADMIRAL was holed on one occasion and the water began to gain on the pumps and then suddenly to drop, much to everyone's relief and then their surprise when it was found that a fish had become wedged in the hole. A cement patch was quickly applied and she sailed off to the repairer's yard. On another occasion one of the small coasters was making her way to Haverford West. The river was swollen by heavy rains and combined with the high tide, the river had overflowed on to the watermeadows obscuring the channel marks. She ran aground and was to be seen high and dry in one of the fields. Fortunately she was safely refloated on the next tide.

At the peak of the slump in the early 1930s, Monroes', who had not made expensive investments in new ships in the early 1920s, began to buy larger coasters around 1,000 tons deadweight coming on the market at rock bottom prices. The smaller 300 deadweight coasters were sold. Up to this time vessels purchased had not been renamed, but with the formation of the Kyle Shipping Co., Ltd., which became the owning company for their ships, names beginning 'Kyle' were used. It was customary to form separate companies to finance the purchase of ships throughout the steam era. The china clay trade was tightly held by Hughes and so Monroes' coasters rarely got clay cargoes. But Monroes were on good terms with Rank's mills and did much business with them, particularly grain and feedstuffs to Belfast. The business became so regular that cargoes were often shipped on a 'turn out' basis. That is, if the voyage turned out to be a quick one, then the charge was about 2/6d per ton. If on the other hand there was a hold up, then a higher rate of 2/9d might be charged. Such arrangements often grew up over the years to the mutual advantage of ship-owners and merchant and much business was conducted by gentlemen's agreements and never written down. The larger coasters were also carrying coal from Ayr to Scotland and from South Wales to Clarence Dock Power Station from its opening in the early 1930s. This contract usually kept three coasters employed until the station was converted to burn oil in the 1950s. Pre-war, one coaster was usually time chartered by Cunard for the Channel Islands fruit and vegetable trade in summer. In the early 1930s Monroes were instrumental in the formation of the West Coast Freight Conference which established the minimum freight rates. Rates had been so low that many ships were running at a loss. This was done by many owners rather than incur the even greater losses resulting from laying up the vessels. Higher rates were needed if the ships running were to be repaired or eventually renewed. Higher rates were agreed but were eventually abandoned when some Glasgow owners undercut them. However, freight rates rose as trade improved in the latter part of the 1930s and minimum rates were no longer needed.

With the purchase of STAGHOUND, Monroes tried the Bergen trade unsuccessfully, but after the Second World War, the Portuguese and Mediterranean trades were entered with the 2,800 deadweight vessels. They also held the contract to carry coal from Barry to the Irlam steelworks on the Manchester Ship Canal and this kept the smaller vessels employed. The Irish coal trade continued to utilise a number of ships and by the time the last gas works was converted to oil, that at Cork, the big four hatch steamer KYLEQUEEN 1919/22 was on the contract. With the steady loss of these large customers, the steamers were scrapped and the motorships used on longer runs. Also the quarries at Carreg-y-llam and Nant which had provided cargoes for the ships returning to Liverpool, had closed down because of the competition from inland quarries with lorry fleets.

Just as Monroes were the main carriers for Carreg-y-llam, Savages were the main local carriers for the important roadstone quarries at Penmaenmawr, near Conway. Captain W.A. Savage's first ship was ZILLAH, launched by Mrs. Priscilla Savage in 1891 from James Harland's yard at Tranmere. She was a little wooden steamer 92 feet long and had twin engines and screws giving a speed of 9 knots. Following the usual custom some of the shares were sold to business friends including a local baker, Walter Brough and shipowner William Rowland. The business prospered and further vessels named after friends and members of the family such as SARAH BROUGH 284/98, were added to the fleet. The latter was built by the Ailsa Shipbuilding Co., Ltd. and had a deadweight of 370 tons which included 20 tons for bunkers. Her compound engine gave eleven and a half knots on her trials. The officer's saloon was well finished and panelled in polished maple and oak. Her first cargo was rock salt from Fleetwood to Widnes. The THORNFIELD 487/13 began the use of names ending in 'field'. The following year ASHFIELD, Plate 79, was delivered by the Lytham Shipbuilding & Engineering Company, and began a long association between owner and builder. They were built with the coal trade to Ringsend Dock, Dublin, in mind but china clay was also carried, though it was never popular with the chief engineer as it always tended to get in the machinery on deck and generally clog things up. By this time the company had moved to Liverpool. Following the First World War, the vessels traded more generally and often carried South Wales coal to France for example. In 1949 the company was taken over by Coast Lines.

One of the later companies to enter the Liverpool coasting scene was R.R. Clark who originally had small steamers running regular services to the smaller ports of North Wales. This business faded and he then formed the Overton S.S. Co., Ltd., to finance his coasting tramps which were given names ending in 'ton' such as OVERTON 426/11. Several vessels were ordered at top market prices at the end of the First World War and the company struggled for many years to pay for them and was finally sold up in 1942 on the death of Mr. Clark. The ships often carried salt to East Coast ports and also took part in the fruit and vegetable trade from France.

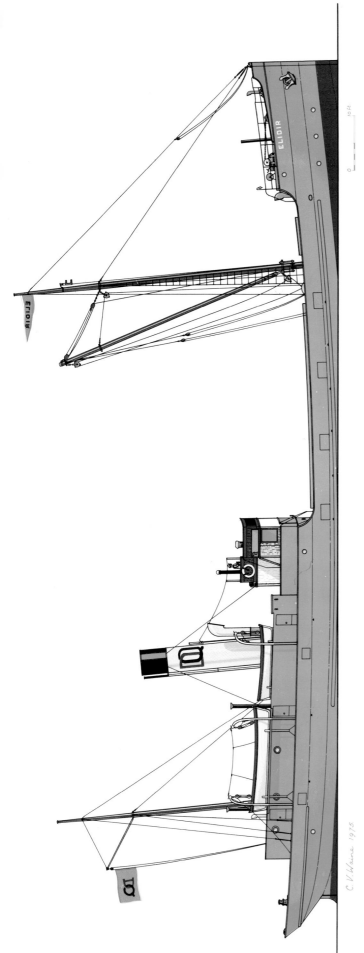

C.V. Waine 1975

0   10 Ft.

Steam Coaster **ELIDIR**

DIMENSIONS: 151'7" x 25'1" x 9'11"

Tonnge 398 gross.

Plate 123

(left) *Steam Coaster* **VELINHELI**

DIMENSIONS: 95'0" x 18'6" x 7'6"

Tonnage 126 gross.

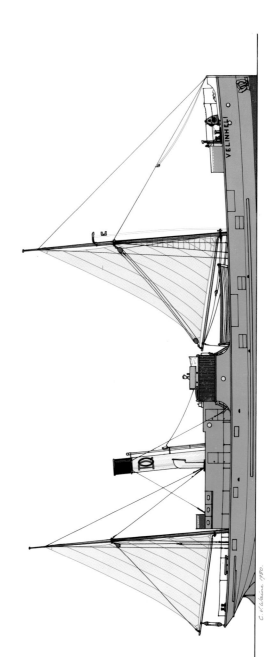

C.V. Waine 1980.

Steam Collier ARUNDEL
GENERAL ARRANGEMENT
DIMENSIONS: 325′0″ x 46′0″ x 22′4″ MLD.

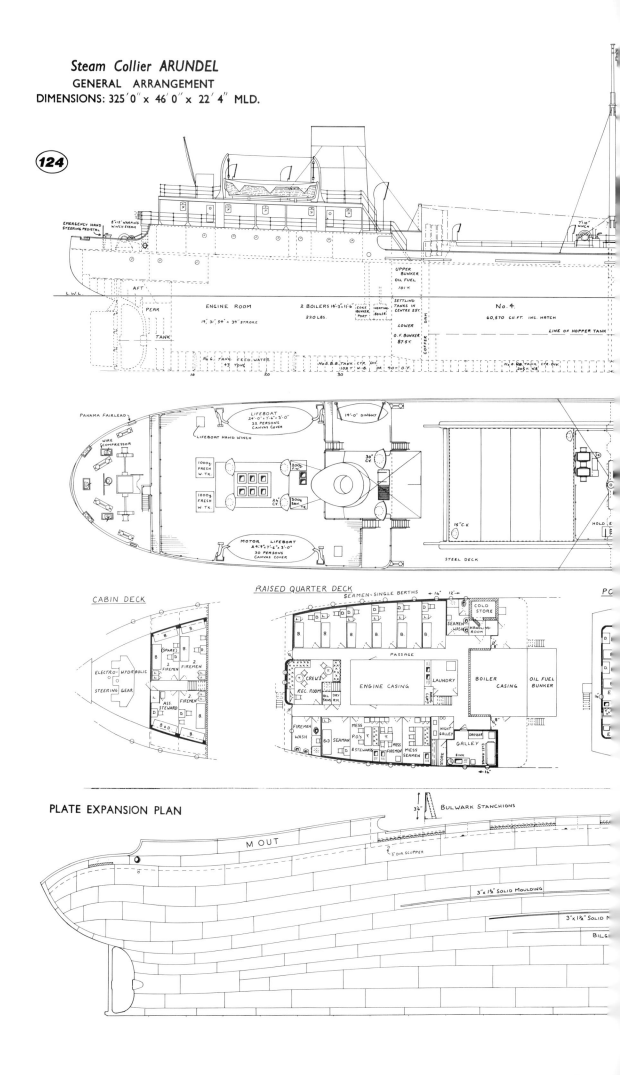

PLATE EXPANSION PLAN

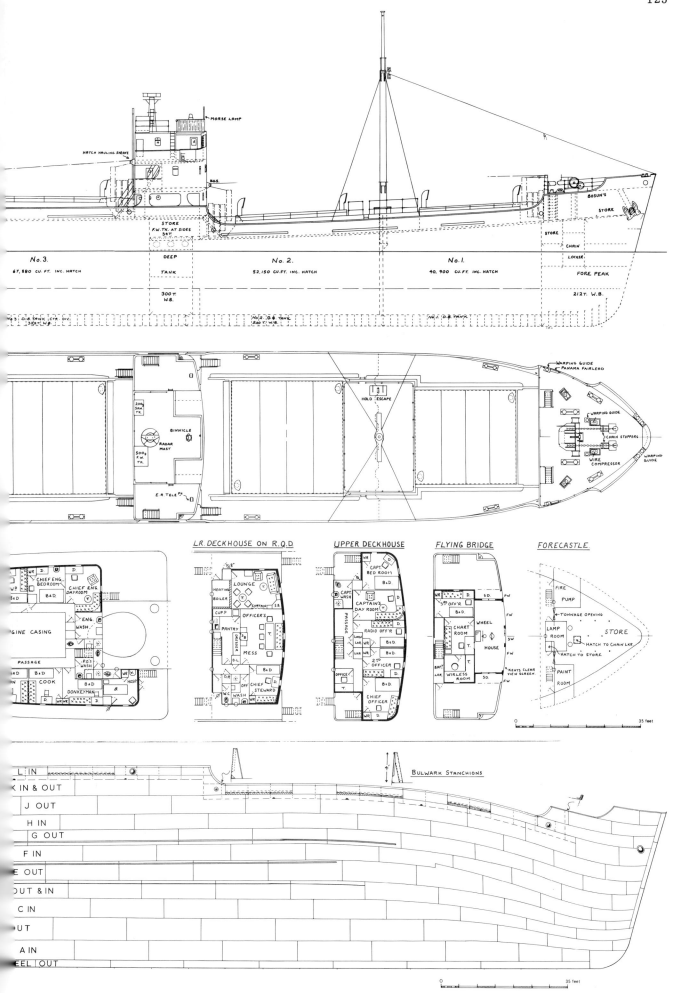

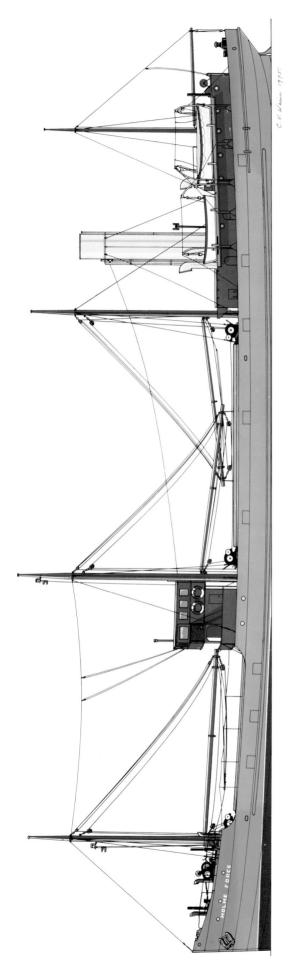

Steam Ship HOLME FORCE

DIMENSIONS: 216′0″ x 34′2″ x 13′7″

Tonnage 1,216 gross.

This short sea trader was completed in 1930 by the Goole Shipbuilding & Repairing Co.(1927) Ltd., for W.S.Kennaugh's West Coast Shipping Co.Ltd., of Liverpool. The vessel was employed carrying a variety of bulk cargoes such as coal, stone and cement between home and near Continental ports. Her triple expansion engine was by MacColl & Pollock of Sunderland. She was torpedoed on the 8th of August 1940 and sank 8 miles off Newhaven while on a voyage from the Tyne to Devonport with a cargo of coal. Six crew members were lost with her.

Plate 126

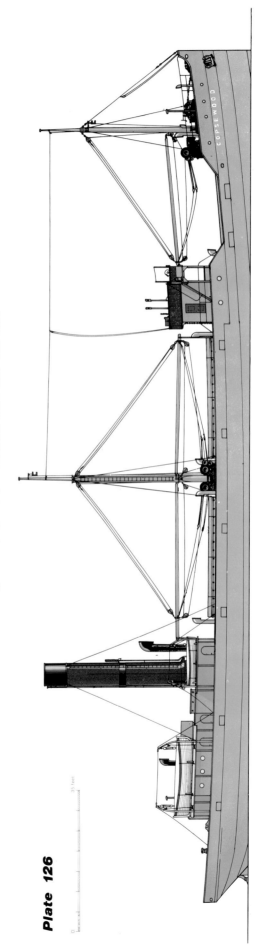

Steam Coaster COPSEWOOD

DIMENSIONS: 198′0″ x 32′4″ x 12′5″

Tonnage 969 gross.

COPSEWOOD was completed in 1925 by Osbourne, Graham of Sunderland for Joseph Constantine of Middlesbrough who was keen on boiler combustion efficiency, giving the furnaces a strong natural draught by fitting a particularly tall funnel. The steam winches, capstan and steering gear were by R.Roger of Stockton-on-Tees. She was mainly employed in the East Coast Coal trade until she was sold in 1939 to Monroe Brothers of Liverpool.

J. W. Fisher, who took over the Mason Shipping Co., at the end of the First World War, had vessels such as ALLANWATER 496/20 and DRAGOON 573/17 in the early 1920s. The ships traded to West of Ireland ports such as Sligo with flour, coal and general cargo. Coal was also carried from South Wales to French ports, particularly Trouville and Rouen. In summer new potatoes were loaded at French ports such as St. Malo. Trade was bad in the early 1920s and the ships were even sent as far as Antwerp in ballast to load scrap for Llanelly and Swansea and some ships were laid up and crews paid off. When this happened Mr. Fisher did his best to find a place in one of the other ships for any crewmen who had been with the company some time. His larger ships carried a steward who provided four meals a day and took 12/6d a week from each crewman to purchase the food. The vessels of the Northwick Carrying Co., came under his control but the fleet was soon sold in the 1920s.

J. S. Sellers & Co., started in the 1890s with old steamers such as THURSBY 496/76 and she is believed to have had a lifting screw for reducing drag when sailing to save fuel. He later formed the Ribble Shipping Co., to finance his fleet. Following the First World War some new ships were purchased including the RIBBLEMERE 489/25. Initially she was used carrying feedstuffs to Silloth and Solway Firth Ports. In the latter part of the 1920s she spent six months carrying stone from Newlyn to various South Coast ports, returning in ballast and bunkering at Portsmouth or Dartmouth. She was sold and he had just one old coaster in the 1930s. Old coasters were often purchased by William Cooper or Richard Abel for their sand and gravel businesses and used to carry sand up the Manchester Ship Canal. One of the main operators of steamers in the post-war period was S. William Coe who acquired various companies such as the Bann Shipping Co., Ltd. and W.J. Ireland's Thorn Line, begun in the 1920s. One of the earliest firms into steam was J.J. Mack who purchased their first small steamer at the beginning of the 1880s, the ADA 85/68. The ANNIE 411/84, with engines amidships, remained their largest steamer for many years. Their last steam coaster FLESWICK 648/00, was sold in the 1930s. There were various other owners with one or two coasters and it is interesting to note that Northwich, some 25 miles from the sea had its own coasting fleet operated by the Northwich Carrying Co. Some companies not primarily engaged in shipping, also owned coasters in Liverpool, the most influential of which was the United Alkali Co., Ltd. which later became Imperial Chemical Industries (Alkali) Ltd, in 1926. They had a number of coasters specially built to carry limestone from their quarry in North Wales, usually to their Burn Naze Works on the river Wyre near Fleetwood. The company also owned a number of sailing and steam flats on the Weaver and Mersey. Vessels such as BARIUM 600/18 saw many years service and were not replaced by motor ships until the 1950s. Another company to run its own ship was the Wigan Coal & Iron Co., who had the BALNEIL 460/86 built to export their coal to Ireland which was replaced by the BALNEIL II in 1909.

The River Dee, with Chester at its head had also long been established as a shipping centre, but was completely overshadowed by Liverpool in the steam era. However, Connah's Quay was a thriving port in the 1880s and shipped bricks from Buckley and Ruabon far and wide. Captain John Coppack who had commenced business in the 1860s with schooners purchased the ASTON 132/67, his first steamer, in 1881. She was used for the rapidaly expanding brick trade to the West of Ireland and the coal trade from Bagillt colliery which was practically on the water's edge. By 1900 his fleet had grown to four steamers and eleven schooners. The schooners were ideal for carrying delicate pipe, tile and faced brick cargoes which needed slow careful handling and the easier motion of sailing vessels to avoid damage. Steamers were profitable only if loaded and discharged more rapidly, but were used to save time on longer voyages. When he purchased EMILY 227/93 in 1899 the firm moved into the French fruit and vegetable trade which was of considerable importance to many coasters. At the end of the season they returned to the coal trade as demand rose for winter. His steamers also entered the china clay trade to Runcorn. The EMILY proving successful, another 125' long Fullerton built coaster, MOURNE (128), was purchased in 1901. She had been built of iron in 1894 for Fishers of Newry at a cost of £4,000 and had a displacement of 352 tons. On the 8th of December she was wrecked on St. David's Head. The wreck was sold to the Mourne S.S. Co. (W.T. Ferris & Co.), salvaged, and rebuilt with a new steel forebody by the Channel Drydock Co., Passage West, Cork. Coppack's new steamer FARFIELD (76) of 1920, was the first of their larger coasters and traded more widely carrying East Coast coal to South Coast ports. China clay was often carried on the return trip to Grimsby for Peter Dixon's paper mills. When the first cargo was delivered it was very carefully inspected to see that no coal had been left in the hold to contaminate the clay and so spoil the paper. The result was that Coppacks carried all the clay for the firm from then on and, in recognition of the care taken by them, the company saw that they received a fair freight rate which was often above the uneconomic rates of the open market. The contract was turned over to Everards in 1952 when return coal cargoes became hard to obtain. By this time motorships such as NORMANBY HALL 332/43 were replacing the steamers, last of which was HOVE, scrapped in 1961. Both often carried flour to Belfast and stone from Carreg-y-llam and Port Rivals for the construction of the M6 motorway and there was friendly rivalry between steamer and motorship as to who could achieve the best passages. Opposite Connah's Quay, John Summers steelworks built up their own fleet of motor vessels and the Point of Ayr Colliery, down river, with a shaft a few yards from the sea, was ideally placed for exporting coal to Ireland at first in chartered vessels and later in their own vessel CLWYD purchased in 1916, but lost the following year in collision. A larger coaster TALACRE 301/17 was built by Crabtree's yard at Great Yarmouth, Plate 2. In her 42 years service she carried hundreds of thousands of tons of coal from the colliery, principally to Ireland as well as the smaller ports of Wales and South West England. Two other vessels were purchased in later years and all were scrapped in the late 1950s.

MOURNE 228/94, at sea, photographed by J. W. Coppack **(128)** PEGRIX loading at Aberystwyth.   J. R. Rix Esq.
circa 1915. Registered dimensions were 125.0'x 20.1'x 9.3'.

The North Wales roadstone quarries relied on chartering the vessels they required, but the limestone quarries had their own fleets. Kneeshaw, Lupton & Co., had schooners before buying their first steamer, TOLFAEN in 1877. Other vessels soon followed, last of which was CALCHFAEN 421/93. No more were built as Robertsons of Glasgow were already carrying much of the limestone and they eventually purchased the quarry. CALCHFAEN had a number of British owners before being sold to A. Toop of Tallin, Estonia in 1937. She was renamed ANNA and successfully escaped to Britain at the beginning of the war and was taken on Government charter. In 1950 she was returned to Mr. Toop, who, not wishing to return to Russian occupied Estonia, renamed her ANNA TOOP and traded her from Cardiff. She was lost on Arklow bank in January 1958.

The North Wales slate quarries also had steamers, operated from their own specially constructed harbours. The Penrhyn Quarries had Port Penrhyn opposite Bangor while the Dinorwic Quarry Company built Port Dinorwic in a narrow valley adjacent to the Menai Straits. Sales of slates grew rapidly in the 19th century and, aided by cheap sea transport, slates were sent out in their millions for roofing the houses of factory worker and owner alike. Penryhn's first steamer was HARRIER 207/92. They had six steamers by 1897, largest of which was PENNANT 648/97 and she alone was used to carry slates to the Continent, often to Hamburg. The Dinorwic Quarry also had their first steamer in 1892, VELINHELI (60b), followed by VAYNOL and DINORWIC in the same year. The latter, together with ELIDIR, Plate 123, made longer voyages to East Coast ports. Velinheli handled Irish sea cargoes to ports such as Newry and kept depots as Preston, etc. supplied. She also discharged directly into ocean ships in Liverpool often carrying as many as three cargoes per week. By the 1920s the slate trade was falling off and the vessels retained did more general coasting. They were always well maintained and the brasswork kept bright. Repairs were carried out by the Company's own drydock at Port Dinorwic which also did work for other local owners.

Anglesey had many sailing shipowners such as William Thomas, Llanrhuddlad who owned square riggers and eventually moved to Liverpool. Thomas Bros., who owned a few steam coasters between the wars, had its origins in the firm and could trace their founding back to the 1870s. The coasters could often be seen discharging stone chippings for the Croft Granite Building & Construction Co. at Widnes. William Thomas & Sons of Amlwch built and owned coasters, both sail and steam. His first steamers were built of wood but he changed to iron with the W.S. CANE 183/83. When the shipping side passed to his son William, a number of second hand steamers were managed from Liverpool such as ELIANUS which was getting 2/3d per ton for stone cargoes from Carreg-y-llam to London. Her cargo of 950 tons was loaded in about three and a half hours. Speedy loading was essential as the ships could load only while the tide was in and in any case the jetty was exposed to the full weight of the Irish Sea and so ships were not kept alongside in case the weather deteriorated. Further down the coast, the lead mines used to ship ore through Aberystwyth, but were closed in the 1920s. One of the last shipments was taken by R.R. Clark's steamer SUTTON 485/20. On her way to Antwerp the cargo shifted in the heavy seas and she was lost with all hands on the 27th of November 1925. The Port of Aberystwyth slowly decayed and TEIFI 244/12, belonging to James Davies, Cardigan had to be quite expert avoiding the silt when delivering her coal cargoes. British Isles Coasters, formed by Mr. James, was also based at Cardigan, the company buying its first coasters in the 1930s including the QUAYSIDER which was well suited to the East Coast coal trade to South coast ports, a trade in which the company were particularly active.

The South Wales Coal field supported a number of owners who mostly owned the larger vessels, suited to the near continental trades, with engines amidships. Smaller shipments were often carried by the smaller coasters based on Liverpool. Llanelly was the home of two coaster fleets, those of Stone & Rolfe and William Coombs. The origin of both was the partnership W. Stone & W. Coombs which purchased the first vessel, ELECTRA, in the 1890s. The partnership was later dissolved, Mr. Stone forming Stone & Rolfe which owned three large, but rather old coasters, by 1918. Fleet expansion was then rapid with the formation of S & R Steamships Ltd., and the vessels were given names ending 'stone' such as the MONK-STONE 867/23. Second-hand ships retained their original names as it was considered bad luck to change a ship's name and in earlier days this custom was closely adhered to. Their largest vessel was SARAH STONE 2473/29. All the ships were active in the coal trade to the Continent, particularly to France, often returning to Llanelly with scrap. ISODORA 1212/15 was lost on a dangerous but profitable voyage; supplying Spain during the Spanish Civil War for which high freight rates were paid. In the post war period, as T. Stone (Shipping) Ltd, they owned a few larger steam colliers, but all were sold by 1959. W. Coombs' coasters were smaller and had names beginning 'Afon' for the most part, such as AFON TOWY 684/19, and also worked in the coal and scrap trades and their last vessels were sold in the 1950s.

Harries Bros. & Co., of Swansea began in the 1890s and by 1908 had expanded to ten ships including the LONGBENTON 924/98. The smaller vessels were sold and larger ships purchased so that in 1927 the 17 vessels in the fleet ranged from BOLBEC 1342/18 to the MANORDILO 2741/11. The fleet was reduced in the slump of the 1930s and their newest ship, GLANRHYD, foundered. She left Newport on the afternoon of Monday 14th of January 1938 with 2,173 tons of coal for the Irlam steelworks on the Manchester Ship Canal. She was last seen heading into a fresh S.S.W. wind that evening. The following day wreckage was washed ashore West of Swansea. All 17 of the crew were drowned. The company sold its last two ships in the 1950s. Cleeves' Western Vallies Anthracite Collieries, purchasing their first ships in 1916 which were initially managed from Cardiff and later from Swansea, began with coasters such as CROSSHANDS, but were soon sold in the 1920s. The collieries and two remaining ships passed to Amalgamated Anthracite Collieries in 1927, the last ship FRED CLEEVES was sold in 1930.

Cardiff tended to be the shipping centre because of the Coal Exchange. One of the oldest of Cardiff's companies was J. T. Duncan & Co., who started with one vessel in the 1890s and held a collier contract with the Admiralty, to supply coal to the fleet. Later the ships worked in the general coal trade and the last ship was sold in the 1950s. Claude Angel's ships were originally ocean traders, but by 1918, his only vessel was CLYDEBURN 553/02. In the early 1920s vessels of Manor Line (London) Ltd., came under his management. The fleet contained vessels such as EMSWORTH MANOR 1289/12 and were often employed to carry coal to south coast ports such as Ramsgate as well as London. This company had a short life, but other owning companies were formed under the management of Angel, Dalling & Co., Ltd., when trade improved in the 1930s such as the Bramhall S.S. Co. One of the oldest companies in the local coal trade from Cardiff was R. Burton & Son. Originating as H. Burton in Newport, they had two small steamers in the 1870s. The Care family, under various titles, managed ships from the 1890s, but never had a large fleet. Specialising in perishable goods, one vessel managed in the 1930s was the PORTHMEOR 449/23 of the Richard England S.S. Co., Ltd. Englands were fruit and vegetable merchants and so the ship was often employed carrying potatoes from Ireland or spring vegetables from France.

Emlyn-Jones & Co., Ltd., managed some coasters for a while but vessels such as the EMLYNMORE 616/19 were paying off their crews and had no work by 1921. Other vessels in the fleet were sold except for the EMLYNMORE herself which had been built as a Q-ship in the First World War. She left Middlesborough for Pembroke with a cargo of plates and angles on the 22nd of October 1927 and was last seen off Dungeness making about five knots in fine weather. She and her crew of 13 have never been seen since. At the beginning of the 1920s a series of coasters were built by Rennie, Ritchie & Newport Shipbuilding Co., at Wivenhoe. Four were completed before the yard was in financial difficulties due to the slump and the fourth, MAINDY COTTAGE was completed after the yard went into liquidation. They were all built for the important South Wales colliery owner Sir David R. Llewellyn who placed them under the management of Merrett Bros. of Cardiff. They were employed in the coal trade to France and one of the vessels, MAINDY KEEP 973/21 was lost on a voyage from Swansea to Bordeaux in 1924. The company was soon reconstructed as Llewellyn, Merrett & Price and became Gueret, Llewellyn & Price in 1925, Mr. Gueret having previously owned colliers in the 1890s. By 1927 only 5 coasters were in the fleet as the larger ships had been sold. They all had names beginning with M. and were similar in size to MEAD 606/19. By 1930 MALLOCK and MANDRAKE were laid up in the Fal and in the latter part of the 1930s just the larger MEARIM 1037/14 remained in the fleet. Another new company formed in Cardiff in the 1910s was the Federated Coal & Shipping Co., Ltd., which had such colliers as the JOYCE LLEWELLYN 1446/24 and traded until the mid-1930s. Cardiff's smallest coasters were those managed by Griffin Bros., such as TORPOINT 214/05. However, by far the largest fleet of small and medium sized coasters belonged to Osborn & Wallis. In the 1890s many of their vessels were large, but they also had smaller vessels for the local Bristol Channel trade. One important run was to Bristol with Welsh steam coal. They had 7 vessels by 1937, largest of which was the DRUID STOKE 486/29. By the 1950s most of the vessels were of this size. Motor vessels slowly replaced the steamers and last to go was DRUID STOKE herself, which arrived at Passage West, near Cork, for breaking up in March 1965. Spillers, the millers, also had their own fleet of coasters and nearly all were given names beginning 'Wheat'. Their first steamer was WANS FELL (73), purchased in 1894. The fleet grew rapidly during the First World War and several new coasters were added in the 1920s, but were soon all sold except for WHEATCROP 523/24 which was used until the 1950s. In later years she was managed from Liverpool and worked in the coasting trade when not needed to carry the company's products.

At Newport Mordeys owned one or two colliers until the 1930s, often with names beginning 'Gwent' as for example GWENTGATE 1600/24. Some steamers were also owned by P. Barr & Co., in the 1870s and 1880s. The other main centre for shipping on the Bristol Channel was Bristol itself. One of the oldest firms was Pockett's Bristol Channel S.P. Co., Ltd., which lasted until the early 1920s. The firm originated as J.W.Pockett, later William Pockett, in Swansea. They began with small steamers in the coal trade including COLLIER herself (46), dating from 1848. Later, moving to Bristol, they entered the local passenger trades, but retained the colliers. However, perhaps the best known Bristol based colliers were those of A.J. Smith which were regularly to be seen discharging at small West Country quays and jetties. One of the vessels owned by them in the 1930s was the COLLIN (Plate 62), while the largest was CALCARIA 569/10 which ventured further afield. T.R. Brown and F.E. Peters used modified coasters for their sand and gravel dredging. United Stone Firms had small coasters such as MULTISTONE 296/10 which ran to their quarries at Porthgain, Pembroke. The Ald Shipping Co., founded in the 1920s used local place names ending in 'combe' such as BROCKLEY COMBE 345/21. Four vessels were owned by the 1940s. Post-war, the larger MONKTON COMBE 1052/45 was traded and their last vessel the motor vessel CASTLE COMBE 535/53 was sold to J.S. Monks in 1960.

James Wood Sully was a coal merchant in Bridgwater on the River Parrett. His first small steamers were TENDER built in 1860 and KATHERINE of 1865. They were joined by BULL DOG 149/66 and later WELSH PRINCE 154/71. The firm subsequently became Sully & Co., Ltd, BULL DOG continuing to serve for over 50 years, eventually to be replaced by CROPILL 190/11 and other steamers. Regular supplies for Bideford merchants were brought to them by the little steamer DEVONIA 98/94 which belonged to them until the 1940s. R. Cock & Sons, the Appledore shipbuilders, built four vessels for their own account between 1917 and 1922, such as ORLEIGH. All were bare boat chartered to Robinson, Brown of Newcastle. Further along the coast at Portreath, the port for Redruth, Bain Sons & Co., started their change over to steam in the 1870s purchasing VERONICA. By 1900 there were eight vessels but after that it declined to four vessels by 1908 including TEST 466/90. She had a very nice round of cargoes; London, load cement, sail Tuesday for Plymouth where the cement was discharged by Friday. She sailed overnight to Guernsey arriving Saturday morning to load stone for London which was discharged by Monday afternoon then she was ready to load cement again. Captain Hewitt of the TEST was never one to miss a salvage job and towed in a number of vessels over the years. Bain's sold their last ships in the 1920s, but John Hampton's County of Cornwall S.S. Co., had a few coasters such as ROSSMORE 627/07 until the 1930s. Hayle, further westwards, was also the home of some early steam coasters, and these belonged to Harvey & Co., Ltd., who were also shipbuilders. They built the iron steamer HAYLE 476/93 as well as her triple expansion machinery and continued with one or two vessels into the 1930s. China clay from Fowey provided a regular source of cargo for locally owned vessels managed by Toyne, Carter & Co. which were built or purchased for various 'one ship companies', beginning in the 1890s. FOY 354/02 was owned, for example, by the Fowey No. 3 S.S. Co., Ltd. FOY, TORFREY and PAR carried clay to Runcorn and Preston usually returning with coal which was often loaded at the Point of Ayr Colliery on the River Dee, for Fowey and other Cornish ports. The ships were sold in the 1920s, the firm continuing as agents. Another company to move in and out of shipping was Renwick, Wilton & Co., who decided to purchase some steamers for their bunker and coal trade based on Dartmouth in the 1900s, starting with old steamers like VANESSA 1166/72 purchased from Cory's in 1903. On taking delivery of KINGSWEAR (109) in 1909 the older vessels were sold and the KINGSWEAR herself was sold in the 1920s after which the company again depended entirely on chartered tonnage.

The beautiful natural harbour of Poole in Dorset has also been the home port of coasters over the years. Henry Burden Junior & Co., Ltd., owned a few vessels at the turn of the century, but all were sold by the 1920s. Though E.C. Burden traded the old coaster DUN-LEITH 292/96 for a while in the 1930s. Modern motor coasters were introduced in the late 1930s by John Carter (Poole) Ltd. Southampton has always primarily been a centre for ocean traders, but Hills operated coasters at the turn of the century and Hemsley Bell Ltd., had a few bunkering tankers continuing until the 1960s. W. Wilson also started in the 1920s with coasters such as TOSCA 449/08 and YORKVALLEY 562/03 which carried coal to Ramsgate and other South Coast ports. They were replaced by motor coasters in the 1930s and the fleet operated until the 1950s. Small vessels have always been owned in the Isle of Wight such as those of the Vectis Shipping, Newport; R.H. Penney & Sons of Brighton have a long history. In the 19th century they concentrated on the New Zealand trade and their barques were often chartered by Shaw, Savill. At the beginning of the 20th century they turned to the Shoreham coal trade and bought coasters such as ALGAMA (131) which often loaded at Goole. All the small ships were replaced by a single larger vessel, ALGOL (102). Peter Hawksfield & Son Ltd of Dover, purchased their first collier in 1929 and operated several vessels in the 1930s such as PETER HAWKSFIELD which regularly carried coal from Methil to Dover for the company.

ALGAMA 774/04, was built by J. Fullerton, Paisley.

F. Atkinson Esq.
BROOMFLEET 854/15, with a timber cargo.

Smaller wharves and harbours of the Thames Estuary largely received their supplies by sailing barges and later in motor vessels owned by Thomas Watson or the London & Rochester Trading Company, both of Rochester. Further up-river at Greenhithe, F. T. Everard & Sons Ltd (the name was originally spelt differently) initially built barges for other owners and then one for themselves in 1890. One of their best known barges is the CAMBRIA preserved by the Maritime Trust. In 1913 they built their first motor vessel, GRIT, but she was soon a victim of a German submarine. They moved into steam coasting during the First World War purchasing vessels such as TOSCA 449/08. A new venture was heralded by the purchase of the tar tanker ALCHYMIST 382/95 which successfully showed that edible oils could be carried in tankers fitted with steam heating coils. This service was soon in such demand that several other steam tankers were built during the 1920s and 1930s such as AGILITY 522/24, the tankers often being used in the whale oil trade from Norway to Britain. As this was outside home trade limits, Captain Dines had to take an extra master with a deep sea ticket. However, many of the whale and peanut oil cargoes were loaded at Shiedam near Rotterdam inside home trade limits. Experience gained with the motor barges was used to enter the longer distance coasting trades with motor vessels at the end of the 1920s. ABILITY and AMENITY were first to be delivered and proved efficient in service. Then at the height of the slump in 1931, Plenty & Son of Newbury failed. Everard ships largely relied on Plenty oil engines, so after careful consideration the factory was purchased. With engine supplies assured, the extensive building programme of the 1930s got under way so that by 1938 the fleet had grown to 43 ships from 3 in 1918. The vessels were firmly established in the coal trade to the South Coast ports, often loading china clay as a return cargo. In later years two quarries were purchased to provide return cargoes. In the Second World War 22 of the ships were lost and so a number of war built standard vessels were purchased to replace them including a few steam tankers. They made voyages to Iceland for herring oil, while vegetable oils from Rotterdam and Amsterdam were carried for Unilever. Everards' success with motor vessels pointed the way for others to follow.

By far the most important coastal fleets operated from London were the colliers which kept the capital supplied with coal from the North East Coast and South Wales, a trade which was very much the cradle of steam coasters. These early vessels were all owned on a 64 parts basis and interested parties would take up shares in the individual ships. The manager or his friends usually controlled at least 33 of the shares in order to retain management. Owners such as Wm. Cory and J. Fenwick, often held shares in ships under each others management. Trading profits and losses were worked out for each ship and separate shareholders meetings held. In early days before the limited company came into use, shareholders had to pay for losses their ships incurred. The intertwined relationships were not resolved until the 1890s, at which time they were sorted out and put on a more modern basis. The first steam collier in which Wm. Cory held shares was the SAMUEL LANG 606/54 and she traded to London for him until lost by collision in 1901. In 1855 four more vessels were built and with the completion of WILLIAM CORY 1578/57, the South Wales coal trade was entered. As there was no distinction between home and foreign trade at this time they traded to the Baltic in Summer. In 1861, in order to discharge his 9 colliers more expeditously, Wm. Cory installed the first floating derricks on the Thames and they were used for some 40 years before being replaced by wharves. In 1896, when the ownership of the colliers was rationalised, a number of vessels managed by Fenwick passed to Wm. Cory. In the same year the colliers of several other owners were also taken over. One was the fleet of Lambert Bros., who had 10 colliers most of which had been purchased in the 1880s. Another fleet built up at this time and taken over was that of Green Holland & Sons. A third fleet acquired was that of J & C. Harrison's 4 coastal colliers with their distinctive names beginning 'Har' such as HARBOURNE 1278/96. When demand for coal fell in summer some of the vessels were sent to the Baltic with coal returning with such cargoes as pit props, while others carried coal southwards returning with Spanish iron ore. HADLEY 1777/01 had more interesting cargoes when she was used to carry coaches from Rotterdam for the electrification of the Metropolitan (Underground) Railway. During the First World War, many were taken up as fleet colliers and transports. In 1920 the well known 'Cor' prefix for names was introduced and colliers belonging to R. & J.H. Rea absorbed into the fleet such as VALEGARTH 1569/13 which became CORBEACH. By 1930 the fleet stood at 21 vessels. In the Second World War 14 ships were lost and the change to motor colliers was begun by CORBRAE 2002/52.

J. Fenwick & Son retained their collier interests after 1896 but their fleet was halved. The position was not helped by the loss of TWIZELL 1717/01 which was wrecked near Cuxhaven when almost new, carrying coal from South Shields to Hamburg, an important customer for British coal at that time. The company then slowly sold off their other ships. Various members of the Fenwick family had long associations with the coal trades, for example, R. Fenwick & Son were sales agents for the hard coals produced by the Earl of Durham's Lambton group of collieries from at least the 1840s. There are records of a letter reporting on the state of the London coal market being dispatched to the Lambton collieries twice a week at that time. The reports were sent, as in the days of sail, no one knew when coal cargoes would arrive, and cargoes were not sold until the vessels reached the Thames, the price depending on the number of cargoes available. The practice was discontinued as steam replaced sail and coal was sold from the pit head or even in the ground. The company became R. Fenwick & Co., in 1861 and by 1888 had a fleet of 33 ships. The name changed to Fenwick, Stobart & Co., in 1893, the Stobart family also having long associations with the Earl of Durham. The company were also 'fitters' (sales agents) for the whole of the output of the Wearmouth Coal Co., for many years. In 1901 the company became Wm. France, Fenwick & Co., Ltd., incorporating Fenwick, Stobart & Co., Wm. France and H.C. Pelly & Co. The latter was a much younger company which had commenced as collier owners in the 1880s and by 1901 had 8 ships, all let on consecutive voyage charters as far as possible, for up to 7 years, mainly to Wm. Cory and the London gas undertakings. Pelly's also chartered vessels to Wm. France & Co., Ltd., for their London-Goole trade, the ships returning with coal. The amalgamation gave a fleet of 16 steamers 3 of which were 'flat-irons' which had been built for H.C. Pelly, to trade up Bow creek which had a low bridge at that time. Captains received £4 and able seamen about £1-8-0d a week and all food, cooking pots and bedding were provided by the crew out of their wages. There was no paid overtime and the crew worked as long as the master felt necessary. Despite these apparently hard conditions there were never any crew shortages and if a ship arrived in the Tyne on Saturday afternoon, every effort was made to load her so that she was not left idle until Monday.

Vessels such as ROOKWOOD 1143/96 with their somewhat smaller hatches were built with the Summer Baltic timber trade in mind. The fleet was renewed and consisted of 10 vessels many of which were new in 1910 like NEEDWOOD, which unfortunately because of bad design was continually flexing, putting the propellor shaft out of alignment. Her shafting problem was settled permanently in May 1917 by a German submarine. Prices of second hand colliers soared during the First World War as everyone tried to replace losses at the same time, and were even higher at the end of the war DALEWOOD costing £162,000 in 1920 compared with NEEDWOOD's £20,500 ten years earlier. To make matters worse she proved to be a structurally weak ship and bunker capacity proved inadequate for more than ten days steaming, and proved too big at 4,600 tons deadweight for near continental cargoes which were around 3,000 tons. She was sold when two years old for just £44,600 by which time the cost of building a 3,000 ton vessel had fallen to £41,500. By 1927 some of the vessels were laid up, but despite this, plans were put in hand for a new generation of colliers with engines placed aft. BUSHWOOD 2314/30 on delivery traded at a small profit despite the low freight rates. The company suffered a serious loss when the American liner PRESIDENT HARDING ran down and sank the new steamer KIRKWOOD 1780/30 at anchor near the Elbe light vessel on her third voyage. The American liner did not admit liability until France, Fenwick had the liner arrested at Southampton. The firm purchased several second hand steamers at favourable prices including some from H. Harrison who was selling off his steamers. HAWKWOOD 2024/34 was their first ship with hopper side tanks while WYCHWOOD 2794/34 was first with a cruiser stern. The war took its toll and several vessels took part in the Normandy landings including the CHELWOOD 2742/28 which carried troops to Arromanches, but sustained much bottom damage including a broken stern frame. However, at low tide the frame was roughly welded and she got off safely, just one of the many war-time incidents. In 1946 France, Fenwick together with other leading collier owners, Cory's and Stephenson Clarke, formed a new company, Coastwise Colliers Ltd, to long term charter vessels to the County of London Electricity Company. The company was wound up in 1949 after electricity was Nationalised. The vessels which had been given names beginning 'Col' reverted to their old names in the respective fleets. France, Fenwick purchased several war built colliers but as the coal trade fell off, vessels such as DASHWOOD were converted to oil burning so that they could trade further afield. During the war the Company managed several old Great Lakes Vessels, brought over to help on the North East coal run. Too slow for the slowest convoys, they sailed without protection, none were lost. Their captains maintained that this was because the convoys always sailed at the same time, consequently the enemy always knew where the convoy would be.

Stephenson Clarke & Co. was set up in 1850 but the family interest in shipping goes back much further. By the 1870s they had several iron steamers in the Spanish trades as well as carrying coal to the South Coast, particularly Shoreham, a trade for which SHOREHAM 491/72 was built. Growth of the fleet tended to be slow as the railway was carrying much coal for this company. When Stephenson Clarke died in 1891, he left 5 vessels to his sons, including the new F.E. WEBB 585/91. The company were doing considerable business with the gas undertakings as they were agents for Durham coal, the best suited for gas making. This trade expanded and the larger colliers like BROOK 1436/06 usually carried coal to the Brentford Gas Co. Trade to South Coast ports, Shoreham, Poole, Southampton and Portsmouth increased

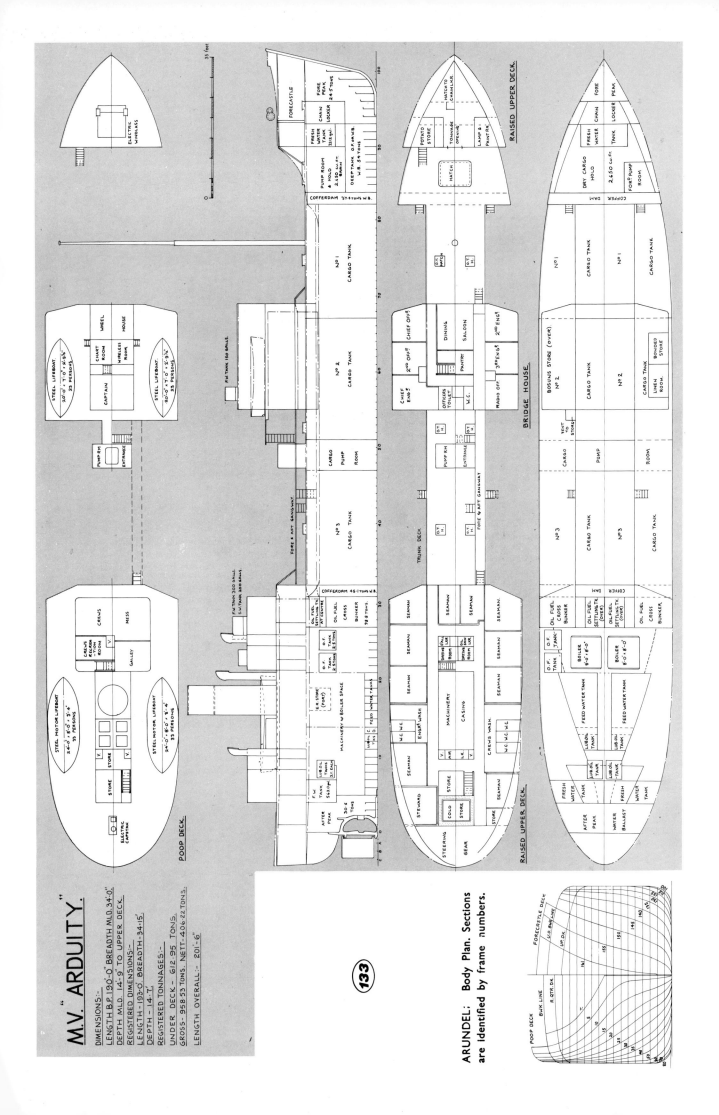

ARUNDEL: Body Plan. Sections are identified by frame numbers.

also as their gas undertakings expanded. Despite war difficulties, a new company, the Normandy Shipping Company was formed with the Powell, Duffryn Steam Coal Co., to carry the latter's coal from South Wales to Northern France. Two new ships were built but both were lost by 1918 and to make good the loss, 5 vessels were purchased from the Shamrock Shipping Co. By 1922 most of the ships had been sold, some back to the Shamrock Shipping Co., and the Company wound up. However, Stephenson Clarke themselves joined the Powell Duffryn Group in 1928. Three new ships were built in the early 1920s largest of which was BORDE 2014/21 and in the latter part of the 1920s further vessels were built to carry gas coal to the South Coast such as WILLIAM CASH 1186/29 to serve Bournemouth via Poole and FLATHOUSE 1546/31 to serve the Plymouth gas works. These ships has a particularly tough time during the war, but they were soon fitted with anti-aircraft guns and armoured bridges for protection. The hazard of drifting mines continued for some years after the end of the war and the BETTY HINDLEY 1771/43 was sunk by a mine in 1947. Most of the post-war colliers were motor vessels but some large steam colliers joined the fleet when the Tanfield S.S. Co., was taken over in 1952. Expansion was steady and ARUNDEL, Plate 6, last of the steam colliers was delivered in 1956.

Stephenson Clarke also managed the fleets of various undertakings. This began in 1911 when the Gas, Light & Coke Co., decided that it was desirable for them to own vessels regularly needed for the gas works at Beckton, adjacent to the Royal Group of docks. Their first ship was FULGENS 2512/12 and their fleet expanded rapidly during the First World War when the Company found it difficult to be sure of chartering vessels and high prices had to be paid for the ships. Ten vessels had been acquired by 1916 and eight new ships ordered at the end of the war, including three 'flat-irons' for the Nine Elms plant at Vauxhall. Further 'flat-irons' were added in 1927 to serve the Fulham works as well. On Nationalisation ships came under the North Thames Gas Board but Stephenson Clarke continued as managers. Eleven new ships were built for the board, but were soon disposed of, as the plants were converted to oil and natural gas was utilised. Electricity undertakings also placed ships under Stephenson Clarke management, foremost of which was the London Power Co., Ltd, who had chartered Stephenson Clarke vessels for many years. First ship of their fleet was the ALEXANDER KENNEDY 1313/32, a 'flat-iron' built to serve Battersea Power Station, then just coming into use. Deptford West was supplied by conventional vessels such as FRANCIS FLADGATE 2268/33. They were named after the important members, or inventors who had contributed towards the advancement of the industry and so followed the early names used by Stephenson Clarke. In 1936 the Fulham Borough Council electricity plant was extended and the Fulham series of 'flat-irons' were managed by Stephenson Clarke as were the colliers HENRY MOON and ARTHUR WRIGHT of the Brighton Corporation plant.

In 1948 the electricity undertakings were Nationalised and the ships were taken over by the British Electricity Authority, but Stephenson Clarke remained managers. New 4,500 ton deadweight colliers were built to supply Littlebrook Power Station on the Thames and Cliff Quay Power Station at Ipswich. The building programme was completed in 1954 with four smaller and faster vessels of 3,600 tons to serve Brighton via Shoreham.

The South Metropolitan Gas Board managed their own ships, and were thrust into ship owning by the First World War and had 9 vessels in 1918 including the new KENNINGTON 1500/18. New ships were built in the 1920s and old ones sold. Similarly the Wandsworth Wimbledon & Epsom District Gas Co. became shipowners, and by 1926 had three new ships to serve their plant, all 'flat-irons' like WANDLE 932/23. These ships and especially those of the South Metropolitan fleet, became the backbone of the South Eastern Gas Board on Nationalisation. The Metropolitan fleet already included a number of successful motor colliers. The ships were all disposed of in the 1960s. The Commercial Gas Co., Stepney, also owned some colliers including small steamers with engines amidships like LIMEHOUSE 562/03. The vessels were disposed of in the 1920s as chartering became favourable again, but two vessels were retained until the 1940s.

John Hudson became shipowners in 1915 when it became impossible to charter the ships needed for the Company's coal business. But to go back a little, in 1905 Samuel Williams obtained a controlling interest in John Hudson (London) Ltd., on the death of Charles Hudson, This company had just been formed to handle the London trade of the firm Charles Hudson, Pearson & Fearney, who had been in the coal trade in Newcastle from the 1840s. The purchase was logical as Samuel Williams owned Dagenham Dock which was handling the coal. Hudsons were agents for Fife coal as well as that from Northumberland and Durham. Their first collier was the OXSHOTT 2124/15. To manage their fleet of 5 vessels, the Hudson S.S. Co., Ltd., was formed in 1920. The fleet changed little until the 1930s. UPMINSTER 1013/34 was built to replace a vessel of the same name lost in 1928. The new vessel had engines-aft and proved so efficient that another was ordered. The fleet like that of other owners was decimated by the war. UPMINSTER was bombed and machine gunned in January 1940 off Haiseborough Sands, killing the Captain and two seamen. The remainder of the crew were saved as the ship went down. LOLWORTH struck a mine off the North Foreland, followed by HORNCHURCH which went down off Southwold after being bombed on July 12th. In November DAGENHAM hit a magnetic mine but was beached on Barrow Sands and later towed to London, discharged, and six months later was back in service. Finally OXSHOTT was lost in a storm the following year. Various second hand ships were purchased and three of the five ships remaining took part in the Normandy landings. At the end of the war two 'Empire' ships were purchased and names beginning 'Hudson' were used for the first time. A series of 4,600 ton deadweight ships were also ordered, but as the coastal trade was obviously going to be much reduced, HUDSON SOUND fitted out as an oil burner and was fitted to carry bulk sugar from the West Indies. Motor ships were next built with this trade in mind and their coasting interests slowly ceased. Harold Harrison's coal business was also taken over by Samuel Williams. Harold Harrison split away from John Harrison who had owned colliers from the 1890s, but did not build up a large fleet until forced to by the First World War. By 1918 he had 14 vessels ranging from GROSVENOR 267/08 to CATERHAM 1777/86. Harold Harrison's first ship was RALPH HARRISON 959/18. John Harrison's fleet was sold off in the early 1920s, but Harold Harrison formed H. Harrison (Shipping) Ltd. which took delivery of a number of new ships such as SEATON 1530/24 and SURBITON 649/26 as well as purchasing a number of second hand vessels. SEATON cost £35,000 and was sold for just £5,600 in the slump, in 1932, when the steamers were sold. Later a few motor ships were built for the company which later came under the management of William Coe while the coal side of the business passed to Samuel Williams. E. T. Lindley similarly bought colliers in the early 1920s and several new vessels were built for the fleet such as HORLEY 929/26. Most were sold in the slump of the 1930s and just the NUTFIELD 1561/19 remained in 1938.

A company which came to England in 1913 was the Shipping & Coal Company, formed by the Dutch firm of the same name. The Dutch company was buying the whole output of certain collieries on a yearly contract basis as was customary at that time. In order to sell the smaller sized coal, as used by Thames power stations, a British office was set up to handle sales. The company was classified as Northumberland coal suppliers and so did not supply gas undertakings which used Durham coal which was best for gasmaking. The contracts with the collieries were fixed in January, whereas it was usual to fix contracts with the Electricity undertakings in April, so there was always an interesting period in the London office during which everyone wondered if all the coal they had agreed to buy would be sold; fortunately it always was. In the 1920s the Dutch company had some 20 colliers carrying the larger 1" and 2" coal to the Continent. A British flag fleet was slowly built up and also had names ending in 'land' such as FORELAND 522/27. In the 1930s another FORELAND 1817/15 joined QUEENS-LAND 1617/28 carrying coal to the Thames as all coal was sold to customers in the South East. West Ham Power Station was supplied by barges loaded overside from ships at Dagenham Dock and Croydon was supplied via Deadmans Dock. Other customers were Associated Portland Cement, Watney's Brewery, Tate & Lyle and Unilever at Purfleet. The steam colliers were all fast, and in their last years were fired by Arab firemen when it became difficult to find reliable English firemen. But sometimes the Arabs tended to be too keen, stoking up quickly if the pressure began to drop going down the Thames, producing the inevitable clouds of smoke. On one occasion this was spotted and the Company fined for allowing the ship to emit black smoke in an area in which it was prohibited. Pre-war, extra tonnage was chartered for Winter. One year the MAURICE ROSE was taken for three months trading, the charter having been arranged by Temple, Thompson and Clarke, the coastal brokers. The fixture did not work out too well on this occasion as her chief engineer would not do more than about 8 knots and so she kept missing her turn to discharge at Dagenham. If he had increased speed she would probably have burned too much coal to be profitable on the charter. Ships were also chartered from E. T. Lindley and H. Harrison (Shipping) Ltd.

Charrington, Gardner, Locket & Co., Ltd, owned a few colliers over the years, best known of which is probably JOHN CHARRINGTON 1576/29. They also chartered a larger number of colliers from other owners for their considerable coal business. For a time during the First World War, Brown, Jenkinson & Co., managed coasters of the London Transport Co., Ltd, but vessels such as RYCKETT 983/17 were rapidly sold in the 1920s under the management of E. J. Heinz. Constants (France) Ltd. and Constants (South Wales) Ltd, had colliers such as SELLINGE 1710/19 which tended to trade outside home trade limits as did those of Denaby & Cadeby Main Collieries Ltd. There were many smaller London owners over the years as, for example, Captain Knapton who took great pride in his little coasters such as HUMBER 280/99 and would always try to find them clean cargoes like grain. One of the last steam coasting companies to be formed in London was British Channel Traders Ltd. This company was created from the coastal tramping interests of the London & Channel Islands S. S. Co. which had been formed by Cheesewright & Ford in 1899 to offer a regular service to the Channel Islands. Vessels not needed for the regular service plied in the coasting trade and often carried stone from quarries at St. Sampsons, Guernsey. In 1937 the JERSEY QUEEN was specially built for coastal tramping and further tramps were built including the TUDOR QUEEN of 1941. Coast Lines acquired an interest in 1936 and the company became a full subsidiary in 1943 in which year the firm's tramping interests were formed into a separate company as British Channel Traders Ltd. which after a few years changed its name to Queenship Navigation Ltd., which became prominent in the 1940s, purchasing a number of war-built steamers such as the BALMORAL QUEEN 1042/45. They were replaced by motor vessels during the 1950s as part of Coast Lines. One of the greatest post-war expansions was that of Comben Longstaff & Co., Ltd. Their first ships such as SURREYBROOK 859/16 were purchased in the mid-1930s. In the post-war period five steam coasters were built for the Company. The relative merits of motor and steam came to the fore when the motor ship CARDIFFBROOK 1812/52 and the steamer CARDIGANBROOK 1780/52 were completed with identical hulls. One more steamer was built in 1954, but after that all were motor. The ships worked in the coal trade and carried considerable amounts of roadstone from Newlyn over the years and in the mid-1950s became part of Amalgamated Roadstone. One of the oldest vessels in the stone trade between the wars was the veteran PANMURE built in 1859 which for many years was on charter to Summerfield & Lang of Liverpool to carry stone for them from the quarries in North Wales and Ireland. She was owned by Tom W. Smyth of London.

The great development of the coastal tanker trades which occurred towards the end of the steam era, was centred on London. The oil companies themselves mainly refined overseas and shipped the refined products to depots at the larger ports from whence it was distributed. The first coastal depots had been set up when the ONEIDA was built by the Anglo-American Oil Co., in 1908. They built few more vessels until after World War Two when there was a great expansion in the demand for petroleum products, as power stations, gas works and industrial users switched to oil which was often delivered by the coasting tankers. Anglo-American Oil became ESSO in 1953 and by 1956 had 10 coasting tankers, half of which were steam. Coastal tankers of Shell and British Petroleum were operated jointly after the Second World War. In earlier times the companies mainly used estuarial bunkering tankers. The pattern changed in the 1940s with the purchase of war-built vessels such as B.P. DISTRIBUTOR 810/44 and SHELL SUPPLIER 1157/46. Motor tankers then followed. National Benzole operated steam coasting tankers from the 1920s. The company refined the crude benzole distillate produced as a by-product of coal gas. Much of this was collected for Thameside gas works by a fleet of tank lighters which were displaced by the pioneer 'through the bridges' tanker BEN SADLER, built 1931. All their tankers had names beginning 'Ben' which were retained after the fleet was merged with that of Shell Mex & B.P. in the late 1950s.

The companies also chartered extra tankers as required, particularly to handle the heating oil demand in winter. Mobil and Regent (later Texaco) relied almost entirely on chartered vessels. The main independent tanker owners were the Bulk Oil S.S. Co., and C. Rowbotham & Sons. There were also various smaller operators such as Coastal Tankers Ltd, Hemsley Bell Ltd. and Burt, Boulton & Haywood Ltd. The latter were among the earliest operators, owning ALCHYMIST 382/95 and later the TARTARY 300/23. This latter vessel was probably intended to be named TARTAR for this was the name applied in brass letters by the builders, Crabtrees, and the 'Y' was painted in at the last minute before the naming. This Company was also a pioneer motor tanker operator, having the NITROGEN 78/12. She became a fleet oiler at Scapa Flow and Harwich during the First World War mainly serving destroyers. Despite being only 79'b.p. and occasionally having trouble with the early Bolinders engine, summer voyages were made to Holland. Post-war, Everards also carried petroleum products, particularly for ESSO. Metcalf Motor Coasters also entered the tanker trades at this time. The Bulk Oil S.S. Co., Ltd., was formed by J.W. Cook & Co., London and commenced operations with converted coasters such as PASS OF BRANDER 524/03 designed for the black oil trade. They also had a small shipyard at Wivenhoe where the tankers could be overhauled. The newly built PASS OF MELFORT 708/26 was used for clean products such as petrol. New vessels were steadily added to the first and in the 1940s, some war-built vessels were acquired. There were six steamers in the fleet when the first motor tankers were built in 1956. They were later taken over by Wm. Cory who had long been bunkering agents for British Petroleum. Coastal Tankers Ltd. began operations with vessels such as OTTERHOUND 860/27. In 1934 the steam tanker BASSETHOUND 1174/34 was completed for Hadley Shipping Co., Ltd., for bare boat charter to Coastal Tankers Ltd. The company ceased operations in the 1950s and BASSETHOUND became a slop barge in the Thames. The main clean products carrier by the 1950s was Rowbotham & Sons who entered the clean products trades in 1927 when the steamer LOCHSIDE was converted. The majority of their tankers were Dutch built motor tankers beginning with TILLERMAN 220/31. She was chartered to Russian Oil Products and the association continued when the company became Regent and then Texaco. There were ten motor tankers in the fleet when the old steam tanker BASSETHOUND was purchased and renamed POINTSMAN. She was towed up to Hull when purchased, for reconditioning by the Drypool Engineering & Drydock Co. This completed, she went on charter to Shell-Mex & B.P. Ltd. and was mainly employed carrying boiler oil from Stanlow Refinery to Herculaneum Dock Power Station for the next 12 years before being scrapped in 1968. She was Rowbotham's first black oil carrier. Prior to moving into the tanker trades, Rowbotham's had a long history in the dry cargo trades. Captain Rowbotham commenced with the sailing ketch PRINCESS in 1879. The first steamer CHEVIOT 258/91 was purchased in 1899. Further steamers were added and by this time the company was very active carrying Admiralty stores. This trade ceased with the reduction in the Navy, following World War One, and the small coasters were sold. In 1922 the Dutch steamer which became WHEELSMAN 1394/20 was acquired and was mainly employed carrying Blue Circle cement from the Medway to the Mersey. When sold in 1935 she was the last dry cargo vessel in the fleet.

Returning now to the dry cargo trades, the Warren Shipping Co., had a few old coasters such as the WARREN CHASE 466/21 which often carried coal to Peterhead for a few years after the Second World War. Names beginning 'Jolly' were used by Walford Lines Ltd. and they also traded the unique ferro-cement steamer ARMISTICE which carried 1150 deadweight. The company was originally Leopold Walford. 'Jolly' names were used later by F.W. Horlock's Ocean Trasnport Co., of Harwich. Originally F.W. Horlock owned MISTLEY 135/06 which was replaced by MISTLEY 487/22 built by the Mistley Shipbuilding and Repairing Co., not far from Harwich. Only the motor barges in the fleet remained in the 1950s. At Ipswich, R. & W. Paul Ltd. had barges prior to acquiring steamers such as OXBIRD 310/16 in the First World War. A few were added in the 1920s and the last of the steamers was disposed of in the 1950s. Beckwith's of Colchester also owned a few coasters.

The best known Hull company in the coasting trade was probably Robert Rix & Sons, founded by Captain Robert Rix in the 1880s. To finance the fleet, a new owning company, Humber Steam Coasters Ltd. was formed to purchase OWAIN TUDUR 234/82 in 1908. The characteristic names ending in 'rix' came into use in the next decade, as for example MAGRIX 314/16. Development was rapid during the First World War, helped by favourable freight rates, and several new ships were built. Immediately post-war, building of larger coasters continued with vessels such as KENRIX 692/21, one of four 900 tons deadweight ships added to the fleet between 1921 and 1924. A further company, Rix Steamships Ltd. was formed to finance some of these later ships. Largest of the ships was MAYRIX 794/20 and she alone was fitted with twin derricks at each of her two masts so that there were two derricks per hatch, a feature usually associated with the liner trades. They proved of use for the loading of timber on summer voyages to the Baltic. On one occasion making one last trip late in the Autumn, she was trapped by ice and did not get back from the Baltic until the following Spring. All the steamers in the Rix fleet were smartly kept and were among the first British coasters to have bow badges, Plate 83. The 900 deadweight vessels worked in the East Coast Coal trade to the smaller wharves and were often used by the Shoreham Shipping & Coal Company for their coal supplies to Shoreham (120), in the latter part of the 1920s. The smaller coasters such as PEGRIX 270/21 ranged widely (128). Unlike most coasters she had two derricks to work the single hatch like the SPURNPOINT (front endpaper), which was also built for Rix. Because of their good cargo gear, they were always popular for shipments which had to be handled by the vessel herself. They were also small enough to load the cargoes of cattle feeds, usually as compressed slabs, which were occasionally sent from the Old Harbour at Hull from the mill of Chambers & Fargus. Prior to the First World War the cargoes were mainly for Kings Lynn and Wells but in later years cargoes were also sent to Scotland, Robert Rix & Sons were quick to see the advantage of the Dutch motor coaster and so the NORRIX 264/30 was built for them in Holland. The name commemorated a steamer lost in 1921 and was also the beginning of the change to motor. In 1947 the three sons decided to split up and the fleet of motor coasters was divided. J.R. Rix formed J.R. Rix & Sons while H.D. Rix and E.B. Rix continued the old firm for some years before going into liquidation. Both had vessels with names ending 'rix', but those of J.R. Rix had green hulls.

The Hull Gates Shipping Co., was formed in 1937 to purchase a new motor coaster, but post-war they operated the steamer HUMBERGATE 1151/45 in the coal trade for a few years. However, the best known steamship operator at this time was the Holderness S.S. Co., Ltd., which purchased many "old timers" sold off by other owners as they re-equipped with motor ships or ceased shipowning. The company was formed in the early part of 1945. Steamers were relatively cheap as most owners were expecting a slump, as had happened at the end of the previous war. In fact it did not occur and the company were able to buy numerous old steamers for as little as £3,000 each as compared with motor vessels which were fetching around £90,000 for a 1,000 ton deadweight ship. They were often a bargain as five steamers made as much profit as one motor ship but cost considerably less to buy and so were attractive to owners with limited funds. All the coasters were given names beginning 'Holder', such as HOLDERNAZE 929/25. The fleet built up quickly to ten vessels by the mid-1950s, but because of their age some only lasted a few months in the fleet before being scrapped as surveys fell due or extensive repairs were needed. They traded all round the coast and Continent wherever profitable cargoes were to be found. The coal burners were all scrapped when freight rates fell in 1958, but the oil burner HOLDERNITH lasted until 1963 before being scrapped, and the company wound up. E.E. Atkinson & Prickett formed the Yorkshire Dale S.S. Co., Ltd., which owned a few coasters, mainly in the 1920s, such as WELTONDALE 883/24 and SWANDALE 966/24 which was on charter to France, Fenwick for a number of years and was eventually purchased by them in 1938 for £18,000, for their London-Goole general cargo trade. The firm ceased shipowning in the 1950s, but continued as agents. John Carlbom's Konnel S.S. Co., Ltd., ceased shipowning a little later. They originally purchased a few old steamers in the 1940s. Thos. Walker & Co. (Hull) Ltd. built up a small fleet of second hand vessels during the First World War but by 1927 only PATRINO 774/96 remained.

The Ouse and Trent were also navigable for steam coasters and a number of owners were based at Goole because of the coal shipments made from Yorkshire coalfields. The coal arrived by compartment boats for the most part. These small square barges, each containing about 38 tons of coal, were towed along the canals in strings (23), hoisted bodily and tipped down shoots into the coasters. John H. Wetherall made the change from sail to steam in the latter part of the 1890s, forming the Wetherall S.S. Co., Ltd.. which by 1908 had five steamers in the Goole coal trade including KNOTTINGLEY (10). The fleet was reduced to two vessels in 1928 and these were sold shortly afterwards. The KNOTTINGLEY had been bought by another local owner, the Hook S.S. Co., and renamed LULONGA. This company was managed by the Goole & Hull Steam Towing Co., who started with barges towed by tugs, but went into coasting shortly after the turn of the century. They expanded this side of the business during the First World War and subsequently retained the small steamers in the coal trade to smaller South Coast ports. However, on one occasion their KNOWL GROVE 370/09 was chartered for a coal cargo for Lerwick. The agents were telegraphed to expect her and the weather was fine and calm. There was some concern when she did not arrive on the appointed day nor on the following day. Finally she arrived three days overdue, having sailed past the Shetlands and got lost. None of the crew had made this voyage before and so were unused to the set of the tides. Most of the old coasting masters relied on landmarks and buoys for navigation. They also interpreted the form of the waves and the colour of the water, especially those who could not read or write. Long years of experience meant that they generally navigated with uncanny accuracy without the aid of charts. Navigation was left entirely to the master and mate, but the responsibility of maintaining the course rested with the seaman at the wheel and he was quite often left to the rigours of the open bridge while the captain retreated to the galley, for a cup of tea where he could keep an eye on the ship's progress in comfort. Sometimes he would appear on the bridge and order a slight change of course and many seamen recall the surprising accuracy with which their captains arrived off some small Irish port after steaming across the Irish Sea for example, having allowed for wind, tide and the tendency of the ship to go off a straight course.

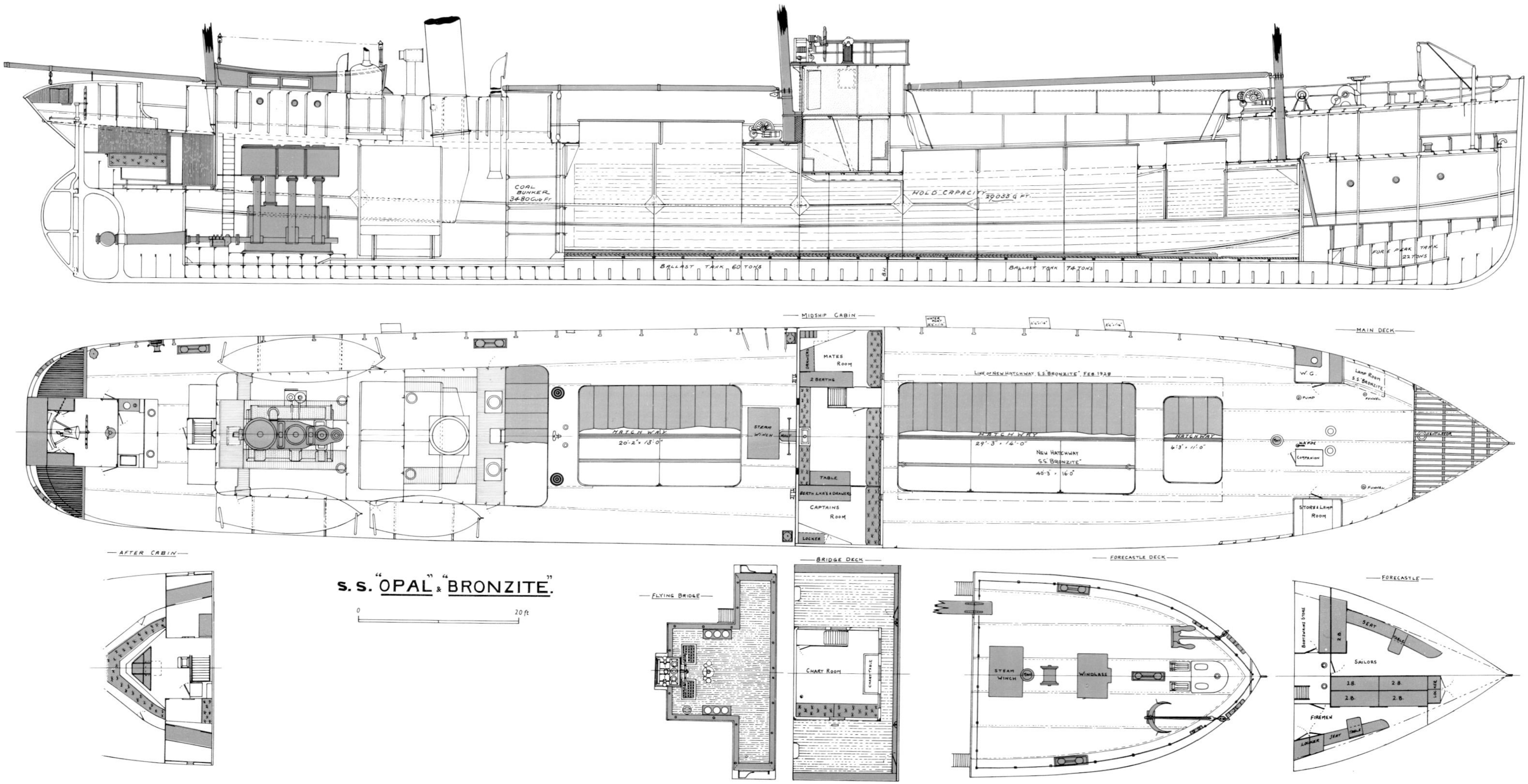

138

S.S. "OPAL" & "BRONZITE."

Plate 138

BRONZITE (ex. Citrine) and OPAL (costing £8,086)
were built by Scott & Sons, Bowling in 1894.

G. B. Wadsworth also made the change from sail to steam in the 1890s and merged with the Goole and Hull Steam Towing Co., in the 1920s. All these firms faced a new rival in 1908 when Captain Atkinson who was 68 at the time, and not liking retirement, decided to become a shipowner instead, purchasing the old steamer RALPH CREYKE in 1908. The Ouse S.S. Co. was founded in 1912 and the first ship built for the company was FAXFLEET 843/16 which began the use of local names ending in 'fleet'. The vessel was similar to KNOTTINGLEY and this type of coaster was popular with Goole owners as their deadweight was around 1,000 tons which was the usual size of Yorkshire house-coal cargoes ordered by merchants in such ports as Bruges, Antwerp and Ghent. However, it was more than two years before FAXFLEET entered the trade as, along with many other colliers, she was requisitioned to serve the fleet at Scapa Flow. In 1919, the BELGE, with engines amidships, was purchased and renamed SWYNFLEET 1168/14. She had been designed for the Danube grain trade and could carry 1,600 tons on the shallow draft of 13'5". This made her ideal for Goole as the river is also shallow with continually shifting shoals, particularly at the confluence of the Ouse and Trent. For example, if there had been a heavy rain storm in the Trent's catchment area, the extra water sweeping down the Trent could alter the shape of the sand banks at the junction overnight. Groundings were common and ships often scraped over the bottom. On one occasion the SWYNFLEET was just touching and kept swinging round, so they made the last part of the journey going astern. SWYNFLEET and BROOMFLEET were both in the Baltic timber trade in Summer, (131). The early 1930s saw the peak of the slump and all four ships of the fleet were laid up for long periods. However the YOKEFLEET was chartered to the Shoreham Shipping and Coal Co. (140) as she could take larger cargoes into Shoreham than the Rix ships and thus show a saving. Other vessels were taken on charter by France, Fenwick to carry the Australian wool transhipments from London in season. At times, Atkinson ships were also chartered by the Goole S.S. Co., Ltd. for their regular sailings to Hamburg and Antwerp. The ships were fully employed in the War and YOKEFLEET even survived the Normandy landings, where she was under fire for several hours laden with 500 tons of ammunition (140). Larger oil burning ships such as MAYFLEET 2020/42 were bought in the post-war period, but because of their size and draft, were mainly used in the Tyne coal trade. The company was wound up in 1961 as the coal trade had declined. Much coal carrying was done for Hargreaves who were selling agents for the Airedale group of collieries, but they later purchased ships of their own, beginning with HARFRY 909/24. In later years their vessels were managed by Comben Longstaff.

The Buck S.S. & Coal Exports Co., Ltd., were also coal sales agents. On completion the CYRILL DANNEELS 1585/24 was the largest steamer that regularly traded to Goole and was used in the coal trade to Belgium. Because of her size, she often got into difficulties, and was sold in the slump of the 1930s, as were the ships of Calvert Colliers, which was started in the 1920s. The East Yorkshire S.S., one of the smaller firms, had COTTINGHAM (141).

Captain William Aiston owned a few coasters in Scarborough during the First World War, but the next important centre northwards is Middlesbrough. Perhaps the best known name in the Middlesbrough coasting trade is that of the Constantine family. They had long been connected with the Baltic and later tramping trades when R.A. Constantine and T.H. Donking formed the Meteor S.S. Co., Ltd., in 1907 and entered the coasting trade. The first ship was CEDARWOOD 654/07 and by 1914 there were four coasters in the fleet, which were mainly engaged in regular cargo services to the Continent. This fleet was sold in the early 1920s and the last ship passed to the Donking S.S. Co., when the original partnership was dissolved as Mr. R.A. Constantine left the company and a new company, T.H. Donking & Sons Ltd. was formed in 1923 to manage the ships. They also managed the Kingdon S.S. Co., which took delivery of DONA FLORA 786/24 and DONA ISABEL 784/24 which were used for the general cargo service. The 'Toft' S.S. Co., Ltd., was also formed and owned five tramps by 1938, such as WHITETOFT 883/24. The last two steamers were both sold to the Holderness S.S. Co., in the 1950s. The main company, engaged in the ocean trades, became Joseph Constantine S.S. Line in 1920 and when building prices were favourable in 1923, ordered their first coasting colliers. First to be delivered was the LEVENWOOD 803/24, followed by sisterships LARCHWOOD 914/24 and COPSEWOOD (88). Some second hand vessels were also bought. The next important step forward was the commissioning of LINWOOD 992/32, which was fitted with an improved type of triple-expansion engine from North Eastern Marine. The ships carried considerable quantities of coal for Associated Portland Cement to Swanscombe and Greenhithe, returning northwards with cement. The bags of cement were loaded in, and left in slings to expedite the discharge. The slings were returned to the cement works from time to time when one of the ships was taking coal to the cement works. Household coal was carried from the Tyne to London for John Hudson and one ship was occupied running coal to Portsmouth Power Station and the dockyard in the mid-1930s. Gas coal was also regularly carried from Seaham to Ipswich. Coal was also carried to near Continental ports, usually Rouen, where a cargo of gypsum was often obtained for the plasterboard works at Greenhithe. Then if all worked well, there could be a cargo of pig iron from Fords works at Dagenham for Grangemouth to provide a northbound cargo. Ten steam colliers were in service by 1937 when the first motor collier was delivered. Further motor vessels were built during the Second World War. However, during this War, all ships were under general requisition and the owners in effect just acted as managers for the Government. Three coasters were lost, but were soon replaced by motor ships. With the post-war decline in the coasting trade, both AVONWOOD and TEESWOOD were sent out to trade in the Canadian Lakes during the summer in the 1950s. Smaller owners in Middlesbrough included Coombs (Middlesbrough) Ltd. and A. Chester who started up at the time of the First World War. The latter handled most of the basic slag shipments out of Middlesbrough for British Basic Slag. In the latter part of

YOKEFLEET, 822/10, on charter to the Shoreham
Shipping & Coal Co., and in their funnel colours.

F. Atkinson Esq.

the 1930s he had four coasters around 500 tons gross such as SOUTHWICK 443/17 which had originally been built for the Anglo-American Oil Co., Ltd.

Further up the coast, the Marquess of Londonderry's investments in his collieries included Seaham Harbour and a fleet of colliers. He was one of the early steam collier owners and had a fleet of 14 vessels by 1885, mostly named after members of the family, including some ocean going vessels. The fleet was much reduced in the 1920s and the last vessels were sold in the 1930s.

Sunderland was also an important coal port and home of James Westoll's fleet. Many of his vessels were engaged in ocean trading and the more distant continental voyages, but there were 17 smaller vessels in the fleet by 1890. Following the First World War, the short sea fleet was down to less than six vessels, but some large colliers were built such as WEST-BURN 2842/29 which was their last ship when sold in the 1950s. The earlier names often ended in 'ent', but later, names beginning 'West' were used. Freear & Dix was founded by Captain Freear who, by 1899, had two colliers. One was the old iron ship ALLERWASH 381/61, purchased in 1897 and often employed in the coal trade from Goole to Shoreham and Gosport (149). A few smaller coasters were operated in the 1920s. Small coasters were also operated from Sunderland by Thomas Rose & Partners. They had built up an important fleet of seven vessels by 1918, but for much of the 1920s and 30s were down to two vessels, by now with names ending in 'side' as in EDENSIDE 366/21. The company expanded for a while in the 1950s, purchasing old steamers for the coal trade to the East coast of Scotland, and later changing to motor vessels and finally concentrating on road haulage.

By far the greatest fleets of colliers were centred on Newcastle-on-Tyne. Many of the companies such as Witherington & Everett, had vessels with engines amidships and often worked outside home trade limits and so will not be considered in detail here. Their fleet consisted of two vessels in the 1890s, but later, management of the John George Hill S.S. Co., Ltd., was taken over and by 1918 the company were managing 12 vessels, mostly with names suggestive of speed like QUICKSTEP 1446/09. The fleet was largely renewed during the 1920s and consisted of 15 vessels in 1927. John Ridley, Son & Tully operated similar vessels particularly prior to the 1920s after which they changed over to ocean vessels. Both firms were active in the Baltic, Mediterranean and near Continental trades. The vessels of the Pelton S.S. Co., were also similar. This company was formed by J. Reay and R.S. Gardiner in 1899 to take over the 8 colliers owned by the Pelton Colliery. The fleet expanded to 16 vessels by 1918 which continued the use of musical terms ending in 'o' such as RONDO 1906/12. Further vessels were built in the 1920s, but by the 1950s the fleet was being reduced in size and mainly carried coal coastwise in vessels such as the LESTO 1893/18 and closed down in 1961 when their last vessel, their only motor ship, was sold. Loading coal was rapid and more than 24 hours in port was unusual. The crews were divided into two watches and after writing down their addresses and leaving a shilling to pay for a recall telegram, those in the watch ashore were over the side almost before the ship was moored. Similar steamers were owned by Broomhill Collieries Ltd., which began with one steamer in the 1880s and owned the port of Amble. The ships regularly ran to London with coal and TURRETHILL 691/95 made many such voyages prior to the First World War, after which a few larger vessels were built and the last sold by the 1940s. The Lambton & Hetton Collieries, later amalgamated with the Joicey Collieries, built up a considerable fleet of colliers. Beginning their fleet in the early days, they had 15 vessels by 1888 which were originally managed from Sunderland by H.T. Morton & Co. Most had local names such as HEDWORTH

(141) COTTINGHAM (left) bound for Goole in ballast and MOORSIDE (right) off Hull.

1081/84. The fleet was largely sold in the early 1920s and the remainder placed under a new company, the Tanfield S.S. Co., Ltd., which had some larger vessels built. The company was taken over by Stephenson Clarke in 1952. In summer their large four-hatch colliers worked in the Baltic timber and the Spanish iron ore trades. Throughout the 1920s rates were below 3/- per ton for Tyne to London and it was not until 1936 that there was an improvement to 4/- per ton.

Sharp & Co., were also long established collier owners with four vessels by 1888. The fleet always remained fairly small and from early days vessels were usually given names beginning 'El' as in ELSDON 1522/14, lost on a voyage to Odense with coal in 1925. The last steamers were sold in the 1950s. E.R. Newbigin purchased steam colliers in the late 1890s and by 1918 had five vessels most of which had names beginning 'Gr' as in the GRIPFAST 1109/10 which was built for the company and lost in 1942. She was replaced by another GRIPFAST 2866/41 which had a rather unfortunate history, for as the STANCLIFFE she had stranded and broken her back on the approach to Sharpness with a cargo of timber from Emden in 1947. Initial salvage attempts failed and finally a local ship repair firm cut her in half and shifted her out of the fairway. After this operation, temporary bulkheads were fitted over the open ends. The two halves were then towed to Newport, Mon., where the ship was reassembled and reconditioned, after which she joined the Newbigin fleet. GRIPFAST and the other steamers were sold in the 1950s and replaced by a new motor ship, the GREATHOPE completed in 1958, but the slump in rates of the late 50s caused her to be sold to the Shipping & Coal Company. In earlier times T.H.Catchside & Co., had traded a few small steamers such as the MOORSIDE (141), prior to World War One.

However, the main operator prior to World War One of the smaller coasters was Robinson Brown & Co., who managed 'T' Steam Coasters begun in the 1890s. Some of the vessels were usually employed carrying coal to East Coast Scottish ports taking both household coal and bunker coal for the drifters. Coal was also carried southwards and JAMES TENNANT 203/93 was the first steamer to the Southwick power station of Brighton Corporation in 1902 with coal for the steam machinery being used on the site. She made many subsequent voyages carrying the steelwork used in construction. The larger coasters were also active carrying packed herrings to the Continent and moving empty herring barrels during the season. The early ships like COASTER 269/03 and FREIGHTER 297/10 which carried about 280 tons on a draft of 12'6".(After the First World War, 9 standard 'Q' ships such as FALCOLNER 621/18 were managed for the Brown Shipping Co. (Newcastle) Ltd, but were soon sold as they were not suited for coasting). The small coasters could not manage more than about five or six days steaming without bunkering so they were best suited to the shorter runs. They were always bunkered with the faster burning Northumberland coal as they could not get good fires with the unscreened Durham coal, burnt by the ocean ships. With the Northumberland bunker coal, they could manage Lerwick or Stornoway and back. In the 1920s they got about 3/6d per ton for coal to Aberdeen, 5/- to Wick and 6/- to Orkney. When carrying coal to Devon and Cornwall, they loaded stone for London from such quarries as that at Grosnez Point, Guernsey. The smallest steamer, TYNESIDER of 160 tons deadweight was built for carrying machinery, but was often used for coal. Of the larger coasters, QUAYSIDER 595/13 was of special note, as she could carry 700 tons on a maximum draft of 12'9" aft, whereas most vessels of her size drew nearer 14 feet. Because of her shallow draft, she could take her full cargo of coal into Par, Cornwall on the best tides. The larger ships also brought in cargoes of bog iron ore from Delfzijl and Esbjerg which were delivered to various gas works where it was used to remove sulphur from the coal gas. Later the ships carried the 'spent oxide' to the Mersey where the sulphur was extracted. Cement was also carried after the First World War in association with Henry & MacGregor. The fruit and vegetable trade usually fell to QUAYSIDER with SOJOURNER 435/20 and ARTIFICER 386/05 helping out. One of the steamers also brought over the French onion men and their bicycles so that they could cycle round the district selling their onions. This done, they assembled for the return trip and paid the company for the charter of the ship. Robinson, Brown's main local competition came from G.T. Gillie who started in 1911 with the purchase of the FERRUM 271/00, of 260 deadweight, for £3,500. She had lain idle in the Clyde for one and a half years after her Glasgow owners had failed. She turned out to be a rather interesting investment because the large engine room was such that the propelling power deduction left a nett tonnage a fraction under 20. Ships under 20 tons nett could trade to the Thames without paying dues and claim certain other advantages. Eventually the Board of Trade decided an error had been made and re-assessed the tonnage at 105. However, with some engine room modifications, the company managed to get a reduction to 95 tons which gave some advantages. A shipowning company, the Ferrum S.S. Co., was formed to own the ship which was soon joined by the ARGENTUM 246/08. The latter made a voyage to Spitsbergen carrying stores and machinery, a long voyage for a little ship of 220 tons deadweight. In 1914 the company became G. T. Gillie & Co., and G. T. Gillie & Blair in 1919. Border Coasters was formed in 1913 and also bought two small vessels. A further company, Cheviot Coasters was formed in 1915 and purchased CRAIGSIDE among other vessels. The more modern vessels were mostly taken for war service and this is why older steamers such as CRAIGSIDE and DEERHOUND 420/82 were purchased. They had engines amidships and did not compare well with the newer engines-aft coasters. As expected, neither was taken for Government service, and so they were soon employed at very favourable freight rates, carrying coal to the South Coast. This was carried a step further when some schooners were traded for a time. The steamer MORAY FIRTH was purchased in 1918 and brought names ending in 'firth' to the fleet which then numbered eleven coasters and two schooners. G. T. Gillie (Coal Exporters) Ltd., was formed and eleven new steamers ordered. First delivered was CROMARTY FIRTH 638/19 which cost £41,200. A potential buyer offered £60,000 for the vessel in 1920 but was refused; in the event, she was sold four years later to William Robertson. The ship and her sister were built with longer voyages in mind. Coal was carried from the Clyde to Iceland where dried fish cargoes were loaded for Bilbao or Barcelona. The ships also traded in the Baltic as far as Leningrad. The company's first motor ship was ARRAN FIRTH 346/21. The Bolinders hot bulb engine gave continual trouble and the ship was a costly failure and was sold at a considerable loss in 1925. The slump began in 1921 and by 1922 a number of the company's ships were laid up. However, ROYAL FIRTH 411/21 and her sister ABINGDON FIRTH, also of 480 deadweight had single long hatches and soon began to get long steel cargoes and machinery. BORDER FIRTH 469/19, purchased at a favourable price in 1923, on one occasion carried a new rudder to Southampton for the AQUITANIA. Two new shipowning companies were formed to take advantage of the cheap second-hand ships coming on to the market, Firth Shipping Ltd., and Northern Coasters Ltd. First ship for Firth Shipping was CROMARTY FIRTH 377/24. Special care was taken with her design and a leading naval architect prepared plans to attain the lowest possible fuel consumption at a speed of nine and a half knots. In service she used under five tons per day saving on bunkers and the fact that only one fireman was needed, except on long runs as the boiler required little attention. The bunker capacity was 62 tons, adequate for 12 days steaming on the longer runs such as Stornoway to Hamburg with herrings. A cargo carried nearer home in the 1920s was Portland stone used in the construction of the Tyne bridge while in contrast MORAY FIRTH made voyages to Casablanca with asphalt, returning with grain. DEEMOUNT 569/33 was built for the Aberdeen coal run while MURRAYFIELD, purchased in 1936, carried the Company's oddest cargo, a circus to Hamburg from Newcastle. Another motor vessel, the CROMARTY FIRTH 538/37 was built and this time proved very successful remaining in the fleet for 20 years. She was taken as an ammunition carrier in the Second World War and was one of the last support ships to escape from Norway. Many of the coasters had traded to Northern France and the ships' captains were able to give considerable assistance in planning the Normandy landings. In the post-war period the change to motor vessels was completed and these traded much more widely. Post-war, Anthony & Bainbridge managed a number of ships and originally began operations with a few vessels in the 1920s. To thirsty crews, the most important coaster throughout the period was James Deuchar's LOCHSIDE 242/05 and later the LOCHSIDE II 368/25 which regularly carried a precious cargo from Montrose to Newcastle; beer from the Lochside brewery. A general cargo service was offered on the return run.

The next main shipping centre northwards is Edinburgh with its port of Leith. Currie Line and George Gibson were primarily involved in the regular liner trade though the latter came into the bulk cargo trades during the 1950s with the gas tankers. The main tramp owner was A.F. Henry and MacGregor, who were agents prior to purchasing the 'puffer' MAYFLOWER 69/82 in 1907 for local sailings. First vessel to have a name to end in 'Head' was KINNAIRD HEAD 190/10 and intended for a service to Fraserburgh. Following the First World War these services were abandoned and vessels such as the RATTRAY HEAD 252/12 continued in the tramp trades, particularly cement from London to East Coast Scottish ports, a trade which they largely helped to develop. The ships carried coal or stone (from Inverkeithing) southwards. The cement trade northwards developed steadily. For example, in 1890, the Lerwick merchants Hay & Co. sold about 100 tons a year but by the 1960s the figure had risen to 6,000 tons. To suit the store size, coasters such as TOLSTA HEAD 673/11 which could carry 640 tons, discharged half her cargo at Kirkwall or Scrabster and took the remaining 300 tons to Hays at Lerwick in the 1930s. A.F. Henry & MacGregor undertook their first major building programme for coasters in 1921 when four ships were ordered, but one was sold on the stocks to other owners. The cement trade helped the company to build up a fleet of 12 coasters by 1939, largest of which was the TOLSTA HEAD, purchased in 1934. In 1941 the company was taken over by the London & Edinburgh Shipping Co., Ltd., but continued to trade as before. Five ships were lost during the war and in the post-war period the pattern of trade was completely changed. The Firth ports had little coal for shipment, so larger colliers were purchased to carry coal from North East England, though they continued to return with cement. One such vessel was DUNVEGAN HEAD 1454/21 which had engines amidships. Two steamers with engines-aft were purchased in 1949, but beginning in 1952 they were progressively replaced by motor ships. The cement trade soon began to decline as cement works were

ROBIN discharging herring barrels at Lerwick prior to 1900.

built in the north. In the post-war period a number of smaller companies came into steam coasting, such as Castle Coasters and G. A. Morrison but only operated for a short time. The Laverock Shipping Co. began in 1951 with a chemical tanker, but when this was returned to Germany, the ENID MARY 582/21 was purchased and chartered to carry agricultural lime from the Tyne to the East Coast of Scotland. The name was changed to the Enid Shipping Co. in 1955 and the steamer scrapped in 1956, though the company continued with motor vessels for a few years. W. N. Lindsay were initially grain merchants and stevedores in Leith, purchasing the CASTLEROCK (ex. Abbotsford) 289/04 in 1932 to carry their grain cargoes. However, the coal trade was soon entered amd further small steamers were bought in the 1940s. A number of old steamers were traded for a few years in the 1950s such as JULIET DUFF 499/20, purchased in 1955 and scrapped in 1957. The first motor vessel ROSELYNE 422/39 began the use of 'Rose' names when purchased in 1955. James Cormack was mainly interested in the Latvian trade, but came into the coal trade nearer home in the winter.

Further up the Forth at Grangemouth J. T. Salvesen operated in the Baltic trades and was not connected with Chr. Salvesen who always had ships in the Norway trade apart from his whalers and was based at Leith. Gillespie & Nicol, formed in 1896, was also mainly active in the Baltic trades, but coal was also carried in the near Continental trades, for example, RAVELSTON 2088/06 loaded coal for Dunkirk on the 5th of June 1929 at Methil. Their last ship was sold in 1945. Buchan & Hogg became shipowners in 1920 with the purchase of the DUNSCORE 176/98 which was put into the local coal trade. Names beginning 'Dun' were generally adopted by the 1930s when they were operating a general cargo service from the North, to London. It was abandoned during and after the war. DUNMOIR was their last ship when sold in 1954. The shipbrokers, Walker & Bain, formed the Shield S.S. Co. in 1911 and purchased the JESSIE 332/01 for coasting. The first new ship was BALFRON 362/20 built for the coal trade to London. She often returned with moulding sand which was loaded at Erith for the foundries of Falkirk. The Kerse S.S. Co. was formed to enter the Baltic Trade, though it was in fact the BALMAHA 1428/24 of the Shield S.S. Co. which was used in this trade and she was their last ship when sold in 1946, the Company continuing as agents.

Fife coal was shipped from Methil and so when Matthew Taylor of Methil purchased his first ship, the WANS FELL 300/82 in 1906, she had plenty of outward cargoes. CAIRNIE 250/91 was soon added to the fleet and Aberdeen became one of her regular runs. She was wrecked in 1941 and was still giving good service despite her age. In season, the larger coasters such as PYLADES 705/03 and GOLFER 377/91 apart from the usual round of coal cargoes to the East Coast of Scotland and the South of England, also carried oats from Scotland to London. They also carried china clay to ports such as Sunderland and brought in a variety of cargoes from the Continent. In the herring season, they were to be seen with stock cargoes (empty barrels) for the fish curers, stacked up to the bridge deck in several tiers, on the stern grating and squeezed in alongside the engine casing. Such deck cargoes were very prone to damage in rough seas and were sometimes lost overboard. Cargo insurers always maintained that many more cargoes were lost overboard when the herring season had been poor and there was a surplus of barrels. In 1921, with the purchase of ABERHILL 1516/15, the Baltic and Mediterranean trades were entered. This was a logical step as Mr. Taylor was an Admiralty coal agent and regularly needed ships to carry coal to Malta and Gibraltar. These larger vessels were also suited to the London coal trade and often fitted in a voyage to London, between Mediterranean voyages. The Mediterranean trade was more profitable and attempts were made to sell the coasters (page 73). Only the steam coasters remained after the war and the last vessel, the steamer MOORLANDS 420/21, sold in 1957, the company continuing as agents.

In Dundee a few coasters were owned in the 1890s, such as those of William Kinnear & Co., though they were sold after a few years. However, J. Barlow owned small coasters such as LITTLE ORME 203/06 for many years and many similar sized coasters were converted for the sand trade, mainly by the Tay Sand Company. The Dundee, Perth and London Shipping Co. were originally in the general cargo liner trade, but as this trade declined, some of their vessels entered the tramp trades in the 1950s, while others were sent to the Canadian Great Lakes for summer trade. The smaller East Scottish ports were largely served by firms such as Robinson, Brown or Gillie & Blair. However, in the 1920s several owners based themselves at these ports. One such owner was J. M. Piggins who left A. F. Henry & MacGregor in 1923 to commence business as a shipbroker in his native town of Montrose. He had latterly been managers of their fleet and was thus well versed in operating steamers. His first ship, CLINT 215/96, was purchased in 1923, (8). She was soon fully employed in the local coasting

trade as an extract from her cargo book shows:
Movements for April and May 1924.

April	9	Wallsend to Berwick	Coal
	11	Berwick to Tyne	Light
	14	Tyne to Montrose/Stonehaven	Soda and Manure
	17	Stonehaven to Leith	Light
	19	Leith to Thurso	Manure
	24	Thurso to Kessock	Light
	26	Kessock/Inverness to Lerwick	Timber
	29	Lerwick to Portmahomack	Light
May	1	Portmahomack to Stockton	Potatoes
	8	West Hartlepool to Montrose/Aberdeen	Salt
	17	Aberdeen to Morrisonhaven	Light
	19	Morrisonhaven to Fraserburgh	Coal
	21	Fraserburgh to Montrose	Light
	23	Montrose to Tyne	Timber
	26	Tyne to Seaham	Light
	27	Seaham to Peterhead	Coal

Other cargoes carried during the year included stones, oilcake and slag. Further coasters were acquired, but CLINT herself was lost off Montrose, outward bound with a cargo of potatoes in 1927. All the steamers were sold at the end of the Second World War as Mr. Piggins felt that trading conditions would not favour steam coasters.

Further North, Aberdeen had long been an important shipping centre for the ocean and coasting trades, local merchants often owning their own ships, especially the coal merchants. One such firm was that of J. & A. Davidson who began as coal, granite and grain merchants in 1865, later purchasing some sailing vessels, before the first steamer BON ACCORD 469/71, was built for the company. Further vessels were then rapidly acquired for Baltic and Mediterranean trading and it was not until 1887 that the company decided to confine shipping activity to the coal trade of Aberdeen. This reduced the fleet to BON ACCORD and BAL-LOCHBUIE 677/80. The Company continued to own up to three vessels throughout the steam era and perhaps the best remembered is TORQUAY 870/14, purchased in 1923, which then served the Company until 1960 during which time she carried close to 2,000,000 tons of coal to Aberdeen. Much of the coal came from the Durham coalfields which had long associations with Aberdeen. The main suppliers were the Earl of Londonderry's collieries and Bedlington colliery. In the early part of the 20th century much of the coal was sold for trawler bunkering, but this trade vanished during the 1950s. The local gas works was supplied as well as industrial users. In summer TORQUAY could be released from the coal run for up to two weeks at a time before more coal was needed, allowing her to enter the general coasting trade.

Ellis & McHardy were established as coal merchants in 1880 and purchased the iron steamer SPRAY 632/72 in 1887, retaining her until 1932 when a new SPRAY was delivered. The third main coal merchants to become shipowners were the Aberdeen Coal Co. in 1902 upon delivery of REDHALL 841/02. Two new ships were delivered to the company in 1919, a new REDHALL 1093/17 and FERRYHILL 1086/19. The two steamers each of about 1,200 deadweight, were both needed to carry coal to Aberdeen in winter, but in summer one was released for general coasting and because of this, the company changed its name to the Aberdeen Coal & Shipping Co. in 1920. The steamer released in summer, often carried coal to North France and at times returned with spring vegetables for Aberdeen. FERRYHILL was lost in 1940 when she struck a mine, but REDHILL lasted until 1959 when she was replaced by a motor ship. The Northern Co-operative society also had a collier, the THRIFT 506/04 which was replaced by THRIFT 648/31 (145), which was one of the last steam coasters trading when scrapped in 1968. Last of the Aberdeen steam colliers to be built was Lewis' steamer MOUNT BATTOCK 396/39 which carried coal to the coal wharf adjacent to the Company's shipyard.

The Aberdeen Lime Co. Ltd. had their own vessels, firstly sail and later steam, owning the LADY CATHCART by 1888, but all were sold by the 1920s. Two companies in the coasting and near Continental trades prior to the First World War were G. Elsmie & Son who managed the North Eastern Shipping Co. Ltd. which had six vessels by 1908 all with engines aft and bridge amidships. Wm. T. Moffatt's steamers were rather smaller and most had names of Aberdeenshire villages beginning with 'C' and ending in 'ie', as for example CLUNIE 227/89, though perhaps CRATHIE is best remembered. She collided with the liner ELBE of Norddeutscher Lloyd in the North Sea in the early hours of the 30th of January 1895; the liner sank with the loss of 334 lives while the coaster continued on her way with damaged bows. In the darkness her crew had not realised the liner had been fatally struck. Moffatt's coasters were locally known as the 'snowball liners' because of the white ball on the blue band just below the black top of the yellow funnel. They were often employed on the coal run to Aberdeen. Wm. R. Aitken also owned small steamers, the first was the wooden steamer BARBARAS 93/88 which was purchased in 1890 and followed by RONA 115/70 in 1900. In 1920 the fleet consisted of WAVE QUEEN 295/03, sold in 1929 and ZEALOUS 324/02 which often carried coal from Sunderland to Aberdeen, until lost in 1944, after which the company continued as stevedores and was later taken over by Cooks who were interested in the Norwegian and Baltic trades with vessels such as GLEN TILT 666/83.

Mitchell & Rae, the grain and general merchants of Newburgh, originally had sailing vessels, but GEM, their first steamer, was built in 1878 and was followed by RUBY 234/82.

(145) THRIFT built 1931.

Steamers were owned until the First World War after which none were owned until a motor-ship was built for the company in 1952. Peterhead was essentially a centre for fishing, but many coasters were regular visitors, bringing bunker coal for the steam drifters. The several coal merchants usually received their coal supplies in 400 to 500 ton shipments. The different merchants usually worked with different suppliers who, in turn dispatched the coal in vessels from different coasting fleets. For example, in the 1940s to 50s, coal for the Co-operative Society usually arrived in W. N. Lindsay's coasters, while that for the Drifter Coal Co. came in vessels such as DEESIDE of Thos. Rose. In the herring seasons of the 1930s, barrels of herrings and stock cargoes were often carried by the coasters of J. M. Piggins and Geo. Couper while supplies of tin-plate for the canning factories arrived in various Irish sea coasters. Fraserburgh had its own coasting fleet from 1940 when Mr. G. A. Sheves purchased the steamer ARCHMOOR 246/08 and further ships were added later, being given names beginning with 'Arch' as soon as war-time restrictions on the renaming of ships were lifted. They traded quite widely until steam became uneconomic and the last to be scrapped was the ARCHGROVE 602/94, in 1957.

One of the most interesting coasters to be built in the 1920s was the TORWOOD 251/21 which was built of wood at Buckie, by Jones' Buckie Slip & Shipyard Ltd. Her machinery which had been made 7 years earlier about 50 miles away by the Rose Street Foundry & Engineering Company of Inverness in 1914. Jones owned her for a number of years and she often carried logs and timber for his Larbert Saw Mills as well as coal and other cargoes. She had no ballast tanks and could be a little difficult to handle in heavy seas when she was empty. George Couper & Co., of Helmsdale purchased three ships for the coal trade from Firth of Forth ports to East Coast Scottish ports in 1932. They were named the BERRIEDALE 614/22, HELMSDALE 717/21 and NAVIEDALE 383/06 and thus 'dale' became the style for Couper ships. The coal trade was much reduced in the 1940s and the last vessel was sold in 1947.

In the early part of this century the herring industry was at its peak with Lerwick as the principal centre. The season began there and as the herring shoals migrated southwards, the drifters followed them down the coast as far as Great Yarmouth. In Lerwick there were still over 40 fish curers operating in the 1920s, each with their own jetty for receiving and dispatching the fish. The herrings were usually lightly cured and so special shipment was necessary if they were to reach the main canning factories in Hamburg in good condition. East coast owned vessels, such as Matt. Taylor's GOLFER, 420 tons deadweight, would bring in empty barrels, often from the factory at Buckie. Salt needed by the curers often arrived in one of R. R. Clark's coasters such as BEESTON, from Runcorn. His coasters often stayed on with the more local vessels, to move stock cargoes or load herrings for Hamburg. At the height of the season, work went on almost round the clock. Each curer would know the quantity and quality of the day's batch by afternoon and would pass this information to the shipbrokers in the herring trade. The brokers then telephoned customers that they thought would be the most interested in the different batches, working from 8 a.m. to 10 p.m. at night. As soon as the orders were confirmed, the loaders would ferry the barrels of herrings out to the coasters waiting in the Sound, often working from 6 a.m. in the morning to 2 a.m. the following morning. Hay & Co. (Lerwick) Ltd. originally operated fishing schooners in the white fish trade, but the last of these was sold before the First World War, the firm concentrating on the merchanting side of the business. Coal was supplied for bunkering and up to 1,800 tons was sold in a week. The coal was usually purchased in 400 to 500 ton consignments. Fife coal often arrived in Matt. Taylor's WANS FELL, but on one occasion PYLADES was accepted with 800 tons. Tyne coal usually arrived in Robinson, Brown's coasters and in the late 1920s, their Appledore ships such as ORLEIGH were usually on the run, bringing 500 ton cargoes.

On the West coast of Scotland the main centre was Glasgow which had many firms both large and small in the coasting trade, best known of which is probably William Robertson. Mr. Robertson began with a coal scow on the Forth & Clyde Canal, purchased in 1852 for £10 and slowly he expanded his interests to sailing vessels and then 'puffers'. The first steam coaster was AGATE built for him in 1878 (67). Two years later he took over the management of vessels belonging to the Carnlough Lime Co., and the movement of limestone became increasingly important, as larger amounts were needed by the blast furnaces of the Clyde, to increase steel production for the shipyards and other industries. The fleet grew rapidly in the 1880s and ten years after the AGATE had been built, there were 15 coasters in the fleet, all named after precious stones. Most had been built by local yards and were now employed in the general coasting trade, carrying coal to Ireland and venturing as far as the Baltic for timber, as well as handling considerable quantities of limestone. They were large compared with the average coasters of the times, with deadweights between 400 and 700 tons. The largest vessel was AMETHYST 552/83 which was built at John Fullerton's yard. Much of the limestone was carried from Kneeshaw, Lupton's quarry in North Wales. The company originally had their own vessels, and these were later managed by William Robertson. The usual round voyage was coal to Ireland, across to the quarry and load for Glasgow or elsewhere as required. The quarry itself was later purchased in the early 1920s. Business was good for steam coasters in the latter part of the 1880s and AGATE was time chartered to Kneeshaw, Lupton for £185 per month, a good rate for a ship of 210 tons deadweight. SYLFAEN was chartered for £300 per month two years later and would rapidly repay the first cost at this favourable rate, to her owners who were Kneeshaw, Lupton. They must have been very satisfied with Mr. Robertson's management of their ships. Growth of the fleet was phenomenal with four of five ships delivered each year during the 1890s, helped by the fact that the cost of new vessels had dropped, for example OPAL 599/94 of 735 deadweight cost £8,086 in contrast to the £12,072 paid for the AMETHYST of the same size ten years earlier. In the latter part of the 1890s a few vessels with engines amidships were built, but the trend was not continued and the company concentrated on coasters. This last spate of orders brought the fleet up to 45 vessels and as trade levelled off few further ships were ordered. In the 1890s some ships were sent to trade on the eastern seaboard of the U.S.A. for a few years. Cargoes carried around the British Isles were very varied as the samples below indicate:

DIAMOND 468/86:   Lerwick to Hamburg with herrings, best time 54.5 hours in 1907.
JACINTH 502/88:   Railway sleepers (10,200) from Ardrossan to Barrow. Wood pulp from Gotenburg to Preston (12.9.96). Malt from Grimsby to Cork (27.4.96). Barley from Liverpool to Dublin (4.4.01).
AMBER 401/92:   Coke (maximum 290 tons in hold and on deck). Liverpool to Dublin. (2.4.10).
CORAL 477/92:   Hay from Limerick to Newport (27.7.07).
CAMEO 394/83:   Empty barrels, coal & coke to Whaling Station, Harris, returning with barrels of oil, glue and bone meal.
OPAL 599/94:   Salt (623 tons) Weston Point to Wick (August 1908).
GIRASOL 602/95:   Soya beans; Rochester to Greenock. Cable (72 miles) Greenock to Plymouth (October 1909). Phosphate from Ghent to Belfast (21.11.04).
ACHROITE 1196/98: Cork waste from Seville to Heysham. South African maize from Southampton to Glasgow.
MALACHITE 743/20: Coal from Glasgow to Cork.

These varied cargoes are typical of the coasting trade at the turn of the century. In addition, in the 1890s some of the ships ran a regular cargo service from Preston to Hamburg, but it was discontinued after some years. It was not until after the First World War that more modern vessels began to replace those built in the 1890s, culminating in FLUOR 914/25. High building prices at the end of the war discouraged them from ordering many new ships, however the company took advantage of the almost new ships coming on to the market as freight rates tumbled. A number of vessels were purchased, especially from the fleets of E. T. Lindley and H. Harrison (Shipping) Ltd. In 1938 the fleet stood at 36 vessels, some of which were on contract to carry supplies for the new Ford plant at Dagenham. However, like most other companies, the majority of cargoes were carried on a voyage basis which meant that captains rarely knew where they would be going more than one voyage ahead, or if trade was bad, it was usual to direct the vessel back to the Tyne, say, for orders in the hope that by the time she arrived, the Company's agent in that port would have found her a cargo.

Usually all went smoothly, as owner and agent knew roughly what size of cargoes were likely to be coming on to the exchange and their frequency. If there were too few ships for the cargoes offering, rates would be pushed up a little and owners would direct ships from elsewhere to take advantage of the more favourable rates. If trade was slack generally, the older, less efficient ships would lay up or be sold for scrap. The good shipbroker would do his best to retain the business for his ships by offering good ships to charterers, who tended to use the same vessels if they had found them satisfactory in the past. In the 1920s and 1930s ships often went considerable distances in ballast to pick up cargoes. Thus when Captain McGlashan received a telegram in Antwerp telling him to proceed to Bonawe (in Scotland), he wired back the usual 'Received wire, proceeding to Bonawe'. This aroused considerable consternation at the office in Glasgow, for the wire they had dictated over the phone had said Boulogne. Apparently, the Scottish operator had misunderstood. Meanwhile the ship was still proceeding to Bonawe and it was not until she reached the Lizard that one of the shore signal stations managed to turn her back to Boulogne. There was no radio in coasters until the 1950s in many cases. Robertsons began the change to motor vessels in the 1930s with the delivery of SAPPHIRE 933/35 and the last steamer PYROPE was built in 1936. The ships were all involved in various ways during the Second World War and perhaps the luckiest survivor was SPINEL, abandoned in Boulogne when overrun by the Germans and found in the Channel Islands in 1945 with nothing more than superficial damage. The steamers were slowly sold as new motor vessels were built in the 1950s. The name Gem Line was brought more into use and the fleet reduced in size as the coasting trade declined. However their limestone quarry came to the fore when it was discovered that the hard crystalline limestone was ideal for making calcium carbide, so good in fact that cargoes were shipped to a Norwegian plant actually built to use the local Norwegian limestone.

The phenominal growth of the Robertson fleet was to some extent paralleled by that of James Hay who set up on his own account about 1880, having left J. & J. Hay. He had a fleet of 17 coasters by 1888, all with names beginning 'Strath'. Unfortunately, he ran into financial difficulties in 1890 and some of his ships were managed by Robertsons until sold. J. & J. Hay continued to be the style of the Hay family's 'puffer' operating company, while John Hay, who purchased his first coasters in the 1890s, was much more successful. The names of his ships were also very characteristic as, for example, THE BARON 367/92 and THE MONARCH 642/04, which were used in the coal trade to Ireland and were soon established in the general coasting trades. There were 15 ships in the fleet by 1908, but little more building was undertaken until the 1920s, when prices were favourable for the larger coasters around 800 to 900 tons gross to be built. The steamers were all sold in the 1950s and J. Hay & Co. did not operate motor vessels until taken over by Everards in 1956.

Paton & Hendry similarly started in the 1890s, beginning with puffers and moving on to coasters. The partnership split up prior to the First World War, J.M. Paton to become Britain's first owner of a large fleet of motor vessels. The McCallums joined the Hendrys to form Hendry, McCallum & Co., who remained in steam. The new partnership added five large coasters in 1915 such as BARSHAW 794/10, giving them a fleet of 19 vessels which included a number of puffers, but all were sold by the end of the First World War. John Paton, having founded the Coasting Motor Shipping Co., placed orders with various yards for numerous small motor vessels. The venture proved disastrous as the engines were unreliable and the war made good engineers unobtainable, so from a fleet of 16 vessels, all with names beginning 'Innis', there was just the INNISTRAHULL 238/13 left in 1927.

Mann, Macneal & Co. Ltd. purchased their first ships at the turn of the century and by 1905 had a fleet of 12 coasters adopting names ending in 'ford', such as SLATEFORD 355/03 and LATCHFORD (5). The owning company was known as the Ford Shipping Co. The company had a number of branch offices on the East and West Coast and the larger vessels ran in the East Coast coal trade. The fleet changed little subsequently and all were sold in the 1920s. J.G. Frew & Co. started in the 1880s with small steamers and had a number of coasters such as TANTALLON 270/00, built by J. McArthur of Paisley. The company failed in the early 1920s. A.F. Blackater started at about the same time and managed the ROBIN 366/90 in the 1890s (143), which after many years in Spain as the MARIA, returned to Britain in 1974 to be restored by the Maritime Trust as a typical example of the once numerous British steam coasters. Ballantyne of Glasgow owned coasters such as MADGE BALLANTYNE 508/95 which was a regular visitor to Connah's Quay from 1900-14 with salt cake for John Summer's steel works.

J. & A. Gardner were originally J. Gardner & Co., the company having been founded by Mr. John Gardner who was in fact a quarry master. He worked the Ballachulish slate quarries and purchased the small vessels ROB ROY and WHARFINGER to carry these slates to Glasgow and then purchased the granite quarry at Bonawe on Loch Etive. In the 1890s there was no mechanisation and the stone was wheeled to the little steamers in barrows and tipped in. Roadmaking always was reduced in winter so that the little ships, able to carry about 150 tons, transferred to the near Irish coal trade. In the early 1900s they were trading too much of Ireland, expecially the smaller ports such as Letterkenny and Dungarvan. The quarry trade continued to be important, chippings and particularly setts were supplied in considerable quantities for the construction of the Glasgow and much of the Liverpool tramway systems. By 1918 there were five steamers in the fleet and names beginning 'Saint' were adopted for the later ships rather than names beginning 'Ard' which had been used for those built at the turn of the century such as ARDACHY 210/04. Five new vessels were built at high prices at the end of the First World War such as SAINT AIDAN 362/20. Fortunately for the company British Aluminium had built a refining plant at Kinlochleven and it was soon arranged that coasters coming to the quarry would bring coke from Glasgow or alumina from Glasgow or Larne. The aluminium ingots were also taken from the plant to a variety of destinations. The stone was carried to Belfast or to the Riverside wharf just in front of the Company's office in Glasgow. Because of this, the captains made sure the coasters looked particularly tidy, while they themselves, resplendent in their bowler hats, supervised operations from the open bridge. In the 1940s the Belfast trade was lost to Penmaenmawr quarry. Some East Coast coal was carried in the 1920s and 1930s often on time charter or on a tonnage basis. There was also a considerable coal trade from Glasgow to Stornoway and to a lesser extent, the other Western Isles. The first motor coaster SAINT ANGUS 392/36 was put on the summer vegetable trade from Jersey and the change to motor vessels continued post-war as the company looked further afield for cargoes. Another quarry, the Eglinton Limestone Company (originally the Eglinton Chemical Co.), also had a few coasters from the 1880s such as GLENARM 300/04, to carry limestone from their quarry on the Antrim coast to Glasgow, and was later taken over by Ross & Marshall. J. Kennedy & Sons had a few coasters in the general coasting trade from the 1890s with names ending 'man' as for example, WELSHMAN 361/93. The last, CRAGSMAN 377/24, was sold in the 1950s. Another small owner was R. Cameron who had a few coasters such as KYLE RHEA 323/21, from the 1920s to the 1940s. Lang & Fulton of Greenock originally managed square-riggers and later ocean tramps before forming Ard Coasters in 1913, when ARDGARTH 770/13. was delivered. Further vessels were acquired and there were four vessels in the fleet by 1918. The company closed down in 1920, but the coasting fleet was taken over by the near-by steel stockholders, P. MacCallum & Sons Ltd., as the ships were often used to carry steel for the company. The steamers were replaced by motor vessels in the 1950s.

A newcomer to the Glasgow coasting scene of the 1920s was John Stewart & Co. John Stewart had been a sale and purchase broker since 1899, and decided to become a shipowner when second hand prices for coasters fell. His first steamer YEWDALE 477/90 was purchased from Earl Leslie of Dundee in 1923. Someone referred to the similarity of the name to 'U-boats' so recently the scourge of the coasting fleets, and so 'Yew-boats' they became from that day on. Further ships were purchased for home tramping such as YEWMOUNT 833/08 (149) and YEWBANK 621/14 which were working Tyne/Blyth to the South Coast and returning with stone from Newlyn to the Thames and then North in ballast. At the end of the 1920s, Mr. Stewart had six new ships built by Scotts of Bowling round six War surplus tug engines and some of the second hand coasters were sold. The ships ran on the East Coast and to the Continent, mainly northern France. Tyne/Blyth to the Thames was one of the more important runs and there were regular contracts with Charringtons and Alfred Blackmore, returning northwards with cement if possible, which was usually the case when coal was carried to one of the cement works. Voyages were limited to the East coast of Ireland, as there were virtually no return cargoes to be had from the West coast and the ships were likely to be delayed by bad weather, especially when in ballast. Similarly, the Cape Wrath passage was avoided as much as possible, because when cleaning fires, the steamers were liable to have difficulty maintaining steerage-way in the strong tides and winds liable to be encountered off the North West coast of Scotland. The company became John Stewart & Co. (Shipping) Ltd. in 1934, and after a period of ill health, Mr. Stewart died in 1936. The company was put up for sale and was purchased by Ian and Edgar Macfarlane, who had recently sold their interest in the 'White Funnel' fleet engaged in the Clyde passenger trade, and now decided to enter the cargo coasting trade. The ships remained on the East Coast trade during the war and YEWDALE among others, was ordered to Dunkirk, rescuing 900 men. The first convoys were not lead by coasters and were soon in difficulties. On one occasion the YEWCROFT signalled that they were getting too near the Banks but, by the time the leading ship saw the signal some were already grounding. After that, convoys were always led by coasters. The first motor ship was purchased in 1939 and further new motor ships were built in the 1950s to replace the steamers. The motor ships continued in the coal trade as they were well suited to the smaller wharves on the Thames around Grays, Essex.

Mr. W.S. Scott left the family's shipyard at Bowling in the 1920s to commence shipowning on his own account in Glasgow, forming the Western Navigation Co. Ltd. The first vessels were MACKVILLE 666/15 and MICKLETON 777/21. Later the larger MOIDART 1262/22 was added to the fleet and was rather exceptional as she ran consecutive voyages Methil to Southampton from 1931 to 1936 at rates of 3/6d to 3/7½d per ton, just making a slight profit. The old MACVILLE was the last to be sold in the 1950s. Post-war, the Aiden Shipping Co. Ltd. and the Mac Shipping Co. Ltd., both ran steam coasters for a short time and the latter firm was taken over by Metcalf Motor Coasters of London.

One of the most delicate cargoes regularly carried by coasters is explosives. Nobel's Explosives Co. Ltd. of Glasgow had the steamer DRUMHENRY from 1875 carrying dynamite, together with later vessels, such as LADY DOROTHY 578/16, delivering explosives to ocean-going ships at the various powder grounds, anchorages which had long been allotted for carrying out the loading operation well away from other shipping and docks. When not needed for this work they were used for coasting and the LADY TENNANT 452/03 was chartered to John Hay for a regular service to Stornoway, sailing every Thursday in 1914 and 1915. The fleet eventually became part of the Nobel Division of Imperial Chemical Industries. Another company absorbed by I.C.I was Kynoch Ltd. Birmingham, the gun cartridge makers. They had coasters from the 1890s for moving explosives to and from the factory in Arklow as well as carrying ammunition to ocean ships. MARIE 191/91 had been joined by six others by 1918, but all were sold after the war. Usually handling the explosives went smoothly, but Tom Coppack in his book 'A Lifetime with Ships' tells when things did not. Kynoch's had opened a factory at Queensferry during the First World War and the guncotton was taken down the River Dee

YEWMOUNT (ex. Hampshire) 833/08 in the Channel circa 1928, courtesy Captain Roberts.

The old iron collier ALLERWASH in her last years.

in two old schooners converted for the purpose and then loaded at the anchorage in Wild Roads into one of the waiting coasters, MAY, MARIE or ELLER for dispatch to Kynoch's treating house at Arklow. On one occasion the ELLER was being loaded when one of the cases fell out of the sling, as it was being hoisted. The crews scattered and ELLER's crew were practically away in the lifeboat before they realised that it was not going to explode. The crews then reassembled, but one member was missing. He was eventually found wrapped round a rope over the stern, fingers in ears still expecting the worst to happen.

On the Firth of Clyde, Rowan & Bain's coasters offered a regular cargo service, but John Campbell of Irvine was in the coasting trade in the 1930s and 1940s with a few steamers such as WALLROY 628/09 and DUNLEARY 480/05 both of which carried bricks from Irvine to the Shetland Isles in the 1930s for a housing scheme in Lerwick. Further south, the next main centres of coasting activity were Maryport, Workington and Whitehaven. The West Cumberland iron and steel trade supported a number of fleets in the 19th century. One was that of Hine Bros., Maryport, who commenced business about 1873 and originally operated square-riggers in the Australian trade, but the first steam vessels in the fleet such as HENRY SCHOLE-FIELD 963/72 made voyages in the home and near Continental trades. Small coasters such as the EARL OF CARRICK 258/75 were built for local trading. In the 1880s some more coasters were added to the fleet including the IVY HOLME 237/83 which was lost on her maiden voyage from Sunderland to Dublin. The ships were often employed in carrying rails and one of the Company's ocean going vessels carried the first consignment for the construction of the Canadian Pacific Railway. The Company closed down in 1911 as trade was now mostly handled in larger ships from Liverpool. In the 1920s and 1930s only the HOLY-HEAD 196/98 belonging to W.E. Fisher was based there.

Workington was the home port of R. Williamson & Son who owned the main shipyard and originally had a fleet of large sailing ships. In the 1890s they began to build coasters for their own account, but were always ready to sell if the price was right. For the most part the names ended in 'ia', such as CORINIA 870/28. Williamson's coasting fleet, by now operating under the name Northwest Shipping Co. was placed under the management of Joseph Constantine, Middlesborough, in 1938, as most of the fleet were running in the East Coast coal trade. Williamson's yard also built many fine coasters for other owners, particularly W.S. Kennaugh & Co., who managed the West Coast Shipping Company, originally at nearby Whitehaven. Their first steamer was SCALE FORCE 229/83, built at Williamson's yard. Starting with relatively small coasters, Kennaugh's soon had larger vessels which were also built by Williamson's yard, the company moving to Liverpool in the 1890s. The West Coast Shipping Co. was formed in 1905 to take over the six coasters and their single ship companies ranging from HOLME FORCE 269/87 to STOCK FORCE 538/05, each named after a waterfall (force), in the Lake District. The fleet was never large, but they became well known in the coasting trade as their ships were not confined to the West coast. They never forgot their connections with Whitehaven and their ships were all registered at that port even after the firm moved to Liverpool. Their grey hulled steamers with a plain yellow funnel were always well kept, Plate 126, and a captaincy in the Kennaugh fleet was much sought after. Though in the general coasting trade, they had a fairly regular sequence of cargoes in the 1920s such as, Newcastle; load coal for Guernsey where stone was loaded for London and from there the ship would sail for Liverpool with cement. A short voyage was then made in ballast to Fleetwood, where soda ash was loaded for Newcastle and from there coal for Antwerp, returning from there with general cargo for Liverpool. Another voyage sequence was Blyth; load coal for Newlyn and stone from there to London and then to Newcastle with cement. The Kennaugh Brothers, Willie and John, had many good contacts so that their ships were rarely without cargo and voyages in ballast were largely avoided, the secret of the successful owner. They liked their ships to look at their best and so avoided carrying the more dusty South

Wales coal as far as possible. The slump in freights and the fact that they were both well past retiring age, made them decide to leave the coasting trade to younger men with motor ships in 1958.

John Pattinson & Son of Whitehaven, originally Pattinson & Winter, started with small ships such as CLINT (8) in the mid-1890s, but had just the single steamer GLENMONA 213/13 by 1927.

One of the oldest West coast firms is James Fisher & Sons of Barrow which was formed in 1847 and had built up a fleet of 70 sailing vessels by 1863. Their first steamer was the SEA FISHER 297/83, completed by McIlwaine, Lewis & Co., Belfast; BAY FISHER 352/84 followed and established the pattern of nomenclature to be used for the fleet. Coasters were steadily added so that by 1908 there were eight vessels in the fleet and the sailing vessels reduced to 18, the last, ELLIE PARK was not sold until 1924. The company became James Fisher and Sons Ltd. in 1926. Various second hand steamers were purchased in the 1920s, but the fleet was down to three vessels at the depth of the slump in 1931. Trade then improved and 12 vessels were owned by 1938. The first motor vessel was built, appropriately, by Vickers-Armstrong at Barrow. Fisher ships often carried steel structures and other items such as guns to the shipyard for Vickers. By the 1930s some of the items being brought to the yard were so large that James Fisher and France, Fenwick formed the Fenwick, Fisher S.S. Co.Ltd. to operate the large collier SOUND FISHER 2950/40 which was designed to carry gun turrets for the new battleships then building at Barrow. The main hatch was 76 feet long and the coamings were bulged out to take the widest part of the turret. All the steamers were rapidly replaced by motor ships in the post-war period and were often used to carry heavy items of power station plant.

Across Morecambe Bay at Lancaster, Robert Gardner operated a few steam coasters beginning in the 1920s with vessels such as GROSVENOR 267/08. They often carried coal to Lancaster from the Mersey and the Point of Ayr Colliery on the Dee. One of the customers in Lancaster was Williamson's linoleum works and cargoes of whitening were also brought from the Thames for the works, as well as from Orr's Zinc White of Widnes. At other times the vessels worked in the Irish coal trade and the local stone trades. The MOUNTCHARLES 286/10 was also owned for many years and lasted until the 1950s when the last ships were sold.

Preston was the home port of J.H. Monks for a short time, but Joseph Gale had a few coasters based there around the time of the First World War. Various firms have been based on the Isle of Man, best known of which was the Ramsey S.S. Co. Ltd., which began during the First World War with steamers such as BEN REIN 212/05 which found ready employment bringing coal to the Island. The fleet grew to six vessels in the 1920s and the ships traded generally on the Irish Sea. Last of the steamers, BEN MAYE 323/21 was scrapped in 1964, leaving a fleet of motor vessels. The salt works at Ramsey had the little steamer MANXSONA 184/22 in the 1920s and 1930s, but the salt works itself closed in 1956 because of mainland competition. The Douglas S.S. Co. started at the same time as the Ramsey S.S. Co., trading small vessels such as TEXA 186/84, but their last vessel was sold in the 1930s.

Many coasters outward bound from Liverpool, found the Isle of Man useful in bad weather as it offered a haven of shelter from winter gales as, if the wind veered, it was always possible to steam round to the other side. As soon as the gale moderated, the coasters would continue on their way to such ports as Belfast which had a number of coasting owners. The largest fleet was that of John Kelly, a prominent coal merchant, his father Samuel having commenced business about 1840 and begun shipowning with the brigantine WILLIAM in 1861 and the business passing to his son John in 1877, who had the first steamer SUSANNAH KELLY 289/90 built for his fleet in 1890 and the sailing vessels sold off. She foundered on a voyage from Ayr in 1897. She was replaced by the steamer BALMARINO 419/98. The fleet grew slowly at first but increased quickly in the First World War to 16 ships by 1918 under the guiding hand of his son, Samuel Kelly, but the company became John Kelly Ltd. in 1911. Apart from the coal trade to Belfast and other Irish ports, the ships were also active in the general coasting trade during the 1920s capturing some of the West coast cement trade which had been carried in Robertson's ships. The vessels returned to the Thames via ports such as Southampton where stone from the quarries of North Wales was discharged. By this time, the larger vessels were running in the East coast coal trade. New vessels like GLEN-MAROON 716/17 had local Irish place names, while second hand vessels often retained their original names. A number of new ships were built in the 1930s including the flagship BARONSCOURT 869/35. The vessels were a common sight lying along Queen's Quay, at Albert Quay or coming up the Musgrave Channel into Belfast. At the outbreak of war there were 46 ships in the fleet. Of these five were lost and 18 were taken for various missions during the Second World War. The larger coasters such as CREWHILL and GLENDALOUGH continued in the East Coast coal trade, facing the dangers of mines, bombs and aircraft attacks in addition to German motor torpedo boats, the last making many attacks, especially off Great Yarmouth. GLENDALOUGH 868/36 was hit by a bomb on the 9th of August 1941 which penetrated the engine room, blowing the stern of the ship apart, killing both engineers, three firemen, the cook and an A.B. However, the after bulkhead of the hold remained watertight and the ship was eventually towed into Grimsby and later repaired, only to strike a mine in the early morning of the 19th of March 1943, off Cromer, sinking almost immediately and taking five of her sixteen crew to the bottom.

Nine of the fleet including the veteran ORANMORE 495/95 now bristling with anti-aircraft guns, took part in the Normandy Landings. BARONSCOURT, for example, had seven machine guns and two rifles, all of which were put to good use against enemy aircraft. So the British coasters, having first rescued the British forces from defeat, returned with them to defeat the enemy, over 350 coasters taking part in the landings and the subsequent supply operations. Kelly's took over several other coal merchants, some of whom had ships, among them Wm. Barkley & Sons Ltd., taken over in 1911, and Alex. King Ltd., whose first steamer was MONARCH 316/85 and they operated the CORBET 468/09 for more than thirty years. John Milligen Ltd., who owned the EVELEEN 434/91 and KATHLEEN 738/02 until the 1940s, was also taken over. John Kelly was itself taken over jointly by Stephenson Clarke and William Cory, but retained its identity. During 1951 and 1952 the 19 steamers in the fleet were all given names beginning 'Bally', such as BALLYKESH given to the BARONSCOURT. In the 1950s six new steamships were built for the fleet. The first of the motorships was purchased in 1953, but it was not until 1958 that the first motor ships were built for the firm.

The Antrim Iron Ore Company had the small steamers CARGAN and VENUS in the 1870s and by 1908 there were four vessels in the fleet all with names beginning 'Glen', such as GLENDUN 1013/03. In later years the ships were involved in the Irish coal trade, and the company merged with coal importers A.S. Davidson Ltd., who owned some coasters in the 1950s and were themselves taken over by the Cawood Group as was the old company Hugh Craig & Co. Ltd. This company originated as Hugh Craig & Co., coal importers, in 1842 and their first steamer was HELEN CRAIG 417/91 which was fitted with a towing hook, so that she could tow the sailing vessels in the fleet. She carried coal to Belfast in the autumn and winter, but took part in the fruit and vegetable trade from the Channel Isles to ports such as Liverpool in the summer. Captain Kennedy had a particularly long association with this ship, joining her as a seaman in 1893 and leaving her, to retire in 1948. In later years, she ran on the firm's general cargo service under the banner of the Belfast & Preston Transport Co. Ltd., becoming such an institution that when she was finally scrapped in 1959, she was given a civic send-off on her last voyage from Preston. The company usually had three or four steamers, most of which had names beginning with 'Craig'.

Samuel Stewart operated some small coasters between the wars and into the 1950s. Isaac Stewart, beginning in the 1930s adopted the names FIRST 243/06, SECOND 328/07 and so on for his old steamers in the 1950s. The FIRST was sometimes chartered by the Point of Ayr Colliery and could be counted on for some tense moments before she finally reached their quay. Her captain was not as familiar with the winding gutterway to the quay and often grounded for a few minutes on the way up. Wilson & Reid's coasters were also in the coal trade, but in the 1920s. One of the vessels in their fleet was the REBECCA 332/95 which had been built for the general cargo trade from Liverpool to Caernarvon, Aberdovey and Barmouth. She often loaded coal at Garston for Belfast and could discharge her cargo of 300 tons or so in a day using her own winches. The coal which had been tipped in was shovelled into bags for discharge. This was normal practice at most smaller ports also, until the 1940s.

The Neill family of Bangor, Co. Down, have long been associated with shipping and coal importing, Robert Neill purchased the RHANBUOY in 1894 and renamed it ROSABELLE 280/93 and she was used to carry coal to Neill's quay at Bangor, Co. Down. She was later replaced by HELEN and finally WHIN 466/20 which was their last ship when scrapped in the 1950s. Further along the coast, The East Downshire S.S., Dundrum, had several successive DOWN-SHIREs from 1898. The Company was formed in 1871 and purchased the LADY ALICE KENLIS 203/68. Lord Downshire was an original shareholder and the next steamer was called the LADY ARTHUR HILL after a member of the Hill family which still own the estate. The Company mainly imported coal, but cattle were shipped out on occasion. The DOWNSHIRE 398/25 was always very smartly turned out, with her casing nicely panelled out and grained, even though carrying coal. On the 12 December 1954 she went ashore on the sands three quarters of a mile west of the bar entrance when trying to enter Dundrum in a strong south-easterly gale. Her coal cargo was discharged overside into the firm's lorries using the ship's derricks. The stern was hard aground and so tons of sand were needed in the fore hold to lift the stern and she was finally towed away for repairs on Christmas morning.

Crossing Dundrum bar in a loaded coaster required good judgement in fine weather. In rough weather all the doors, ventilators and skylights had to be closed to prevent the waves which broke over the ship from flooding her when coming through the broken water over the bar. At the turn of the century the men were paid 17/- a week for discharging the DOWN-SHIRE's coal and 1/- extra if she managed three cargoes in a week.

Joseph Fisher of Newry had a considerable fleet of steam coasters and originated from the Newry & Kilkeel S.S. Co., whose first vessel was the CLANRYE, built in 1884. The fleet grew rapidly and the number of owning companies under Fisher management increased and the names of trees became general for vessels in the 1890s. By 1908 there were 14 ships grouped under two owning companies, the Frontier Town S.S. Co., and the Newry & Kilkeel S.S. Co. Ltd. Further new vessels were added until the 1920s like ALDER 341/09 (front end-paper). The ships were mostly quite small and well suited to the Irish coal trade to the smaller ports and wharves. Little change took place in the fleet during the 1920s, but several new vessels such as BAMBOO 360/36 were built in the 1930s. The last steamers to be built were the sisterships BALSA 405/457 and EBONY 405/47, for the coal trade to Newry and Dublin. The change to motor vessels began in 1938 and this firm was also eventually taken over by Cawoods. At Dundalk, Samuel Lockington & Co. Ltd. had SHELLIE 358/05 and the MARGARET LOCKINGTON 460/21 running until the 1950s.

Perhaps best remembered of Dublin's coasters were those of the Alliance & Dublin Consumers Gas Co., who acquired coasters in the First World War to ensure their coal supplies and had the GLENAGEARY 446/20 and the GLENCULLEN 448/21 built to bring their fleet up to four vessels which carried coal from Partington or Garston to Ringsend Dock, Dublin, year in, year out, until the 1960s when replaced by motor vessels. The collier W.M. BARK-LEY was purchased by A. Guinness Son & Co. Ltd., from John Kelly in 1913 to carry their stout to Liverpool and Manchester returning with empty casks. The vessel had engines amidships and so was not ideal. Three engines-aft colliers were taken over from John Kelly in 1914 and two, CARROWDORE 599/14 and CLARECASTLE 627/14 were fitted with cooling equipment to carry Guiness to London, but were soon taken for war service. By 1930 the shipments to London had become so important, that a new steamer GUINNESS 1151/31 was built for the run, carrying 800 tons of stout in the cooled and insulated hold. Shipments continued until the London brewery was opened in 1938. The first motor ships were built in 1952 with bulk tanks which could be lifted out.

Tedcastle, McCormick & Co., apart from operating regular services from the late 1880s, also had steamers in the coal trade. W.O. McCormick also had the single steam coaster DUNLEARY 470/05 built and retained her until 1932. However, the first Dublin coal merchant to go in for steam appears to have been Thomas Heiton & Co., who purchased the old iron collier ARBUTUS 356/54 in 1880. The collier was not quite as old as the firm which had been founded in 1849. She was a success and a new collier, SAINT KEVIN 477/83 was built by McIlwaine & Lewis and the ARBUTUS sold. The next steamer, SAINT KILDA 479/84 had the then modern innovation of a triple expansion engine. Further vessels were built in the 1890s to replace those lost or sold and the ships were now trading quite widely, making voyages to the Continent. The next spate of building occurred in the 1920s as for example SAINT FINTAN 495/21. The first motor ship was SAINT EUNAN 436/37 and a further motor ship was purchased in 1947, both had been sold by 1955, the company continuing as coal and builders merchants.

J.J. Stafford & Sons Ltd. originally Wexford Steamships Ltd., were engaged in the general cargo and cattle trade from Wexford. J.J. Murphy of Waterford acquired some small old steamers such as BRAEBEG 165/78 at the time of the First World War, but sold them after a few years. John Christopher's steamer CARGAN 274/16, brought coal and other cargoes to Waterford until the 1930s. A. Maloney & Sons, who were merchants in Dungarvan had the lovely old steamer THE LADY BELLE 331/00 throughout the 1920s and 1930s. R. McCowen & Sons Ltd. of Tralee had steamers by the 1890s and the DERRYMORE 485/05 was built for them and replaced by another new vessel KERRYMORE 509/21 which traded until the 1950s.

The steamers of the Limerick S.S. were well known as they concentrated on the general cargo liner trades in later years. However, the earlier vessels such as MUNGRET 515/13 were used to carry bulk cargoes to Limerick and other Irish ports. J. Bannatyne & Co. had steamers from the 1880s, one of which was the GARRYOWEN 403/54 which was not sold until the 1920s. Mullock & Son, who were coal merchants, had such coasters as KERRY HEAD 825/13 in the 1920s and 1930s and continued as agents after the sale of the ships. The Sligo S.N. Co. of Sligo carried bulk cargoes such as coal, as well as general cargoes in their earlier steamers such as SLIGO 525/13, but later owned cattle boats. At Londonderry, Thos. H. Corbett had CARRICKLEE 334/04 in the 1920s, the company continuing as agents. Larne was the home port of the Shamrock Shipping Co. which began in the 1890s. The firm were soon established in the coal trade from the East Coast and South Wales to the Continent. There were 18 vessels in the fleet by 1918, such as CLONLEE 1012/99. By 1938 the fleet had shrunk to seven vessels. Howden Bros. of Larne, later taken over by John Kelly, began in the 1890s with steamers such as FERRIC, which mainly carried coal to Larne. The fleet expanded to 9 vessels by 1918 when several new vessels were built such as GALGORM 450/18, though most were smaller like FINVOY 374/20, which was one of the last to be disposed of in the 1950s. Two larger steamers were used for a short lived general cargo line in the 1960s.

The Channel Islands have long been the home of the coasting firm of Onesimus Dorey & Sons, St. Peter Port, Guernsey. The company was formed in 1898 and used the steamer ROSSGULL in the coal trade to the islands. By 1918 there were eight vessels in the fleet under the names Anglo-French S.S. Co. Ltd. and the Sea Transportation Co. Ltd., which had vessels like LAKEWOOD 570/19. Anthracite from Swansea was a common cargo and used for heating the Islands' greenhouses. Coal was also brought for the gas works. By 1938 the fleet had increased to 16 vessels and a similar number were operated in the 1950s. Oil replaced coal for heating and the fleet declined to a few motor vessels. It was the end of the steam era.

Index

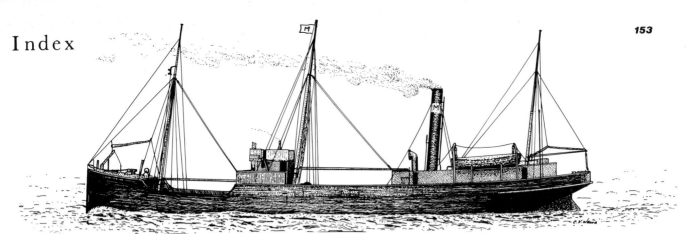

Ships

Companies etc.

Glossary

Shipyards

SEE OPPOSITE for LIST of SHIPYARD PLANS
and MAP, Plate 17 for LOCATIONS.

Plans

page	name	built	gross	nett	deadweight (summer)	registered dimensions (feet)	summer draught	bunkers (tons).	hold (cu. ft.)	water ballast (tons)	diam. cyls. -stroke	boiler press. (lbs). *twin boilers	horse-power	engine builder	speed (kts)	builder	source
8	Clint	1896	197	74	?	125.0x20.0x9.0	9'6"	?	?	18t	16,32-24	120	43r	Ross & D		Fullerton, Paisley	(o)
13	Deemount	1933	569	274	716	165.5x27.2x9.7	12'1"	80c	32622	218t	13,21,34-24	180	70r	Lewis	9	J.Lewis, Aberdeen	(ds)
20	Pearl	1896	678	277	700	185.0x29.1x10.8	13'3"	66c	34813	178t	16,26,42-33	160	90r	Muir & H		J. Shearer, Glas.	(o)
26	Ophir	1908	469	172	?	155.1x26.2x10.5	12'9"	47c	20337	167t	18,40-27	130	94r	Ross & D		Ailsa, Ayr	(mm)
47	125' Collier	1852	402	171	333	125.0x28.0x15.3	12'0"	?	?	?	(2) 24-27	20	60h		9	(Russell's treatise)	
48	Eagle	1853	479	361	419	149.0x28.0x15.3	12'0"	?	?	?	(2) 24-27	20	60h		8	(Russell's treatise)	
49	W. ballast Stmr.	1854	597	470	496	166.3x28.0x15.0	12'0"	?	?	?	(2) 36-30	12	100h		9½	(Russell's treatise)	
50	Warkworth	1874	533	334	?	160.8x27.1x12.9	12'9"	102c	27190	170t	21,41-28	80	70h	Ch'e, G.		C.S.Swan, Newc.	(nmm)
52	St. Seiriol	1886	140	68	150	95.0x20.0x7.9	8'5"	23c	7040	12t	14,26-20		30r	J.P. Ren.		C.S.Swan, Newc.	(nmm)
55	Moonlight	1952	164	64	188	85.6x19.5x9.3	9'8"	25c	8400	?	12,24-18	140	200i	Yarw'd	7½	Yarwood, Northw.	(a)
59	Ailsa	1904	100	30	?	66.5x18.3x8.8	?	?	?	?	10,20-16		7r	Denny		Denny, Dumbart.	(nmm)
60	Raylight	1963	177	73	220	88.0x20.8x10.1	?	8d	9894	?	6cyl. 2SCSA		?	Crossley	9	Scotts' SB & E.	(o)
60	Velinheli	1892	126	50	125?	95.0x18.5x7.5	8'6"	18c	5471	12t	13,28-18	120	40r	W.Kemp;	9½	McKnight, Ayr	(a)
62	Collin	1915	287	107	287	120.8x22.1x9.1	10'0"	30c	?	25t	14,30-22	135	87r	Jeffrey	8	Jeffrey, Alloa	(a)*
63	Indorita	1921	203	110	260	108.6x22.1x9.4	10'6"	5d	12500	?	6cyl. 2SCSA		?	Crossley	9	Abdela & M., Q.	(a)
65	Lucena	1913	243			114.0x23.6x11.1					16,33-24				9½	Hawthorns, Leith	(ssr)
66	Doris Thomas	1924	266	99	270	120.0x22.1x9.1	10'1"	36c	12388	42t	15,32-21	130	41r	M. DD.	8	Manchester DD.	(mm)
67	Agate	1878	178	59	210	120.0x20.1x9.6	9'4"	24c	8850	50t	16,28-22	70	35r	W.King		Seath, Rutherglen	(o)
68	Calatum	1908	293	93	?	120.5x22.1x9.6	10'1"	?	?	25t	15, 32-22	130	57n	Ross & D		Williamson, W'ton	(a)
69	St. Modan	1910	237	89		122.2x21.6x9.4	10'3"	?	?	21t	14,30-24	135	35r	Fishers		Scott, Bowling	(pnt)
70	Florence Cook	1923	294	109	275	130.1x22.6x9.5	9'7"	60c	12160	111t	17,34-24	130	62r	Shields	8	Hepples, S.Shields	(pnt)
71	Shotton	1909	300	110	330	135.0x23.1x9.3	10'7"	41c	14100	40t	17,36-24	130	62r	Holmes	9	Cochrane, Selby	(b)
74	Belford	1920	366	147	420	135.5x23.6x10.0	10'4"	44c	19000	47t	17,34-24	130	62r	Shields	9	Morris, Newcastle	(o)
77	Cornish Trader	1920	470	189	?	141.9x25.1x11.6	12'2"	58c	?	65t	18,38-27	130	74r	McColl &	8½	Abdela & M., Q.	(a)
78	Briarfield	1920	446	172	512	142.2x26.0x11.5	12'10"	50c	23315	81t	14,22,38-24	180	88n	Lytham	8½	Lytham SB, Lyth.	(mm)
79	Farfield	1921	468	192	530	152.0x25.2x10.8	11'10"	66c	24100	69t	13,23,37-24	180	85r	Holmes	9	Cook, W. & G., Bev.	(o)**
81	Helmsman	1903	458	207	?	160.0x25.0x10.2	11'11"	?	?	129t	14,22,36-27	180	75r	N. E. M.		Wood, Skinner, N'c.	(o)
82	Sligo	1913	515	215	560	175.7x27.4x10.3	12'11"	63c	29500	190t	15,26,41-30	180	85r	McColl, B.		Dublin DD. &c.	(o)
82	Cromarty Firth	1919	638	300	770	175.4x28.3x10.1	12'6"	72c	33000	300t	14,23,38-27	180	99r	Beard'e		Ardrossan D. &c.	(o)
85	Annaghmore	1924	583	271	770	165.0x27.0x11.1	13'3"	65c	33140	176t	14,24,39-27	180	83r	Lewis	9	Lewis, Aberdeen	(ds)
86	Broomfield	1938	657	268	800	171.0x28.8x11.2	13'2"	65c	34775	270t	13,21,36-24	200	88r	Lytham	9	Lytham SB., Lyth.	(mm)
88	Copsewood	1925	969	537	1316	198.0x32.3x12.4	14'7"	108c	63000	376t	16,27,44-30	180	131n	Clark	9	Osborne, G., Sund.	(o)
89	Stepney	1916	808	375	1114	186.3x29.4x12.4	14'4"	110c	52000	202t	14,23,37-24	180*	99r	Beard'e	8	Williamson, W'ton	(o)
91	Kylebrook	1927	870	426	1165	188.3x30.0x12.4	14'4"	107c	54687	221t	14,24,40-27	200	99r	Beard'e	9	Williamson, W'ton	(hm)
92	Yewpark	1930	827	410	1150	195.0x31.1x11.9	13'7"	102c	50000	216t	15,25,40-27	180	90r	Davey, P.	9½	Scott, Bowling	(mm)
94	The Duchess	1924	799	356	1025	190.0x29.7x12.1	13'11"	94c	45363	290t	16,27,44-30	180*	137n	Beard'e		C.Rennoldson, Sh.	(pnt)
96	Busiris	1929	943	426	1066	215.7x31.1x12.3	13'11"	148c	51000	218t	16,27,43-33	200*	154n	Ailsa	11	Ailsa SB., Troon	(o)
97	Holme Force	1930	1216	645	?	216.0x34.2x13.6	15'3"	130c	78000	411t	14,24,40-27	180*	144n	McColl &		Goole SB., Goole	(b)
98	Empire Kew	1945	1052	568	1437	205.0x32.8x13.7	15'3"	110c	69660	318t	14,24,40-27	200	?	Lewis	9	J.Lewis, Aberdeen	(pnt)
100	Island Queen	1920	689	355	910	173.5x28.1x12.9	13'5"	74c	45000	100t	14,22,36-30	180	97r	Swan		Swan, Hunter, Sld.	(nmm)
101	Islington	1924	1494	836	2440	240.0x37.2x17.7	17'3"	244c	101919	528t	18,29,49-33	180*	168n	McColl &		Swan, Hunter, Sld.	(nmm)
102	Kylebrook	1924	1578	920	2727	245.3x37.0x18.7	18'0"	251c	116000	505t	18,29,48-33	180*	180n	N. E. M.	9	Dobson, Newcastle	(o)*
105	Cordene	1924	2345	1322	3610	284.5x42.1x19.6	19'5"	188c	168000	1004t	21,34,56-39	180*	247n	Grey		Swan, Hunter, New	(nmm)
107	Fulham	1936	1598	878	2390	238.1x38.3x16.5	16'8"	105c	117380	806t	17,28,46-33	200	185n	N. E. M.	10	Burntisland SB.	(a)*
111	Lady Charrington	'52	2154	1096	2920	275.1x41.0x22.1	18'0"	166c	136500	1118t	17,29,48-33	220*	850i	N. E. M.	10½	S.P.Austin, Sld.	(a)*
113	Louie Rose	1924	1596	955	2500	250.5x37.1x16.4	17'3"	148c	107000	583t	19,31,50-36	180*	226n	Ross & D		Fullerton, Paisley	(pnt)
113	Cardiganbrook	1952	1780	871	2268	258.1x38.2x15.6	16'11"	143f	117328	470t	17,29,47-30	225*	1150i	Lewis	12	J.Lewis, Aberdeen	(a)*
116	Eastwick (Tk.)	1920	526	261	750?	157.9x26.2x12.3	12'6"	68c	35298?	136t	12,20,34-23	180	77r	Beard'e		Swan, Hunter, Newc	(nmm)
117	Esso Preston (Tk)	'56	1965	721	2790	280.0x42.0x ?	17'4"	209f	89168	1049t	17,28,47-30	225	1300i	Hall, Ru.	10½	Hall, Rus., A'deen	(a)
119	Ben Hebden (Tk)	1947	410	184	390	138.6x25.0x11.2	11'5"	38d	13600	74t	6cyl. 2SCSA		560b	B. Polar	9½	Rowhedge IW.	(ms)
123	Elidir	1903	398	152	455	151.6x25.1x9.9	12'4"	?	?	150t	14,23,37-27	170	91r	Ross & D	9	Ailsa SB., Ayr	(a)*
124	Arundel	1956	3422	1754	4555	325.0x46.0x ?	20'0"	303f	221500	1602t	19,31,54-39	220*	1450i	Clarke &	10½	Austin & Pick, Sld	(a)
133	Arduity (Tk)	1946	959	406	1043	193.0x34.1x14.7	13'6"	?	?	108t	4cyl. 2SCSA		640b	B.Polar	10½	Grangemouth D.	(o)
138	Bronzite	1894	602	237	735	180.0x29.1x10.6	13'4"	79c	29055	162t	17,27,44-30	160	108n	Muir & H		Scott, Bowling	(o)
158	Sonority	1952	589	304	750	176.7x27.6x9.4	11'6"	23d	41000	277t	5cyl. 2SCSA		?	Newbury	11	Fellows, Gt.Yar.	(o)
159	Norrix	1920	576	283	?	165.0x27.0x11.0	?	?	?	?	13,22,36-24	?	84r	Earle's		Cochrane, Selby	(o)

NOTES: Key to Engine builders; Ross & Duncan, Glasgow (Ross & D). Muir & Houston, Glasgow (Muir & H). Christie, Gutch, N. Shields (Chi,G.). J. P. Rennoldson, S.Shields (J.P.Ren). Shields Eng. & Drydock, Shields (Shields). McColl & Pollock, Sunderland (McColl &) McColl, Belfast (McColl, B.). Beardmore, Glasgow (Beard'e). Davey, Paxman, Colchester (Davey, P.). North Eastern Marine, Newcastle (N. E. M.). G.T.Grey, Shields (Grey). G. Clark & N. E. M. (Sld) Ltd (Clark &).

Key to Sources: author's collection (a), shipbuilders (b), Don Smith Esq. (ds), Hull Museum (hm), Merseyside Museums (mm), Motor Ship (ms), National Maritime Museum (nmm), P. N. Thomas Esq. (pnt), Shipbuilding & Shipping Record (ssr), Shipowners (s). All plans above are from the original shipyard drawings or surveys of the vessels by the author. *indicates a plan of a less detailed nature made by Board of Trade or other surveyors or small scale plan. **indicates a drawing based on the builders plan with additional details, mainly the masts, from photographs. All the coloured drawings are based on original plans with the addition of details from photographs and conversations with crews etc.

Key to bunkers; coal (c), marine diesel (d), boiler oil (f). Key to horsepower; brake (b), indicated (i), nominal (n), registered (r).

BIBLIOGRAPHY

Admiralty. Naval Marine Engineering Practice. Vols. 1 and 2. H. M. S. O., London, 1959. Details of steam machinery.

Anderson, E. B., Sailing Ships of Ireland. Morris & Co., Dublin 1951. Much information on steamship owners also.

Anderson, R., The Port of Coleraine - A Short History. Impact Amergin, 1976. Coleraine ships and shipowners.

Bowen, F. C., London Ship Types. East Ham Echo, 1938. General information on the different vessel types to be seen.
Ships We See. Sampson, Low 193?. Similar work of a more wide ranging nature.

Dunn, L., Ship Recognition - Merchant Ships. Ross, 1952. Critical analysis of the features of various ship types.

Coppack, T., A Lifetime With Ships. T. Stephenson, 1973. Autobiography of a coasting sail and steamship owner.

Donaldson, J., The Practical Guide to the Use of Marine Steam Machinery. Wilson, 1881. Small steamers machinery.

Fenton, R. S., W. S. Kennaugh & Co and the West Coast Shipping Co. World Ship Society Monograph No. 1., 1979.

Hocking, C., Dictionary of Disasters at Sea During the Age of Steam (1824-1962). Vols. 1 & 2. Lloyds Register, 1969.

Le Fleming, H. M., abc of British Coastal Cargo Ships. Ian Allan, 1954-60. Four editions of fleet lists.

Mitchell, W. H. & Sawyer, L. A., Empire Ships of World War II. Sea Breezes, 1965.

Pollock, W., Small Vessels. Walter Pollock, 1946. Small shipbuilding methods, mainly motor vessels.

Pollock, W., Building Small Ships. Executors of Walter Pollock, 1948. Similar to above title.

Pursey, H. J., Merchant Ship Construction. Brown, Son & Ferguson, Glasgow 1963. Basic construction details.

Ripper, W., Steam Engine Theory & Practice. Longmans, Green, 1908. A general introduction to the subject.

Russell, J. Scott, A Modern System of Naval Architecture. Russell, 1864. Detailed drawings and descriptions.

Sennett, R., & Oram, H. J., The Marine Steam Engine. Longmans, 1908. A general introduction to the subject.

Smellie, J., J., Shipbuilding & Repairing in Dublin. McCorquodale, 1924? Shipyard practice used for steaers.

Talbot-Booth, E. C., Ships and the Sea. Sampson Low, 1938. A general reference work.

Walton, T., Steel Ships: Their Construction & Maintainence. Griffin, 1901. A general reference work.

Winchester, C., (Ed.), Shipping Wonders of the World Vols. 1 & 2. Amalgamated Press, 1936.

Annual Publications: Lloyd's Registers (1840-1972). Lloyd's Register. Mercantile Navy Lists (1858-1949). HMSO.

Periodicals: Journal of Commerce & Shipping Telegraph, Sea Breezes (new series), Ships Monthly, Marine News, (monthly journal of the World Ship Society), Shipbuilding & Shipping Record and Motor Ship.

Nºˢ 356 & 357.
GENERAL ARRANGEMENT ~ PROFILE.

SCALE :- ¼" = ONE FOOT.

FELLOWS & COMPANY Lᵀᴰ.
SOUTHTOWN DRY DOCKS.
GREAT YARMOUTH.

4. 4. 51.

DIMENSIONS:
LENGTH B.P.   174'-0"
BREADTH MLD.   27'-6"
DEPTH MLD.   11'-7"

SONORITY and SEVERITY were built for Everards in 1952.

158